Plays: 1

**The Waters of Babylon, When is a Door not a Door?,
Live Like Pigs, The Happy Haven, Serjeant Musgrave's Dance**

The Waters of Babylon: 'This wild, acidly funny and oddly tragic story of London low-life . . . reveals Arden's tough linguistic freedom and the free-wheeling ease with which he switches from prose to verse and back again.' *Sunday Times*

Live Like Pigs: 'Thrilling theatre . . . a rumbustious delight, outrageously funny, powerfully dramatic and, when you least expect it, genuinely moving . . . a modern classic.' *Daily Telegraph*

The Happy Haven (written with Margaretta D'Arcy): 'This rare and excellent revival perfectly reflects the play's bizarre atmosphere, its potent mixture of farcical prose, rhymed poetry, its marked avoidance of schematic moral codes.' *Time Out*

Serjeant Musgrave's Dance: 'This is spell-binding, mind-challenging drama that touches greatness; and what is more it is written in that wonderful Arden language that seems to be hewn out of granite.' *Guardian*
'A modern classic . . . a white-hot piece of work . . . Since its first appearance in 1959, the play has advanced towards us as if in a slow prophetic march.' *The Times*

Also included in the volume is *When is a Door not a Door?*, a one-act 'industrial episode'.

John Arden was born in Barnsley, Yorkshire, in 1930. While studying architecture at Cambridge and Edinburgh universities, he began to write plays, four of which were premièred at the Royal Court Theatre: *The Waters of Babylon, Live Like Pigs, Serjeant Musgrave's Dance* and *The Happy Haven*; while a fifth, *The Workhouse Donkey*, was produced at the Festival Theatre, Chichester. For a year he held an Annual Fellowship in Playwriting at Bristol University, and Bristol Old Vic produced *Ironhand*, his free adaptation of Goethe's *Goetz von Berlichingen*. *Armstrong's Last Goodnight* was first produced at the Glasgow Citizens' Theatre and later at the National Theatre. *Left-Handed Liberty* was specially commissioned by the Corporation of London to commemorate the 750th Anniversary of Magna Carta and was produced at the Mermaid Theatre. Recent revivals of Arden's plays include *Live Like Pigs* (Royal Court Theatre, London, 1993) and *Armstrong's Last Goodnight* (Edinburgh Festival, 1994). He is married to Margaretta D'Arcy, with whom he has collaborated on many plays. Arden's first novel, *Silence Among the Weapons* (1982), was short-listed for the Booker-McConnell Prize for Fiction. His other novels are: *Books of Bale* (1988), *Cogs Tyrannic* (1991), which won the PEN 'Silver Pen' Award, and *Jack Juggler and the Emperor's Whore* (1995). He also won the V. S. Pritchett Award in 1999 for his short story 'Breach of Trust'.

JOHN ARDEN

Plays: 1

The Waters of Babylon
When is a Door not a Door?
Live Like Pigs
Serjeant Musgrave's Dance
The Happy Haven

with a preface and introductory notes by the author

Methuen Drama

METHUEN CONTEMPORARY DRAMATISTS

1 3 5 7 9 10 8 6 4 2

This collection first published in Great Britain in 1994
by Methuen Drama

Reissued 2002

Methuen Publishing Ltd
215 Vauxhall Bridge Road, London SW1V 1EJ

Methuen Publishing Ltd Reg. No. 3543167

The Waters of Babylon first published by Penguin Books 1964
Copyright © 1964 by John Arden

Live Like Pigs first published by Penguin Books 1961
Reprinted in *Three Plays* by Penguin Books 1964
Copyright © 1961 by John Arden

The Happy Haven first published by Penguin Books 1962
Reprinted in *Three Plays* by Penguin Books 1964
Copyright © 1962 by John Arden

When is a Door not a Door? first published in *Soldier, Soldier and other plays*
by Methuen & Co Ltd in 1967
Copyright © 1967 by John Arden

Serjeant Musgrave's Dance first published by Methuen & Co Ltd 1960
Reprinted in first edition of *Arden Plays: One* 1977
Copyright © 1960 by John Arden

Preface to this collection copyright © 1994 by John Arden

The right of the author to be identified as the author
of these works has been asserted by him in accordance with the
Copyright, Designs and Patents Act, 1988

ISBN 0 413 68800 3

A CIP catalogue record for this book
is available from the British Library

The front cover shows a detail from *Der Jungbrunnen* (The Fountain of Youth) by
Lucas Cranach the Elder (1546, Gemäldegalerie, Berlin)
Photo: Archiv für Kunst und Geschichte, Berlin

Typeset by Wilmaset Ltd, Birkenhead, Wirral
Printed and bound in Great Britain by
Cox & Wyman Ltd, Reading, Berkshire

Caution

All rights whatsoever in these plays are strictly reserved and application for
performance etc., by amateurs and professionals, should be made before rehearsal to
Casarotto Ramsay & Associates Ltd, 60 Wardour Street, London W1V 4ND.
No performance may be given unless a licence has been obtained.

Contents

Chronology

Note: The initials '(JA/MD'A)' or '(MD'A/JA)' indicate a
collaboration between John Arden and Margaretta D'Arcy.

(MD'A/JA)	*The Ballygombeen Bequest*, performed by 7:84 Theatre Company at Edinburgh Festival	1972
(JA/MD'A)	*The Island of the Mighty*, in three parts, Royal Shakespeare Company at the Aldwych Theatre, London	1972
(JA/MD'A)	*Keep Those People Moving!*, schools' radio	1972
(MD'A/JA)	*Non-Stop Connolly Show*, in six parts, performed in Dublin, Ireland	1975
(MD'A/JA)	*Vandaleur's Folly*, toured by 7:84 Theatre Company	1978
(JA)	*Pearl*, BBC radio	1978
(JA)	*The Adventures of the Ingenious Gentleman Don Quixote*, BBC radio, in two parts	1980
(JA)	*The Old Man Sleeps Alone*, BBC radio	1982
(JA)	*Garland for a Hoar Head*, BBC radio	1982
(JA/MD'A)	*The Manchester Enthusiasts*, BBC radio, in two parts	1984
(JA/MD'A)	*Whose is the Kingdom?*, BBC radio series, in nine parts	1988
(JA/MD'A)	*A Suburban Suicide*, BBC radio	1994
(JA)	*The Little Novels of Wilkie Collins*, BBC radio series	1998
(JA)	*Woe Alas! The Fatal Cashbox*, BBC radio	1999

Novels by John Arden:

Silence Among the Weapons	1982
Books of Bale	1988
Cogs Tyrannic	1991
Jack Juggler and the Emperor's Whore	1995

Preface

Before I write anything about plays, let me first explain the cover-illustrations I have chosen for this book and its companion volume. They are parts of a large crowded composition by Lucas Cranach the Elder: *The Fountain of Youth*, which he painted in 1546. I would guess that he had heard the stories so recently brought home from the New World, of just such a magical fountain somewhere in the hinterland of Florida, known to the indigenous Americans; and vainly sought by Spanish conquistadors (notably Ponce de León), blind to the way their own greed was destroying not only the native peoples but that very concept of a Golden Age which had made such a sweet legend plausible.

Cranach's imagination was something of an oddity, split down the middle with intriguing contradiction – which may well have cost him more self-struggle than is superficially apparent.

On the one hand he was a strong Lutheran Christian, who made many spectacular religious pictures and many devoted portraits of the German reformers and the princes who supported them. His patrons were successive Electors of Saxony, of the house that upheld Luther in his darkest hour when papal agents were out to kill him. Cranach was a court-artist: he was also Burgomaster of Wittenberg and a prosperous property-owner in the town – the town of Luther's great gesture, the nailing of his revolutionary Theses to the church door. Which was all very solemn and sober.

But Cranach was also a creature of the Renaissance; he dreamed with a portion of his soul of an ancient Golden Age, a pagan Paradise where naked human beings of warm and naughty beauty disported themselves among forests and

half-wild gardens, in harmony with each other and with all
the gorgeous beasts of the animal kingdom. He painted
innumerable young women, sometimes entirely nude, sometimes mysteriously (and libidinously) accoutred with
jewelled collars, heavy gold chains and plumed hats the size
of cartwheels. At times they had male companions, some in
armour, some as naked as the women; more often little boys,
Cupids, bare and playful. I believe his dream was absolutely
genuine, a concept of sincere poetry: he perceived a lost
ideal which Christianity (and especially the new Protestant
Christianity of the north) viewed with at best incompre-
hension and at worst a determined hostility. And yet he
painted (or his workshop painted) scores, maybe hundreds,
of such images. Who was buying them, and for what
reasons?

The answer, alas, is obvious. Dirty Old Men; and rutting
young ones. Such paintings, in the sixteenth century, would
have been hung in the private cabinets of gentlemen,
churchmen and wealthy merchants; with curtains drawn in
front of them, only to be opened when ladies were not
present – or at any rate, ladies of the family and (of course)
their female attendants. While the rest of the house would be
adorned with the scriptural icons of its public and official
piety.

Now *The Fountain of Youth*, as we have it, fits well into
this category. It shows the Fountain, carved in the Germano-
Vitruvian taste and crowned with a statue of a nude goddess,
in a stone-rimmed square pool surrounded by pastoral
countryside: there are mountains and a city and a bridge over
a river in the far distance; on the right stretch meadows and
bright-leaved fruit-trees; on the left, precipitous crags sur-
mounted by a dour fortress, and thickets at the base of the
crags, dark and rather ominous. Broken old women, disfig-
ured by the pain of age, muffled up in hoods and scarves, are
being brought from among these thickets, some in carts, one

on a stretcher, one in a wheelbarrow. Most of their conductors are middle-aged workingmen, except for one or two young women who look like maidservants. At the edge of the pool the crones are helped to undress, totally exposing their used and worn-out bodies. In the pool they flounder grotesquely, until one by one they reach the middle. Suddenly they are young and lovely: delectable golden-skinned nymphs who might have frolicked in a backwater of Propontis, as visited by the wandering *Argo*. (You'll have to find the second volume if you want to know just what they look like. Not entirely a cynical catchpenny: the details of the picture are too small to allow more than a bit of it to be reproduced at one time.)

Then they climb out of the pool at its right-hand margin. They are greeted by a gallant young knight and shown to a dressing-tent where they will find resplendent raiment for all the pleasures that await them – we see these pleasures between the fruit-trees: music, dancing, feasting, the amorous company of more young gallants. It is implied there need be no end to them; for the pool is always there for a subsequent re-immersion.

In short, Cranach's purchaser had before him a discreditable fantasy – 'if only all the old hags could be given a swift bath by Hans of the Stable-yard and Gretchen of the Backpantry, what a wonderful time for all good men! Doxies and chits for the asking, always smiling, never refusing a kiss, drinking with you pint for pint of best-vintage Rhenish.' A conveyor-belt of lubricious fulfilment.

But if that's what the purchaser thought, I am not sure that Cranach did. He knew his market well enough; but he also knew that the Fountain of Youth was a non-sexist amenity. Men could be rejuvenated just as well as women. So why did he not show it? Well, partly because part of him was as much a Dirty Old Man as any of his customers. His secret lusts, as it were, underlay the Lutheran aspect of his temperament as well as the pagan Renaissance side, and as an acclaimed artist he had a vast advantage over all the other respectable Wittenberg citizens: he could (without risk of prosecution) invite young women to undress in front of him and submit for hours to his courteous scrutiny; and even if Frau Cranach came into the studio and found him at it, there would be no legitimate cause for her to complain. This has to be stated; because it has long been a traditional feature of the artist's way of life, and its underlying dubiety as a piece of human behaviour (social? moral? even political?) ought not to pass unnoticed.

But now that I've noticed it, I'll leave it alone. Because I prefer to assume that (although his Dirty Old Man symptoms probably prompted Cranach to start off by painting women and only women in the Fountain) he intended more. I have no historical warrant for this: but I think he planned a second picture, the same subject but with the sexes reversed, where his old men would have been just as hideous, his young men just as beautiful, as the women in the painting that exists. He had made such a pair before: two satirical illustrations of the mediæval 'January and May' theme, old persons (repulsive) embracing young persons (mercenary): in one picture January is male and May female, in the other vice-versa. Grim juxtaposition of pathetic sexual explorations. As Webster says of the gates of death in his *Duchess of Malfi*, 'such strange geometrical hinges, you may open them both ways.'

If my guess is on the mark, the missing *Fountain* has either been lost, which is not at all impossible; or he never got around to painting it. The latter would have been a harsh irony, for Cranach was 74 in 1546; he only lived for seven more years, during which he seems to have given over much of the work of his studio to his son, surely not from inability to *imagine*. He was hindered by weariness, no doubt, maybe tremors in his hand; he felt he could no longer *execute* with the confidence he had once enjoyed. Was it not his age more than anything else that gave him cause to choose this subject?

74 is old for some people, merely elderly for others. Let's say Cranach at that age had suddenly become aware that he was, very shortly, about to be *old*. 1546, moreover, was the year of the death of Luther, his great spiritual hero. So he brooded (as I see him) upon such sad matters as time, the futility of human wishes, the decay of the human body . . . and the frequent refusal of the human mind, its desires, its hops, skips and inconsistent little jumps, to decay at a parallel speed. For one thing is clear from Cranach's later work: if *his* mind did suffer senility, it was not until he was close to the grave's edge.

The Fountain of Youth, therefore, is a very personal representation; its exact relevance to Cranach's life can only be conjectured, but it is certainly as contradictory as it is complex. I find in it, without being quite able to fix it against all argument, the shape of an undeclared allegory upon the glorious self-renewal of artistic creation. Every time you set yourself to paint a picture, or make a song, or tell a story, or write a play, the act itself is another plunge into the pool of the fountain. Happily to complete the picture, the song, the story, the play, brings you out at the far brink, young again, naked and glorious, fully capable of all that comes next. It is a parable that (deliberately? courageously? blindly or foolishly?) takes no account of so beastly a concept as the Law of Diminishing Returns.

*   *   *

I am now 63; I have (insidiously rather than suddenly) become aware that I am about to be *elderly*. For example, I don't find it easy to climb over a drystone wall if I'm out on a country walk. It vexes me, and why not? I sometimes think that a practicable Fountain of Youth would be a very good idea. But then I think: is it necessary? I am still imagining, still writing; in fact, according to the terms of Cranach's allegory, I slide myself regularly into the *idea* of such a Fountain, and get my limbs across it as speedily as ever.

*   *   *

Which brings me to the specifics of my own work; or rather, of items of it which I wrote more or less on my own and finished by 1969. In that year I became 39, and Margaretta D'Arcy and myself and our four young sons went off to India for thirteen months. Afterwards we lived permanently in Ireland. It was a year of great change in my life. In those days I could emerge from each plunge in the Fountain's pool scarcely smoother in the skin and darker in the hair than I was when I entered the water: I remind myself of this with some surprise as I look at these plays, for the first time, all together.

They are in fact a finished chapter.

For most of my theatre work over the last quarter-century has been as much Margaretta D'Arcy's as mine – *more* hers than mine, a good deal of it. So therefore it has been quite different, in its purpose and its subject-matter as well as its style. (If you want to know how different, there is a short bibliography at the end of this preface.)

Several of the plays have their own individual prefaces; so I will not say much about them here. Just a few anecdotes of how I came to think of them, and so forth. Thus:–

The Waters of Babylon
In 1956 I had a play about the Arthurian legends rejected by George Devine at the Royal Court. I was very cast down. My flatmate, Tom Austin, an Irishman who worked in the same architect's business as myself, told me I was an ass to send a poetical-historical epic to a theatre which had just made its name by presenting *Look Back in Anger*. Why didn't I 'look

around' rather than attempt so pretentiously my own 'look-ing back'? 'For instance, there's that cranky bald-headed political refugee or whatever he is, who works in the inner drawing-office; someone really ought to put *him* on the stage. Why not you?' So I did, by way of a highly artificial plot which I stole from the Elizabethans (a queer, 'corrupt' text called *The Blind Beggar of Alexandria*). The character of Charlie Butterthwaite came from my father's tales about a notorious political chancer who had ruled Barnsley for years between the wars. The rest of the play was by and large a young Yorkshireman's wide-eyed view of London and its astonishing jumble of people who had not been born there – I myself was brand-new to the capital and still had a lot to find out about it.

When is a Door not a Door?

This play was a pot-boiler, which I was proud to be asked to do: it showed that someone regarded me as a proper craftworker who could turn his hand to anything. A school of drama wanted a script for the final-year showpiece of a particular group of students, which imposed certain string-ent conditions without which my work would be literally useless. The number of performers and their respective genders were specified, together with the length of the piece: a large cast for a very short episode. It needed, I concluded, a quite simple main action without too many participants, surrounded by a general in-and-out of mixed humanity. It took me a long time to think of this main action and then I remembered –

A year or so earlier, in 1956, I was lying ill with flu in the flat I shared with Tom Austin, in Walton Street just behind Knightsbridge and Harrods. The street at that time was a curious little survivor of a Victorian working-class ghetto. The houses even had gas-light; and our landlady, Miss Mahon, was straight out of a novel by Trollope (where she would have administered the digs of some thin-in-the-pocket young clerks from a minor government department). There was an old Welshman across the road who kept a 'dairy'. Nowadays it would be a self-service branch of Londis. A couple of trendy bistros had made their appearance, one for high-class bohemians, the other for hooray-henries; and within a year an infiltration of primrose-yellow front doors marked the end of the old order. While I was ill – as ill as one sometimes can be without actually causing 'grave concern' – Miss Mahon had in some carpenters to repair goodness knows what on the staircase. My bed was against the lath-and-plaster that divided my room from the first-floor landing.

In semi-delirium I listened all morning to every word of their conversation (it included reflections upon Suez and Anthony Eden), interspersed with the exigencies of their work. I did not exactly repeat it in the play: but the hallucinatory clarity with which it stuck in my mind gave me at last my main action, the 'still centre' of a highly-stylised little farce.

Live Like Pigs

After *The Waters of Babylon* I felt I should try something for the Royal Court of a more 'realistic' nature, politically acute, relevant, committed, as the jargon went – Lucas Cranach in his Lutheran mode, in fact. Or, no. That's what I should have felt, and that's what the critics assumed that I *had* felt. What actually happened was that a violent little episode from the police-court reports in my home-town paper, *The Barnsley Chronicle* (which my father would sometimes send), caused me to hoot with amazement at the capacity of seemingly mild and decent folk to set themselves off like fireworks when other people refused to live 'on right lines.' I told the story to various friends as an example of bred-in-the-bone Barnsley; and then I went to see Brendan Behan's *Quare Fellow*. I was immediately struck by his use of a succession of short sharp scenes, each one of a different flavour, to build up the picture of different groups and individuals in a gaol, sometimes mixing, sometimes following their separate preoccupations, and basically divided into two inimical blocs, the prisoners and their keepers. I set the notion of this technique alongside the story of the Travellers-versus-householders row from Barnsley, and *Live Like Pigs* resulted.

The rhythm of the ballads between each episode came to me from a public house in Ladbroke Grove, close to the street where Margaretta and I had set up our home. An Irish labourer, one night as we walked past the pub, was chanting an interminable traditional song – he paused at intervals between stanzas; a roar of bar-room conversation flooded instantly into the gap. Then the song would continue and the spoken clamour die down. I suppose there was an exceptional acoustic effect, deriving from echoes in the saloon, the half-open doors to the street, and the relative positions inside of singer and general crowd. It was clearly impromptu and not a regular 'music-pub performance'; but the singer did seem in some strange way to be *conducting* an entire symphony of music and multitudinous chatter through the command of his single voice.

The play, incidentally, caused a brief political storm in Barnsley – 'Local dramatist besmirches the town', *etc*. In order to defuse this (and also, it must be said, to grab hold of any handle of publicity for a production that was doing badly at the box-office) the theatre invited the Mayor of Barnsley to come and see *Live Like Pigs*. He felt very flattered, very grateful; he praised the actors and the author and everyone. He said, 'Of course, we did have a bit of trouble o' that sort, there's no denying. But we locked 'em all up and then ran 'em out of town. What else could we do wi' such a filthy pack o'knackers?'

Serjeant Musgrave's Dance

During the dress-parade of *Live Like Pigs* I was sitting at the back of the Royal Court, watching the actors in their drab costumes move about in the new set, a monochrome of various shades of gray. I thought, 'Oh yes. That's what I asked for, that's what I've got. Gritty realism, right? a black-and-white socially-conscious movie. Wouldn't it be nice to have at least one character in a bright red coat like an old-fashioned soldier?'

Later on, when the play itself was shaping itself in my mind, sprung off by this incident as much as by the hideous contemporary activities of the British Army in Cyprus, I talked about it to the folk-music authority, the late A. L. Lloyd. He was at the Royal Court to sing the between-scene stanzas in *Pigs*, to tunes of his own digging-out. And thereupon he dug out, for me, a whole set of eighteenth and nineteenth-century ballads about the old pre-Kipling red-coat soldiery. I put one of them straight into the play (Sparky's song, Act One, Scene One), and the rest into the coal-box of my working imagination – together with my father's collection of photographic postcards of his own old regiment, the East Yorkshire, taken at the end of the Victorian era in their garrison at Beverley. The album with these pictures had been one of the treats of my childhood, only to be looked at with washed hands.

The Happy Haven

This play arrived in a dream. I dreamed the whole shape of the plot – the only time in my life such a very useful thing happened to me with such completeness – and I have no idea to this day how or why. It is of course Cranach's theme from *The Fountain of Youth*, but I was not aware of that picture then, nor did I think in particular of *The Happy Haven* when

I was asked to suggest a cover illustration for this book. It all seems to have worked out subconsciously.

One scene in the play I did *not* dream. It is the Hopscotch episode (Act One, Scene Three) between Mrs Phineus and Mr Golightly. Margaretta D'Arcy had already written this as a one-act play in its own right. She thought it might fit into the *Haven*; with a little modification it did; the joint, I think, is seamless — at any rate no-one has noticed it — it serves not only to fill out the two characters concerned but also the first part of the middle of the play. Without it there would be a beginning and an end, as in my dream, but the essential middle would have remained a dead gap. I had been sorely stuck until she came to my rescue, by no means for the first time and certainly not the last.

*   *   *

Collaborative texts by J. Arden & M. D'Arcy (all published by Methuen):

Arden/D'Arcy (aka *D'Arcy/Arden*), *Plays: One* (1992).

The Island of the Mighty (1974).

The Non-Stop Connolly Show (1986).

Whose is the Kingdom . . . ? (1988).

To Present the Pretence (1977): essays, including an account of the script-and-stage history of *The Non-Stop Connolly Show*.

Awkward Corners (1988), essays etc.

Preface to an earlier version of *Arden, Plays: One* (1977: in the 'Master Playwrights' series), a kind of valediction to the established theatre.

John Arden,
Corrandulla, Co. Galway, Ireland.
May 1994

The Waters of Babylon

To Gwalchmei Francis Arden

Who put his head out in October,
Kept it out until November,
Drew it in then.

      Please remember:
He was young enough to take his choice.
What he did not like he did not have to face.
We who are older
Must needs be bolder.

The pen must crawl:
The black ink fill the waiting space:
For tortoise and child alone
The shell is an honourable home.

               J.A.

First produced at the Royal Court Theatre, London, on 20
October 1957 and directed by Graham Evans

List of Characters

KRANK (Sigismanfred Krankiewicz)	a Pole
PAUL	a Pole
CONOR CASSIDY	an Irishman
CHARLES BUTTERTHWAITE	an Englishman
ALEXANDER LOAP	an Englishman
COUNCILLOR JOSEPH CALIGULA	a West Indian
HENRY GINGER	an Englishman
AN ENGLISH POLICEMAN	
BATHSHEBA	a West Indian
TERESA	an Irishwoman
BARBARA BAULKFAST	an Englishwoman, an architect

SCENE: London, early in 1956.
NOTE: As the scenes of this play are, to some extent,
unlocalized, the sets should in no way be realistic. Where it is
necessary to indicate a particular locality, this must be done
rather by suggestion than by outright illustration.

The sort of scenery I had in mind was the eighteenth or
early nineteenth century sort, which involved the use of
sliding flats or drop curtains which open and close while the
actors are still on stage – a method still in use in provincial
pantomimes.

ACT ONE

KRANK *is discovered, yawning and stretching. He is a slight, fair man, aged anywhere between thirty and forty-five, with an undistinguished Central European face, steel spectacles, and receding hair. He is wearing a dirty jersey with a vee-neck, and trousers, and gym-shoes: no more. He has a coffee-pot, a cup, and a sandwich. There is a macintosh lying about.*
As the curtain opens, there is heard a crescendo then diminuendo of noise, as of an Underground train passing.

KRANK (*confidentially, to the audience: he has a light foreign accent*). Half past seven of a morning. What kind of day is it? Cold, I think, yes, cold, rainy, foggy, perhaps by dinnertime it will snow. No? Perhaps not snow, it is after all spring. March, April, May, even in London. I do not think – even in North London, perhaps, not snow. Breakfast, what sort of breakfast, this coffee it is not very fresh, is it? After the nature of an archaeological deposit, more water more coffee into the pot every morning, but at the bottom it has been there six weeks, seven, it's like drinking bitumen. Why don't I wash my cups and plates more often than only once a week? 'Cause I am a man of filthy habits i—

bone Barnsley; and then I went to see Brendan Behan's *Quare Fellow*. I was immediately struck by his use of a succession of short sharp scenes, each one of a different flavour, to build up the picture of different groups and individuals in a gaol, sometimes mixing, sometimes following their separate preoccupations, and basically divided into two inimical blocs, the prisoners and their keepers. I set the notion of this technique alongside the story of the Travellers-versus-householders row from Barnsley, and *Live Like Pigs* resulted.

The rhythm of the ballads between each episode came to me from a public house in Ladbroke Grove, close to the street where Margaretta and I had set up our home. An Irish labourer, one night as we walked past the pub, was chanting an interminable traditional song – he paused at intervals between stanzas; a roar of bar-room conversation flooded instantly into the gap. Then the song would continue and the spoken clamour die down. I suppose there was an exceptional acoustic effect, deriving from echoes in the saloon, the half-open doors to the street, and the relative positions inside of singer and general crowd. It was clearly impromptu and not a regular 'music-pub performance'; but the singer did seem in some strange way to be *conducting* an entire symphony of music and multitudinous chatter through the command of his single voice.

The play, incidentally, caused a brief political storm in Barnsley – 'Local dramatist besmirches the town', *etc*. In order to defuse this (and also, it must be said, to grab hold of any handle of publicity for a production that was doing badly at the box-office) the theatre invited the Mayor of Barnsley to come and see *Live Like Pigs*. He felt very flattered, very grateful; he praised the actors and the author and everyone. He said, 'Of course, we did have a bit of trouble o' that sort, there's no denying. But we locked 'em all up and then ran

And that? Oh that's the Irishman upstairs. That's Mr Conor Cassidy, that's another foreign man lives in this London. *He* does not like getting up in the cold mornings, neither, Cassidy.

More banging.

Cassidy. Will you stop, please, your bangings and crashings over my head. Over the head of my bed. Over my breakfast. What is the matter with this salami? I think, somebody, they've dropped it on the floor. It would disgust a drain-layer. But not me. For me, breakfast is to be enjoyed.

He enjoys it.
Enter BATHSHEBA, *a very pretty black girl, dressed for the street.*

BATHSHEBA. Mr Krank.
KRANK. Get out.
BATHSHEBA. I'm feeling so tired, Mr Krank.
KRANK. Well so am I tired. I've told you before, between half past seven and eight o'clock of the morning I am neither elegant nor delightful.
BATHSHEBA. Not to look at, Mr Krank, no sir, indeed you're not.
KRANK. Nor to talk to, nor to make love nor nothing else. I have slept alone tonight, I am an Englishman this morning, Bathsheba, I have bad temper like a grindstone, and where is my *Daily Mirror*, you haven't even brought it?
BATHSHEBA. I left it upstairs, I guess.
KRANK. In Cassidy's room, no?
BATHSHEBA. I was never in the room of that boy.
KRANK. No?
BATHSHEBA. Never.

have at least one character in a bright red coat like an old-fashioned soldier?'

Later on, when the play itself was shaping itself in my mind, sprung off by this incident as much as by the hideous contemporary activities of the British Army in Cyprus, I talked about it to the folk-music authority, the late A. L. Lloyd. He was at the Royal Court to sing the between-scene stanzas in *Pigs*, to tunes of his own digging-out. And thereupon he dug out, for me, a whole set of eighteenth and nineteenth-century ballads about the old pre-Kipling red-coat soldiery. I put one of them straight into the play (Sparky's song, Act One, Scene One), and the rest into the coal-box of my working imagination – together with my father's collection of photographic postcards of his own old regiment, the East Yorkshire, taken at the end of the Victorian era in their garrison at Beverley. The album with these pictures had been one of the treats of my childhood, only to be looked at with washed hands.

The Happy Haven
This play arrived in a dream. I dreamed the whole shape of the plot – the only time in my life such a very useful thing happened to me with such completeness – and I have no idea to this day how or why. It is of course Cranach's theme from *The Fountain of Youth*, but I was not aware of that picture then, nor did I think in particular of *The Happy Haven* when

KRANK. I don't think I believe you. Even if you tell me the truth, so what? You were sleeping with someone, weren't you?

BATHSHEBA. Well, if that's not what you want me to do . . .

KRANK. But not with people I know, not people who live here in my house. You must not confound a proper commercial business with . . . with all sorts of other things, with my friends, with your friends, with all my other businesses. O.K.? Now where's my *Daily Mirror*? I want to read it before I go out.

BATHSHEBA. I don't want you to read it. I want to hear you sing.

KRANK. In the mornings I don't sing.

BATHSHEBA. Yes, you do.

KRANK. Get out.

BATHSHEBA (*producing some notes of money*). There's the money.

KRANK. What money?

BATHSHEBA. My last night's money. What you sent me out to earn.

KRANK (*counting it*). Is this all of it there is?

BATHSHEBA. I'll give you the rest when you sing me your song.

KRANK. What song?

BATHSHEBA. The song, you once called it your Dolorous Song.

KRANK. Oh. In the mornings I do not sing.

She waits.

O.K. The true story, this song, of the life of, of the life of me, of Krank. This was myself, you see, at an altogether different time of the world. I make the song so that I can sometimes remember.

BATHSHEBA. Remember?

KRANK. Remember what perhaps by now I ought to have forgotten. After all, more than ten years . . . I will sing.

(*Singing.*)

> As I went down by Belsen town
> I saw my mother there
> She said, go by, go by my son, go by,
> But leave with me here
> Your lovely yellow hair.
>
> As I went down by Buchenwald town
> My brother looked out of the wall
> He said, go by, go by my brother, go by,
> But leave with me here
> The lovely strong tooth from your skull.
>
> As I went down by Auschwitz town
> And there for my sweetheart I sought
> But she whispered, go by, Oh my darling go by,
> You leave with me here
> The lovely red blood of your heart.

Noise of train passing.

BATHSHEBA. I don't understand all that song, what it's about. All the names of them foreign places you been? Man, you must have travelled wide.

CASSIDY *enters. He is a young Irishman of cunning and insolent appearance. He is wearing London Transport uniform.*

KRANK. Get out.

CASSIDY. I will not. Why, hello, Bathsheba, and you irrigating the morning wilderness of London with your tropical two eyes.

KRANK. Cassidy, you madden me with your noise. For your room this week, the rent is outstanding.

CASSIDY. And I'd come to pay it, so. Here y'are, fifteen silver shillings, count it yourself, all genuine and resonant like icicles. Ting, ting, jingle, jingle.

KRANK (*taking the money*). You had a woman in with you last night. I'm not deaf. Is five shillings extra.

CASSIDY. There was nobody with me at all. There's all the second floors. Number six the Attic's after barring up and fastening his door. I couldn't be in at him without bursting the lock. What'll you do about that?

KRANK. Look, I let you pay reduced rent so you help me run these lodgings, I leave it to you what to do: O.K.? Five shillings extra for last night. I'm not deaf.

BATHSHEBA. Mr Krank, there's all the money I owe you, Mr Krank, I always pay all the money I owe anybody, always.

KRANK (*pocketing this further money*). H'm.

BATHSHEBA. Mr Krank, will you give me some breakfast?

KRANK. There's some coffee in that pot. And finish my sandwich. Tonight, Bathsheba, you can have a vacation. Tonight you sleep with me. There's too many very untrustworthy people around here. When you're not on the streets you come in with me. O.K., *Mister* Cassidy?

CASSIDY. Well then, won't that cancel out my extra five shillings? Let alone allegations of . . .

KRANK. You'd best go to work, you'll be late. I don't want to be there before you.

CASSIDY. Plenty of time, now. I've a piece of information for you, Mr Krank.

KRANK. Oh.

CASSIDY. At the Brompton Oratory, after Mass, last Sunday morning . . .

KRANK. I wasn't there, last Sunday.

CASSIDY. Sure I know you weren't, but this young fellow was. He seemed to be expecting you.

KRANK (*sharply*). What young fellow?

CASSIDY. One of your own lot. Some sort of foreigner. He

knew me. I don't know how: he says, 'Where's Mr Krank?', he says.

KRANK. Well?

CASSIDY. So I says to him, 'I don't know.' So he says, 'Tell him I'll see him soon,' he says. He gave me his name. After the Holy Apostle . . .

KRANK. I can guess it. Paul was his name.

CASSIDY (*disappointed*). Why, sure it was, too. Then I've told you no news at all. I'll be off to me work. Oh, there's a fellow in the passage asking for you now. It's not the same one. Will I send him away?

KRANK. I don't want to see him. . . . Send him down here.

CASSIDY. I will. Oh, this boy at the Oratory, I didn't like his face at all. It was a face in a cold broken mirror, all kinds of bits that didn't fit, all full of bad luck. Not like Bathsheba, now: sure you could look at *her* face until . . .

KRANK. Out.

CASSIDY (*calls off and upwards*). You can come down, Mister, he'll see you. Watch the steps in the dark, they're fitted with the most perilous declivities.

Enter BUTTERTHWAITE. *A miserable elderly man, of shabby genteel appearance, cadaverous and with a West Riding accent.* KRANK *is reading and* BATHSHEBA *eating, so he finds himself ignored.*

CASSIDY. Here he is, and here I'm away. Begod, I love you, Bathsheba.

Exit CASSIDY.

BUTTERTHWAITE. Er. Are you Mr Krank?

KRANK (*without looking up*). Sometimes.

BUTTERTHWAITE. Good morning. Er. Good morning, Miss. My name's Butterthwaite. You wrote me a letter. (*He takes a letter out of his pocket.*)

KRANK. Indeed? I write a great many letters to a great many people. What did I write to you?

BUTTERTHWAITE. Er . . . well . . . I . . . er . . .

KRANK. Read me what I wrote to you.

BUTTERTHWAITE. Well, you just wrote like . . . er, 'Come next week and see me, and have some breakfast. Together we will talk business.' That's all. I was right puzzled I can tell you . . . I don't reckon you recollect it was in the bar at the 'Coach and Horses', you asked the barman to pass me this note, I mean, I wondered . . .

KRANK (*looking up at last*). Oh yes, I recollect it. Bathsheba, will you go away please. I made a mistake about the breakfast. I never eat breakfast, so I haven't any to offer you: I am sorry. You come back here tonight, Bathsheba.

Exit BATHSHEBA.

Now look Mr er . . . Butterthwaite, I've been delayed this morning, I am very late for my business. So we waste no time, O.K.? First, I'd better explain why I asked you to call and see me. I have been informed that you are in some sort of authority upon the complications, the intrigues, the tricks, traps, and tramlines of your English bureaucracy.

BUTTERTHWAITE (*showing interest*). Ah.

KRANK. Is it true?

BUTTERTHWAITE. Well now, if you'd asked me that about twelve years ago, I'd have answered you downright, Mr Krank: aye it's true.

KRANK. But now it is not.

BUTTERTHWAITE. Oh no, I wouldn't say that. Not right final, like that. But since I was last in practice, there's been a lot like of changes, you know. I'm bound to be a bit rusty.

KRANK. In practice. What is your profession?

BUTTERTHWAITE. I was a Napoleon.

KRANK. I beg your pardon?

BUTTERTHWAITE (*livening up*). A Napoleon of Local Government, I was. The term is not exactly mine, but it was coined in the provincial press. But it meant me, Mr Krank . . . me, Charles Butterthwaite. 'Vote for your Uncle Charlie and get pudding to all your dinners.' And they did. And they got it. Though I say it myself.

KRANK. You fascinate me.

BUTTERTHWAITE.

Aye. I'll tell you the tale.

As a young lad I began in Trades Union Offices.

Railways, smoke, black steel, canals, black stone.

That were my town, and where sets the power?

Mill owners: I saw that. Hundredweights of them.

Murky money. But not for me, not for our Charlie.

Conjure up the adverse power from out the crowded smoke:

Union Headquarters. Only a young lad: I begin: I go on:

From Union on to Council, Councillor to Alderman,

Alderman to Mayor, unfolded power of scarlet

Broadening back and belly: but that weren't the secret:

It's not gold chain nor scarlet carries right power.

Committees. Chairman of this one, Secretary of that one,

Housing Development, Chamber of Trade,

Municipal Transport, Hospitals, Welfare Amenities.

Eat your Christmas Dinners in the Lunatic Asylum,

Colliery Canteens, in the poor old Borough Orphanage,

Weekly photo in the paper in a paper hat and all

Cheery Charlie Butterthwaite: there was puddings to them dinners.

KRANK. Indeed, indeed.

BUTTERTHWAITE. But not any more. I've forgot the taste of puddings.

KRANK. What happened to you?

BUTTERTHWAITE. I had my misfortunes, like. So do we all.

KRANK. Ah yes, indeed.

BUTTERTHWAITE. What have I been once and look at me now.

KRANK. Yes. I need someone to advise me, Mr Butterthwaite: over these difficulties I am running in, with – what you call – the Local Authorities. English process, and so on, it is still somehow strange . . .

BUTTERTHWAITE. Ah well, of course, you being as you might say, a foreigner it would no doubt. . . . You'd be a kind of Czechoslav, I take it.

KRANK. I would not. I am not a Czechoslav, nor yet am I Lithuanian, nor yet Byelo-Russian. I am a Pole. O.K.

BUTTERTHWAITE. Eh, no offence, you know.

KRANK. Will you work for me, Mr Butterthwaite?

BUTTERTHWAITE. Nay, I don't know. Where's the advantage?

KRANK. Advantage?

BUTTERTHWAITE. Well, what do I get out of it?

KRANK. A fair proportion, certainly, of whatever I can get out of it.

BUTTERTHWAITE. It's difficult, you know. I'm like a foreigner myself in this city, and I'm that long out of touch. Exactly what is it you want me to do?

KRANK. I'll explain, I'll explain. But look, now I must go to my business, I take a bus to the Baker Street Underground Station, if you come with me we can talk as we go. I'm sorry about the breakfast, come on.

The noise of a train is heard.
KRANK *puts on mackintosh and they walk together. Scene closes.*

BUTTERTHWAITE. Well, that's all very well, you know, but I mean to say, I mean . . .

KRANK. Do I understand you, Mr Butterthwaite, that you're asking me for money? I have no money. How can I give you money? When you have assisted me as I require, then we shall both have money.

BUTTERTHWAITE. There is such a thing as a retainer, you know, like, a little on deposit . . .

KRANK (*crossly giving him a note*). Oh, take ten shillings. Now I shall have to go without my lunch, very likely.

BUTTERTHWAITE. But exactly what is it you want me to do for you?

KRANK. My house, you've seen it. A well-conducted lodging-house. I have eighty people in it . . .

BUTTERTHWAITE (*flabbergasted*). In that house — eighty people . . .

KRANK. Certainly. The most of them West Indians, East Indians, Cypriots, so forth, so on. Thirty shillings a week, one room one bed, I provide packing-cases if they wish to make any additional furniture: one lavatory: one gas-ring every landing: and a tap for cold water.

BUTTERTHWAITE. Well, I don't know: I say, I'm not surprised you're in bad favour with the Council.

KRANK. I *have* had to indulge in certain, ah, subterfuges. Eighty people, they say, is too many for the one building. Also I charge extra if a lodger wishes a guest for the night. I don't see, why is not that legitimate? But yet I have had this trouble . . . they *will* talk about a disorderly house. To be frank, they are persecuting me. And that, I come to England to avoid. O.K.?

BUTTERTHWAITE. But I don't reckon you need *me*, a good solicitor's what you want.

KRANK. No, no, no, no, no. A good solicitor would defend me, would he not, against the bureaucracies; but I, Krank, am not any longer in this a man of defence. I am to attack. In this I must be positive. So, I see you: I know you're more useful than a whole palatinate of solicitors. To begin: I intend to acquire a second house, to convert it to similar lodgings.

BUTTERTHWAITE. That's asking for trouble. The Sanitary
Authority alone . . .

KRANK. . . . must be on my side. You will find me a way to
arrange it. O.K.?

BUTTERTHWAITE. Eh, I don't know . . .

KRANK. Well, here we are at the Underground station. Good
morning. I'm sorry about the breakfast. Oh, get into
touch with me, come early of a morning to my house: or in
the evenings, shall I say, always I can find *you* in the bar of
the Coach and Horses? Good morning, Mr Butterthwaite.

BUTTERTHWAITE (*bewildered*). Good morning, Mr Krank.

Exit BUTTERTHWAITE.

KRANK *comes forward as the scene opens. Discovered are a
characteristic London Transport signboard, reading 'Baker
Street' and another reading 'Gentlemen'.*

KRANK (*walking round by one side of the stage*). Baker Street
Station. Here is that extremely convenient arrangement, a
gentleman's convenience with a door at either end of it. A
most remarkable, and, I think, beautiful phenomenon. I
am about to be reborn: in this twentieth-century peculiar
ceremonial womb, glazed tiles and electric light beneath
the golden pavement stones of London, hygienic underground renascence, for *me*, is daily routine. Where is the
lavatory attendant? Wash and brush-up fourpence.

Enter CASSIDY *with a mop and bucket, and a hold-all.*

CASSIDY. Ah hello now, Mr Krank, you're a little late this
morning. Here's a neat cubicle vacant for you, and here's
your clothes all ready.

KRANK *goes behind a screen and changes his clothes.*

Would you be after reading your *Daily Mirror* now you
took from me?

KRANK (*from behind screen*). I have looked at it, yes.

CASSIDY (*industriously mopping the floor*). And is there any news in it? I hadn't had time at all.

KRANK. News. Oh yes there is news.

CASSIDY. Some Royal Occasion perhaps? Or some praiseworthy betrothal announced combining Saxon Spectacle with warm Levantine money and money with true love – and how nice if we could keep all the teenagers off the streets.

KRANK. This morning no Royalties nor no Betrothals.

CASSIDY. But some sort of threat no doubt to popular morality. Some new and abominable traffic in the souls of men, or the hearts of women, or the bodies of youth; some beast in clerical or scholastic shape unmasked.

KRANK. Nothing so interesting, I'm afraid; one item only, it caught my attention. (*He comes out from behind the screen, dressed in a dark suit, made-up bow-tie, white shirt, carrying an umbrella. He had changed his spectacles for heavy horn-rims. He hands his original clothes in the hold-all to* CASSIDY.) The Russians are coming to London.

CASSIDY. Glory God, the whole atheist lot of them? Trampling through my lavatories, with their feetfuls of frozen snow – I'm going to put in for a thirty-shilling raise and bedamn it: I'll do it this day.

KRANK. Not quite the lot of them, only two of importance. I expect you'll have heard of them. The paper thinks they're funny, it calls them the Bulge and Crush, how amusing, read for yourself, I make haste to my office.

CASSIDY (*accepting the paper*). Why sure, Mr Krank, sure, I'll see you in the evening. What a desirable bright day it is for subterraneous employment.

Exit CASSIDY.
KRANK *comes forward as the scene closes.*

KRANK. Indeed. My employment, as you observe, is now immaculate, professional, appropriate to this body sparkling new from its matutinal rebirth, you see, I am a man of no one condition having no more no country, no place, time, action, no social soul. I am easy and able to choose whatever alien figure I shall cut, where and wherever I am, in London: not any place in London but all places of London, for all of it and none of it is mine (Central European paradox). Now Ladies and Gentlemen, my respectable existence, a skilful Polish architect in a good English office, reputable West End address, liberal working hours nine-thirty to five-thirty, and my name is not quite just Krank.

The scene opens to discover a drawing-table with architect's instruments, etc., and a telephone. BARBARA *enters, a square-faced young woman, age thirty-five, in a smock. She is not unattractive, but businesslike.*

BARBARA. Sigismanfred.

KRANK. Good morning, Miss Baulkfast.

BARBARA. You are late again.

KRANK. Everywhere this morning I am late. I miss the train, I meet a sort of person I have no wish to talk to, he talks to me two hours and a half.

BARBARA. When I appointed you my senior assistant, I told you I expected you to set an example to the rest of the office.

KRANK. Forgive me, Miss Baulkfast. It *is* 'Miss Baulkfast' today, I think, not 'Barbara'?

BARBARA (*rather grimly*). I think it had better not be Barbara again.

KRANK. Now why that, gracious lady?

BARBARA. Because I think it is better. We have a new client coming to see us this morning. He wants a house built.

KRANK. Let us build him one. It is what we are here for, no?

BARBARA. Have you completed the Contract Drawings for that school up at Hampstead?

KRANK. Not yet.

BARBARA. Why not?

KRANK. Not yet had time, Barbara . . . Miss Baulkfast. Forgive me.

BARBARA (*angrily*). Oh, for God's sake, Sigismanfred, I asked you to have them finished last night.

KRANK. Sigismanfred?

BARBARA. Mr Krankiewicz. It's a ridiculous name, anyway.

KRANK. It's a very interesting name, is mine. Sigismanfred. Did I tell you ever how I came to be called it?

BARBARA. Yes. These are the electrical layout drawings for the Willesden factory contract. Check them, please.

KRANK (*aware that she is taking no notice of him*). My grandfather, his name was Axel Krankiewicz, he was born in Warsaw, 1848. It was always his romantic sorrow, he had not been born twenty years earlier, so he would have been able himself to take part in the great and splendid events of that year throughout the nations of Europe. When my father was born, he named him Sigismanfred.

Enter LOAP, *a man of about forty with elderly and petulant manners. He is immaculately dressed as for Westminster. Neither* KRANK, *who is talking, nor* BARBARA, *who is studying drawings, notices his entry.*

Not after any national or liberal leaders of the age, for that would have had a taste perhaps of journalistic vulgarity, but after two most overweening heroes of poetry and history respectively. They possessed the soul of my grandfather. They were Manfred, the creation of your English Lord Byron, who defied the laws of God's greater creation: and Sigismundo Malatesta, the Italian Renaissance Tyrant, the wickedest man in the world.

LOAP. God bless my soul.

BARBARA (*startled*). Oh. I beg your pardon, I didn't hear you come in . . .

KRANK (*unabashed*). And *I* the eldest son of my father, received his identical name of Sigismanfred, to remind me doubtless of how different the fate of Poland, had my grandfather been born some twenty years earlier.

LOAP (*uneasily*). How very extraordinary, er . . .

KRANK (*introducing himself with a short bow*). Krankiewicz. Sigismanfred Krankiewicz. *I* am not the man to liberate my country. All my efforts are devoted to the liberation of myself.

BARBARA (*crossly*). Mr Krankiewicz, *please*. I beg your pardon, sir . . . er . . . good morning . . . er . . . can we help you in any way?

LOAP. Miss Barbara Baulkfast's office?

BARBARA. Yes, I am Miss Baulkfast.

LOAP. My name is Loap. I had an appointment . . .

BARBARA. Of course, Mr Loap. Do take a seat. This is Mr Krankiewicz, my chief assistant. Mr Krankiewicz: Mr Alexander Loap, our – prospective – client. He is a Member of Parliament for . . .

KRANK. Loap, Loap, Alexander Loap. You are Member for the Constituency in which I live, Mr Loap. The wrong side of the park. Most remarkable.

LOAP (*with professional enthusiasm*). Well, well, *really*, a Constituent. I am indeed delighted, sir . . .

KRANK. I do not have a vote. I am not a British Subject. Don't worry.

LOAP. Oh.

BARBARA. Now, Mr Loap, business. You wish us to design you a small house, do you not?

LOAP. That is correct. A commodious, but by no means large, ah quite small, in fact, ah, house in the country . . . it will not exactly be for myself . . . it, ah . . .

Enter TERESA, *a splendid Irish girl, with red hair worn very long. It is evident that a considerable amount of money is being spent on her adornment.*

TERESA. Certainly not for himself. It's for me.

LOAP (*very out of countenance*). Why, Teresa, my love, I did not expect you here today . . . ah. Miss Baulkfast, may I introduce . . .

BARBARA (*too flustered to know better*). Mrs Loap, how do you do, your husband has just been . . .

TERESA. He's not my husband. But he's building me a house all the same. I don't trust him to tell you what I want and get it right, so here I am to control him. I heard him say the house will be small. It will not. I want a good size to it so I'm not always cannonading against the corner of the bath when I'm trying to get into the kitchen . . . (*She sees* KRANK.) Oh God, who am I looking at? It, it isn't little Krank . . .

KRANK (*taking her up very smartly*). Krankiewicz is my name, gracious lady. I don't think we have had the pleasure . . .

TERESA (*slyly*). Oh is that it? Sure, maybe you're right. Mistaken identity after all. You're an architect, are you, mister?

KRANK. I am the assistant of Miss Baulkfast.

TERESA. Why, isn't that lovely, now, and I'm the harlot of Mr Loap.

BARBARA. I am afraid . . .

LOAP (*sweating with embarrassment*). Excuse me, must introduce, very glad to, ah, Miss Delaroy: Miss Baulkfast, our architect, Miss Delaroy, my . . .

TERESA. All right – let's talk about the house. I'll tell you what I want. There's to be a good-size parlour or drawing-room or whatever you'd call it, and a dining-room separate. I don't eat in annexes any more at all. And the kitchen with everything in it, freeze, cook, wash, dry, everything, and the bathroom must have two showers, one over the bath and one in one of those transparent sentry boxes, and a spray nozzle affair additional between the taps of the bath. Oh God, and I want a bed like a Cathedral, with purple quilting going right up the wall behind our heads and two, three mirrors I can take a survey of meself in, top to toe front to back, whenever the notion takes me. And carpets as soft as custards in every room and corridor. Now you know what I want, Alexander, you arrange it with this good lady.

BARBARA. Well, Mr Loap, I have here a few sketches which might give you some idea of the sort of thing we can do for you . . .

KRANK. Not those, that's the Willesden factory, I think.

BARBARA. Oh dear, I'm unaccountably confused. Thank you, Mr Krankiewicz.

BARBARA *and* LOAP *study the drawings at the table.*

KRANK. Your name, Teresa, it was not always, 'Delaroy'.

TERESA. Neither was your name always . . . whatever you said it was.

KRANK (*seriously*). Ah, there you are in error. Long before I was anything else my name was without doubt . . . But yours used to be . . .

TERESA. Flaherty was it, or maybe Delaney? When you first picked me up on Euston arrival platform and perfect gentleman you were, carrying me string bag, you asked me so compassionate, 'Would I be the young lady seeking domestic service in a decent Catholic family?' and I says to you, 'I would,' and little did I know of the ladder of shame and sorrow you'd set me tender feet on: till today there's a house to be built for me for £5,000 . . . That day when I met you, I said me name was . . .

KRANK. Lonegan.

TERESA. It was not. That was me first lie in London. Me real name is Cassidy. I didn't dare to use it, I was afraid the 'domestic service' 'd get home to me mother or worse to me grandmother, or worse still, me brother Con.

KRANK. Con . . . Conor Cassidy?

TERESA. Of course.

KRANK (*carefully*). He is, I suppose, still living in Athlone?

TERESA. Somebody said, no. I think he's come to London. Some sort of job with the Transport Executive I shouldn't wonder. Oh he's always the boy for ambition is Con.

KRANK. Yes, I know what you mean.

TERESA. And why do you work in a place like this? Sure you made a lot more money the way you were before.

KRANK. Yes, but I was not . . . like here, I can find myself in touch, with, if you like, Members of Parliament. Architecture, building, it is a trade, I thought I'd learn it, then see what happened. Always useful, no? But I have not abandoned other interests and businesses. *Now* I send assistants to meet the Irish Mail for me, when they have time. You know, I *do* take great credit for you, Teresa – you had never met me, where would have you been now?

TERESA. And to think that my first one, you found him for me, sold bad apples off a barrow at the corner of Praed Street . . .

The telephone rings.

BARBARA. Oh, damn the thing. – Hallo, Barbara Baulkfast's office. Miss Baulkfast speaking . . . (*coldly*) Oh. It's for you, Mr Krankiewicz.

KRANK. Thank you. Hello, here is Krankiewicz . . . Who? I've never heard of you . . . Oh, *Paul*, is it you, is it? Now look, I told you, I am not to be telephoned at the office . . . No, no no . . . Proszę mówić po Polsku. Ktoś mоэе

podelechiawać. . . . Khrushchev, Bulganin? Nie wyglu-
piaj się . . . (*Abruptly.*) Nie ma o czym mówić . . .* No, I
can*not* see you, Paul. If you are going to be waiting for me
always on the Oratory steps, I shall never go to Mass
again. Then you will be punished eternally. Good-bye.
(*Rings off.*) Excuse me, I tell him not to telephone me here
– he telephones.

LOAP. Khrushchev, Bulganin?

KRANK. I beg your pardon?

LOAP. I don't wish to seem inquisitive, sir, but I did
overhear . . .

KRANK. Oh no, nonsense, Mr Loap, two Polish words, quite
different, no connexion whatever.

LOAP. Naturally I am not one to interfere with, independent
thought, all have of course great sympathy, refugees, ah,
iron-curtain of totalitarianism: but the Government is
exceedingly anxious, and so indeed, is the Opposition that
the forthcoming visit should in no way suffer from,
ah . . .

KRANK. Indiscreet demonstrations.

TERESA. Or boys throwing bombs?

LOAP. Be quiet, Teresa. This is a serious matter.

KRANK. Mr Loap, I do not throw bombs; neither do I
demonstrate. It is not in my nature to do such things.
Don't worry.

LOAP. I see. Thank you. Now, Miss Baulkfast, I have an
appointment at the House in precisely half an hour, so I
shall take my leave. As I say, I am impressed by the quality
of your work, but *cost*, Madam, cost, is the key note. I
shall have to give the matter much further thought.

TERESA. Indeed. So all is beneficence and bounty as usual.

---

* Please speak in Polish. Someone may eavesdrop . . . Khrushchev,
Bulganin? Don't be silly . . . There is nothing to talk about.

LOAP. Good morning, Miss Baulkfast. Do you accompany
me, Teresa? I will see you to a taxi.

Exeunt LOAP *and* TERESA.

BARBARA (*in a strained voice*). What has there been between
you and that girl?

KRANK (*airily examining a drawing*). Nothing, dear Miss
Baulkfast, that need cause you to lose your sleep.

BARBARA (*indicating herself*). What has there been between
you and *this* girl?

KRANK (*as before*). Nothing, dear Miss Baulkfast, that . . .
(*Turning on her very suddenly.*)
Now listen to me: To look for true love in a naked bed
It is more dangerous, perhaps more vain,
Than burgling a house on fire,
Pearl diving under a whirling roof of sharks,
Hewing pit coal when the narrow air hangs dead along the
    galleries.
Where is your gain?
You do not have to do it for a living.
You do not have to fight it as a war:
You look for too much, and you look too far.
That way you find nothing but another person's pain.
And then you delude yourself, it's a fit pain for *you* to bear:
Though all you know about it is a muttering you would
    hear
Drift into your ears when you think you're asleep in bed.
Alone in bed, I mean: *I* never talk in my sleep.
It looks like I've lost a page from the Specification of the
    Hampstead school. Do you know where it might be?

BARBARA. You are a great deceiver of women, Sigismanfred.
One day, I think, one of them will finish you.

KRANK (*airily*). Oh, I don't imagine that is very likely.

BARBARA (*exploding*). No, no? Do you ever imagine anything, do you have the smallest conceivable scruple of a notion of a grain of an idea . . .

Enter PAUL, *a haggard man in a dark duffle-coat.*

What do *you* want?

PAUL (*like* KRANK, *he has a light foreign accent*). I beg your pardon if I intrude. I am from the Holocaust Heating and Engineering Company. Always trusting to meet your every requirement. I understand you wish to use our products in a factory at Willesden. I could discuss the contract with you, Madam, now, if you desired, or some other time . . .

BARBARA (*unsteadily*). My assistant will discuss the contract with you. I – I think I have another appointment. Mr Krankiewicz, entertain the gentleman.

Exit BARBARA.

KRANK. So. A heating-engineer are you now?

PAUL. I am. I am, in fact, my dear friend. Do you wish to talk about heating your factory?

KRANK. No. I wish to know why the devil you come here, I have given up going to church because you lie in wait for me behind the confessionals: I have given up answering the office phone because you terrify me over it continually. At least you do not know where I live. Or do you?

PAUL. Yes.

KRANK (*resigned*). It is clear there is to be no escape, Paul, will you tell me, please, what it is you want?

PAUL. I want *you* to remember, you are a citizen of Poland.

KRANK (*wearily*). Dear Paul, I am no longer a citizen of anywhere.

PAUL (*dramatically*). The Russians are coming to London.

KRANK. I read now and then the newspapers.

PAUL. What are we going to do about it?

KRANK. *Me*, I intend to do nothing about it.

PAUL. There are others who do not so intend.

KRANK. Let me point out to you – it has been officially requested by the leaders of the Polish Community in England that nobody does anything to disturb Queen Elizabeth's peace. I have no doubt some *gentle* kind of a demonstration, some carrying of banners and laying of wreaths, may likely take place. But strange, Paul, you are not a man I can envisage . . . you laying of wreaths . . . no.

PAUL. No. What I intend to do is not gentle, it is not passive, nor floral, nor processional, Sigismanfred, I am going to blow them up.

Telephone rings. Enter BARBARA.

BARBARA. That'll be for me. It's that bloody headmistress up at Hampstead. Hello. Barbara Baulkfast's office. Miss Baulkfast speaking. . . . Good morning Miss Fisher. . . . Yes . . . Yes . . . I quite understand. You want the colour scheme for the infants' classroom as it was before, the dove-grey and signal-red . . . Yes, Miss Fisher, they *have* started painting it blue. I'll order them to stop . . . Good morning. You heard that, Krankiewicz. Send out another Variation Order. After all, she's the client. (*She turns to leave.*)

KRANK (*to* PAUL, *from whom he has not taken his eyes*). You must be out of your mind.

BARBARA. Are you talking to me?

KRANK. No. I er . . . it's the Willesden factory, he wants to put in an oil-burning boiler instead of the gas. But . . .

BARBARA. Arrange it to your satisfaction. Only, remember, all these things have got to be paid for.

Exit BARBARA.

PAUL. No, Sigismanfred, I am not out of my mind.

KRANK. God's mercy on to London, Paul, how do you possibly think you can . . .

PAUL. It will be perfectly easy. I have my job . . . I work for a firm making boilers, radiators, taps, screws, gas-pipes, electrical appliances, all of them things that each, with skill, can provide some necessary part of the – bomb, mine, infernal machine, or what you'd call it. Everything that is . . .

KRANK. Except your explosive.

PAUL. Ah, yes. The explosive will be furnished by Wladyslaw. As you know he has means of access.

KRANK. I did not know.

PAUL. It's true, he has. All we want, Sigismanfred, is somewhere safe to assemble our device.

KRANK. *And* somewhere safe to go and set it off.

PAUL (*humourlessly*). That is being planned for.

KRANK. Why not assemble it in your radiator factory? If all the parts are manufactured there . . .

PAUL. Don't be a fool.

KRANK. Thank you.

PAUL. You owe me five hundred pounds.

KRANK. Oh, no I don't.

PAUL. In 1946 that money was lent to you by Josef, my second cousin from Poznań. Some disreputable deal, I don't care to remember . . . But *I* have taken over the debt from Josef in settlement of a – a private dispute between us. Here is your acknowledgement of the loan. Your signature is incontestable. (*He produces a paper.*)

KRANK. So?

PAUL. I want it. Five hundred pounds.

KRANK. I haven't got five hundred pounds.

PAUL. Yes: it is, perhaps, so large a sum, you cannot immediately realize it; so, I will permit you to pay me in kind.

KRANK. What kind of kind?

PAUL. The use of your house at the end of next month for the purposes I have already implied.

KRANK. No.

PAUL. Yes.

KRANK. But you cannot carry out political conspiracies in my house. I will be ruined. Anyway, there's more than enough goes on there as it is.

PAUL. It is the only safe place. I know your elusive habits, Sigismanfred. Wladyslaw has had you observed for quite a long time. You are not so clever as him, but I think you may be more clever than English Security. All *our* premises are liable to be watched. *We* are too well known to the M.I.5 as indefatigable patriots: but you are known only as . . .

KRANK. Never mind what. You are over-rating me. *My* 'elusive habits' were designed to protect me from women, from creditors, from my tenants, from my own old convictions: not from the Special Branch.

PAUL. It does not matter. When we are ready, we shall expect a room, and privacy, and such assistance as we ask. In return, I forget the five hundred pounds, and also I forget to do my Honorary Englishman's duty of informing the police about all your different businesses in the northern part of London. You will hear from us soon.

Enter BARBARA.

In the Willesden factory, Mr Krankiewicz, a gas boiler would be by far the most suitable. I will prepare estimates accordingly. Good morning madam. Always trusting to meet your every requirement.

Exit PAUL.

BARBARA. Gas boiler.

KRANK. Yes, on this particular contract, I think . . .

BARBARA. Very well, I'll leave it to you. Did he give you a price?

KRANK (*vaguely*). Five hundred pound . . .

BARBARA. What?

KRANK. Er . . . no. He didn't give me a price. We shall hear from him later.

BARBARA. You never told me what you had to do with that girl.

KRANK. Just old, old acquaintance is all. Don't worry.

BARBARA. Just old acquaintance. Like me?

KRANK. Not very much like you. Don't worry. Half past twelve. Are you not lunching with a client today?

BARBARA. Good heavens, so I am. I must fly.

KRANK (*airily*). O.K., dearest Barbara, you fly. Good-bye.

BARBARA. God destroy your bloody breath, Sigismanfred.

Exit BARBARA.

KRANK. Not until somebody gives me five hundred pound. Keep these people away from my house. . . . Bombs, violence, conspiracy, all of it again, pale faces, sweaty fingers, jigging on my heart, hooded fanatic eyes like letterboxes watching me. I was alone, and confident, and uninvolved. Now look at me. Should I tell the Police? Police: No. I am Krank. I must stand uninvolved. Five hundred pound. At least I have over a month to get it.

He sings and dances a little step dance between the stanzas.

> O when I was young
> I played with a gun
> And all the other children in a row
> I shot them through the head
> Till they lay down dead
> And then I did not know
> Where to go,
> Where to go.

But the children they arose
And came creeping from the ground
And they fired silver bullets up my stair
They woke my true love,
Who was sleeping up above,
Till she ran from me
Tearing out her hair,
Out her hair.

They drove down the doors,
And set fire to my roof,
And they pulled away the pillars of the wall;
I stood in the street
With the rain upon my feet;
While my house so majestical
Did fall –
Oh did fall.

CURTAIN

ACT TWO

Noise of train passing. CASSIDY *discovered. He is not wearing his uniform, but a black suit.*

Enter BATHSHEBA.

CASSIDY. Are you after meeting the boat train, Bathsheba?

BATHSHEBA. Man, half the week I've been meeting it. Waterloo, Victoria, Charing Cross.

CASSIDY. Anybody on it?

BATHSHEBA. Two today from Trinidad and there was one from Jamaica. I brought them along for to see Mr Krank. Will he keep them, maybe? No, I don't know. Not what I'd call real proud-jetting young women, not what I'd call flying fish or torpedoes. No sir, just kind of sad and quiet gentle sea-weed laid out dark on a hard cold beach. You've been along to meet a train too?

CASSIDY. The Irish Mail, no less. And there they stepped down from it, six beautiful doxies. Sea-weed? – No sea-weed but all roaring gorse, wild whitehorn, a chiming tempest of girls, turned that dirty Euston into a true windswept altitude, a crystal mountain-top for love. Or for Mr Krank's finances, which is more to the bloody purpose.

BATHSHEBA. Did you bring them here?

CASSIDY. I did not.

BATHSHEBA. Why not?

CASSIDY. Sure they'd a pair of chattering old magpies of nuns with 'em, 'March strictly past the wicked enticing man, girls, straitly away past him, and drop your eyes to the platform, God preserve us from the man, God help us and save us'. And who goes to Mass more commonly than

Cassidy? What would you call me but the epitome of religion, what's Baker Street station but crumb of a warm loaf expansive to my leaven of perpetual devotion? Royalty and strength to His Holiness the Pope.

BATHSHEBA (*uncomprehendingly enthusiastic*). Royalty, Royalty.

CASSIDY. And may the bones of Oliver Cromwell crumble in the ground. Crumble and rumble, rumble and crumble.

Enter BUTTERTHWAITE *full of excitement. He carries a great bundle of newspapers.*

BATHSHEBA. Glory hallelujah.

BUTTERTHWAITE (*sings*). Hallelujah, hallelujah, hallelujah! Every Christmas up north we'd reckon to do 'Messiah'. Ah, there's a good thundering work-through into the fling of that chorus, I'll tell you, and then, what about the Refiner's Fire, eh? Hear *that* one holler, as it comes running up shaft. (*Sings.*) 'For He is Li-i-ike a Refi-i-i-ner's Fi-ire' . . . (*He holds up papers.*) But I've got it, I've got it. Your Uncle Charlie's got it, every detail fixed and prized for him. Where is he? Where is he? I'm bawling at his door.

CASSIDY. He's above in the house passing words with some women.

BUTTERTHWAITE. Words d'you call it, what I've got here it's more than words, I can tell you, it's Power, it's Potential, it's congenital Might and Force. And between you and me, Mr Cassidy, it's money. (*Sings.*) 'The Trumpet shall sound and the Dead sha-all be wakened.'

Enter KRANK *in his mackintosh and a cloth cap.*

A Merry Christmas, Mr Krank.

BATHSHEBA. Merry Christmas.

CASSIDY. Merry Christmas, many of them, barrel-loads of bloody beer.

KRANK (*annoyed*). Merry Christmas, we only just had Christmas: what the hell you all talking about? Is more noise down here than when the Underground goes past . . .

The train passes and drowns his words.

When the Underground goes past. Three young ladies upstairs, what is it you think they think of it all? Howling and screaming like a cellarful of gelded cats, like I kept a brothel house down here, like you all wanted the police in here after us. Is that what you want? I tell you, these days, that is the *last* thing must be let to happen in this house. O.K.

CASSIDY. Oh, and how long is it you've been so respectful to the police?

KRANK. Never mind: do as I tell you. I hope, Mr Butterthwaite, you are come here to some practicable purpose.

BUTTERTHWAITE (*a little dashed*). Aye, well I am: but, er . . . if you're not in right mood, like, I can . . .

KRANK. I am in the right mood for good sense; not for foolishness. What have you for me?

BUTTERTHWAITE. What have I for you? I've got everything for you. I've got such a scheme here – who said I'd no notion, who said I'd lost my touch; who said that Cheery Charlie Butterthwaite there was nowt left of him but press cuttings? I'll show 'em.

KRANK (*looking at the bundle of papers* BUTTERTHWAITE *gives him*). I don't know what all this is. What is it? What will it do for me?

BUTTERTHWAITE. What you want it to do. It'll put you and the Borough Council together like that. (*He holds up crossed fingers*). Two mouths, ten fingers, four little feet, in a big brass bed, that's you and them: Mister and Missus, and devil take the lodger. 'Course, you'll have to play it careful. Bold, aye, but careful. Stands to reason, you know.

KRANK. Indeed? You fascinate me. But at this present unfortunate moment I am no longer concerned with the coition of myself and the Borough Council. What I would like to know: will your scheme, Mr Butterthwaite, bring to my imminent pocket five hundred pounds?

BUTTERTHWAITE. Five hundred pounds? It'll bring you thousands.

KRANK. So? But how long, how long?

BUTTERTHWAITE. Ah, it'll take time: but I reckon we could guarantee you five hundred in no more than a month or two. Of course, that warn't exactly, you know, what you'd set me on to find out. But still . . . Now then, for details. What I'd reckon'd be best . . .

KRANK (*studying papers*). One moment, wait. Cassidy, Bathsheba; if you please – out.

BUTTERTHWAITE. I thought, maybe, Miss Bathsheba, she maybe, might be of help to us.

KRANK. Indeed? O.K., Bathsheba. Stay.

CASSIDY. If she stays, I stay. What the hell should Bathsheba do, that you keep secret from me? Carry on, Buttery boy, let's hear the story.

BUTTERTHWAITE. A matter of interest, what do you want the five hundred for? Because if . . .

KRANK. Never you mind.

BUTTERTHWAITE. Oh very well, very well. So long as I get my percentage.

BATHSHEBA. And for me, Mr Krank? Me too, for a percentage?

KRANK *takes her on his knee and fondles her as he reads.*
A train passes.

CASSIDY. Percentages on the house me boys, tonight, hey?

KRANK. As well as I can make it out, your extraordinary handwriting, Butterthwaite: what is here, it is some sort of arrangement for swindling the electors of this Borough out of their savings?

BUTTERTHWAITE. Swindling – Mr Krank, the scheme is in the nature of a Municipal Lottery, as you'll see.

KRANK. To start with it's illegal, I'm afraid.

BUTTERTHWAITE. Eh, it's not illegal. If the Borough Council sets it up for us . . .

KRANK. The Borough Council. But how . . . ?

BUTTERTHWAITE. It's nowt but a modification of what's always been successful, years ago, up north, scores of Corporations, I tell you I'm *experienced*. The Borough Council first sets up . . .

KRANK. But how to hell we can get the Borough Council to set such things up for us?

BUTTERTHWAITE. But that's where our Joe comes in. Now as I was saying . . .

CASSIDY (*bemused*). Oh God, I'm dancing on the twirly water, who's this fellow Joe, anyway?

KRANK. Quiet.

BUTTERTHWAITE. The Borough Council first sets up a Municipal Savings Bank. Connected, very like, with Cooperative Society. Now then, your Bank might not do too well, so what happens? You offer a Premium, every month, every quarter, when you want, and you draw for it, and the winning ticket gets – whatever you want to give. Folk put their money in. Who draws it out? We do.

KRANK. By what means?

BUTTERTHWAITE. That rather depends on how well we get on with Joe.

CASSIDY. I'd rather you told me, Mister, who the bloody hell is Joe?

BUTTERTHWAITE. Oh aye, Joe. I thought I'd made that clear.

KRANK. No. You had not. Please to make it clear. Who is Joe?

BUTTERTHWAITE. Joe is the new Napoleon of this Borough. Leastroads, he will be, by time I'm through with shaping him. As soon as you'd done talking to me the other week, I said to myself, 'What this Borough needs is a new Napoleon, and what Mr Krank needs is to be like Grey Eminence, behind him.' I'd have taken on the job myself, but you know, I'm an old man – I don't reckon I've got right stamina any more. So I took a look at your Council, took a good look at all of them, and out of them all I selected Joe.

BATHSHEBA. Joe – Joe for Joseph – why, man, it's Joseph Caligula you got on your mind.

BUTTERTHWAITE. That's right – aye, she's right, Joe Caligula, the very lad I mean.

BATHSHEBA. But that one, he comes from Barbados, just like me, Mr Krank, all away from Barbados, and look at him now . . . so marvellous and main, he sits and he rules the Council of the town.

KRANK. You know him, Bathsheba?

BATHSHEBA. It's all of we spades we know him, Mr Krank. He's a real famed boy, Joe Caligula. Oh yes, he's the black bully ruler, he's the stamping boy to prove no faster blood in London than Joe's jump of life.

Noise of train passing.

KRANK. Joe Caligula. Councillor Joseph Caligula. Yes, I think I have heard of him. I think I had better meet with him. O.K.

BUTTERTHWAITE. O.K. It's two o'clock, it's Sunday: I'll tell you where he'll be. Speakers' Corner, Hyde Park, he goes every Sunday, he stands on his platform, he makes speeches all afternoon. He does work hard at his trade, you know. Perhaps you'll like to go and listen?

KRANK. Excellent thought. Let's all go and listen.

They come downstage as the scene closes.

How wonderful a symbol of your English democracy: The Corner of the Park. So sylvan, so arcadian, so pregnant a lesson to the errant Totalitarian. So joyous an expanse of sweet Independent Liberty informed by true reason and the dictates of Conscience. Let us all go there and listen.

There are discovered three speakers' stands, as follows:
JOE CALIGULA's with a placard reading, 'Joe Caligula. Only friend of Coloured Londoners. Destroy Discrimination';
HENRY GINGER's, reading, 'England and the Foreign Peril. We are betrayed'; LOAP's, reading, 'Our Foreign Policy is a Balanced Road to Peace.'
CALIGULA is a spectacular black man, very big and bold, well dressed in a camel-haired greatcoat and grey homburg.
HENRY GINGER is a seedy little man, with long grey hair and a reedy cockney voice. When the scene opens they are all three talking at once. Throughout the scene their speeches, unless otherwise indicated, are addressed directly to the theatre audience.

CALIGULA. I stand for the Right of the Coloured People in this Country. We are loyal subjects of the British Government, but we must have full liberty, we must have freedom, we must have freedom.

HENRY GINGER. There are untold thousands of criminal foreigners in this country. They are being let in by the British Government, a monstrous threat to our liberty, a threat to our freedom, to all our freedoms.

LOAP. The considered Foreign Policy at the present time, of

this Country, Expand the Good Influence of the British Government.

CASSIDY. Well, and here we are. Now which of these three is the glorious Napoleon?

BATHSHEBA. Do I have to tell you? Oh, see him with your eyes, man.

KRANK (*indicating* LOAP). One thing you didn't tell me: *he* was going to be here. How exceedingly inconvenient. I must not be observed. (*He turns his collar up and pulls his cap down.*)

CASSIDY. I don't see the Irish Republican Army today . . .

KRANK. Quiet.

HENRY GINGER. I know very well that I'm not listened to, but I shall fearlessly continue to deliver the truth . . .

CASSIDY. That's his usual place, there, where that little fellow is.

CALIGULA (*in a sonorous Old Testament voice*). Five years, six years, I have lived in this London. What do I find in the streets and high houses of this city, what do I find for my people beneath these aching pavements and up under these glittering roofs . . . for my people, whose skins are of the dark coal forest and whose spirits are the fire and wonder that hides inside that trodden coal, O my dark people; I find we still are told, Go down, Go down, here is enough warm light already, you are come among us uncalled-for, as smoke and shadows to drench out our fire in alien ugliness and our own guilt for it. But I say no man can hold us down, shall send us down again, shall choke the sweeping hinges of our wide wide progress and our open pride of life: for we are breaking up and out into our own time of the world, and we never shall go down.

BATHSHEBA. Glory, glory yeah man.

KRANK. Are you quite sure he is the most suitable for our purpose?

BUTTERTHWAITE. Nay, what good's a Napoleon, without he's got strength?

CASSIDY. Oh Lord, to me he's just a roaring nigger. Let's go and listen to one of the others, for God's sake. (*He goes over to* LOAP.)

LOAP. We feel, and, I say, the Prime Minister feels, that, to this circumstance, that is to say, the forthcoming visit of the Russian Leaders – as a necessary if indeed a not entirely inappropriate manifestation, or, yes, a trend towards possible peace, ah, mutual co-operation, co-habitation . . . co-, to coin a phrase, co-existence with the mighty Soviet Union. This momentous visit, must not, I have made it my personal, my personal charge, to see that it must not be marred or spoiled, that all should concerning it . . .

CASSIDY. Oh what the hell do you think you're telling us? You tell *me* a thing, Captain.

LOAP (*to* CASSIDY). What is that, sir?

CASSIDY. My brother Seamus comes across the water to live in London, he's a peaceable decent man like yourself, and what happens to him? They make him join the British Army.

LOAP. I fear, I . . .

CASSIDY. Two bloody years, Captain, oppressing Minorities in the English Colonies, and putting the bayonet into pregnant women . . . that's what they're after making him do. Now he has a friend, see, his name's Paddy Riley, *he* comes to London. 'Begod,' says he, 'I want to be a fireman in the Brigade.' 'What's your nationality?' they ask him. 'Holy Ireland,' says he. 'Begod boy,' they tell him, 'there's no place for you in the Fire Brigades of London, you're no more than a bloody foreigner,' they tell him. Now is that justice, Captain, I put it to you square, should you call that justice?

LOAP. I, ah, I don't – I was endeavouring to discuss – Mr

Khrushchev and Marshal Bulganin, sir, is my subject. I must ask you to let me keep to it.

CASSIDY. O, Mary in Heaven, there's no justice at all.

He goes towards HENRY GINGER.

CALIGULA. You think I am a bitter man, I am cruel, full of revenge, I want racial wars and bloodshed – no, it is not true . All I want, all I demand, is the knowledge in this country that my people are your people, the Queen of England's people, that we have some claim to live in London without being feared, suspected, laughed at, sniffed at, we don't stink, you know, and we do change our underwear as often as most of you; sniffed at, sneered at, patronized, entertained with that wrong friendliness that says, 'I know you are inferior, but I am such a jolly fellow, such a gay dog, that I can forget it – unlike some of my unneighbourly neighbours. So have a drink, old fellow. Let's hope we're not observed.' Perhaps above all we claim our rights to live without being preyed upon by the avarice of pimps and landlords, black or white, disguised as human beings, into whose malevolent houses are trepanned so many cold bewildered travel-tired dark strangers before they've even been in London half an hour.

KRANK. Oh dear.

CASSIDY. Sure, that one's the noisiest black man I ever heard in me life! I can't catch one word this little creature's discoursing. Speak up, speak up will you, and let's have some notion of your argument.

KRANK. For the sake of heaven, Butterthwaite, what sort of convenient Napoleon is this?

BUTTERTHWAITE. Now don't you try and cross the Trent when you've not yet got as far north as Luton. Everything's . . . (*To* CALIGULA, *who comes down from his stand.*) Good afternoon, Councillor Caligula, I trust as how you're in health?

CALIGULA (*when not orating, he has a grave courteous manner*). Why, Mr Butterthwaite, I am indeed most happy to see you. I am your debtor, sir, for the decent invaluable assistance you have rendered both to me and my work. I have put your project before the Borough Council and it has found favour. There is much work to be done, sir, in the ward I represent, and in many others. Evil houses to be pulled down, vicious tenants to be evicted, plague spots to be burnt out. Your Savings Bank Scheme, properly used, will give us great help, Sir.

BUTTERTHWAITE. Aye, well, the Lottery should act as a bit of an inducement . . .

CALIGULA. Yes, indeed. Particularly among my improvident countrymen.

BUTTERTHWAITE. I wonder, Councillor, if I might introduce to you a gentleman who . . . (*He turns to look for* KRANK *but finds him shaking his head and taking evasive action.*)

Meanwhile BATHSHEBA *thrusts herself in front of* CALIGULA. *He is not to realize that she is associated with* KRANK *or* BUTTERTHWAITE.

BATHSHEBA. Councillor Caligula, it's Bathsheba. I'm from Barbados, just same as you, you know my folks back there . . . or maybe, maybe you know 'em, you bet you know'em. My pappy he was a man like a black old battle remembered in a song. Only one eye left to him, only one ear, all cut about to the shape of a scallop shell, 'Half-past-two-half-past-three' they used to call him 'cause them times of every day he was wild wild drunk, he would go and he'd fight against the sailormen for gold rings and dollars, way down along on Silver Beach . . . You know him Mister?

CALIGULA. No, child, I never knew your pappy – but I know you and I know the way you choose to live in this town.

BATHSHEBA. I keep a gentle warm bed, Councillor, wide and gentle. I could rock you to sleep easy as a swooning ship in a loud storm. I could be the arrow-compass for all your ranging dreams, Councillor. Oh yes.

CALIGULA. What could you do in London you couldn't in Barbados? Only here, there's more money and more wicked men after it. Child, you may be wide and gentle, you may have pretty tits and hips, child, but all you are with them is just a waggling fool.

BATHSHEBA. Oh.

BUTTERTHWAITE (*recapturing* KRANK). Councillor Caligula, this is Mister Alfred Cash, the Polish gentleman I was telling you about, Councillor. Mr Cash is as it might be the moving spirit behind our Savings Bank . . . it were his own original idea entirely, let's be proper modest about it. He's the one worked every bit of it out.

KRANK (*frantically aside*). What did you say is my name?

BUTTERTHWAITE. I reckon he's got a right name for it, eh, Alfred Cash, Cash means money. . . . Good Cash brings you the Good Cash, eh? (*He laughs uproariously and nudges.*)

BATHSHEBA. Councillor, I'm going.

CALIGULA (*to* KRANK). I am very honoured, sir. You must be a person of great financial acumen.

BATHSHEBA. Good-bye Councillor, I'm gone.

Exit BATHSHEBA.
Enter PAUL *unremarked by the others.*

HENRY GINGER. But, I stand here and fearlessly say it, it is the monstrous army of foreign agents calling themselves Political Refugees, who for years have been insinuated, O with cunning, into the midst of our Society . . .

CASSIDY. Where's your evidence?

HENRY GINGER. . . . And we have welcomed them. Refugees? Where do they come from? Czechoslovakia, Yugoslavia, Lithuania, Hungary, Rumania, and, perhaps above all, Poland.

PAUL. What is that you say?

KRANK (*recognizing* PAUL). Oh my God, I get out of this quick, Excuse me, Councillor, but . . .

CALIGULA. Are you going, sir? I too will have to take my leave, I have a meeting . . .

HENRY GINGER (*to* PAUL). I have documentary proof that half the Poles in this country were nothing more than active collaborators with the Nazi Gestapo . . .

Exit CALIGULA *with his stand and placard.*

PAUL (*furiously*). That is a lie. I will not speak of myself, but there, over there, I see one of my compatriots, he will support me. Sigismanfred Krankiewicz. Sigismanfred, come here.

LOAP. I repeat, in extending the hand of friendship . . . (*He breaks off, noticing* KRANK.)

GINGER *writes in a notebook.*

KRANK (*who has almost managed to sneak away*). Paul, is it, Paul, there seems to be some mistake . . .

PAUL (*magnificently*). This man has been in Buchenwald. I know it for certain. Now will you dare to tell *him* what you have been saying to me . . .

HENRY GINGER (*doubtfully*). He may have been in Buchenwald, oh yes, that's very likely.

PAUL. And I myself was two years in Siberia, prisoner of the Soviets, and after that for two years I fought in most bloody campaigns, in Italy I fought . . . Who captured Monte Cassino?

LOAP. I repeat in extending the hand of friendship to our Russian friends . . .

HENRY GINGER. And that is another thing. I have heard unimpeachable information that there is a clear plot, a Polish plot, to sabotage the visit next month of Comrades Khrushchev and Bulganin . . .

PAUL. You have heard nothing but unimpeachable dogs-vomit, you foul old man; I will not stand here and listen . . .

HENRY GINGER (*very fast and nervous*). What I'd ask you is this, why didn't the Poles go back after the war? I'll tell you why not . . . they were afraid, because they knew that the People's Government in Warsaw knew that they'd worked for the Nazis. And now they're all working against a just peace settlement with the Russian people and the Progressive Soviet Statesmen. They're all criminals and traitors, that's what they are.

PAUL. Lies, lies, lies, pull him down, the dirty slanderer . . .

HENRY GINGER (*shouting into* PAUL's *face*). Yah, warmonger, where's your Iron Cross, where's your Swastika, you Fascist?

PAUL *pulls* HENRY GINGER *off his stand and jumps up himself.*

PAUL. Now hear my words, Englishmen. I am a Pole. I am proud of my nation. I did not ask to be an exile in this country, I did not ask to have my own country betrayed into the belly of the atheist tyrants . . .

CASSIDY. Ha, ha, hurrah.

PAUL. Nor did I ask to walk the streets of London and look on in silence while the vile murdering butchers who have killed my family and enslaved my friends walk and talk and smile among your graveyards and your picture galleries, and smear the gloves of your delicate Queen crimson with the reek of their hand-grasp.

LOAP (*to* PAUL). Sir, if you please, I must beg you to moderate . . .

CASSIDY. Send him down, David.

PAUL (*to* LOAP). Roll back into your mudwallow, you slobbering crocodile.

LOAP (*to a* POLICEMAN *who has already wandered across the back of the stage once or twice during the scene*). Officer, Officer, for heavens' sake restore order . . .

CASSIDY *pulls* LOAP *off his stand and damages his placard.* HENRY GINGER *scuffles with* PAUL.

HENRY GINGER. Nazi, Fascist, Reactionary, Warmonger, Anti-British, that's what he is, why don't you arrest him, Officer – he's Anti-British, I tell you . . .

KRANK. Cassidy, come here, will you come back here . . .

CASSIDY. Ha, ha ha hurrah, where's the police, where's the bloody peelers . . .

POLICEMAN (*strongly clearing the stage*). Come on, come on now, break it up. You there, you there, come on, move along, out of it the lot of you. Oh, it's you, is it, Henry Ginger, you behave, old man, or you'll find yourself inside again for Inciting a Breach. Come on, come along now, break it up, can't you?

Exeunt all save LOAP *and* POLICEMAN. HENRY GINGER *carries away with him his stand and placard.*

LOAP. Thank you very much, Officer. Much obliged to you.

POLICEMAN. That's all right, sir . . .

Enter TERESA.

. . . Here, you, young lady, we've got too many of your lot round here already; get moving.

TERESA. Well, I declare.

LOAP (*embarrassed*). It's all right, Officer, I, ah, I know this lady.

POLICEMAN. Eh? Indeed? Well, if you say so, Mr Loap. Good afternoon, sir. (*Exit* POLICEMAN.)

TERESA. And the same of it to you, Superintendent. You after enjoying now an agreeable half-hour with your politics, Alexander?

LOAP (*following her*). How many times . . .

TERESA (*looking at what is left of his placard, etc.*). They don't seem to have left much of your little platform for you.

LOAP. Teresa, how many times have I to tell you . . .

TERESA. This Balancing, now, it must be a difficult art. I used to live once with a boy from the circus, he made out he was an Equilibrist, but not after dark begod he wasn't. I only let him have me for a fortnight – the lunatic grunting crab. It was like sharing your pillow with a steam-shovel.

LOAP. Teresa. *Will* you listen to me.

TERESA. Oh, what's the matter now?

LOAP. Time and time again I have told you I will not have you hovering around me in public places. It was quite bad enough in that architect's office, but in . . .

TERESA. And what about the architect's office, anyway? If you're to build me a house at all, I'm going to have some sort of opinions, I imagine, and not let your generous money be thrown away on a pie-dish of a cabin that wouldn't be appreciated by a pigman. Besides, I became reacquainted with a very old friend in that office, and that's one pleasure you'd never begrudge a girl surely.

LOAP (*reflecting*). A very old friend. So you did. I knew he was familiar. Bulganin, Khrushchev.

TERESA. What?

LOAP. Khrushchev: Bulganin. Of course . . . Good heavens. Your old friend, Teresa, how well do you know him?

TERESA. Oh, well enough.

LOAP. Do you know where he lives?

TERESA. I know where he used to live.

Enter BARBARA *in some agitation. Unobserved she stops to listen.*

LOAP. Where?

TERESA. Never you mind. Anyway, I think he's moved.

LOAP. Now understand me, Teresa. If you are to get this new house as I promised, you are going to have to earn it.

TERESA. *Earn* it. And what do you think I'm after doing every other night for the past six months . . .

LOAP. Be quiet. You find out where this fellow, Krankiewicz, where he lives now. I want you to go to his house, and I want you to watch what he's up to.

TERESA. What he's up to . . . What should he be up to?

LOAP. Never you mind.

TERESA. Then what the hell am I supposed to . . . Oh, and, how extraordinary, here's the Architect-lady herself.

LOAP. Oh, good afternoon, Miss Baulkfast.

BARBARA. Good afternoon, Mr Loap.

LOAP. Are you . . . ah . . . taking a walk, Miss Baulkfast?

BARBARA. Yes, I – I am taking a walk. The park, it is, it is so delightful in the sharp weather, is it not? Miss Delaroy, I think?

TERESA. I am captivated with the renewed opportunity, Ma'am. And how are your affairs?

BARBARA. Very well, thank you. (*She takes* LOAP *aside.*) I wonder, Mr Loap, you didn't happen to see my assistant anywhere round here recently, did you? My Polish assistant, you know. I thought I saw him among the crowd, and now he seems to have vanished. I wanted to tell him . . . er . . . something rather important, connected with the office actually.

LOAP. No, I haven't seen him, no. I am sorry.

TERESA, *now up on* LOAP's *platform, starts to sing.* LOAP *and* BARBARA *attempt to carry on their conversation.*

TERESA.
Oh I built my love a castle
Of the marble stone so strong
And fastened up the doors on her
So she could do not wrong
I stood to guard her bedroom
With me pockets full of gold
But the wind blew down
the corridor
And I caught my death of cold.

BARBARA. I hoped you like the sketch designs for the house I sent you last week.

LOAP. Yes, indeed, they were most interesting. I'll be calling on you some day very soon to go into it more fully; but I can tell you now, Miss Baulkfast . . .

LOAP (*cont.*). Teresa, I would be obliged if you would go and do what I asked you to do.

TERESA.
I'll finish me song first.
Oh if you love a lady
And you know she loves you good
You can lie her down in thorns and briars
Or in a wild green wood
But if she sees the thicket
Has a fence or wall around
She'll climb by night and take her flight
And leave you on the ground.
Isn't that the truth, now, Miss Baulkfast? Oh, God, Alexander, and now for Mr Krank.

Exit TERESA.

BARBARA. Mr Krank?
LOAP. Miss Baulkfast. About the house . . .

BARBARA. Krank? Krankiewicz. Krank. You have seen him, haven't you?

LOAP. Now, now, Miss Baulkfast. . . .

BARBARA. And that girl knows where he is. Or she will know where he is. And she is going to him. That's enough for me.

LOAP. Miss Baulkfast, don't go. I mean, I meant to ask you before, but . . . Miss Baulkfast, will you have dinner with me tonight?

BARBARA (*losing patience*). Oh, you stupid god-damned . . . can't you see . . . no sense of time or place or of . . . God, what would you know of decorum, anyway. No, of course I won't have dinner with you, you pompous political idiot.

Exit BARBARA *after* TERESA.

LOAP. Well. What an unbusinesslike young woman. Do you imagine that she treats all her clients like that? Yet she was highly recommended to me. And by a Cabinet Minister too. I don't understand it.

Exit LOAP *with his stand and placard. The Scene closes.*

Enter HENRY GINGER.

HENRY GINGER. Sigismanfred Krankiewicz. I've wrote him in my book – if there's anything to find out, I'll find it out. Buchenwald, he says, does he? We shall see, we shall see. I wish I knew what the other one was called. Very violent character: tst, tst. But I'll catch him. I'll catch the both of 'em, I know 'em. Foreigners, doing down the interests of the English working man. But they've got to be smart to outreach Henry Ginger:

> Henry Ginger quick and hot
> Against Conspiracy and Plot,
> Though the fool policeman sleeps
> Henry Ginger wakes and creeps.

> He tracks down Subversive Threat,
> And he'll rescue England yet.

Krankiewicz was he called? I've wrote him in my book.

Exit HENRY GINGER.

Noise of train passing. Enter KRANK *in old jersey and trousers.*

KRANK. Butterthwaite. Butterthwaite, where are you? Where the devil are you?

The scene opens to discover BUTTERTHWAITE *sitting reading a newspaper on a flight of steps which run up from the rear of the stage as from an area up to the street which is suggested by a platform across the back at a height of about five feet from the stage floor.*

BUTTERTHWAITE. I'm out here in your basement area, Mr Krank. Getting a grip on some fresh air.

KRANK. Oh. What is it you think you are doing out here? I don't like you out here. You might be seen from the street.

BUTTERTHWAITE. You just listen to this. 'Councillor Joe Caligula's scheme for a borough Savings Bank and Public Lottery in which no one can lose is proving a great success. The popular Coloured Councillor told Pressmen today. The promise of bumper annual prizes has encouraged many North Londoners to invest in the new Bank. Asked when the draw for the first Premium would take place . . .'

KRANK. The popular Coloured Councillor said, 'Not for a long time,' I hope.

BUTTERTHWAITE. Something of that, Aye.

KRANK. Look here, how much money already we got out of this scheme?

BUTTERTHWAITE. Well, I . . .

KRANK. How much?

BUTTERTHWAITE. Nigh on a hundred.

Exit BUTTERTHWAITE, *above*.

CASSIDY (*to* BUTTERTHWAITE). Oh sure, sure.

KRANK. Now – *who* is watching the lavatory? Police?

CASSIDY. I don't think so.

KRANK. Wladyslaw?

CASSIDY. Who?

KRANK. A big thick man, black moustache. Polish, like me.

CASSIDY. Oh no, it's not him. It's that little fellow was preaching away against the foreigners in Hyde Park. Henry Ginger, I think was his name, now.

KRANK. Oh? Oh. I wonder what it can be *he* is after? Has he seen *me* there, my uses of that place?

CASSIDY. I couldn't tell. I wouldn't be surprised at all.

KRANK. This I do not like. (*Suddenly angry*.) There's other things I do not like, neither, Conor Cassidy. If it was not for you making abusive behaviour and your so amusing little riotings in Hyde Park, that man would not now be watching me into your lavatory. It is a great part of your fault, I tell you.

CASSIDY. Hey, wait a minute, now . . .

KRANK. And other things I do not like. If you were less interested in pinching the buttocks of the girls who come to this house, and were more interested in collecting the money that they owe me, there should be the less reason for me to revile you. Now get upstairs and gather in some rent from my tenants. There is a lot of it due, O.K.?

CASSIDY. Oh sure, sure. But you watch the tones you're talking to me with, Mr Krank, I'm not a man to . . .

Enter from the wings BATHSHEBA.

BATHSHEBA (*singing to a blues tune*). He laid me down, he laid me down, he laid me down, Oh Lord. He laid me down so low.

CASSIDY. He's in a battering bad mood tonight, take care of

your manners, now. And you take care of yours, Mister Conor Cassidy's no bloody Hebrew slave in Egypt, you know, despite his occupation.

Exit CASSIDY *into the wings.*
Noise of train passing.

KRANK. Where have you been?

BATHSHEBA. Where you told me to go. Where you asked me to go. Where you begged me to go, Mr Krank. Where I couldn't have held myself from going, if you was to stake me down to your kitchen floor, with nails of burning fire. And what have I got for it? What have I got from Councillor Joe Caligula, that proud lovely roarer of this town? I got as much joy as is water in a kettle after five hours a-boiling: and that's all I gone and got. From any living man I never met less. I'm real downright shamed. Am I old, Mr Krank, are my round haunches withered, my belly shrunken-in, my bosom dropped to nothing? Is my face and lips a ploughed field full of dirty thistles? What am I like, Mister, that I get no joy at all? 'Cause I don't seem to have given none, the first time in my life.

Noise of a motor vehicle arriving, door slams, knocking.

KRANK. What's that?

BATHSHEBA. Up at the back door, I think.

KRANK (*calls*). Cassidy, Conor Cassidy, see what is happening.

CASSIDY (*from off and above*). I think it's some fellows at the door are looking for lodgings.

KRANK (*calls*). Well see to them yourself. I'm busy down here. Considering it, Bathsheba, you need not go to Caligula again. You never told him, did you, that you came from me?

BATHSHEBA. No indeed. You said not yet to tell him.

KRANK. O.K. That damned fool Butterthwaite, he seems to be managing all my plans for me. I don't know why or where, or whatever he is doing. So perhaps it is better you should not go any more at present.

What are you like Bathsheba?

Thistles in a sour field?

That I do not see.

Nor do I see these witherings and wrinklings and shrinkings you talk of

I am no man for no woman, truly, Bathsheba:

I am a sort of a hole pinched into the wall of the world

Letting in the strong wind to knock down the chimney-pots.

I am a sort of pocket in the serene sky

Rattling and bouncing the royal passage of airliners.

What reason can there be for *me* to so continually couple with these girls,

Black girls, white girls, yellow girls, all lamp posts in the fog . . .

Stamping and banging above.

More noise, more. What goes on up there? Cassidy?

Enter TERESA *above.*

TERESA. Delaroy is the name, Mr Krank, I'll thank you to remember.

KRANK. Teresa. You should not have found your way here. I never told you I was living in this house.

TERESA. I've not come on a sociable visit. I've been sent. I've been sent to spy on you, Krank. What do you think of that for a tale?

KRANK. Sent? By whom? Scotland Yard?

TERESA. Not at all. Alexander Loap, M.P. He thinks you want to murder the Russians.

KRANK. He makes a mistake, then, is all. I am at peace. So tell him, Teresa.

TERESA. I don't know that I'll tell him anything. It's none of his damned business. This house of yours, you know, it's a great improvement on your last. But begod, it's not any tidier, is it? Who's the lady?

BATHSHEBA. Bathsheba's my name.

TERESA. And mine's Teresa. Hello there. (*To* KRANK.) You were kissing her when I arrived? Don't let me interrupt you.

BATHSHEBA. You hear what she says, man?

Enter BARBARA *above and unnoticed.*

TERESA. Put your arms around his neck, now, lovely, sit on his knee . . . he's small and he's bristly and he's short-sighted, and the sweaty little hands on him tremble like telephone wires: but with it all, if there's seven hundred people in a street and he out in the middle of them quite away from the sight of your eyes, you'd know he was there, you'd know he was there, always you'd know he was there.

BATHSHEBA. Not always the happiest thing you could know, is it, Mr Krank? But I don't scare as easy as I can lie down, ah no.

KRANK (*kissing her*). No? No? So, so, so.

He sees BARBARA.

Tonight it seems to be for me to be watched upon by everyone. Please come in, Miss Baulkfast. This is indeed a great honour. The humble little slum of poor Sigismanfred. Introductions: Miss – Delaroy, you know, do you not? And this is . . .

BARBARA. Miss Delaroy, I certainly know. I must admit, Sigismanfred, you astonish me. I felt sure I would find you in somebody's arms, but I thought . . .

TERESA. You thought at least they would be white and Irish?

BATHSHEBA. But they're not, they're not, lady. They're dark as a dolphin in the sea. I guess they're warmer than a dolphin, yes indeed.

KRANK (*getting up*). Yes indeed. Barbara you are making me exceedingly angry.

BARBARA. Then we'd better get together again, hadn't we – see, we have just one thing left to us in common.

BATHSHEBA. You and me, lady, we seem to have something in common as well, but I tell you I don't want to get together with you, not one mouthful.

TERESA. We've got all the three of us that something in common: but as none of us appear to have been having it simultaneous, I don't see any reason for hate and distaste. (*She takes a whisky bottle from her handbag.*) Here's a much better thought. We will have a portion of this? Will we reconcile together our broken lives of Krank, or whatever you'd call them?

BARBARA. Certainly not. You're an outrageous trollop. (BATHSHEBA *and* TERESA *laugh.*) Sigismanfred Krankiewicz; you need no longer attend my office for architecture or for any other purpose. The money that is due to you will be sent on through the post.

The banging, etc., above is suddenly repeated and prolonged.

CASSIDY (*offstage*). Mr Krank, Mr Krank, Mr Krank, for God's sake . . .

Enter CASSIDY *in a panic.*

For God's sake, come up above, man, and stop their bloody nonsense.

KRANK. What bloody nonsense?

TERESA (*aside*). Holy Joseph and Jacob. The transport executive.

CASSIDY. How the dancing devil should I know what it's

about? These fellows they come trampling in with all their
clanking junk, and all over the passage and the bottom two
flights of stairs . . . Authorization, they say they've got, to
deliver it to Mr Krank's – Have they got Authorization?
What the hell next? Have I got a Hydrogen bomb in me
hip pocket?

KRANK. Hydrogen bomb? No, it can't be. These men, who
do they tell you they are?

CASSIDY. I don't know who they are. They've come in a van
called the Holocaust Heating or something. Are you truly
having rows and rows of radiators put into this house?

KRANK. Holocaust – radiators – No. At least, maybe I am, I
don't know. But not yet, not yet, in God's name, they
can't be wanting to come in *yet* . . .

Enter PAUL *above.*

PAUL. Excuse me.

KRANK. No, so soon.

PAUL. So soon. I hope it is not too great inconvenience for
you, Mr Krank. Good evening, Madam, I think . . .

BARBARA. I think we have met, at the office? I didn't know
you were doing private work for Mr Krankiewicz.

PAUL. A little contract only, Madam, one good friend to
another.

BARBARA. Of course. Good night, Sigismanfred, I am sorry
I have to go: but there is an invitation to dinner which I
have just remembered. Good night, Mr . . . er . . .
Holocaust.

PAUL. Good night, Madam. Always trusting to meet your
every requirement.

BARBARA. Good night, Miss Delaroy. Do enjoy your
whisky, and whatever bed you find access to tonight.

Exit BARBARA *above.*

CASSIDY (*looking at* TERESA, *puzzled*). Delaroy . . .
KRANK. Paul, come here.

> PAUL *starts to descend. The two girls are reclining volup-
> tuously and passing around the whisky bottle.* CASSIDY
> *drinks.*

KRANK. I owe you five hundred pounds.
PAUL. So I believe.
KRANK. Today, I have not got it.
PAUL. Not?

> HENRY GINGER *walks quietly across the stage above.*

KRANK. But I am getting it, do you see, Paul, I am getting it.
PAUL. And so?
BATHSHEBA (*sings*). He laid me down, he laid me down, he
laid me down, oh Lord . . .
KRANK. I do not understand your hurry. I did not expect
your, your radiators to be installed till next month. Why,
the Foreign Tourists are not to be here till at least the
month after that.
BATHSHEBA (*sings*). He laid me down so low.
KRANK. I cannot deal with this sinister ironmongery in my
house. Will you ask, please, your gentlemen to take it
away.

> HENRY GINGER *passes quietly across above.*

PAUL (*grieved*). So, we are not to be welcomed here. I am
disappointed. I had thought, Sigismanfred, that your true
Polish spirit . . . Nevertheless, this house of yours it is so
very convenient a place for us, I do not want to have to
change now. Any other arrangements must be expensive
and very difficult.
KRANK. But for five hundred pounds?
PAUL. You are not able to pay it.

KRANK. But soon, very soon. I *can* give you *one* hundred . . .

PAUL. Insufficient, my friend.

HENRY GINGER *passes quietly across above.*

But as you are my friend, I will not embarrass you more than I can help. Give me my five hundred by the end of this week and we will leave your house alone. Meanwhile I am moving into that vacant room at the back.

KRANK. It is not vacant. There are three Pakistani bus-conductors to come into it tomorrow.

PAUL. They must find somewhere else. I'm sorry.

Exit PAUL *into the wings.*

BATHSHEBA. That's not a kind man, Mr Krank. He's neither kind nor joyful.

CASSIDY (*who has been looking at* TERESA *puzzled*). Excuse me, miss, your face now, it seems some piece of it familiar – I wonder would you ever have travelled to Athlone?

TERESA (*dryly*). I wonder.

CASSIDY (*still puzzled*). I wonder, would you have ever worn your hair something of a different colour?

TERESA (*stung*). *Indeed*, I would never so.

Noise of train passing. CASSIDY *recognizes his sister.*

CASSIDY (*beginning quietly, then bursting forth, scandalizing*). No, no more you would, no more you would at all. But sure, when you were younger, sure, you were a young girl as rapid as a housemartin, but you had the grace and decency of religion to wear it all roped-up under some proper hat, you did, or some scarf or some shawl – you never paraded the walks of the Shannon the likes of this, with a great long battle-flag of incontinence flattering into the eyes of every randy man.

TERESA. What are you talking to me about, Con Cassidy?

CASSIDY. It's not to you I should be talking, Teresa Cassidy, no, it's here's the fellow's done it, here's the beastly fellow's brought you to such grief and shame . . . (*He has turned on* KRANK.) in the very flowering of your maiden's beauty.

TERESA. Gracious save us all.

CASSIDY (*thrusting his face at* KRANK). Whatever bed, was the word, whatever bed she finds access to tonight. Now listen to me, Mr Fornicating Foreigner . . .

KRANK (*cuts him short.*) I will talk to you in one minute, will you give me *one minute*? – be quiet for just *one minute*? Thank you.

CASSIDY (*considerably cowed*). The beastly fellow, the beastly filthy fellow . . . (*He turns away muttering and helps himself to whisky.*)

BATHSHEBA. That's not a kind man, Mr Krank.

BUTTERTHWAITE (*calling offstage*). Mr Krank, Mr Krank.

BATHSHEBA. I think he's doing you wrong, Mr Krank.

KRANK. Mind your own . . .

CASSIDY (*lurching downstairs and growling at the audience*). Wrong, is it, she says wrong, who's done my sister wrong, look at her, will you look at her, lusting away like a bloody female sea-lion, and she one time the most virginal white darling in all the world..

BUTTERTHWAITE (*entering*). Mr Krank . . .

KRANK (*very fiercely*). Well Mr Butterthwaite, what bad news have you brought me?

BUTTERTHWAITE. I've just been to the Town Hall. Do you know what Joe Caligula's been and gone and done?

KRANK. He's not been and found out, has he?

BUTTERTHWAITE. No, it's not that, but it's very near as awkward. He's arranged the draw for first prize in the Lottery; Mr Krank, it's day after tomorrow.

KRANK. God above us. But now I shall never get that five hundred pound in. It will take us months and months.

BUTTERTHWAITE (*very miserable*). God knows it will and all. I'm right sorry, Mr Krank. It looks like I've made a miscalculation.

BATHSHEBA. That's not a kind man, Mr Krank. He's neither kind nor joyful.

KRANK. Wait, wait, but one moment, is there maybe an answer? How much is he offering as the Premium Prize?

BUTTERTHWAITE. Four-fifty.

KRANK. It is enough. It is more than enough, Mr Butterthwaite, we must hold the winning ticket.

BUTTERTHWAITE. How can we do that?

BATHSHEBA (*sings*). He laid me down, he laid me down . . .

KRANK. Teresa, here is five shillings.

TERESA (*taking it*). Mary in Heaven.

KRANK. Tomorrow you go to the Town Hall, and you buy with it one Municipal Savings Bank Certificate. O.K.?

TERESA. Anything at all to give you gaiety.

KRANK (*to* BUTTERTHWAITE). Is there anyone in the Savings Bank Office now?

BUTTERTHWAITE. No.

KRANK. Then let us go there and see what we can plan. And this time there has got to be no miscalculation.

Exeunt KRANK *and* BUTTERTHWAITE *up steps and above.*

CASSIDY. Give that money to me.

TERESA. No, I will not.

CASSIDY. Then buy your bloody certificates, and – oh the shame and the grief of it – how well I remember the day your sainted grandmother, rest her soul in peace, St Patrick, St Bridget, St Mary Gipsy, pray for her soul, gave you your first rosary – 'Teresa,' said she, and the tears of love were like snow on the cheeks of her . . .

TERESA. Indeed and indeed? And what would she think of

you, High King Conor Transport Executive Cassidy, and
you nothing more than a little foreigner's personal pimp.

CASSIDY. Do you tell me that? Me own sister tell me that.

Enter CALIGULA *from the wings.*

What are *you* doing here. How did you get in?

CALIGULA. I came here, sir, to see a compatriot of mine who
lodges in this house. I entered quite normally through the
front door.

CASSIDY. Well, your friend's not down here. But sure and I
know you. The roaring nigger, that's who you are. Joseph
Caligula.

CALIGULA. You are not mistaken.

CASSIDY. Councillor Joseph Caligula,
He pulls down the houses
Where we cheat the bloody niggers.
He runs the local Savings Bank
And cooks the bloody figures.

CALIGULA. Thank you.

CASSIDY. Thank you, Mister Councillor, thank you very
very much. Teresa, you've taken the whisky, you bitch.

CALIGULA (*to* BATHSHEBA). Hello, child.

BATHSHEBA. Hello, Councillor. You come a-looking for
me?

CALIGULA. No. I came looking for this house. I had heard it
is an evil house for our people.

BATHSHEBA. You think so, Councillor?

CALIGULA. I *know* so, child. And you ought to know it too. I
had heard of the man who runs this house. I have never
seen him, but they say his name is Krank. A bad name for
a bad man.

BATHSHEBA. Oh not so bad. No no no, Councillor, not so
bad as that.

CASSIDY. Sure it's a bad name. And it's not the only one he
carries, neither. You'd find it highly interesting, wouldn't

you now, if you heard his other, Councillor? Perhaps you know it already, they call him . . .

TERESA *hits* CASSIDY *over the head with the bottle. He falls unconscious.*

TERESA. When he has the drink taken he behaves irresponsible. Before you came in, Mister, he was just after slandering his own grandmother. I have the drink taken too. So, I'm behaving irresponsible.
(*Sings air: 'The Wearing of the Green.'*)
> My love is like a thornbush
> On the middle of the moor.
> The winds have blown it black and bare
> Except for one white flower.

BATHSHEBA *and* CALIGULA *are facing one another from opposite sides of the stage.* CASSIDY *lies between them.*

BATHSHEBA. Councillor, you've been running away from me.
CALIGULA. No.
BATHSHEBA. Yes.

They begin to circle slowly round CASSIDY, *each keeping as far from each other as the size of the stage permits. They keep their eyes fixed on each other.*

TERESA (*singing*).
> The only road to reach it
> Runs mad with rocks of stone
> And underneath the branches lies
> A heap of soldiers' bones.

A very irresponsible song, bloody hell, it's an irresponsible song. Good night to the both of you. (*Exit* TERESA *up the steps and above.*)
BATHSHEBA. Or maybe, Councillor, I've been running away from you.

CALIGULA. What do you mean?

BATHSHEBA. You don't run in a straight line, I don't run in a straight line, but round and round: who follows who?

  Say I was the moon, you was the sun,
  Each one as near and as far from each one,
  Draw a circle, walk it round,
  Draw a circle on the ground.

CALIGULA (*determined not to let her bewitch him*).

  You don't play that game with me.

BATHSHEBA.

  No? Say I was a rat and you was a black cat,
  You'd tear me down and break my back.

CALIGULA.

  No.

BATHSHEBA.

  Say I was a mackerel and you was a whale,
  You'd swallow me under, head and tail.

CALIGULA.

  No.

BATHSHEBA.

  Say I was the thorn-bush and you was the south wind,
  You'd strip off my leaves and my flowers and my
    rind.

CALIGULA.

  No.

BATHSHEBA.

  No? Draw a circle, walk it round.

CALIGULA (*beginning to be caught*).

  Draw a circle on the ground.
  Say I was the lantern and you was the dark.

BATHSHEBA.

  You could thrust at me though, wherever I'd lurk.

CALIGULA.

  Say you was the reaper and I was the corn.

BATHSHEBA.
>I'd feed on your heart and your husk I would burn.

CALIGULA.
>Draw a circle on the ground.

BATHSHEBA.
>Draw a circle, walk it round,
>Say I was the red meat.

CALIGULA.
>And I was the fork.

BATHSHEBA.
>Draw a circle, walk it round:
>Say you was the lantern –

CALIGULA.
>And you was the dark.
>Draw a circle on the ground.

BATHSHEBA.
>Say you was the railing and I was the park:

CALIGULA.
>I am the lantern

BATHSHEBA.
>I'm all the dark.

She breaks from the circle and runs up the steps and out, above. He follows.

Upstairs, upstairs, Councillor. I've got a room in this evil house. Wide, wide and gentle. Easy, gentle and dark.

She runs out and he runs after her.

CASSIDY (*groaning and sitting up*). Somebody's hit me on the head. I can't remember who. I was going to tell a man something: I can't remember what. I *do* remember whisky. Somebody's taken that. Oh God, what a world – it's nothing but misery – fornication, shame, and misery: and never a drop of whisky in between.

CURTAIN

ACT THREE

Enter HENRY GINGER *with his notebook.*

HENRY GINGER. Oh, very violent, very dangerous, I know, but I mean to have my words with him. Here he comes. I don't like his looks:
> But what care I for such malice.
> If Truth he brought to Birth:
> I am H. Ginger, fearless I stand forth.

Enter PAUL.

Hello. I'd like a word with you.

PAUL. You. How dare you present yourself before my face? How dare you?

HENRY GINGER. Fearless I stand forth.

PAUL *offers to hit him.*

That don't do you no good, you know. You don't want to hit, you want to listen. It's true, isn't it, you've got a plot to kill the Soviet Leader?

PAUL. Of course it is not true.

HENRY GINGER. You've got a plot.

PAUL. Oh no. You prove I've got a plot: go on, prove it to me.

HENRY GINGER. I didn't say I could prove it. Didn't say I knew your details. But I do know your confederate.

PAUL. Confederate?

HENRY GINGER. Mr Sigismanfred. Mr Buchenwald. Mr Krank.

PAUL. Well . . . he is a *friend* of mine, certainly.

HENRY GINGER (*pointing offstage*). Is *he* a friend of yours?

PAUL. No. I would not say so.

HENRY GINGER. Then let's get out of his way. I've got a lot to talk to you about.

Exeunt.
Enter CASSIDY *in uniform, suffering from a hangover.*

CASSIDY (*vaguely invoking the audience*). Who'll buy me a drink, now? That's all I need, boys, just one glass of the whisky, sit me down easy, and let me sort meself out. Bloody hell to it, I don't know, I'm all shocked and shook up. Would you believe me when I tell you, I've wandered every room upstairs and down, in the house of that, that copulating Croesus, that – oh never mind – the dark house of Krank, anyway. I've wandered every room, and not one drop, in one bottle, or one glass, or anything at all. And me head, oh me head, the back of me head, boys. What about the back of me sister? Ah, she's done more travelling on that part of her body than on either of two legs, and that's shameful certain. Two legs. Two keys, I've got two keys, you know, to every room in Krank's house. That's what he doesn't know. He thinks I've only got one. So, when he takes from me just one of those ones, I go straight to the room concerned: I want to know his purpose. Now what purpose do you suppose he has in making a bloody great bomb? Central-heating is it? I'll Central-heat his continental arse for him. I know about bombs, I do: I used to work for the Republican Army. Not as exciting as the London Transport, but maybe more educational. Here's Charlie Butterthwaite. If only he'd buy me some whisky, boys, it'll clear out me brain for me, and I'll know what way to go. Then you'll understand what I'm talking about.

Enter BUTTERTHWAITE *carrying a pair of large brass cymbals.*

Buy me a drink of whisky, will you? There's not been such discomfort to an Irishman since Wolfe Tone lost his shoehorn in the bog.

BUTTERTHWAITE. I don't reckon you'd better have any more. You've got to do an important job for us at this meeting tonight.

CASSIDY. Sure I'll do the job. I'll do any job you want.

BUTTERTHWAITE. Look, if you make just one little mistake, the whole show's mucked up. You've not forgot the signal, have you? (*He makes as though to clash the cymbals.*)

CASSIDY (*clapping his hands to ears in agony*). Oh, God, don't do that, don't do it now. I can remember it.

Enter TERESA.

TERESA. Ah, Mr Butterthwaite, so I've found you at last. Here's the Savings Certificate. I bought it yesterday. Krank told me to give it to you. It's number Three Two Four.

BUTTERTHWAITE. No, no Miss, you want to keep that, you'll need it. All I want's the counterfoil.

TERESA. I haven't any counterfoil.

BUTTERTHWAITE. I hope you haven't. It's supposed to be left with the clerk at the Town Hall.

TERESA. Oh I see. So it was, too. How are you going to get it?

BUTTERTHWAITE. I'll get it, love, I'll get it. Quickness of the hand deceives the eye, eh? Come tonight, we'll need to be even quicker.

CASSIDY. Ah, the brave boys.

TERESA (*indicating* CASSIDY). And what part's he going to play in this prestidigitation? You're not trusting him for anything reliable, I hope?

CASSIDY. What part is it, what part? What part are you after playing these last five years, but sorrow and trouble upon the grey heads of them that has loved you . . . ?

TERESA (*angrily*). Oh take him away, will you, take him away? The minute he sees me he thinks he's on the stage of the Abbey Theatre, or something. For Godsakes, take him away . . .

Enter KRANK *in his smarter suit, with a flower in his buttonhole and a fancy waistcoat.*

CASSIDY. Ah, the brave boys. What they need, now, is a new opportunity. All for the lack of a little central heating.

BUTTERTHWAITE. What are you talking about?

CASSIDY. The Irish Republican Army.

KRANK (*aside to* BUTTERTHWAITE – *gives him some money*). Get rid of him, Butterthwaite. Buy him a drink, why don't you?

CASSIDY. Oh, the tall gallant fighters – all them grand machine-guns they stole, and what the hell did they do? They left them in a warehouse at the back of the King's Cross for the bloody peelers to discover.

BUTTERTHWAITE (*gives some of the money to* CASSIDY). Look, Mr Cassidy, you go round the corner, and buy yourself a bottle. I'll come and join you in a minute.

CASSIDY. Will you so, truly?

BUTTERTHWAITE. Aye, I will too. Go, you go on.

CASSIDY. Another thing they did, they sent a poisonous mince-pie to the Chief himself of the Ulster Constabulary: and then they sent a message after to tell his wife not to eat it. Oh, the gallant fighters, so cruelly betrayed.

Exit CASSIDY.

KRANK. Is everything arranged for tonight?

BUTTERTHWAITE. Aye, aye, I reckon so.

KRANK. Well, let us just consider again what we have to do. You and me and Calilgula are on the platform. O.K.?

BUTTERTHWAITE. O.K. There may be others, you know.

KRANK. What others?

BUTTERTHWAITE. Oh, some of the councillors and that, very like. Most of them won't be there. They're not altogether so fond of our Joe, now he's working up as a Napoleon. They reckon there's a right place for right folk, but not as long as they're black, eh?

KRANK. I see. Now then: tedious speeches first are to be made. We come then to the great event. The drawing of the ticket. They're all in a drum, O.K.? The drum is whirled and whirled around. It stops whirling. And then the winner is drawn out by . . .

BUTTERTHWAITE. By Miss Bathsheba.

KRANK. *Bathsheba*. But that is not what was decided . . .

BUTTERTHWAITE. I forgot to tell you. Joe Caligula, he's fell for that girl at last. This is all his idea, this is. Very nice, too, eh, very sentimental.

KRANK. Does she know: does she know what to do?

TERESA. Sure I've told her what to do. As soon as the signal's given, every light in the building goes off. When they go up again, there she is with the ticket and, hey presto, she's drawn it out of the drum. Number Three Two Four.

KRANK. But when is she going to get hold of the ticket?

BUTTERTHWAITE. I'll put it into her fingers when the lights are gone out. It couldn't be easier.

KRANK. This is getting very complicated.

TERESA. There's one thing, though. Suppose somebody recognizes you, Krank? You appearing in public for the first time . . .

KRANK. But not as Krank. As Cash. No one in this part of London has ever seen me in this suit, or these spectacles, or washed, or shaved, or brushed. Except Loap . . . Oh God. Loap.

TERESA. He'll not be around.

KRANK. Not?

TERESA. Sure, he's soaring and rutting after that whore of an architect of yours. He'll not be finding his politics in any

Public Halls for a day or two, I dare say . . . Do you know
– there's one of my lady-friends tells me of a Cabinet
Minister, no less, is looking for a new lady. Very good
situation, first-floor flat in Pont Street, generous allow-
ances, only required Thursday nights and Saturdays, rest
of the week's your own, and he's not at all jealous. If Loap
can give me an introduction to him, I'll promise not to tell
the Sunday papers about Loap.

KRANK. Yes. Now, there's only one thing not fixed. What is
to be the signal?

BUTTERTHWAITE. My cymbals.

KRANK. What?

BUTTERTHWAITE. Aye, it's what I said the other night, we
must carry off this meeting with a bit of high style. Loud
and Cheery, you know. Half the audience are going to be
West Indians, and the other half'll be chronic Telly-
gawpers looking for one of them give-away games. You've
got to make it dramatic. Besides, the noise has to carry to
Cassidy at the switchboard. That's underneath the stage.

TERESA. Con Cassidy, you've got Con Cassidy . . .

BUTTERTHWAITE. There's nobody else . . .

KRANK. You have tested it. It will carry?

BUTTERTHWAITE. Aye, it'll carry. (*He clashes cymbals.*)

KRANK. Let me try, too. (*He takes the cymbals and clashes
them.*) Good. Very good, I think. Yes. Use them by all
means. (*He clashes them again.*)

Enter PAUL *followed by* HENRY GINGER, *who keeps
obscurely in the background.*

PAUL. Sigismanfred.

BUTTERTHWAITE *exits with* TERESA.

KRANK (*jauntily*). Aha, Paul, aha. I have something to tell
you. Tomorrow at this time, either five hundred pound, or
else a little iron bed in Pentonville Gaol.

PAUL (*drawing a revolver purposefully*). Sigismanfred. I am your bed-maker. I would like you to go easily to sleep. (*He aims the gun at* KRANK.)

KRANK (*backing away*). Oh, Paul. No, please, please point it some other way.

PAUL (*grim*). No other way. You have been my friend.

KRANK. Oh, Paul. Had you not better tell me the reason?

PAUL. Reason, I cannot believe it that you do not know. (*To* HENRY GINGER.) Come on, come here. He wants to know the reason.

KRANK. So. Henry Ginger, is it not? Sir, I hope you found your hours well spent in the Baker Street conveniences?

HENRY GINGER. Oh yes, very well spent, yes, I make no doubt of that.

PAUL (*to* KRANK, *sobbing*). You said to me, you said to me, that you were two years in the Buchenwald Concentration Camp. Did you not say it?

KRANK. Certainly I said it. It was the truth.

PAUL. But he says . . .

KRANK. Well, what does he say?

PAUL (*with a tremendous effort*). He says to me, that you were in Buchenwald yes, but Sigismanfred, you were no prisoner.

KRANK. Henry Ginger, words of truth, how should Henry Ginger know? He was not there?

HENRY GINGER. No, I wasn't, no. But what about them as was, what about Constantin; what about Ranewski; or Joachim Klarakiewicz, what about Braunstein, you know him, a little Jew with three warts under his jowl; what about Jean-Pierre Dumaurice, I think he was a Frenchman?

KRANK. So? What about them?

HENRY GINGER. All of them was once in Buchenwald. Now then, you see, all of them are living in London. They've told me some curious things, Mr Krank. When you was in Buchenwald? You used to be . . .

PAUL. . . . You used to be . . .

KRANK. I used to be a German soldier in Buchenwald. I helped to garrison the camp. And my principal occupation was to clean the officers' boots: but nevertheless, I was a German soldier, a volunteer, I used to wear the grey uniform, all right now, Paul, you have heard Henry Ginger's truth, all right, you shoot me.

PAUL (*terribly upset*). Why, I do not want to shoot you. What is the good to shoot you? All I want − I want to shoot myself. You have been my friend. I *must* understand this. (*He lowers the gun.*)

KRANK.

You know, there's nothing difficult, psychological, obscure

It's a most easy story, not very long. I will tell you.

1939, my part of Poland is invaded by the Russians,

So I find it convenient to join the Russian Army.

I clean the officers' boots. Amusing. Then, 1941.

My part of the Russian Army is destroyed by the Germans.

So I find it convenient − so, once again, I find . . .

I clean the officers' boots. Amusing? I did not ask

To be posted to Buchenwald. That was the time of the world

That I know to myself I have no year, town, or family,

The house of Krank is to be always an empty house.

Eighty people in it, lodgers? For me it is empty.

In Buchenwald was I prisoner, was I convenient soldier . . .

So many thousands of people all lost in that cold field.

Who knows what I was?

PAUL.

We know what you were.

KRANK.

> But I don't know what *you* are.
> Or you, Henry Ginger, or all of the rest of you,
> With your pistols and your orations,
> And your bombs in my private house,
> And your fury, and your national pride and honour.
> This is the lunacy,

Exit HENRY GINGER *furtively*.

> This was the cause, the carrying through
> Of all the insensate war,
> This is the rage and purposed madness of your lives,
> That *I*, Krank, do not know. I *will* not know it.
> Because, if I know it, from that tight day forward,
> I am a man of time, place, society, and accident:
> Which is what I must not be. Do you understand me?

PAUL.

> No.

KRANK (*violently*).

> The world is running mad in every direction.
> It is quicksilver, shattered, here, here, here, here,
> All over the floor. Go on, hurtle after it.
> Chase it, dear Paul. But I choose to follow
> Only such fragments as I can easily catch,
> I catch them, I keep them such time as I choose,
> Then roll them away down and follow another.
> Is that philosophy? It is a reason, anyway,
> Why I am content to hold such a disgusting lodging-
>   house,
> And why I'd be content to get you and your bombs out of
>   it.

PAUL. I do not know what to think of you. I was going to
shoot you, but how can I shoot a man who does not
understand why I am shooting him? My bombs, did you
say? Where is Henry Ginger?

KRANK. Where indeed?

PAUL. Gone, gone. I have been led into a trap, yes, surely, why, now he must know – I'm going after him.

KRANK. Wait – Paul.

PAUL. After him, Henry Ginger. Led into a trap. (*Exit* PAUL *in a frenzy*.)

KRANK (*wiping his brow*). That is a man I never feel safe with. He's mad, you see, terribly mad. I am now on my way to meet another madman, not quite so unsafe but not so far from it. I don't think he has a gun. (*He walks up and down the stage*.) Councillor, Councillor Caligula. Are you here? This is me Alfred Cash. I am waiting to see you.

CALIGULA (*off*). Coming, Mr Cash. I won't be a moment.

KRANK. Good, he sounds jocund. I wonder is Bathsheba with him. Yes, so she is. How remarkably fortunate.

Enter CALIGULA *with* BATHSHEBA.

CALIGULA. Well, Mr Cash, I think everything is ready. I am most honoured that you are to be on the platform with us, on this pioneer occasion.

KRANK. It's a pleasure, sir.

CALIGULA. For me, indeed sir, a true pleasure. I would like you to meet the young lady who has consented to make the draw for us tonight. Bathsheba, this is Mr Alfred Cash: Mr Cash, meet Miss Bathsheba.

KRANK. I am delighted.

CALIGULA. She has been a victim, you know, of the devils and sharks of this part of the town. Against whom I fight, Mr Cash. Yes, sir, against whom Joe Caligula does not hold himself meek. Krank is the name, she lived in his house, but not any more. That man I have marked, Mr Cash . . . Mr Butterthwaite, I presume, will be with us tonight?

KRANK. Yes, I am sure that he will.

CALIGULA. I don't think any of the councillors are going to

attend. I am conscious, nowadays, of a coldness towards our scheme, which I had not expected. But not among the people, no. There, there is enthusiasm. However, Mr Loap has promised to come along, later.

KRANK (*startled*). Mr Loap.

CALIGULA. Our Member of Parliament. Now he has shown consistent interest in the scheme. I believe even the Cabinet have expressed interest. You may find yourself a famous man, Mr Cash.

KRANK. Yes; I rather think that I may.

CALIGULA. I must hurry from you now. I have last-minute arrangements to make. I'll see you on the platform shortly. You coming, Bathsheba?

BATHSHEBA. I'll just be in the way if you're busy. I'll stay with Mr Cash, till the meeting.

CALIGULA. If Mr Cash does not mind . . .

KRANK. It will be a pleasure.

CALIGULA. Well, sir, till the meeting.

KRANK. Till the meeting.

Exit CALIGULA.

What the devil do you laugh about? Everything, everything is ruined.

BATHSHEBA. Ruined, why ruined?

KRANK. The Member of Parliament. He knows me, Bathsheba.

BATHSHEBA (*disconcerted*). Oh, lady, that's bad. But he's not coming right away. You've still got time for the draw, man.

KRANK (*suddenly*). Let's hope so, by God. How intimate have you become with Mr Caligula?

BATHSHEBA *grins*.

I see. Where did it happen?

BATHSHEBA. Your house, Mr Krank.

KRANK. So, so? What was he doing there?

BATHSHEBA. Prowling around. Oh lady, can that councillor prowl?

KRANK. Can he indeed. How much does he know?

BATHSHEBA (*voluptuously*). Everything I could show him, plenty more besides.

KRANK (*sharply*). I did *not* mean that.

BATHSHEBA. Are you really going to beat the signal with *these*?

KRANK. Yes. They belong to Butterthwaite. When he was a young lad. In the Trades Union Offices, I believe.

BATHSHEBA (*laughs and clashes the cymbals*). There goes the signal. Draw out the ticket. Does it win? (*Clash.*) Lords, Gentlemen, it does. Give the money to Mr Krank. (*Clash.*) Oh Mr Krank, you certain are grand and elegant tonight.

KRANK. Why should I not? Perhaps my last opportunity.

BATHSHEBA. Sing me a song, Mr Krank.

KRANK. A dolorous song?

BATHSHEBA. Not that one tonight. You sing me a loving song, instead.

KRANK. For you and Joe Caligula?

BATHSHEBA (*sings*).

> As I lay sleeping
> There came to my bed
> My love with no clothes on
> But a crown on his head,
> But a crown on his head.
>
> Oh he was as black
> As the night without stars
> His eyes were like steamboats
> Racing from afar.
>
> He came to my bed
> And he lay in my bed
> And he loved me all night

    From my feet to my head,
    My feet to my head.

CALIGULA (*off*). Ha, Mr Cash. (*Enter* CALIGULA *agitated.*)

CALIGULA. Mr Cash, Mr Cash, have you seen Mr Butterthwaite?

KRANK. Has he not arrived?

CALIGULA. No, he has not. I have been waiting for him, what can have happened? We shall have to start without him, Mr Cash.

KRANK. Without him. But we can't do tha . . .

Enter POLICEMAN.

POLICEMAN. Good evening, gentlemen.

CALIGULA. What can we do for you, Officer.

POLICEMAN. Councillor Caligula, I believe?

CALIGULA. Yes.

POLICEMAN. I'm Police Constable Robinson, sir. I am reporting as detailed to be present on your platform at the Drawing of the Premium.

KRANK. What for?

POLICEMAN. Just a matter of form, sir. In an observatory capacity, as you might say.

KRANK. Really.

CALIGULA. You haven't seen Mr Butterthwaite, have you?

POLICEMAN. No, I'm afraid not, sir. As a matter of fact, sir, between you and me, I'm not at all sorry I've been picked for this duty tonight. Me and Mrs Robinson, sir, as you might say, we have a bit of an interest ourselves. Only a couple of five-bob certificates, you know. But there's always a chance, isn't there? Of course if I was to win, being on the platform at the time, do you know what they'd call it, down at the police station, don't you? They'd call it Evidence of Criminal Collusion – laugh. Oh there's a lot of funny jokers in the force.

KRANK. Very diverting. Ha, ha.

The tabs open to a flourish of music. The full stage is discovered laid out for a public meeting – the audience being represented by the theatre audience. In the centre is a table draped to the floor with Union Jacks. On it are the usual carafe and glass, etc., and a kind of miniature milk churn, on trunnions, which is the drum for mixing the tickets. There are chairs behind the table. Hanging from the flies is a large poster reading 'Look after the pennies and the pounds will come running', 'Sixpence today saved is a pudding for dinner tomorrow'. There is a telephone on a small table.

Enter CALIGULA, BATHSHEBA, *and* KRANK, *and take their places behind the table. The* POLICEMAN *follows and remains standing upstage.* BATHSHEBA *lays the cymbals carefully on the table.*

CALIGULA (*knocking for silence*). Ladies and Gentlemen of this Borough: or shall I say my good friends – you all know me. I'm Joe Caligula. I'm the man the newspapers call the 'Chocolate Dynamo of North London' and the 'Black Banker with the Premium Punch' and various other things. And you all know what I'm here for. I'm here to give you that Premium Punch. I'm here for the drawing of the first ticket for the first prize in the first scheme of this nature ever to be put before the English public. With me on the platform was to have been Mr Alexander Loap, your Member of Parliament. I understand he has been delayed – an important committee at the House of Commons, I believe . . . But he will be along, he assured me, in plenty of time for the draw. Also I had hoped to be supported by another gentleman – indeed I had intended he should have taken the chair – for without him, I can freely tell you, this scheme would never have begun to carry any sort of shape at all. I refer, friends, to Mr Charles Butterthwaite, like myself not a native of London, but . . .

BUTTERTHWAITE *crawls forward out from under the table.*
He is wearing a mayoral gown of scarlet and a gold chain and
clutching a half-empty whisky bottle and a black cocked hat.
Although he is very drunk the clarity of his speech is
unimpaired.

BUTTERTHWAITE. . . . . But the erstwhile Napoleon of the
north. Cheery Charlie Butterthwaite. Councillor you've
begun without me. Why? (*He addresses the audience.*)
Hello one and all. Here I am, then, in the flesh, large as
life, me lads and lasses. Your old Uncle Charlie. Hark to
your Uncle Charlie and get pudding to all your dinners.
I'm sorry, I seem to have got a bit too much pudding to
mine already. Alfred, your fault, you should never have
sent me . . .

KRANK. Ladies and Gentlemen . . .

BUTTERTHWAITE. Well then, let's get this meeting moving.
Just at present it's like one of them snooty fancy parties
where the time stays seven-o'clock-cocktails-and-bits-of-
biscuits till half past eleven at night, and nobody so much
as splashes their boots. Councillor, the folk want livening,
we all want livening, this is an occasion . . .

KRANK. Ladies and Gentlemen . . .

BUTTERTHWAITE (*scornfully*). Nay, that's not how to do it.
You're giving them nowt but dishwater, when they're
bawling for mulligatawny. 'Ladies and Gentlemen.' Look
at me. Here's the very gown that I was Mayor of our town
up north in; nine times I was voted for Mayor, three times
three is nine, and when I retired they give me a testimonial
like, this gown, aye this gown and this chain, real gold,
you know, none of your brass for tarnishing . . . and the
old cocked hat as well. Here's how it should go on, fore
and aft, aye like this eh, I look a proper Charlie, don't I?
But put it on like this . . . (*He alters it to a sideways
position.*) Then what do you get? Napoleon Bonaparte,

that's what you get . . . (*He suddenly becomes very melancholy.*) Napoleon Bonaparte, erstwhile, erstwhile. . . .

    Three times three
    Did my conquests run
    Against the moon, against the sun,
    Three times three, Humber shall drain,
    Ere Charlie Butterthwaite rise again.
    Talk to 'em, Alfred. Have a go. Tell 'em the tale.
(*He subsides forlornly.*)

KRANK (*very willingly*). Ladies and Gentlemen: after so exuberant an introduction, my few words, my very few words, are bound to appear a little lacking in excitement. Like Councillor Caligula I am not by birth English. Poland is my country: since 1939 I have the misfortune to be a political exile. But in so far as the place of my exile has been your wonderful, your beautiful city, London, by so much, so far, I cannot call it truly a misfortune. It is to me a great honour . . .

BUTTERTHWAITE (*with his hand on his bosom, moodily*). Austria, Prussia, and Russia.

KRANK. . . . a great honour . . .

BUTTERTHWAITE. Austria, Prussia, and Russia. I conquered the first two, lads and lassies, no doubt about that. But Russia, ah Russia, there was a miscalculation.

KRANK. It is to me a great honour, a great delight, to be able to play this very humble role . . .

BUTTERTHWAITE (*rudely*). On shut your cake-hole, Alfred. This meeting wants livening up. Let's hear from the true Working People, let's see if they can't make a bit more noise. (*He addresses the audience, dividing them into groups.*) Now then, all you lot to the left of my hand, you're Austria. You lot to the right, you're Prussia. And you lot up top, are you listening? You're Russia. Now what I want you to do is to tell me who you are, and tell me all at once, when I give you the one-two-three. It's a grand way to get a gathering going this. They say old Wilf Pickles used it to warm up his legless pensioners before his broadcasts. All right now, on the one-two-three: Austria, Prussia, and Russia. Shout them names out, and shout 'em loud. (*He picks up the cymbals and prepares to clash them.*) One, two . . .

KRANK (*violently checking him*). No. Not now.

BUTTERTHWAITE (*recollecting himself and laying the cymbals on the table*). Oh aye. Aye. We'll do without them. Now then . . . one, two, three . . . Eh, there could have been a lot more noise there. Again let's have it. One, two, three . . . And again then. One, two, three . . . Oh you disappoint me, you know, there's no two roads.

KRANK. Don't you think, Mr Butterthwaite, we should be getting on to the draw?

BUTTERTHWAITE. Eh lad, there's plenty of time.

KRANK (*fiercely*). No, there is not.

The telephone rings. The policeman answers it.

BATHSHEBA (*aside to* BUTTERTHWAITE). The counterfoil, Mr Butterthwaite, my counterfoil?

BUTTERTHWAITE. Eh, oh don't worry. (*He confidently puts his hand to his breast pocket. His expression changes and he begins a frantic search through all his pockets.*)

CALIGULA. Friends, I think it would be as well for me to explain the method of the draw. In this drum are all the counterfoils of all your certificates. (*He shows the drum full of tickets. The* POLICEMAN *has finished telephoning and whispers in* CALIGULA's *ear.*)

BATHSHEBA (*aside to* BUTTERTHWAITE). Man, have you got it, have you got my ticket?

BUTTERTHWAITE. Eh, God, I don't know.

CALIGULA. Friends, I have just had good news. That telephone call was from our Member, Mr Loap. He regrets very much he has been delayed, but he is on his way here at this moment, and should be with us almost immediately. Of course, we will defer the draw until he comes.

KRANK. No.

CALIGULA (*surprised*). Mr Cash?

KRANK (*wildly*). I said, no . . . (*In his precipitancy he leans right across the table and with his elbow knocks the cymbals off the edge.*)

BATHSHEBA. Mind the cymbals . . .

BATHSHEBA, KRANK, *and* BUTTERTHWAITE *all leap to catch the cymbals which fall one upon the other on to the floor with a considerable clanging. The drums of tickets is also overturned. All the lights go out.*

BUTTERTHWAITE (*in the darkness*). I tell you I've lost it, I've lost it I tell you . . .

CALIGULA. Keep your seats, friends, please keep your seats. It seems to be a power failure. The lights will very likely . . . (*The lights come on again.*) Ah.

KRANK *and* BATHSHEBA *are discovered on their knees by the pile of tickets.* BUTTERTHWAITE *is sitting on the floor as though turned to stone.*

BUTTERTHWAITE. Austria, Prussia, Russia.

CALIGULA. Oh dear, the tickets. Perhaps we had better . . .

POLICEMAN. Just one moment, if you please, sir. I think it would be better that nobody should handle the tickets at all, before the young lady takes her pick.

CALIGULA. But we must put them back into the drum.

POLICEMAN (*good-humouredly*). I think it would perhaps look better, if you didn't, sir.

BUTTERTHWAITE. Moscow's bloody burning.

POLICEMAN. Why don't we blindfold the young lady and let her have a stab at the heap on the floor?

CALIGULA. An excellent idea. It quite solves the difficulty. Thank you, Officer. Bathsheba. . . .

KRANK. Use my handkerchief, gracious lady. (*He ties it on for her. Aside to* BUTTERTHWAITE.) Did you give her the ticket? (*Aside to* BATHSHEBA.) Did he give you the ticket?

CALIGULA. Ready, Bathsheba? (*He leads her forward.*) Here is the pile. You just bend down and pick a ticket. Nobody can say they aren't shuffled now.

BATHSHEBA (*bends down resignedly and picks*). I've got one. Here it is.

CALIGULA (*takes the ticket and unfolds it*). Friends, I am about to read out the winning number of the first prize in our first pioneer premium draw. This ticket is number three hundred and . . .

TERESA (*shouting from offstage*). Mine.

CALIGULA (*the rest of the number has been inaudible*). And here is the lucky lady of tonight.

Enter TERESA *from the wings.*

And her prize, my friends, for one five-shilling Savings Bank Certificate is four hundred and fifty pounds.

POLICEMAN (*with considerable diffidence*). Excuse me a minute, sirs.

CALIGULA. Yes, Officer?

POLICEMAN. I didn't quite catch the number of the ticket, as read out – the lady was so quick.

CALIGULA (*slightly surprised*). Number three hundred and seventy three was the number I read out.

POLICEMAN (*embarrassed*). Oh, but that's my wife's ticket, sir. Three-seven-three. There must be some mistake. Here look I've got the certificate. (*He produces it.*)

CALIGULA. It can't be a printer's error, surely. May we see your certificate, Madam?

TERESA (*realizing something has gone wrong*). I think there is a mistake. It's number three-two-four. I must have misheard you. I'm sorry, I was so excited, you see. (*She hastens to leave the platform.*)

CALIGULA. Pardon me, Madam, but have we not met before?

Enter CASSIDY *from the cellar.*

CASSIDY. Aha, well, so you've had the draw, have you . . . and who's won the prize – Teresa, so it's you. I'd never have believed it. Has he given you the cheque yet? Give her the four-fifty, Mister Councillor, and sign it neat and good for her. Cassidy's her name. And *here's* the splendid fellow, Mr Alfred Cash himself, the moving spirit, milords, behind this fervour of financing. And I put it to you all, who is he? Mister Councillor, I put it to yourself, who is he? I was for telling you two days since, but there was reasons well known to you already. It's *Krank*.

BATHSHEBA.	BUTTERTHWAITE.
No, no, no.	Waterloo, Waterloo, Waterloo.

TERESA (*furiously*). Don't you be paying any attention to this drunken knacker. Sure he's me own brother, but for all the good of that I'd pour sewage on him in the street. Get inside with you, you dirty nasty fragment of a catechist's carnal mediation, you . . .

CALIGULA (*knocking for silence*). Wait a moment. Let us have quiet, please, quiet, please. (*To* KRANK.) Sir, this man had called your name, Krank. I know of one Krank: a subtle and wicked enemy to the peace of life of many of my people. I also know that this man is both drunken and malicious, yet, as he lives in Krank's house, I cannot entirely ignore his accusation. What have you to answer, sir?

KRANK (*very winningly*). It is true my name is Krank. And because I had heard of your hatred to this Krank, I told you it was Cash, so you should not hold against me the faults of my brother.

CALIGULA. Your brother.

KRANK. My brother Krank. Very disreputable. I know you will think there seems to be a lot of new brothers and sisters so suddenly appearing, but . . .

CALIGULA (*sombrely*). I do think it, yes. And I do not believe you. Although I am a politician, I will admit I am not a very quick thinker. But my mind is slowly moving to another, and I fear catastrophic, conclusion. This Savings Bank, this Lottery . . .

KRANK (*savagely*). This Lottery has been won by Mrs Robinson, the Constable's wife. I can assure everyone there is no trickery about *that*.

CASSIDY. What, my four-fifty pounds, you've let it be stolen by a bloody peeler? What the hell have you all been playing at, up here?

POLICEMAN. That's a very good question. Now I'd like to know a thing or two about . . .

KRANK (*decisively*). O.K. O.K. Gentlemen, Ladies. I am Krank. Yes, I have no brother. I run a disorderly house and I exploit my under-privileged fellow men. Mr Caligula, you do right to be horrified. *But*, Mr Caligula, your horror would do you the more credit if it was not that you yourself have been, in more than a manner of speaking, a satisfied patron of my premises. Bathsheba, is it or is it not the fact that Councillor Caligula spent a night with you in my house, in bed?

BATHSHEBA. Oh, you shouldn't have said that. That's a bad cruel thing of you to say.

KRANK. Is it or is it not the fact?

CALIGULA. Yes sir, it is the fact. Let me make this clear to you, Mr Krank, to all the people in this hall. I'm not a preacher, I'm only a councillor, I have a body and a heart of love and they will drive, and I'm a warm man then, I'm a man of rash peril, like a pounding motor-bus in your thick streets of London, or a strong heavy bowl among the nine-pins. And who's to tell the ride of love where it is to blame? Here's me, here's my woman, we make children together. What else on this world are we for? But to squat down in your black hell, your basement kitchen, counting and counting of moneys . . . You've cheated last night from the guests within your doors, where that is to blame anyone can tell. And I'm anyone. For the matter of the Savings Bank . . .

Enter from the wings LOAP *and* BARBARA.

LOAP. Constable, will you please see that nobody leaves the hall.

POLICEMAN. Why, Mr Loap, sir . . .

LOAP. Let nobody leave the hall, Constable.

POLICEMAN. Well, yes, sir – there's some funny things going on around here.

LOAP. I can well believe it. Pray be seated, my dear Miss Baulkfast. Councillor Caligula, Ladies, and Gentlemen, Electors of this Constituency, Fellow Citizens, as you know, my chief concern as your duly elected representative in Parliament has been my indefatigable support to a declared policy of renewed intercourse with the Mighty Soviet Union – to be achieved by the momentous means of meeting at the Summit. It is therefore with the gravest concern that I have discovered neither more nor less than a plot to murder the celebrated Leaders of the Mighty Soviet Union, during their forthcoming visit – yes; murder them, Fellow Citizens. In London. With a bomb.

CASSIDY. With a bomb.

LOAP. With a bomb. Miss Baulkfast, my dear, you told me that you had information incriminating at least two persons.

BARBARA. Yes.

LOAP. Do you see either of them here?

BARBARA. One of them.

LOAP. Who?

BARBARA (*harshly pointing to* KRANK). That man. He is Sigismanfred Krankiewicz. He is in league with another man, whose name I do not know. Under pretence of having a Central Heating system installed, he is fabricating the bomb in his own house.

BUTTERTHWAITE. St Helena.

KRANK (*quietly*). Gracious lady. You have what kind of proof for all this?

LOAP. Well, Officer, you heard the lady; arrest him.

POLICEMAN. He has a point, you know, sir, proof. I'm afraid till things are sorted out a bit more, I can't very well . . .

LOAP. His house is being raided, at this very moment, Officer. I can assure you that in less than five minutes you will receive orders to carry out the arrest.

POLICEMAN. I don't know, sir, it's a question of exceeding my duty . . .

The telephone rings.

LOAP. You'd better answer that, Officer. I think it will be for you.

The POLICEMAN *answers the telephone.* LOAP *again addresses the audience.*

Fellow Citizens, this man, he has tried to destroy our chances of peace in the world. At his house is a bomb. The police will by now have found it.

HENRY GINGER (*appearing at the back of the stage*). Oh no they won't.

LOAP. I beg your pardon?

HENRY GINGER. They'll find no bomb. Me, Henry Ginger, I've just been to that house. There's no bomb there no more. Somebody's whipped it away.

KRANK (*bewildered, but thinking fast*). Whipped it away? But how to whip away what was never there?

HENRY GINGER (*bitterly*). It was there once, all right, all right. You've had a bomb there, all right. Concealing of Evidence, that's what you've been doing.

KRANK (*sincerely*). I'm certain I have not.

CASSIDY. And I'm certain too. Oh, he's a truthful boy is Krank. Now what would he or any other Christian at all be wanting with a bomb? Up the I.R.A.: ha, ha . . .

POLICEMAN (*his telephone conversation finished*). Seems like you're right, for once, Henry Ginger, old man. (*To* LOAP) That was the Superintendent, sir. He says there is nothing in the nature of bombs to be found anywhere on the premises in question. Now, Henry, I'd like to know what you think you're doing here.

HENRY GINGER. I've come to watch our Mr Krankiewicz. I'm watching him.

> Though the fool policeman sleeps,
> Henry Ginger wakes and creeps.

PAUL *bursts in at the back of the stage with his gun out.*

PAUL (*distracted*). But not for too long, no, Henry Ginger, you, you, you, you, you, you . . . what have you done with my bomb?

HENRY GINGER (*terrified*). Nothing with your bomb. What are you talking about? Officer, he's a Fascist, he's mad. He's a mad Fascist, Officer, he's going to shoot me, help.

PAUL. Yes, Henry Ginger, I'm going to shoot you . . .

HENRY GINGER *dodges in panic behind* KRANK. PAUL *shoots and hits* KRANK.

PAUL. Oh no, but not you, not *you*, Sigismanfred – you are my friend – I did not mean . . .

HENRY GINGER. He's dangerous, he's Anti-British . . . you

ought to have run him in long before this, you know. (*Exit into the wings.*)

POLICEMAN (*approaching* PAUL *dubiously*). I am arresting you on the charge of Attempted Murder, in possession of firearms; it is my duty to caution you . . .

PAUL. And *I* caution you, do not come any nearer. There are yet bullets, five of them in this gun. Sigismanfred, I have killed you, I have killed you.

KRANK. What did I say, that you are a lunatic, Paul: this quicksilver I told you, too difficult for you to catch. I'm not going to die, I don't think. Go on: quicksilver: run.

PAUL (*helplessly*). I thought to have helped, for the people of Poland, for freedom from violence, I had thought. . . . For what value to kill Henry Ginger, even; a little poisonous screech-owl, is all . . . Nobody follow me. I swear I will shoot. Good-bye, Sigismanfred. I did not mean to do it.

Exit PAUL *into the wings.*

POLICEMAN. Here, you come back here . . . Stop him, stop him . . .

Exit POLICEMAN *after* PAUL. *Shouts and police whistles die away offstage.*

KRANK.
I said I was not going to die;
Truth? I am afraid, I think it was a lie.
So, only a few minutes to live,
I must see can I not give
Some clearer conclusion to this play
To order your lives the neatest way,
For when after the voters have gone home.
Mr Loap and lady, there is no bomb.
Let the Bolshevik tyrants arrive:
Conviviality shall thrive

And the ceaseless peace no doubt ensue.
Councillor, that quick girl with you tried with me to cheat
   you, true.
Forgive her. She had a clever master:
But I'm almost sure you now can trust her.
The bomb, Cassidy, I think you stole it.
I hope your brave boys can control it,
For is it not the nature of such ammunition
To perpetuate partition?
Of your sister imagine no more evil.
She is now reaching Ministerial level.
So use respect. Good-bye, Charlie.
A pity the cymbals have had to clang so early.
Your Hundred Days were short I fear.
Ladies, come here . . .
Bathsheba, Teresa, Barbara – Miss Baulkfast:
I'm going to declare my identity at last.
Place and time, and purposes,
Are now to be chosen for me.
I cannot any longer do without knowing them . . .
So many thousands of people
In a so large a cold field.
How did they get into it?
And what do they expect to find?

KRANK *dies.*

BARBARA.
Deceit upon his tongue. Quicksilver in his mind.
TERESA.
No money in his pocket. Shouting in his house.
BATHSHEBA.
Songs in his throat, lightning and thunder in his bed.

BUTTERTHWAITE.
Notwithstanding, Krank is dead.
I'm going to sing you a song:

He sings (Air 'The Ash Grove').

We're all down in t'cellar-hoyle
Wi't'muck-slaghts on t'windows.
We've used all us coyle up
And we've nowt left but cinders.
When t'bum-bailey comes,
He'll never find us
'Cause we're all down in t'cellar-hoyle
'Wi't'muck-slaghts on t'windows.
Not let's divide up like and sing it as a round
Then after that all the folk can go home. . . .

The song is sung as a four-part round as follows:

Part one: BUTTERTHWAITE
Part two: CASSIDY and TERESA
Part three: BATHSHEBA and CALIGULA
Part four: BARBARA and LOAP
BUTTERTHWAITE *clashes the cymbals three times.*

THE CURTAIN FALLS

When is a Door not a Door?

An Industrial Episode

WHEN IS A DOOR NOT A DOOR? was first produced at the Embassy Theatre, Swiss Cottage by the Central School of Drama on 2 June 1958 with the following cast:

MR HENDERSON, Managing Director	Bernard Dandridge
MR GOLDSWORTH ⎤	Nicholas Simons
MR GURNEY ⎦ of the Office Staff	Graham Heppel
MR STOBO, a Trade Union Official	Jeremy Kemp
FIRST WORKMAN ⎤	John Scarborough
SECOND WORKMAN ⎦ Carpenters	Giles Phibbs
MISS BROACH, Packing Shop Manageress	Helen Willett
SALLY, Mr Henderson's Secretary	Eva Huszar
TEA-GIRL	Clare Stewart
FIRST WORKING GIRL ⎤ of the	Shuna Black
SECOND WORKING GIRL ⎦ Packing Shop	Joan Clevedon

Directed by Robert Cartland

The Scene is a factory, in England. The office of the Managing Director's Secretary; between the Managing Director's office and the office corridor.

The time is the Present, about ten o'clock in the morning.

Notes for Production

Characters:

HENDERSON. He is youngish, brisk, intolerant and high-voiced. Very energetic.

GOLDSWORTH. Middle-aged, very serious, pompous; and rather slow.

GURNEY. An ex-officer type, and incompetent.

STOBO. Pushful and aggressive, but good-humoured.

FIRST WORKMAN. In the prime of life. With strong opinions.

SECOND WORKMAN. A young man, fairly respectful towards FIRST WORKMAN.

MISS BROACH. Of a certain age. Easily offended and generally harassed.

SALLY. A pretty girl in early twenties.

TEA-GIRL. Same age as SALLY, but a few social strata below.

WORKING GIRLS. Tough good-humoured young women, with some strength of character.

General Notes:

The two WORKMEN do not take any notice of the conversation and actions of the others, except where indicated in the text. They may now and then look up, but without any apparent interest or comprehension of the events taking place. Their work upon the door should be carried out completely realistically, and should be rehearsed so as to terminate properly where the stage directions say. The job should be seen to be properly done before they leave the stage. The scenery need not be more than sketched into place: but the door and doorframe between the outer office and the corridor must be real.

The scene is divided in the middle by a partition. One side represents a corridor, and the other side an office. In the rear wall of the office is a door marked 'Managing Director'. In the partition is a door, standing ajar, marked 'Managing Director's Secretary'. In the Office SALLY *sits typing at a desk, upon which is an inter-office speaking installation.* TWO WORKMEN, *carrying a heavy toolbag, come along the corridor and stop outside the door.*

FIRST WORKMAN (*studying a piece of paper*). Well, here we are. 'Doorway between outer office and corridor.' Outer office: right? Corridor? Right.

SECOND WORKMAN. Right.

FIRST WORKMAN. It says: it won't hold shut. Let's have a see. (*He tests the door by opening and shutting it several times. Seeing* SALLY, *he nods casually.*) Morning.

SALLY. Good morning.

SECOND WORKMAN (*to* FIRST WORKMAN). It's warped, see. Sticks in the frame. (*He tests the door also.*) Take it out, won't we?

FIRST WORKMAN. Right.

They stand back in the corridor and study the door.

SALLY. Do you know that door's been jamming since before the Christmas holiday. It's dreadful. I've had to stay all of last Saturday in bed with a stiff neck. So I told Mr Henderson. I mean, if nobody else . . .

SECOND WORKMAN (*to* FIRST WORKMAN). Top or bottom?

FIRST WORKMAN. Top corner. Take it off with the plane. Eighth inch. Quarter inch. Should do.

SECOND WORKMAN. Nothing to it, really.

FIRST WORKMAN (*sucks his teeth*).

HENDERSON *comes briskly down the corridor and strides past them into the outer office.*

HENDERSON. Good morning, Miss Nuttall.

SALLY. Good morning, Mr Henderson. (*She indicates the* WORKMEN.) Oh, Mr Henderson, the door . . .

HENDERSON (*impatiently*). So I see. So I see. Mr Gurney in this morning?

SALLY. I think so, Mr Henderson.

HENDERSON. Buzz for him, will you? I want him *now*.

He goes into his office and slams the door.

SALLY (*buzzing the desk-speaker*). Mr Gurney? Mr Henderson's just asking for you, sir . . . Yes sir. (*She clicks the button to transfer the line.*) Mr Gurney's on his way, Mr Henderson.

She clicks off, and returns to her typing: which she continues intermittently throughout the play.

FIRST WORKMAN. The little driver ought to do it. (*The* SECOND WORKMAN *hands him a small screwdriver from the bag.*) Right. (*He starts to unscrew the hinges of the door.*) Just hold her up so she don't fall out as I unscrew, will you . . . Hoo ah: stiff devil, this one . . . ah!

GURNEY *comes hurrying down the corridor and goes straight through into the outer office.*

GURNEY. Morning, Sally: how's the love-life?

SALLY (*chillingly*). Please, Mr Gurney. I think you're wanted urgently.

GURNEY (*disconcerted*). Oh. Oho. Is he waiting?

SALLY. Of course, Mr Gurney.

GURNEY. God save us. What's he after now? What's the racket this morning, hey?

SALLY (*chillingly*). I really couldn't say, Mr Gurney. I'm sorry. You'd better walk straight through: he's waiting.

GURNEY *knocks at the inner door and opens it.*

GURNEY. Morning, F.H., what's the panic?

He goes in and shuts the door behind him.

FIRST WORKMAN. Now hold her steady while I take these lads at the bottom out. (*The* SECOND WORKMAN *is supporting the leaf of the door as the hinges are unscrewed.*) Right. All scroffed up with paint, these . . . You see, it's what I say all the time. It's apathy. Well, look at it. Apathy. I mean, take Russia.

SECOND WORKMAN. What's Russia got to do with it?

FIRST WORKMAN (*disgusted*). That's what I mean, then . . . You stand there: and you ask me what's Russia got to do with it. If it wasn't for your apathy, you'd know.

SECOND WORKMAN. Oh, draw it mild, mate . . .

FIRST WORKMAN (*scornfully*). 'Draw it mild, mate, draw it mild' – You're no better than *he* is, 'cept you put it in different words.

SECOND WORKMAN. Better than who is?

FIRST WORKMAN (*jerking his thumb towards the inner office*). Him. 'Morning, Sally: how's the love-life?' I mean – 'scuse me, miss – I mean, listen to it.

SECOND WORKMAN. Oh, *him*. They all talk like that, these fellers. It's the way they learn 'em, y'know. 'Course, they get paid for it according.

FIRST WORKMAN. What you gain on the swings, you lost it on the hoop-la . . . O.K. O.K. Let's lift her away. (*They lift the door out of its frame, backing with it into the office.*) Careful, steady, *to* you.

SECOND WORKMAN. 'Scuse us, miss: we'll take it in the corridor, eh? (*They carry the door out of the office.*) *To* you. Steady.

FIRST WORKMAN. Careful.

SECOND WORKMAN. Steady.

FIRST WORKMAN. Down.

The door is set down against the wall.

SECOND WORKMAN. Well, there we are. Have a drag?

FIRST WORKMAN. Don't mind. Ta.

They light a pair of half-smoked cigarettes, and stand easy.
The desk-speaker buzzes.

SALLY (*answering it*). Hello, Mr Henderson's secretary. Can I
help you? . . . Oh, Miss Broach. Yes . . . Good gracious
me . . . But he'll be furious. Oooh . . . Oh dear, oh dear,
and on a Monday morning, too. It just seems everything's
to happen on a Monday, and just after thē holidays, too, I
mean . . . Yes, Miss Broach, I'll get you through to him
directly. (*She clicks to transfer the line.*) Oh, Mr Henderson.
Miss Broach on the line. She says the girls in the Packing
Shop have stopped work, Mr Henderson . . . Yes . . .
Oh, I'll put her on directly, Mr Henderson. (*She clicks the
apparatus again.*) You're through to Mr Henderson, Miss
Broach.

She clicks off.
The TEA-GIRL *comes down the corridor, pushing a trolly
loaded with teapot and cups, etc.*

SECOND WORKMAN. Oi oi, tea's up.

TEA-GIRL (*passing him coldly*). You're not allowed to smoke
in the corridors.

SECOND WORKMAN. Who says?

She goes into the outer office.

TEA-GIRL. Tea-time, dear.

SALLY. One extra this morning, Doris, please. Mr Gurney's
in with Mr Henderson. I think . . .

TEA-GIRL. Looks a bit draughty here this morning.

GURNEY *comes out of the inner office.*

HENDERSON (*from within*). And tell him I'm not having it!
I want an answer by Wednesday, or I'll know the reason.

GURNEY *hastens away down the corridor.*

SALLY. Well, he *was* in with him, anyway.

The TEA-GIRL *pours out tea.*

TEA-GIRL. They're going on strike in the Packing Shop, did you know, dear?

SALLY (*discreetly*). Well, yes, I did hear *something*.

TEA-GIRL. It's true. Imagine. Well, I mean, I'm not surprised. It's that frozen in there this weather, I'd do it meself for half the money. Why don't he put in radiators that *work*? He can't expect . . .

HENDERSON (*appearing at the door*). Miss Nuttall!

He goes in again.

SALLY. Coming, Mr Henderson. Oh lord, where's his sugar . . .

She hunts around for the sugar and succeeds in upsetting her own cup of tea.

TEA-GIRL. Watch out!

SALLY (*furious*). Oh!

TEA-GIRL (*rather sulky*). Not my fault.

SALLY *goes into the inner office with a cup of tea, sugared, and her notebook. The* TEA-GIRL *mops up the spill, clucking with annoyance.*

FIRST WORKMAN (*selecting a plane from his toolbag*). You see, the trouble is: I've always said it: it's not rightly a question whether they're right or whether they're wrong. It's the basic *impressions* that count. And don't tell me no different. Basic. Now take Suez.

SECOND WORKMAN. You take it.

FIRST WORKMAN (*beginning to plane the edge of the door*). Well, what happens? He says: it's lah de dah this, and it's lah de dah that, and play the game, Britons, play the game.

And what does Nasser do? He walks in, *don't he?* He nicks the old canal. And wouldn't you? He's a smart man, Nasser, he knows the Old School Tie when he sees it. 'You play the game, me boys, and I play dirty.' That's what *he* says.

SECOND WORKMAN. Huh. And what about Eden's free holiday at Bermudas, eh? What about *that?* After all that shambles. Just like, in'it?

FIRST WORKMAN. Look, you go back to the yard this afternoon. You tell our boss: 'Look here, boss, you said go and see to that doorway, it's jamming. We gone and done the window by mistake: what are we to do?' And what does he say to that? He says: 'All *right*, my lad, don't you worry, my lad, all you done, boy, is make an error of judgement. Anyone could do it. So take yourself a week at Brighton and credit it to the firm.' It's likely, *in'it?* Bleedin' likely.

The TEA-GIRL *wheels her trolly out again into the corridor.*

SECOND WORKMAN (*intercepting her*). Here, lovey, let's have a cuppa . . .

TEA-GIRL (*tartly*). This is for the offices, this is. There's a canteen for *you*, across the yard.

GURNEY *comes back along the corridor.*

SECOND WORKMAN (*to* TEA-GIRL). Ah, who's to know . . .

GURNEY. Tea, tea, do I see tea!

He rapidly pours himself out a cup and carries it into the outer office.

SECOND WORKMAN (*still wheedling*). Come on now, just a quick one . . .

TEA-GIRL. I've got me cups counted. You leave them alone.

GOLDSWORTH *comes along the corridor.* GURNEY *enters the inner office.*

GOLDSWORTH (*to the* WORKMEN *in passing*). No smoking in the corridor, please.

GOLDSWORTH *enters the outer office as* SALLY *comes out of the inner office.*

TEA-GIRL (*triumphantly to the* WORKMEN). See.

She wheels her trolly away.

GOLDSWORTH (*to* SALLY). Is he in, Miss Nuttall?
SALLY. He's waiting for you, sir.

GOLDSWORTH *knocks and enters the inner office.* SALLY *sits to her table again and continues typing.* GURNEY *comes out of the inner office.*

GURNEY (*flustered*). Last week's packing schedules, Sally: where are they?
SALLY (*coldly*). In the General Office, Mr Gurney, where they always are. You'll have to ask Miss Hawkins.
GURNEY. Oh, blast and bloody . . . (*She looks at him, and he becomes more flustered.*) I *beg* your pardon. Yes, I'll ask Miss Hawkins. (*He goes out into the corridor, muttering as he passes the* WORKMEN.) There's a lot I'd like to ask Miss Hawkins. There's a lot I'd like to tell Miss Hawkins, Miss Hawkins . . .

He goes out, cursing to himself.

SECOND WORKMAN (*continuing the previous discussion*). Well, how do you account for it, then? I mean, Bermudas and that.
FIRST WORKMAN. Why, it's all the same; he plays their game, they give him a holiday. But as for anyone getting anything *done*, I mean *results* – oh ho ho no. Now see, take the Olympic Games.

MISS BROACH *enters along the corridor and goes into the outer office.*

MISS BROACH. Is Mr Henderson disengaged, Miss Nuttall?

SALLY. Mr Goldsworth's in with him, Miss Broach. Just a moment, I'll see . . . (*She clicks the desk-speaker.*) Mr Henderson, Miss Broach is here . . . Yes, Mr Henderson. (*She clicks off.*) He won't be a moment, Miss Broach . . . Is it going to be a proper strike, do you think?

MISS BROACH. How should *I* know, my dear?

SALLY. Well, what's it all about?

MISS BROACH. I'm only the Shop Manageress, my dear; I'm told nothing. Except one minute they're all at work, and the next minute they're all in the toilets laughing their heads off.

SALLY. What about?

FIRST WORKMAN. The Russians win the lot. I mean, by and large, they win 'em. Now why? It's 'cos of apathy. 'Cos there's no *passion*, that's why.

MISS BROACH. I'm sure I can't imagine, my dear. It's quite beyond *me*, I can tell you. It began with some nonsense about Dirty Money because of those gunmetal manifolds that had to be packed in grease, and then . . .

FIRST WORKMAN. What do they say to the English team before they go out on the field, eh?

SECOND WORKMAN. I dunno.

FIRST WORKMAN. Well, I'll tell you. It's 'Play the game, chaps, oh play the game. It doesn't matter who wins, only play the game.' But to these Russians – oh oh: 'You'll win the lot and you'll win bloody records; or there's cold breakfasts in Siberia . . .

GURNEY *re-enters along the corridor, carrying papers, and goes into the outer office.*

GURNEY. Ah, Miss Broach!

MISS BROACH. Good morning, Mr Gurney . . .

FIRST WORKMAN. . . . till Charlie Khrushchev tells you different!'

GURNEY (*savagely*). So the Packing Department's stuck its arm in up to the elbow again! As usual on a Monday.

MISS BROACH (*offended*). If we technical people had the proper co-operation from the office staff, there'd be no need at all for that sort of language, Mr Gurney.

GURNEY. And the best of luck!

He enters the inner office.

MISS BROACH. It's very well, very easy, to put the blame on me, but I don't control the wages policy, nor *yet* the annual holidays.

GOLDSWORTH *comes out of the inner office.*

GOLDSWORTH. Miss Broach, if you please.

GURNEY *comes out of the inner office.*

GURNEY. Just a moment, just a moment. Sally, F.H. is asking for . . .

HENDERSON (*from within*). Gurney!

GURNEY (*confused*). Yes, er – yes, F.H.?

HENDERSON (*from within*). Not the red one, you idiot, the blue!

GURNEY (*furiously to* SALLY). The blue one, the blue one – why can't you have these things ready? He's going to break my collarbone in a minute . . . Yes, there, you silly girl!

He snatches a blue-covered file off her desk and goes in again.

GOLDSWORTH. We'd better go in, Miss Broach.

MISS BROACH. Very well, Mr Goldsworth.

He takes her into the inner office.

FIRST WORKMAN (*completing the planing and standing up*). I think that ought to do it: what do you say? Just sand down the angle, and then we'll set her up again, then give a lick of paint. And Bob's your uncle. Hokey cokey.

SECOND WORKMAN (*looking in the toolbag*). We ain't got that much sanding left, you know. I thought you said there was some in the bag.

FIRST WORKMAN. Well, there is, in't there?

SECOND WORKMAN (*holds up a piece of sandpaper*). There's *this* piece. Like, rough, in't it? Not much, for us? I mean, there's none of the proper smooth.

FIRST WORKMAN (*vexed*). Ow.

SECOND WORKMAN. I thought you said there was some in the bag.

FIRST WORKMAN. That young lad said he'd put some in. He said it this morning. I'll sandpaper his backend for him, we get back at the yard. They're no better than a lot of Teds, these fellers.

SECOND WORKMAN. Ah, we'll make do with this. It's a botch, but it's a job.

FIRST WORKMAN. It's a botched job and that's *all* it is. You see what I'm telling you, you see what I'm telling you, there's no passion these days, there's no what I call a lust, it's a botch all round, six ways on the compass. Look at Hitler.

He tests the edge of the door with a square, and begins sandpapering, carefully.

STOBO *and two* WORKING GIRLS *come along the corridor and into the outer office.*

STOBO (*with an air of command*). Ha-h'm.

SALLY (*a little flustered*). Oh. Yes? Good morning.

STOBO. It's a deputation.

SALLY. Mr Henderson's in conference at the moment, I'm afraid.

STOBO. Tell him it's a deputation, Miss Nuttall. I've called these girls out and I'm here to tell him why.

FIRST GIRL. He knows why.

SALLY. Miss Broach is in with him, you know.

STOBO. That's neither here nor there. Miss Broach is Miss Broach. *We're* on about double rates for holiday shifts and we want the head-man.

SALLY. I'll see what I can do. (*She clicks the desk speaker.*) Mr

Henderson, there's Mr Stobo here from the Trade Union, and some of the Packing Shop people in a deputation . . . Yes, Mr Henderson. (*She clicks off, and repeats the answer, nervously apologetic.*) He says: 'Stobo comes in and the rest stay out,' Mr Stobo.

STOBO (*humorously*). All right: he's frightened for his life, is he? You stay here, me dears: I'll call if I need help.

FIRST GIRL. Good luck, Harry boy.

SECOND GIRL. Tell 'em the tale.

STOBO *goes into the inner office.*

FIRST WORKMAN. He's a soldier. He's seen life. And more than that. He's suffered. He was a corporal, see. Then they put him in prison. I mean, he knows the force of strength, doesn't he? I mean, like, you're Hitler: I'm Chamberlain. So I come along with the old umbrella up, *crawling*: 'Oh play the game, old boy, play the game.' Well what do you do!

SECOND WORKMAN. I dunno. What do I do?

FIRST WORKMAN. You march into Poland! Stands to reason you do. Come on, come on!

SECOND WORKMAN (*with a laugh*). Where, Poland?

FIRST WORKMAN. All right, laugh. But I've seen experience. I know these things.

FIRST GIRL (*chatting to the* SECOND GIRL *as they wait*). I said to him, 'Why not Butlins? We've never been, and it's not expensive . . .'

SECOND GIRL. It *is*.

FIRST GIRL. We-ell. It couldn't be worse than that place in Llandudno, three-and-six a day extra just 'cos we wanted a bit of pork pie to our breakfasts. And Dad got his hernia there.

SECOND GIRL. They didn't charge him for that, did they?

Both GIRLS *laugh.*

FIRST WORKMAN (*finishing the sandpapering*). O.K. . . . Let's take her in. (*They lift the door.*) Up, two. *To* you. Steady.

They back into the outer office with it, squeezing the GIRLS *against the wall.*

SECOND WORKMAN. Steady. 'Scuse us, love. *Up* yours, *down* mine. Steady.

The door is held up in its frame again.

FIRST WORKMAN. Right. I'll hold her this time, you screw.
SECOND GIRL (*laughs*).
FIRST WORKMAN (*to* SECOND GIRL). I'll tell your mother!

He supports the door while the SECOND WORKMAN *begins to refix the hinges.*
High voices, unintelligible, are heard in the inner office.
GURNEY *shoots out of the door.*

GURNEY (*passing the* WORKMEN). My God, don't let him catch you smoking! He'll burn my hair off!

He hurries away along the corridor.

FIRST GIRL. Sounds like Harry Stobo's bringing in the ceiling a little, don't it?
SECOND GIRL. Aha, he knows his strength, does Harry.

GOLDSWORTH *comes out of the inner office.*

GOLDSWORTH. Where's Mr Gurney?
SALLY. I don't know: he went off!
GOLDSWORTH (*harassed*). Oh dear . . .

He goes in again.

SECOND GIRL (*to* SALLY). Dunno why your mob don't do it.
SALLY. Do what?
SECOND GIRL. Well, same as us. Walk out on it. You don't tell me they serve *you* any better – worse, *I* know, 'cos we've

got the Union, all you got's your flannelling Staff Association. That lot couldn't kick a donkey through a gate.

SALLY (*embarrassed*). I don't know, I'm sure . . . I've got to do these letters.

HENDERSON (*within*). All very well, that's all very well . . .

STOBO (*within*). Mr Henderson . . .

HENDERSON (*within*). But that's not just money you're asking for, you know . . .

STOBO (*within*). Mr Henderson . . .

GOLDSWORTH (*within*). On a wider front and a long-term policy . . .

HENDERSON (*within*). It's not just a question of an extra sixpence, you know, to buy lipstick for fifty silly girls: it's the life-blood of this industry . . .

STOBO (*within*). Mr Henderson!

GOLDSWORTH (*within*). We have to consider the reactions not only of the shareholders . . .

HENDERSON (*within*). Mr Goldsworth . . .

GOLDSWORTH (*within*). But also the Parliamentary Commission . . .

HENDERSON (*within: in a great bellow*). Mr Goldsworth, *I am talking*!

The noise from the inner office now drops suddenly.

FIRST GIRL. Cor blimey.

SECOND WORKMAN. It's one thing talking. But passions, lusts and that – hold her steady, mate, I'm not bang on the hole here . . . O.K., O.K. – Passions, lusts: I mean, what is it you want?

FIRST WORKMAN. What I'm *telling* you. It's everywhere around these days; there's nothing matters, is there? You want a bit of sense of truth of life, man. (*He starts to sing in a melancholy tuneless fashion.*)

For life is hard and life is cruel
And hits you where it hurts:

It's better to fight and die on your feet
Than fatten in the dirt.

It's good philosophy, it is . . . What's the matter – can't you manage the last two turns? Here: you need a *wrist* on this job. (*He takes over the screwdriver and continues singing.*)

I hid my money under the floor
Tied up in a woollen bag:
But the rats they came and ate it all
And left me never a rag.

GURNEY *re-enters along the corridor, and goes into the outer office.*

GURNEY (*to* SALLY). I can't find it anywhere – where is it, where is it?

SALLY. I don't know what you're talking about, Mr Gurney, I'm afraid. What's got into everybody this morning? It's not a bit nice working here, and there's no use my pretending it is. If you can't remember your manners . . .

Offstage office noise.

GURNEY. Oh lord, oh lord . . . (*He turns on the* WORKING GIRLS, *in a despairing appeal.*) Now honestly: is there any real need at all?

SECOND GIRL. Need for what?

GURNEY. Oh, *you* know. I mean, there's Harry Stobo in there, we all know, hitting F.H.'s desk for him and bellowing away like a radioactive hairbrush, but . . .

HENDERSON (*within*). No no no . . .

FIRST GIRL. He's not the only one bellows, is he, Mr Gurney?

HENDERSON (*within*). It's no good, Stobo; it won't wash, man, it won't wash . . .

SECOND GIRL (*satirically*). Ah, it's the old old agony; it's all right; so long as we don't shout, everybody's happy.

FIRST GIRL. It's models of industrial co-ordination.

SECOND GIRL. It's managers-labour co-operation, class-consciousness barriers broke down . . .

FIRST GIRL. A demi-bloody-paradise, write in the papers . . .

SECOND GIRL. Just for so long as *we* don't shout!

GURNEY (*a little overwhelmed by their outburst*). Now, wait a minute . . .

FIRST GIRL (*aggressive*). Wait a minute, wait a minute; don't you go telling us to wait a minute . . .

SECOND GIRL (*nearly dancing with scorn*). Lah de dah, lah de dah, Boss Henderson's bloody dog, bow-wow . . .

FIRST GIRL. Doggy doggy, bow-wow, wow, wow-wow-wow!

SECOND GIRL. Down, y'devil, *down*!

They both laugh.
GOLDSWORTH *appears at the door of the inner office.*

GOLDSWORTH. Gurney! Where in earth have you been, Gurney? Mr Henderson wants . . .

GURNEY. In two shakes!

GURNEY *goes out down corridor.*

HENDERSON (*within*). No no no . . .

STOBO (*within*). No no no no, it's no good, Mr Henderson. I'm not taking *that* . . .

HENDERSON (*within*). I don't give a damn what the blasted woman says . . .

MISS BROACH, *weeping, runs out of the inner office, and away down the corridor.*
STOBO *appears at the door of the inner office.*

STOBO (*strongly*). Come on, girls, come on: there's no good for us in this place, no! We're going out and we're staying out – that's all the Packing Shop, Mr F.H., and you'll be lucky if it's not the Bottling Line and the Gum-kibble Floor as well!

FIRST GIRL. Transport and General ought to come out in sympathy.

STOBO. Well, they might at that. So you'll lose your lorry-men and the canal-hands, and all, and then where will your orders be! Come on, girls!

GURNEY appears in the corridor, indecisively.
STOBO goes out down the corridor in a rage.
The GIRLS follow him, barking and laughing at GURNEY as they go.
GURNEY goes out again.
HENDERSON comes out of the inner office.

HENDERSON. Miss Nuttall! Take a letter!

SALLY. Yes, Mr Henderson.

She starts gathering up her notebook and pencil.
HENDERSON begins dictating without giving her a minute. As he talks, he goes back into the inner office, and SALLY follows him, desperately trying to take down his words.

HENDERSON. To Amalgamated Iron Hooks Limited, for attention Mr Longhandle. Dear Sirs, We are in receipt of yours of etcetera etcetera – get the date off the relevant file – and have pleasure in confirming herewith our acceptance of your quotation for the supply and delivery of thirteen-gross pattern – pattern whatever it is – ah – those hooks we ordered, find out what they are, and complete as usual. Send a copy to Haskins and Judson . . . (GURNEY *enters down the corridor and into the outer office, as* HENDERSON *reappears at his door, which has remained open.*) Gurney, I thought I asked you to check last week's packing schedules.

GURNEY. Yes – ah yes, F.H. I've got the figures here, yes . . .

HENDERSON. Are they collated?

GURNEY (*taken aback*). Well, ah, not exactly . . .

HENDERSON. Then for God's sake collate them! If there's going to be a full-blown strike, how the devil am I expected to handle it without full knowledge of our resources? Mr Goldsworth, I've told you what I want you to do.

GOLDSWORTH. Yes, Mr Henderson. By lunch-time. Yes.

He hurries industriously away, down the corridor.

GURNEY (*fumbling*). O.K., F.H., right-ho, smart as lucifer, right, right, at the double . . .

He follows GOLDSWORTH.

HENDERSON *re-enters his office and slams the door.*

The WORKMEN, *having fixed the hinges, are now examining the effect of the contents of a pot of paint taken from the bag. The* SECOND WORKMAN *has dabbed a small patch on the edge of the door and they stand back and regard it.*

FIRST WORKMAN. That's not a bad match at all. What do you think?

SECOND WORKMAN. It's a bit light, you know.

FIRST WORKMAN. It ought to dry down dark enough. You've got the shine on it, you see, with it being wet. Anyway, your door fits right, there's no question.

SECOND WORKMAN. Bit on the small side, maybe: you'll get draughts.

FIRST WORKMAN. Ah, not to signify. 'Course, it might sing.

SECOND WORKMAN (*painting the door, where they have planed it*). Sing?

FIRST WORKMAN. With the wind in it, like. Being warped, and then trimmed. My old grandma's kitchen door used to sing, something violent. Like a regular aeroplane. The Sopwith Camel, we used to call it, when we was kids. Bzzz, hmmm, bzzz! You'd have to wait for a windy day to test this one, though.

(SALLY *comes out of the inner office and sits at her machine.*)

Excuse me, miss. We've done.

SALLY. Oh, thanks ever so much. What a relief to be able to

work with the door shut at last. Or work at all, if it comes
to that.

FIRST WORKMAN. 'Course, it might sing. If you've a windy
day in the east and it sings, give us a call at the yard and
we'll come and sort it. Morning to you.

He goes out into the corridor.

SALLY (*puzzled*). Sing?

SECOND WORKMAN. Yeah, sing. Give us a call, we'll sort it.
Morning.

*He, too, goes out into the corridor and shuts the door carefully
behind him. They pack all their equipment in the toolbag.*

SALLY (*as the door closes*). Good morning, I'm sure.

FIRST WORKMAN. You see, what I tell you. That's a nice girl,
but she's like the rest of 'em in a place like this. They're
walking dummies. They've no passion, they've no *heart* on
the job at all. Offices *or* the assembly-lines, it's the same
thing everywhere. All rush – no urgency . . . Don't let
'em catch you smoking here, mate . . . Apathy all over.

SECOND WORKMAN. The bigger the firm – the less the
initiative.

FIRST WORKMAN. No passion. Nothing. Ah, it needs a crafts-
man to feel an honest rage about the world. I mean, take
Khrushchev. He's been a collier, hasn't he? He's worked in
the pits, he's seen life: he's suffered. We-ell . . .

As they are about to leave the stage they meet the TEA-GIRL
*pushing her trolly. They go off, past her; one of them apparently
having pinched her bottom on the way.*

TEA-GIRL (*furiously*). Get aht of it!

SALLY, *typing furiously, makes a mistake, swears to herself,
tears out the paper, and starts again.*

SALLY. Oh, *Oh;* what a morning. I don't know *where* I am . . .

(*The desk-speaker buzzes. She answers it.*) *Yes*, Mr Henderson . . .

The TEA-GIRL *comes into the outer office.*

TEA-GIRL (*loudly*). Empties!

SALLY (*angrily*). Oh, shut up, Doris, I'm trying to hear Mr Henderson . . . Yes, Mr Henderson . . . Yes . . .

TEA-GIRL (*very surly*). How many cups inside?

SALLY. Very well, Mr Henderson . . . How should I know? Go and see!

TEA-GIRL. *I* can't go in there; you know I can't.

SALLY. Yes, Mr Henderson. (*She clicks the desk-speaker off.*) Look, can't you just wait a minute, while I'm on to the boss, for goodness' sake? Yappity-yap . . . God's sake, here's your tea-cups, and . . . (SALLY *shoves her cup across the desk: it drops on the floor and breaks.*) Well, it serves you right.

TEA-GIRL (*furious*). Here, who's going to pay for this? It's not going to be stopped out of *my* wages, I can tell you . . .

SALLY. Oh, shut up!

TEA-GIRL. You shut up yourself, you smarty stuck-up cat!

SALLY. Don't you talk to me, you – you – you little tart, you! This is *my* office, *mine*, how dare you . . .

The desk-speaker has buzzed again, but they ignore it in their anger.

HENDERSON (*from within*). Miss Nuttall. Miss Nuttall! *Miss Nuttall!*

The desk-speaker buzzes continuously.

Live Like Pigs

Seventeen Scenes

Introductory Note

When I wrote this play I intended it to be not so much a social document as a study of differing ways of life brought sharply into conflict and both losing their own particular virtues under the stress of intolerance and misunderstanding. In other words, I was more concerned with the 'poetic' than the 'journalistic' structure of the play. The reception of the production at the Royal Court seemed to indicate that I had miscalculated. On the one hand, I was accused by the Left of attacking the Welfare State: on the other, the play was *hailed* as a defence of anarchy and amorality. So perhaps I had better declare myself. I approve outright neither of the Sawneys nor of the Jacksons. Both groups uphold standards of conduct that are incompatible, but which are both valid in their correct context.

The Sawneys are an anachronism. They are the direct descendants of the 'sturdy beggars' of the sixteenth century, and the apparent chaos of their lives becomes an ordered pattern when seen in terms of a wild empty countryside and nomadic existence. Put out of their fields by enclosing landlords, they found such an existence possible for four hundred years. Today, quite simply, there are too many buildings in Britain, and there is just no room for nomads. The family in this play fails to understand this, and becomes educated in what is known as the 'hard way', but which might also be called the 'inefficient way'.

The Jackson's are an undistinguished but not contemptible family, whose comparative cosiness is not strong enough to withstand the violent irruption into their affairs that the Sawneys bring. Their natural instincts of decency and kindliness have never been subjected to a very severe test. When they are, they collapse. I do not regard them as being necessarily typical in this. They are the people I have chosen for the play, because they illustrate my theme in a fairly extreme form.

To any producer interested in presenting *Live Like Pigs* may I offer one or two suggestions?

(i) The play is in large part meant to be funny.

(ii) The Old Croaker-Blackmouth-Daffodil group have much the same effect upon Sailor's household as the Sawneys in general do upon the Jacksons.

(iii) The singing of the ballads should be in some way integrated into the action or else cut out. At the Court they were unsuccessful because the singer was put on the stage between the scenes and quickly taken off again so that no one was really clear whether he was in the play or out of it.

The setting is the interior and exterior of a typical council house. I do not think it necessary to build a whole house on the stage. This was done at the Court, and had the effect of slowing down the action considerably. Distinction between upstairs and downstairs can be made quite easily by arranging the upstairs rooms behind or beside the downstairs ones with only a foot or so difference in level. I have written all the stage directions in terms of a real house; but these can be modified by a producer without strain. The exterior scenes do not really need a complete front wall to be provided for the house (or houses, for the door and one window of the Jackson building are required). The sort of council house I had in mind is the dull sort – not one of the agreeable designs given prizes by County Planning Committees.

The Housing Estate has only too obviously been laid out by an unimaginative Borough Surveyor. It is wearisome to look at and contains no real feeling of a living town. Col's criticism of it to Doreen in Scene Three is entirely justified.

The room in the house are as follows:

Downstairs: Living-room

Hall, with staircase, front door, and door
into kitchen

Upstairs: Large bedroom
Small bedroom
Landing, with door into bathroom.

The kitchen and bathroom are not seen on the stage.

The Characters

SAILOR: He is a strong broad-shouldered old tyrant of seventy. He walks with a limp. His white hair hangs to below his shoulders and he has a long drooping moustache. He is the most barbarous yet least savage of the group.

RACHEL: A tall handsome termagant aged about forty, and carrying it easily. She has very long hair worn loose and an alarming tigerish laugh. Arrogant and harsh-voiced.

ROSIE: In her early twenties, short and stocky, and apparently sullen. Obviously put in the shadow most of the time by Rachel. She has, however, a basic sense of satire and true depth of passion. She is also very weary.

COL: Is a loutish youth of eighteen or nineteen, with a rather more urbanized approach to life than the others: though he stops very far short of being a genuine Teddy-boy. His clothes do have certain hints in that direction, but no more. He is much given to uncouth noises to supplement his speech, and has swift and violent mannerisms.

SALLY: Is a wicked little ten-year-old girl with Woolworth spectacles, and a great capacity for loud excitement. She idolizes Col.

BLACKMOUTH: He is described as half-gipsy, and looks it. He is twenty-eight years old, lean, and sexy. He is both insolent and obsequious, and can put on a kind of false joviality that does not take many people in. (It does take Col in, for a while.) When crossed, he gives clear indications of underlying mental unbalance.

THE OLD CROAKER: Has a voice from which her name clearly derives. She is a batty old hag, alternately skittish and comatose. Her voluminous rags make her look like an outlandish bird. When scared, she can be very self-effacing. So can her daughter.

DAFFODIL: Aged about seventeen, she has an old, old face like that of a malicious fairy. Her sideways smile is caused by a white scar that runs up from chin to cheekbone. She has some of her mother's mannerisms, as well as a sly juvenile lechery which is all her own.

MR JACKSON: Is a man of forty-five who is in process of being promoted from the working-class proper into the lower-middle. There is nothing much to be said against him. He knows he has a dull life and feels very hurt that when he looks for a little mild excitement he should receive so much more than he bargained for.

MRS JACKSON: Has grown older quicker than her husband and has not had a figure for several years, but does not mind. She loves her gossip, and in general much resembles her neighbours.

DOREEN: She is a shop-assistant, eighteen years old, very nice, simple, pleasantly dressed. She is not particularly well versed in the contemporary 'Teenage Culture' of her friends, but likes to think she is.

THE OFFICIAL: A typical junior-grade Local Government employee, middle-aged and well meaning. He wears an old Burberry which looks as though he slept in it and a bowler hat on the back of his head. His outer pockets are stuffed with documents and his inner ones with pens and pencils.

THE DOCTOR: Is a lady doctor and not a very pleasant one. She is impatient with the members of her panel and by no means inclined to put herself out for their convenience. Her diagnoses are accurate. She is fifty years old.

THE POLICE SERGEANT: He is motorized and therefore wears a peaked cap and not a helmet. If his methods are irregular and his manner overriding, this is principally when dealing with those he despises. He is honest enough: and no more of a bully than he would claim to be necessary to preserve the peace.

The Songs

The stanzas of song at the beginning of each (or nearly each) scene are intended to be sung as an introductory statement either just before the set is discovered or while the lights are coming up. This song needs no instrumental accompaniment, and the same tune, basically, could be used for each scene. It should be a typical melancholy street-ballad, dragging and harsh, and sung with the peculiar monotony associated with the old fashioned street-singers. The same singer need not sing each stanza if it is considered that a better effect would be produced by varying the voices.

The first stanza of all should cut very violently into the hushed hum-and-shuffle that normally comes between the lowering of the house-lights and the rise of the curtain.

The songs sung by the actors in the course of the play should be to airs of the usual folk-song variety, and unaccompanied.

First presented by the English Stage Society at the Royal Court Theatre, London, on 30 September 1958, with the following cast:

An OFFICIAL *of the Local Housing Department*	Alfred Lynch
BIG RACHEL	Anna Manahan
ROSIE	Margaretta D'Arcy
SALLY, *her daughter*	Daphne Foreman
COL, *Rachel's son*	Alan Dobey
SAILOR SAWNEY	Wilfred Lawson
MRS JACKSON	Peggy Anne Clifford
DOREEN, *her daughter*	Jacqueline Hussey
MR JACKSON	Nigel Davenport
BLACKMOUTH	Robert Shaw
THE OLD CROAKER	Madge Brindley
DAFFODIL, *her daughter*	Frances Cuka
A DOCTOR	Anne Blake
A POLICE SERGEANT	Stratford Johns

Directed by GEORGE DEVINE *and* ANTHONY PAGE

Décor by ALAN TAGG
Ballads set and sung by A. L. LLOYD

TIME: The Present
SCENE: A post-war Council Estate in a north-country industrial town

Scene One

SONG

O England was a free country
So free beyond a doubt
That if you had no food to eat
You were free to go without.

But if you want your freedom kept
You need to fight and strive
Or else they'll come and catch you, Jack,
And bind you up alive.

So rob their houses, tumble their girls,
Break their windows and all,
And scrawl your dirty words across
The whitewashed prison wall.

Interior. Evening.
The OFFICIAL *is discovered half-way up the stairs, discoursing on the house.* ROSIE *sits in the living-room with her baby in a shawl and* RACHEL *stands in the hall. Both women have brought in several untidy bundles.*

OFFICIAL. And up the stairs we're into the bedrooms. There's the two bedrooms, one big, one small; and there's your bathroom off the landing. You didn't have a bathroom down on the caravan site, did you? Mrs Sawney! I say Mrs Sawney; aren't you coming up to look at your bathroom? (*He comes back down into the hall.*) Oh come on, missus, I've not got all day. Blimey, you'd think I was showing you round a condemned cell or summat.

ROSIE. Did you say it was a bathroom?

OFFICIAL. God help us. Of course, love, I said it was a bathroom.

SALLY *has entered through the open front door.*

SALLY. Bathroom? Is there water? Is there taps of water, mister?

RACHEL (*slapping her*). You shut your noise, Sally.

ROSIE (*angry*). Don't you go knocking her, she's not yourn, she's not yourn to go knocking her like that.

SALLY *howls.*

ROSIE. Shut your noise when you're told.

ROSIE *slaps her.* SALLY *shuts up and then begins stealthily climbing the stairs.*

OFFICIAL. Now look here, missus, do you want to see upstairs or don't you?

RACHEL. Why? We've no choice, have we? You've put us to live here. Why can't we take our own bloody time looking at the place? So what if we *don't* like it? We've got no bloody choice.

OFFICIAL (*exasperated*). Eh God, I'm a reasonable man . . .

The baby cries and ROSIE *rocks it and croons.*

OFFICIAL. But where did you get all this fat nonsense from, hey? 'No choice', 'put you to live here' – *who* put you to live here?

RACHEL. You put us. Coppers put us – all the lot of narks.

OFFICIAL. Now wait, wait. I'm not the police, I mean look at me, Mrs Sawney, did you ever see a policeman my shape of figure? All that's happened is: your old place down by the caravans has had to be condemned, well I mean: rightly – I mean a broken tramcar with no wheels no windows, I wouldn't put pigs – all the rain coming in on you and all, why . . .

RACHEL. Our place, mister.

OFFICIAL. But *this* is your place. *This is* your place. You've to pay rent, of course, it's not much, though. You'll easy afford it; if not, you can go on the Assistance, you see . . . Why it's a *good* house. It's only five years old at most: I mean look at it . . .

There is the sound of running water from the bathroom into which SALLY *has slipped. The* OFFICIAL *turns angrily and hurries up the stairs.*

OFFICIAL. What's that? Sounds like running water. . . . Where's that kid gone – God help us, in the bathroom. Hey lovey, hey, little girly, hey hey, what do you think you're playing at with them taps, water all over the bloody floor.

He goes into the bathroom and SALLY *comes running out, down the stairs, and off through the front door. The* OFFICIAL *turns the taps off and comes slowly down himself.*

OFFICIAL. I don't know. I don't know. A lovely house, I'd call it. I've not got a house like this, you know. *I* have to live in furnished lodgings, and like it.

There is a pause.

RACHEL. It's time Col was here with Sailor and the barrow. Why don't he come?

ROSIE (*nervously to* OFFICIAL). Can we: can we – is that . . . ?

OFFICIAL. What is it, missus?

ROSIE. Upstairs, you chased the kid off, she was only running water. Who's to tell us when we *can* run water?

OFFICIAL. What are you talking about? Nobody's to tell you. It's your bathroom. You can use it when you like.

ROSIE. Then what for do you chase the kid off? She was only running water.

OFFICIAL. She'd left the plug in the basin, it was all over the floor.

ROSIE. She's not your kid to chase. She was just having her play, that's all.

RACHEL. They ought to be here with the barrow. Wait all the bloody evening.

OFFICIAL (*embarrassed*). Well, I'll have to be off to the Town Hall. I've given you the keys, I've done my job, and precious thanks I've got for it. (*He moves to the door.*) Just a while, and you'll get settled all right, Mrs Sawney. You know, you'll like living here. Honest, you will.

SALLY *runs in again.*

SALLY (*very excited*). He's coming, he's coming, Col's coming, Col's coming. Col, Col, Col's coming.

She dances up and down. SAILOR *and* COL *come in through the front door pushing a home-made barrow consisting of a packing case mounted on pram wheels. It is loaded with a great pile of household junk, topped by a chamber pot and an old-fashioned horn gramophone. They also both carry bundles. We hear their voices before they appear, grumbling angrily.*

SAILOR. Two men to pull the barrow, one man pulls the barrow, one man walks beside it, that's *his* way.

COL. Ah, hold your old gob, will you, I'm leading as much of the weight as you –

SAILOR. One man to pull it, one man to walk beside – it's the strong lad, he walks beside; the old man, he has to pull; that's *his* way. (*He sees the* OFFICIAL.) Who's this?

COL (*to the women*). All the road up from the back bottom of the hill, he's carrying-on. Why don't I smash his face for him? (*He sees the* OFFICIAL.) Who's this?

OFFICIAL. Mr Sawney? I'm from the Corporation, I've just been opening the house up for your good ladies and like

showing them around. I think everything's in right order
for you – if there's anything you want to know about –

SAWNEY. Want to know, is it? Do *you* know where we've
been living, mister, until today, d'ye know *that*?

OFFICIAL. Yes, I know. Down the far side of the railway
yard, on what they call the caravan site. No drains, no
fresh water, no nothing.

SAILOR (*satirically*). Ye wouldn't keep pigs in it, hey?

RACHEL. That's what he said to *us*.

SAILOR. Oh hoho, he's the grand man to talk. And look at
the grand palace he gives us. (*He goes up the stairs*.) Look at
it. Lovely. Lovely . . . Mister!

OFFICIAL. Er, yes?

SAILOR (*calling sharply from the big bedroom*). Whose is this
house?

OFFICIAL. Well, er –

SAILOR. Whose is it?

OFFICIAL. Well, you might say it's yours, now, Mr Sawney.

RACHEL. That's what he said to *us*.

SAILOR. Then that being so, Mister, then that being so – I'll
give ye one half minute to get off of this ground.

COL (*violently*). Go on, you heard him, go on. Jump your
bloody feet to t'other side o' that door.

OFFICIAL. Now just a moment, you can't do this sort of
thing here –

COL. Are you going?

OFFICIAL. This is very silly of you, you know, this is very
silly indeed . . .

He hurries out of the house as COL *advances threateningly*.

RACHEL (*shouting after him*). Calling us pigs, would you!
How'd you like a real screaming sow to raven your paunch
for you, hey?

COL. I'll show him pigs.

SAILOR. Has he gone?

COL. Aye, he's gone. Ought to have put the boot through him. I'll show him pigs.

SAILOR. Bring the dunnage into the house, Col. Here we are and here we've got to live. But we're keeping *them* out from us, every bloody one of them. (*He stands astride and terrible.*) They call me Sailor Sawney and no man slaps his natter at *me*. Rachel, Rosie, help Col carry the dunnage.

COL *and the women bring in more possessions from outside, including a very battered pram into which* ROSIE *puts her baby and leaves it in the living-room.*

SALLY. Col told him, Col told him right proper. You told him proper, didn't you, Col?

COL. Get out the road, kid. Run away to Sailor.

SALLY *creeps timidly upstairs and peeps at* SAILOR *in the bedroom.*

SAILOR. Come away in, Sally, come away in, to Sailor.

SALLY. It's water in there. Taps of water. He chased me cos I run it. He did.

SAILOR. Never you mind for him, little daisy, little sparrow. You run it when you're minded. Our house, our taps of water.
(*He sings.*)
> Oh when I was a strong young man
> I wandered on the sea
> And many were the ladies
> That called unto me:
> With golden hair and scaly tails
> And eyes of bright green
> So many were the mermaid girls
> That swam all in the stream.

Scene Two

SONG

To every woman is a man
Or two or three or four:
And she that has not got a man
Must fight a terrible war.

Like mermaids in the ocean wild
With babes upon their breast
Will cross the bow of a roaring ship
And sink it both keel and mast.

Exterior. Morning.
ROSIE *is sitting on the doorstep rocking the baby in the pram by pushing it backward and forward with one hand while she sorts a basket of clothes-pegs with the other.* RACHEL *comes out to the doorway, with a cigarette in her mouth.*

RACHEL. Where's Col gone?

ROSIE. He's gone out.

RACHEL. I know. I said where?

ROSIE. He went down the town. He says 'if my mam asks where I've gone, I've gone for a job' he says.

RACHEL. What like of a job?

ROSIE. He says, there's new building work along beyond of Woolworths –

RACHEL. Aye I've seen it – they say offices for the Corporation. Are they taking men, are they?

ROSIE. Col says any labourers you want to ask. It's four bob an hour.

RACHEL. He didn't tell me he wor going.

ROSIE. He said for me to tell you, if you wanted to know.

RACHEL. Who are you to tell me – he's *my* lad!

ROSIE. You warn't around, so he said it to me. He said four bob an hour.

RACHEL. Well it's time there's *someone* brought it in. We've got rent to pay for this bloody dump. It's time Sailor went for some work. The bad leg of his been better six months, seven. He could work.

ROSIE. Well, you tell him then.

RACHEL. You tell him, he's your dad.

ROSIE (*stung*). He'll work when he's ready. There's no one can touch that old Sailor once he's got his strength in. My mam, when she wor living, he'd be out on a job, wind a crane, dig drains, heaving barrels, what you like, all day he'd be at it; then into the boozer till closing – likely fight a pair o' men into canal dock, knock a copper over after – then home like a traction engine and revel her three times down to Rio without he'd even take off his boots. That's what my mam said.

RACHEL. Ach, your bloody mam.

ROSIE. And before that, when he wor a right sailor. He comes home from his voyage one time, and he says to her, 'Every water's got its wavetops, every house got its roof, but there's only one sailor's got *you*,' he says, 'and there's only one bloody sailor keeps you.' That was his last voyage of all, that. He come into Hull from Archangel on the ice and he lived with my mam till she died. What do *you* know about him?

RACHEL. I know he's been young and now that he's old. But I'm not old and I'm still with him. So that tells you. That bloody tells you. Telling me, you dirty bitch. What about the feller give you these two kids of yourn – call *him* a wavetop on the burning water, hey? You living with *their* daddy till you die? Burning likely you're living with him, hey?

ROSIE *takes no notice and plays with the baby*.

I said: Burning likely you're living with him. I said: Where he is, you'd *love* to roll and slumber. I said: Where he is, *you'd* carry your belly to the cookhouse door, wouldn't you, where *he* is, hey? why don't you follow him —

While she carries on, MRS JACKSON *comes out of her house and begins to sweep the steps. This is only an excuse for her to be out, however.*

— You don't *know* where he is, you never *did* know. In one night, he serves you pretty Sally; in another night, serves you the other here. Off with the sunshine and where does he go? Or was it the rain?

ROSIE (*sullen*). Rainy days. All you know of rainy days is stand under the arches at closing-time, isn't it? — 'Come in out of the wet, dearie, nice bit o' fun wi' Rachel, only ten bob, dearie, call it sheltering while the rain comes down and never tell a word to the Missus.'

RACHEL. And what about it so?

ROSIE. I've nothing about it. 'Cept there's some as offers for *five* bob. Young redheads and all.

RACHEL *laughs with a bitter hiss and turns angrily awry.* MRS JACKSON *comes across to them.*

MRS JACKSON (*very friendly*). Excuse me: it's Mrs Sawney, isn't it? The rent collector give me your name, he said you were coming to live here, so I thought, well, I'd just pop round the door and have a word — like, it's your first day here, and why not be neighbourly, I thought, and give 'em a call? Eh, isn't it a lovely day?

RACHEL. Who are you?

MRS JACKSON. I live next door, you see, so I thought why not be neighbourly; like, it's such a lovely day. Jackson's the name. My husband, my husband he works for Co-op you know; like he's their agent, drives around the villages all day in his van to the local branches; just in the grocery he used to be, but he got made Agent last year. By, he wor pleased, I can tell you. He's got his van, you see: he's like his own master now. . . . What do you think to the Housing Scheme?

RACHEL (*dourly*). Housing Scheme, is it?

MRS JACKSON. Well of course, I mean, we think it's lovely. We've been here nigh on two year. I'll tell you where we used to live – you know when you went past the Town Hall, down by the Catholic Church – all them little mucky streets – eh it wor terrible. But they moved us out, moved us all out and pulled the lot down. That's where they're building new Corporation Offices, you know, now. Isn't it lovely here, though? Wide streets, bits of garden, and all. Of course, it's a long way from the shops and there's only the one public. But my husband, he reckons that's a good thing. He says –

RACHEL. Oh go to hell, you and your fizzing husband.

MRS JACKSON (*stopped gasping in midstream*). I beg your pardon! . . .

SALLY *runs out of the Sawney house and stares at* MRS JACKSON.

RACHEL. I says go to hell. You're not wanted here. Keep to your own garden, you like it so much.

SALLY. Mam, mam, she's as fat as a pig, ent she?

SAILOR (*from indoors*). Rachel! Rachel!

RACHEL (*shouts back*). Oh so you're out of your bed at last! What d'you want then?

SAILOR (*appearing at an upper window*). Chase that bloody cow out o' here, and get me a sup o' tea. Well, move to it!

He shuts window.

RACHEL (*to* MRS JACKSON). Go on, get out of it.

MRS JACKSON. Well! Well . . . Of all the –

RACHEL *goes into the house.*

ROSIE (*wearily*). Why don't you folk leave us alone? We didn't come here cos we wanted; but now we *are* here you ought to leave us be. (*To the baby.*) It's time you had your dinner, Geordie. In we go, in we go, in we go to dinner.

ROSIE *goes in too.*

SALLY. Pig, pig, pig pig, fat fat pig.

MRS JACKSON. Why, you little – (*She offers a blow to Sally, but* SAILOR *indoors shouts again:* 'Rachel!', *and* MRS JACKSON *nervously lets her arm drop.*) I'll tell my husband of this. I never heard the like.

She goes into her house.

Scene Three

SONG

Wages at four bob an hour
What labourer will decline?
Yet you can earn you much more than that –
And I don't mean overtime.

Exterior. Evening.
COL *enters, from work, with an army haversack across his shoulder. He approaches the Sawney's door; but instead of going in, he stands outside and shouts.*

COL. Hoy oy, where are you! Who's at home tonight?

SALLY (*appearing at a window*). Sailor and Big Rachel gone to the boozer.

COL. Gone to the boozer.

SALLY. Me mam's gone selling clothes-pegs. Then she's to the boozer too. Left me to watch our Geordie. He's asleep.

The baby howls indoors.

Oh he's woke up again. I give him a clothes-peg to suck but he don't keep quiet. He don't, Col, he don't. You going to the boozer, Col?

COL. Maybe later. I only got one and six. They didn't have no more nor that in their pockets this morning: so where'd they get it from, hey?

SALLY. Big Rachel found, like, a wallet. In the road she found it. Three quid in it, see. Me mam had a half-a-dollar too. That mister he dropped it in the bathroom yesterday when I wor running the taps. He dropped it, see. Then me mam made me give it to her. Then there's her clothes-pegs and all.

COL throws his haversack down and takes out a number of carpenter's tools.

What you got there, Col?

COL. Off the building site, these. How much for 'em, Sally, eh? Two quid? Sell 'em to Charlie, up the Sheffield Road. He'd give me two quid; two quid ten maybe?

SALLY (*laughing*). Ey, Charlie, Snotty Charlie!

COL (*joining in with her*).
Filled his pockets with oats and barley
Some for cakes and some for loaves.

SALLY. And some for sticking up his long red nose!

They both laugh. SALLY *climbs out of the window, carrying the gramophone and three records.*

SALLY. Col! Col! will you play us gramophone?

COL (*ungraciously*). Gramophone . . . Out here, then. I can't abide inside, you'd be a tortoise or summat, you've to live in this dump. . . . There wor four records. I say you've only brought three.

SALLY. It broke.

COL. Oh it did, eh? It's about time somebody broke *you*, you little . . . Here's the music for Col, boy. Listen at this one:

He puts on a record: 'Cigareets and Whisky'. He and SALLY
*listen with great absorption, joining in the words of the song at
intervals and beating time wildly.* DOREEN *enters from the
street and goes up to her front door. She opens her bag for her
latchkey and cannot find it. After a moment's indecisive
fumbling she rings the bell. There is no answer.*

DOREEN. Oh dear.

COL (*enthusiastically picking up the refrain as the record ends*).
'Drive you insane!' 'Drive you insane!' There's the boy he
wrote that, knew the truth.

DOREEN (*looking at him dubiously*). I say –

COL (*glances at her, and then turns to the gramophone*). We'll
put it on again, kid. God, he's a good song, this: *he* knows
a man's life, he knows it. 'Cigareets and whisky and wild
wild women –'

DOREEN. Excuse me . . .

COL *looks at her and says nothing.*

Are you the new people that's come next door?

COL *makes an uncouth noise which she takes for affirmative.*

I've done ever such a soft thing, I went out to work this
morning and left my key behind. Dad's not in while seven
o'clock tonight, and it don't look like my mum's in,
neither. So I shall have to wait in the garden.

COL (*rudely*). Ah?

DOREEN. You're not very friendly, are you?

COL. Take it one gate, take it t'other. Here's your garden,
here's ours. Can talk your head off.

DOREEN (*offended*). Well I don't know, I *must* say – (*She turns
away.*) I think I'd better go and wait round the back.

COL. Hey.

She pauses.

Come here.

She comes, carefully.

Here's a song for *you*. (*He puts on the record again, and lifts off the needle after a few lines.*) It's a true song, see. I can tell you.

The baby howls.

SALLY. There's that Geordie again.
COL. Go in and stay in, kid. God's sake shut him up.
SALLY. Col, I want to hear records . . .
COL. Go on.

SALLY *goes.*

'Drive you crazy, drive you insane' . . . it happens, you know. This kid's dad, he used to –
DOREEN. She's your little sister?
COL. Ach no, Rosie's kid, she is. It's like her dad, he goes right crazy some days. He gets out after six month, eighteen month, or whatever, and then, boy, it's the cigareets and these women, and (hoo hoo) the whisky. Then he comes for Rosie. 'Away out of it,' she says. 'For me, you're a dead damned man and that's all.' And she won't take him these days – not since wee Geordie, nowise. So he goes crazy like the song. Wild crazy. Then inside again. Six month, two year. It's a true song, that.
DOREEN (*disparagingly*). It's an old song, isn't it? Must be all of nine or ten years old. Don't you have no up-to-date discs? It's awfully corny, that song is.
COL. Corny? It's truth of life, *I'd* say. I tell you, experience. What it is, you see, them kids' dad, he's half of a Romany.
DOREEN. A Romany? You mean, you're gipsies?
COL. *We're* no gipsies. But *he's* half of a Romany, you see. What we say – it's: they stink like foxes, them Romanies . . . What's your name?
DOREEN. Doreen. Doreen Jackson. What's yours?
COL. Col.

DOREEN. Col what?

COL. Just Col. They call us Sawney, cos of old Sailor, see. While Big Rachel's with Sailor, we're all of us, like, Sawneys. But that's not to last. You call me Col.

DOREEN. Oh.

There is an awkward pause.

COL. Hey, how do you live?

DOREEN. What?

COL. I say how do you live?

DOREEN. Well just like anybody else, I suppose.

COL. Here?

DOREEN. Why not here?

COL. We come here last evening, just.

DOREEN. Well?

COL. Look at it. You got a house you got a house. Then you got a bit of garden. Then there's a house and house. Then you got a bit of garden. A house a house a bit of garden. Then you got the concrete bloody road and two blue coppers thumping up and down it. I'll tell you, I'm going off me nut already . . . You work all the day, don't you?

DOREEN. Yes.

COL. *Then* what d'you do?

DOREEN. Well we watch the telly sometimes. Or we go to the flicks. Or Sheila and me (Sheila's my friend at the shop, nylon counter, you see – I'm lingerie) we might go to the Pally Saturday nights. Do you like dancing?

COL. The way *we* dance – I've been at one of them Pallies one time – 'Away out with you!' he says: and we'd not been in the place five jumps . . . Here's to dance, judy! Way *we* go dancing, hey?

He puts on another record – an old-fashioned ragtime tune. He dances to the music in a very strange barbarous fashion, flinging out his legs and arms and whooping. The general effect

*is almost as though an unskilful person were trying to do a
Highland reel to the wrong accompaniment. Suddenly glancing at* DOREEN *to see her reaction, he discovers that she is
laughing. Immediately he knocks the gramophone needle off
and recoils, stung.*

You think it's to laugh at, do you?

DOREEN. I'm sorry, I didn't mean to –

COL. All right! But there's more of us than me – *we* don't
think it's to laugh at.

DOREEN (*upset*). Oh look, I *didn't* mean, honestly –

MRS JACKSON (*from the street*). Doreen!

DOREEN. Here comes my mum. Dad's with her, and all. She
must have gone to meet him at the Co-op. I wonder –

MR *and* MRS JACKSON *enter.*

MRS JACKSON. Doreen, come inside at once.

DOREEN. But mum . . .

MRS JACKSON. You heard what I said.

DOREEN. Oh, O.K., mum . . . (*she whispers to* COL.) So
long. See you again, soon, eh?

DOREEN *and her mother go indoors.* JACKSON *comes round to
the Sawney's door.* COL *bends over the gramophone, adjusting
it; and ignores him.*

JACKSON. Her-hum. My name's Jackson.

COL (*without looking up*). Get out of it.

JACKSON (*embarrassed and pompous*). I believe my wife was
round here this morning. She was talking to the lady of the
house.

COL (*startled*). The what's that?

JACKSON. Mrs er Mrs Sawney, ent it? Is she in?

COL *shakes his head.*

Oh. Have you any idea what time –

COL *gets up with the gramophone and takes it into the house.*

JACKSON (*in vain*). I say have you any idea what time she *will* be in. . . .

COL *shuts the door in his face.*

JACKSON. Oh. Well *I* don't know.

JACKSON *raises his hand to knock on the door; thinks better and turns away.* RACHEL *has entered from the street and is looking at him.*

RACHEL. You ringing at that door?
JACKSON. I – I was thinking of it, aye . . .
RACHEL. He's not in.
JACKSON. Who's not?
RACHEL (*who is somewhat flushed with liquor, and speaks bitterly*). Sailor the gaily Sailor. He's voyaging to Archangel on the wave-tops of *my* money, mister. And he turns me home from the boozer while he spends it. What sort of a man, what sort of a man.
JACKSON. Are you Mrs Sawney?
RACHEL. So?
JACKSON. My name's Jackson.

RACHEL *laughs.*

Now look here, Mrs Sawney.
RACHEL. Look here, Johnny Jackson mister. Hold out your hand.

He does so automatically.

Cross the tall tart's palm with silver and who'll tell you your fortune, will she? I'll tell you *yours* without. You wor sent to tell me your wife tells you we tell her the dirty road to go today.
JACKSON. Why as a matter of fact –
RACHEL (*she takes his hand and caresses it mockingly*). Oh, you're a strong big man, you shouldn't worry what the

ladies say, Johnny. You know what they did? They put us
in this house the last day. And they're holding us in it and
all. They've even put a bathroom for us, to be certain sure
we're clean for their snow-white garden paths. I don't go
for baths regular. It's not my common life. But I'll strip
me down one day for this one, and you can be there to see
me do it. Then you tell the copper and the Council that Big
Rachel's had her bath, all like they like it. There's a
pleasure for you, mister. I'll tell you the day . . . So *let* him
got to Archangel, I'll tilt his keel, his bloody keel, I will.

She sits down on her doorstep. MRS JACKSON *opens her door a
crack and calls softly to her husband.*

MRS JACKSON. Ben? Ben? What did she say?
JACKSON (*going over to her, bewildered*). Oh – she must be
drunk. Couldn't get any sense out of her at all.
MRS JACKSON. Well, I call it a right disgrace. If it goes on I
shall make a complaint. They've no right to send people
like that to live here.
JACKSON (*dubiously*). They may settle down. They're like
gipsies or summat . . .
MRS JACKSON (*significantly*). Our Doreen, Ben . . .
JACKSON. She'll be all right. I don't reckon –
MRS JACKSON. Well I do. Anything might happen. Come on
in.
JACKSON. Aye aye, love.
MRS JACKSON. Kettle's boiling. (*She goes indoors.*)
JACKSON. Aye, aye, I won't be a minute, I'll just sort these
milk bottles for you.
MRS JACKSON (*inside*). What?
JACKSON (*making a clatter with the bottles on the step*). Milk
bottles, love. I'll not be a minute. (*He tiptoes over towards
Rachel.*) I say, Missus . . .

RACHEL *turns and grins at him like Burt Lancaster.*

JACKSON. It's just come to me. I've seen you afore.

RACHEL. Huh?

JACKSON. In the passage outside the Earl Fitzwilliam, selling matches and that . . . More than matches, and all, aye . . . (*He laughs nervously. Change the subject.*) Look, about my Missus, I dunno who started it this morning, but she *does* let things sometimes get a bit, like on top of her – if er well – I'm all for being neighbourly, you know – are you still around over at the Earl Fitz?

She shakes her head.

Aye, well, maybe, some other time, er, some other er – now and again, eh? er –

MRS JACKSON (*inside*). Ben!

JACKSON. Be with you! 'Night, Missus – er, 'night . . .

He laughs nervously. He goes into his house. RACHEL *sits brooding in the doorway. The night darkens in.*

Scene Four

SONG

Good rest and warm inside the house
For all who come along:
Here's a piece of meat, and there's drink, me boys,
And set you up with a song.

Interior. Night.

RACHEL *is lying on a pile of bedding in the big bedroom.* ROSIE *is in the living-room feeding the baby.* SALLY *is with her, eating out of a tin bowl.* COL *and* SAILOR, *fairly drunk, are on the stairs with bottles. Also on the stairs, is the gramophone playing the third record – a military march by a brass band.*

SAILOR. They call me Sailor Sawney. They call me a killer. You know why they call me that?

COL. You tell me why they call you that.

SAILOR. They gave me that name. Times I sail the sea they gave it. So take you one look at 'em: forcsle, deck, or captain's bridge – 'Watch out for that boy, he's a killer.' That's the word they'd use. True?

COL. You say so.

SAILOR (*savagely*). I say so. I say it: and it's true. (*He grabs* COL *by his neckcloth.*) Killed a Finn one day. Puts a witch on me, does he, a witch's curse. I knew him. Third mate, but a bloody Finn he was. *What* did I do to him!

COL (*breaking loose*). Killed him. You killed him. O.K.

SAILOR. A witch's curse. In there – (*He points to the closed door of the big bedroom.*) In there. She'd turn your eyes to charcoal, that one – you look at her straight. *Rachel!*

COL (*laughing stupidly*). Rachel . . .

SAILOR. Rachel.

He batters at the door with his fists, and COL *beats on the wall – both shout 'Rachel!'* RACHEL *gets up, listens to them a while, then suddenly opens the door.* SAILOR *staggers into the room, and kicks the door shut in* COL's *face.* COL *returns to his bottle.*

SAILOR. Go on, go on then, witch me, you power of fury – you!

He goes at her passionately and they wrestle. They fall down together and they roll on the floor, biting one another and howling in their throats.

SALLY. Mam, mam, what's happening?

ROSIE. It's Sailor and it's Rachel, that's all it is, lovey.

SALLY (*gleefully*). He'll break her heart, won't he, mam, Old Sailor will, eh? Break it, eh?

ROSIE. He'll have his try. He'll have it one time or the last.

The front door opens and BLACKMOUTH *comes in cautiously. The gramophone has now ceased playing.*

BLACKMOUTH (*to someone outside*). Here's the place. Wait while I make sure. (*He comes into the hallway proper.*) Hey ey!

COL. (*looking down the stair and recognizing him*). Hey ey!

BLACKMOUTH (*enthusiastically*). Col, me boy, me little Colly-O . . .

ROSIE *hears him and listens tensely.*

COL. We've had a few jars tonight.

RACHEL *forces* SAILOR *off her and he falls with a crash against the door.* BLACKMOUTH *looks questioningly at* COL.

Sailor and Big Rachel.

BLACKMOUTH. Rosie with you? Eh?

COL (*jerks thumb at living-room door*). Rosie.

BLACKMOUTH. In there? Away hey, then, let's have a look at her. (*He flings open the door and stands gaily on the threshold of the room.*) Ah me bonny Rosie, here I stand in the door!

SAILOR *comes out of the bedroom and stands at the top of the stairs.*

ROSIE (*hostile*). I'm giving these kids their suppers. We don't want you.

BLACKMOUTH (*very charming*). You don't?

ROSIE (*trembling*). No I bloody don't.

SALLY. Mam, is that my dad?

BLACKMOUTH (*taking some toffee out of his pocket*). Aye Sally, it's your dad. Here, look, I've got a bit of spice for you. All the road from London it comes. D'ye want it, d'ye want it, all the road from London and here it is for Sally . . . (*He dangles it in the air and she jumps after him trying to reach it.*)

SALLY. Give it, give it, give.

BLACKMOUTH. You've got to catch it first. Come on, kid; jump now jump; whoop where's it gone?

SALLY *succeeds in seizing the toffee.*

SALLY. Ah! I've beat you, I've got it. Eh I do like it when my dad comes.

ROSIE (*bitterly*). Do you? Begod you're about the only one as does.

SAILOR *comes down the stairs, followed by* RACHEL, *who goes across the hall to glance out of the little window beside the door.*

SAILOR (*at the living-room door*). Is he here? Is that dirty dog-fox Romany here, is that black-mouthed bastard –

BLACKMOUTH (*smiling*). Aye I'm here. Good old Sailor, always the same. Come on, man, you've drank three jars already, Col's drank two of them, I've not been offered none yet. Let's be having some warm in us, hey?

SAILOR (*hard*). What are you doing here, Blackmouth?

BLACKMOUTH. Wah wah wah, spit on the hearthstone, always the same. Friendly faces *I* get, don't I?

SAILOR. We thought you was still Inside.

BLACKMOUTH. Wah wah wah, what's Inside? Well I'm outside now, aren't I; and I've not eat for nigh half a week. Go on: she feeds my kids all right. Liverpool lobscouse she gives for *them*; but not for bloody Blackmouth. Oho. He's only their dad.

RACHEL. Why don't you give him eating? He comes in from the road. It's foul outside, he's not had nowt. Give him it. Go on, Col.

COL *goes into the kitchen.*

BLACKMOUTH (*jovially*). Ah me old Rachel –
RACHEL (*hard*). Who did you bring with you, Blackmouth?
BLACKMOUTH. Eh?

RACHEL. I says: bring with you. You left two outside in the dark. Who are they?

BLACKMOUTH (*embarrassed*). Oh aye, them.

COL *brings in a pan of stew, which* BLACKMOUTH *takes.*

Here's the stuff, Col, here's the eating for a man. Aha! (*He eats greedily.*)

SAILOR (*watching him closely*). Who are they?

BLACKMOUTH (*with affected ease*). Ah, you're a grand cook, Rosie. . . . Them two, you see: it's only the Old Croaker. I picked her up at Macclesfield. (*He eats with an eye on* ROSIE.) There's Daffodil with her.

ROSIE *knocks the pan out of his hand, and hits him on the side of the head.*

BLACKMOUTH (*parrying the blow*). Eyey, ey, Rosie, steady your heart now . . .

ROSIE (*white with anger*). You bring that Daffodil here?

BLACKMOUTH (*reasonable and pleading*). Well now, what else? Look: they wor after her in Macclesfield, see. So I meet up with them, chancy, on the road, the Old Croaker's half-daft: where are they going, what are they to do? See, Daffodil: like, poorly – I don't know what, she's *poorly*. And then there's some of them Scotchmen we met, you know, Jocky Faa with the one eye, his lot – through here Tuesday with their wagon, he says they've been giving to you Sawneys a right living house here, warm and roof and all . . . You're not going to turn us out now. Why, Daffodil's gone all wrong. And with travelling nights and all. We come here on a lorry. Spewing sick every mile.

SAILOR (*still hard*). Bring her in.

BLACKMOUTH (*relieved*). Ah well, you've room enough – I knew it.

SAILOR. Blackmouth clever-mouth, aren't ye? Go on, bring her in.

BLACKMOUTH (*opens the front door and goes out calling them*). Hey ey there, come on in!

COL (*with lecherous anticipation*). It's that Daffodil, is it? I've heard a word or two of *her*, me boys. Heh heh heh.

SAILOR. She'll try no turnings here, and that's for certain. Oh, not in Sawney's place.

RACHEL. Let 'em all come. If they put us here off of the roads, why not us bring the rest from the roads: who're *wanting* to come?

BLACKMOUTH *brings in the* OLD CROAKER *and* DAFFO-DIL, *all carrying bundles.* DAFFODIL *seems weak and sick.* RACHEL *greets them.*

Here's the Old Croaker, she's daft and she's dizzy, but she can shovel in the scouse, me lovely, can't you?

ROSIE (*cold*). You're Daffodil, they tell me. You're feeling poorly, they tell me.

DAFFODIL. Who are you?

ROSIE. Oh don't mind as to *my* name. I'm no one as counts. That's so, ent it, Blackmouth?

BLACKMOUTH (*vexed*). Don't talk so soft. She's Rosie, Daffodil. You've heard of her.

DAFFODIL. Rosie. Oh aye, Rosie. (*She laughs venomously, and turns upon* BLACKMOUTH.) You never tell me *she* wor going to be here!

BLACKMOUTH. Ah, now, now, Daffodilly –

DAFFODIL (*hysterical*). You never tell me! You smarty bastard, aren't you. Look, I'm proper poorly. I'm all shaking like a west wind. Get me somewheres to lie down, Blackmouth, I'll pass out on you again.

She huddles down on the floor shuddering. CROAKER *is eating the stew from the pan.*

BLACKMOUTH. Let's get her to a bed, eh. Where can we kip her down?

RACHEL. Upstairs. There's a room over the front. Col's in it. He'll not mind that, I daresay.

COL *laughs.*

BLACKMOUTH (*in mock admiration*). Upstairs begod. We've got an upstairs! Come on, Daffodil. Give us a drain for her, Col. You can sleep in the passage, boy. (*He seizes a bottle from* COL, *and gives it to* DAFFODIL.) Swallow this lot down, eh? (*He leads her upstairs and takes her into the small bedroom.*)

CROAKER (*sings*)

    Tom Tom the piper's son
    Plays his pipe when he was young
    And all the tunes that he could play
    Was over the hills and far away.

Where's Blackmouth?

RACHEL. You eat your scouse and shut up.

CROAKER. That's my girl, that Daffodil. Eh she's a bold one. Do you know what she went and did? In Police Station. I saw it. She did. She said: '*I'll* wash your nasty floor for you,' she said, and she stood and – he he he, she did it –

SAILOR. She'll try no turnings here.

CROAKER. Right there on the floor in front of all them female coppers. He he he. Eh she's my girl, my lovely girl.

BLACKMOUTH (*tucking* DAFFODIL *up in the bedding on the floor*). Here you are now, kip you down. You'll be a right dragonfly by morning eh? Bright and lively.

DAFFODIL. You never tell me she wor –

BLACKMOUTH (*fervently*). O begod, now Daffodilly. Rosie, Rosie – it's over two year since I wor in ten mile of Rosie – what you worry about *her*, God help us?

DAFFODIL. Now you listen to me, Blackmouth. I know your

goings, I do. You can't nancy me, you know. You come here for that Rosie. If I warn't so bloody poorly I'd have known of it afore.

BLACKMOUTH. Well *I* didn't know of it, neither.

DAFFODIL. Don't you tell me! You only brought me with you because I hung on to you like a flaming padlock –

BLACKMOUTH. There's more to it than that.

DAFFODIL. Aye, there's more. We'd seen you: that's what's more. And how to keep us quiet except you bring us with you, eh? I know.

BLACKMOUTH (*sourly*). If you think like that, I'm off downstairs. Let's have that bottle.

DAFFODIL. I need it. I'm shivering. I tell you.

BLACKMOUTH (*going to door*). All right.

DAFFODIL (*earnestly*). Look, Blackmouth. I'm over poorly to do owt about it now; but remember: padlocks bites tight.

BLACKMOUTH *snarls, leaves the room, and comes downstairs. At the living-room door he finds* RACHEL.

BLACKMOUTH (*with a parody of courtesy*). Upstairs and downstairs and under me lady's armpit. The Sawneys at home. 'May I make so free, ma'am, as to come for to go for to pass beside you into your commodious apartment? Thanking you in anticipation, ma'am' – (*He passes her and enters the room.*) Hi Rosie.

ROSIE. Ah no. You don't touch me.

BLACKMOUTH (*giving her up and turning to* SAILOR). She ought to have a doctor, you know.

SAILOR. What's wrong with her?

BLACKMOUTH (*shrugs*). Fevered and that. Christ, I don't know . . .

SAILOR (*confronting him strongly*). Laugh or not laugh over it, it's Sawney's place is this place. It's long time since you was with Sawneys, Blackmouth.

BLACKMOUTH (*airily*). Ah well, I'm on my road, soon. I

didn't *want* her with me, you see. Nor the Old Croaker neither, but –

CROAKER (*sings*). All round his hat he wears the green willow.

CROAKER ⎱ (*singing together*). He wears it for his true-
SALLY ⎰ love who is far far away.

BLACKMOUTH. But what to do about 'em, you tell me. Besides, you don't know *who* she goes talking to.

CROAKER. Meet all the old folks, tell 'em the old tale. Packet o' chips and a bottle o' stout and all o' that too – eeh, lovely days.

She starts to tear up a piece of cloth she has found on the floor.

RACHEL. Hey, you leave that alone.

CROAKER (*complacently*). I tear it all up, don't I?

BLACKMOUTH. And then the other thing. They look for me on the roads. I'm always on the roads, eh? eh? They'd never look in a house, would they? (*He starts beating the walls and floor with his hand.*) Walls, you see? Roof, you see? Floor. Clench you close and safely.

RACHEL. Who *should* be looking for you? Anyplace?

BLACKMOUTH (*showing signs of unbalance.*) They had me Inside all of for two year, this go. But I showed 'em. I came out of it. God-quick: this go. Rah bah rah! (*He goes through the motion of kicking, stabbing, and punching low.*) There's one blue screw to bite no padlocks on to no poor boys no more. Look at his two eyes all smoking hot tar, they are, black full of the blood. Ss. Ss. Set to look at *me*, eh? I showed him where.

COL (*delighted*). Oh, ho ho, you did him proper, didn't you, Blackmouth?

SAILOR (*dangerously*). Are you calling yourself killer?

BLACKMOUTH. Eh?

SAILOR. *My* name, Blackmouth. And I ain't no reeking fox, ye know.

RACHEL. *Easy, Sailor.*

SAILOR (*brushing her off*). Let alone, will ye! So ye're in my place, Blackmouth. Then watch it how ye go. And mind your work with Rosie, my Rosie. You mind.

BLACKMOUTH *meets his challenging glare with another one, but thinks better of it, and slides aside from the defiance.*

BLACKMOUTH. O.K. O.K.

RACHEL (*to* SAILOR). What if they come after him?

SAILOR. No one comes after no one into Sawney's place. No one. I'm the killer here and all the rest they clap their gobs afore I clap 'em for 'em. Rachel, ye bloody leprosy, come up to the bed.

He lurches upstairs to the big bedroom and RACHEL *follows.*

BLACKMOUTH. Rosie –

ROSIE. Get out of here. Me and the kids is going to sleep. And take her with you. (*She indicates the* OLD CROAKER.)

BLACKMOUTH (*calm but menacing*). Aye aye, me old Rosie. Go on, Croaker, there's your place. (*He pushes her into the kitchen.*) Aye aye, me old Rosie. Come on, Col boy, what about a drain.

He and COL *go and sit on the bottom of the stairs with a bottle.*

CROAKER (*singing in the kitchen*).
He wore it for his true-love for a year and a day
And when they come to hang him on the gallows
He cried 'Where is my true-love? Oh, so far so far away.'

Scene Five

SONG
They build a wall to keep you in,
It serves to keep them out.

So when they set their feet on the wall
Beware what you're about.

Exterior. Morning.
COL *is sitting on the Sawney steps.* BLACKMOUTH *leans out of the window beside him.* DOREEN *comes out of her front door on her way to work. Her mother appears in the doorway behind her.*

DOREEN. 'Bye, mum.

MRS JACKSON. Doreen, you've forgot your plastic over-shoes.

DOREEN. I don't need them today, mum, it's not raining.

MRS JACKSON. It said on the forecast –

DOREEN. Oh the forecast –

MRS JACKSON. Well. If it's wet tonight you might be ten minutes waiting for a bus, catch your death of cold, you never think on what I try to tell you –

DOREEN. Eh mum, all right then – come on, I'm going to be late for the shop, Mr Holroyd's been on to me already twice last week – (*She snatches the overshoes and hurries away.* MRS JACKSON *shuts the door as* DOREEN *turns to call.*) Goody-bye-ee!

BLACKMOUTH (*rudely*). Good-bye-ee!

COL (*shutting him up*). Tst! Hey, kid . . .

DOREEN (*nervously*). Look, I'm late –

COL (*coming down to her*). Don't you take no note of him – he's a dirty jumper, all he is – eh, Blackmouth?

DOREEN. Mustn't let my mum see you talking to me, Col – she's been on and on about it –

COL. Ah what the hell –

DOREEN. Please, Col, you mustn't –

COL. It's tonight, ent it, dancing, you said –

DOREEN. Well, but Col –

COL. At the Pally.

DOREEN. I don't know.

COL. I'll be there. You *said* you was going. You said with your friend – Sheila, ent it, eh?

DOREEN. Col, I'm going to be late for the shop.

COL (*turning back towards the doorstep*). Pally, right, I'll see you?

DOREEN. I don't know . . .

She hurries off down the road.

BLACKMOUTH (*appreciatively*). Take that one up in a barn loft, she'll learn ye some places for the straw to scratch you, heh heh heh.

COL (*considering it*). Why not, eh? What d'you reckon, Blackmouth?

BLACKMOUTH (*sings*).

> If you want to be a soldier
> You must learn to carry your gun,
> Learn to march and to encounter,
> And to turn you around and run.

But go for her, Col boy.

> The route is for the land of Flanders
> The route is out of Germany
> Tow-ri-ah the doodle addy
> Tow-ri-ah-di the doodle-ay.

She'll swerve you fair and nicey.

COL (*with admiration*). *You* can tell 'em, can't you, Blackmouth? I dunno though. You ever been to these Pallies, like, dancing?

BLACKMOUTH. Aye, sure.

COL. She's not like the sort I went with ever . . . Ah – I dunno . . . It's time I was to work. What time is it?

BLACKMOUTH. I dunno.

COL. I can't get the time at all, living in this dump. All times of day looks the same round here. He says last week, 'If you're late again, you're off of this job.' He says, 'Ain't you got no clock to look at?' I says, 'Bloody no we aint.' He says, 'Don't you tell me.' I says – where's me snap tin?

BLACKMOUTH *passes him out through the window a sandwich tin, which* COL *puts in his haversack, together with a bottle of cold tea.*

BLACKMOUTH. And your cold tea, boy. A man's drink for the good work!
COL. O.K. O.K. See you, Blackmouth. Is that doctor still upstairs?
BLACKMOUTH. Aye.
COL. She takes her time, don't she? I thought you said your Daffodil wor getting better.
BLACKMOUTH (*shrugging*). I dunno.
COL. O.K., O.K. See you.

He goes out down the road, leaving BLACKMOUTH *at the window.*

Scene Six

SONG
The Doctor's trade's a very good trade
To raise the dead to life:
But some of them no man should raise
For they died of a needful knife.

The Doctor's trade's a dangerous trade
For who can know for sure
If dust and bones that stand and walk
Will walk where they walked before?

Interior. Morning.
SAILOR *and* RACHEL *are sleeping in the big bedroom.*

BLACKMOUTH *is lounging moodily in the hall. In the small bedroom the* DOCTOR *is taking the pulse of* DAFFODIL (*who is in bed with a thermometer in her mouth*). CROAKER *is squatting in a corner moaning and tearing up a sheet of newspaper. The* DOCTOR *takes and examines the thermometer.*

DOCTOR (*to* CROAKER). I asked you please to leave the room if you can't be quiet.

CROAKER. Quiet?

DOCTOR. If you can't be quiet.

CROAKER. That's my girl, you know. Her.

DOCTOR. So you told me.

CROAKER. You're the doctor, aren't you? Doctor.

DOCTOR. I'm the doctor.

CROAKER. Ee ee, a female doctor. Female coppers and female doctors. You don't know where you are these days. I think I'll go for a soldier meself – how about it? You give her physic.

DOCTOR (*writing a prescription*). She can take two of these every four hours.

CROAKER. Physic.

DOCTOR. Two of these. They're tablets.

CROAKER. He give it in a bottle, afore, he did. He didn't give her none of them things.

DOCTOR. Who didn't?

CROAKER. Doctor didn't.

DOCTOR. What doctor?

CROAKER *sucks her teeth and sways on her haunches.*

DAFFODIL. Macclesfield it was.

DOCTOR. Well, I wouldn't know about that –

DAFFODIL. But it wor after that I got took, on the road, see; got took sick, doctor.

DOCTOR. There's nothing seriously wrong with you that a few days in bed won't cure.

CROAKER. Eh but she's proper poorly, doctor.

DOCTOR. A few days in bed.

CROAKER. Proper poorly. Spewing sick. You should have seen her.

DOCTOR (*to* DAFFODIL). But you ought to be looked after. Are you married?

CROAKER *cackles*.

Well, who do you live with? Who else is in the house?

CROAKER (*in great delight*). Blackmouth, she means. Married. Eee, Blackmouth.

DOCTOR. Please be quiet.

DAFFODIL (*urgently*). Here, doctor, here . . . The way they are in this house, they'd throw me on the street, give 'em a quarter chance of it. They would, you know. Aye. You tell 'em I'm proper poorly. Go on, you tell 'em. Tell 'em if they make me move I'll die.

DOCTOR. I shan't tell anybody anything of the sort. You've only had a mild chill. Stay in bed for a couple of days and then you can get up. Come and see me in my surgery on Monday if you're still not feeling right. (*She goes out on to the stair-head.* CROAKER *stands aside at the door for her. She speaks to* CROAKER). This house is appalling, you know, the condition of it: appalling. Look at the state of this room. Supposed to be a sickroom, filthy. (*She goes down the stairs and* BLACKMOUTH *accosts her obsequiously at the bottom.*)

BLACKMOUTH. She all right doctor?

DOCTOR. Who are you?

BLACKMOUTH (*evasive*). Oh I'm just – She all right, doctor?

DOCTOR. She would be if she were properly fed. There's no reason why not, these days. Does she work?

BLACKMOUTH. Oh aye. Now and then.

DOCTOR. What at?

BLACKMOUTH (*greasily*). Oh – not to give it a name, doctor.
You know . . .

> Up the lane behind the wall:
> Lying down or standing tall . . .

Ah you know: we've got to live, doctor.

DOCTOR. Do *you* work?

BLACKMOUTH (*still evasive*). Is it me? We all have our lives,
like. Like: you're a doctor, make folk well. She'll soon get
better. Won't she, doctor?

DOCTOR. I have no doubt.

SAILOR (*waking up*). Who's that – there's someone in the
house!

RACHEL (*waking too*). Go to sleep, it's the doctor.

SAILOR. Doctor for that Daffodil.

RACHEL. That's right. It's time she was bloody better.

SAILOR. Time she was better and out. (*He shouts loudly*.)
Make her better, doctor!

DOCTOR (*taking no notice*). Filthy. I was appalled by the
bathroom, appalled. This is quite a new house. You ought
to know how to treat it properly.

SALLY *comes out of the kitchen and looks at the doctor.* ROSIE
appears nervously in the kitchen door, carying the baby.

SALLY. She the doctor, dad?

DOCTOR. Yes, I'm the doctor.

SALLY. Ee-ooh.

DOCTOR (*to* BLACKMOUTH). She's your child?

BLACKMOUTH. Aye. Oh aye.

DOCTOR. Is it her mother upstairs, then?

BLACKMOUTH. Oh no. No.

ROSIE. No, it's not. I'm her mother and so what's that to
you?

DOCTOR (*looking closely at* SALLY). How long has she had these sores on her face?

They are silent.

Hasn't the school doctor seen them? . . . You do see the school doctor, don't you, little girl? . . . She does *go* to school? You do *go* to school?

They are still silent.

Why doesn't she go to school?

ROSIE. Why should she go to the school? They'd not learn her nowt there. They'd knock 'em about there. *I've* heard of it. Hurt her. Keep her book-reading at night when she ought to be having her play and her sleep. We'll not let them take my Sally for the school. Oh no, no, we don't.

DOCTOR (*giving her up*). Well it's none of my business –

ROSIE. And that it's not.

DOCTOR. But you can be made, you know. Brought before the courts. I don't understand your attitude. Present day and age. House in this condition, child needs attention – what do you imagine the Health Service is for? Why don't you take her to the children's clinic? Here's the address: look. (*She gives* ROSIE *a card.*)

ROSIE. Why should we?

DOCTOR. Oh good heavens. Well . . . well . . . if that's the way you want to – Good morning.

BLACKMOUTH (*politely*). And to you, doctor.

The DOCTOR *leaves, and shortly after we hear her car start up outside.* ROSIE *looks at the card irresolutely and then drops it to the floor.*

SALLY. Mam, have I to go to the school?

ROSIE. No lovey, you've not.

SALLY (*frightened*). I'm not going, I'm not going.

BLACKMOUTH (*indulgently*). Hey hey Sally, *who's* off to send

you to school? Anyone to send you to school, they've to
sort wi *me* first: let 'em sort it with your dad, what about it?

ROSIE (*sardonic*). Aye, what about it?

BLACKMOUTH. Away to the back room, Sally, I want to talk
with your mam.

SALLY. I'm not going to the school.

BLACKMOUTH (*fiercely*). Off away with you, kid. Go on!

SALLY *goes into the kitchen unwillingly.*

BLACKMOUTH. She says Daffodil's getting better.

ROSIE. She does, eh?

BLACKMOUTH. Aye . . . Ye see what it means, don't you?
Old Sailor'll want to put us out. The killer, he. Ss . . . I
dunno about Rachel.

ROSIE (*sardonic*). Ach Rachel.

BLACKMOUTH. Well. She don't know her mind one day into
the next, Rachel. She takes us in to spite her Sailor, that's
all.

ROSIE. So.

BLACKMOUTH (*passionately*). Look, what the bastard hell,
Rosie – I don't want that pinchy tart of a Daffodil! Not any
more begod, anyhow. I want you.

ROSIE (*bitterly satirical*). Ohoho, you do? The third time he
says it. First time's for Sally, next time's wee Geordie, so
for your third time – O.K. Here on this hard house floor
just like you cry for . . . And then what?

BLACKMOUTH (*rather puzzled*). Well and then we –

ROSIE. Well and then we get up again; and you wipe yr dirty
gob wi' the back of yr hand and you say: 'Aye aye me old
Rosie, never tell 'em Blackmouth don't know how to love
you.' And then there's two years, and then you come back;
and begod here I am with another little Blackmouth set
puking on me knees. And so we start again. And so we
start again for number *four*!

BLACKMOUTH (*trembling and shaken*). You didn't ought to talk to me like that. That's the road you send men off their nuts, I'll tell you. You remember the last time.

She turns away.

Look, now look; Rosie! We get out of here, now. You come with me. Afore there's Daffodil on her feet again we're out and travelling, and she nor nobody never knows where. Come on, come on, Rosie, *now*.

SAILOR *comes out and stands on the stairs.*

ROSIE (*doubtful despite herself*). You don't mean it true . . .

BLACKMOUTH. I do so. I want you. I'm bloody starving for you.

ROSIE. You don't mean it. Besides, there's coppers chasing.

BLACKMOUTH (*violently*). I don't care a donkey's hiccup for any o' that. Rosie, will you come?

SAILOR. Blackmouth!

BLACKMOUTH. Hallo?

SAILOR. I hear ye, ye letchy polecat. Now you hear *me*. You say you're wanted by the Polis: right. Now let there stand one more word atween you and my Rosie and you go bang away out o' this without her: and run your own chances with every flatfoot in the land!

BLACKMOUTH (*shaking even more*). You didn't ought to talk to me like that, Sailor.

SAILOR. I talk how I want to who I want.

BLACKMOUTH (*in a vicious whisper*). I'm not afraid of no blue coppers. You say Go – all right all right . . . (*He moves towards the front door.*) Sawney's, eh? Good friends to all, eh? I'll tell the boys along the road, I'll tell 'em. Ss ss. Good friends, good friends. *I'll* tell the bloody boys –

He slips out, trembling and jerky.

RACHEL (*who has also come on to the stairhead*). Off into the sunshine; or is it raining today?

SALLY *comes out of the kitchen.*

SALLY. Where's my dad gone?
ROSIE. He's gone off, lovey.
SALLY. I want him back, mam.
ROSIE. Shut up, will ye. Sailor, maybe he comes back, you know.
SAILOR. Ach, for that . . . He's only a dirty Romany, so.
ROSIE. He makes me scared.

CROAKER *comes out of the small bedroom.*

CROAKER. Ee ee? she wants her dinner.
RACHEL. What's that?
CROAKER. Her dinner. She wants it.
RACHEL. Dinner?
CROAKER. Dinner. My Daffodil, my girl. She does. Oo hoo hoo . . .

Scene Seven

SONG
Oh why do you laugh and why do you cry
And why do you walk alone?
I'm hunting down a tall woman
To make her all my own.

Interior. Afternoon.
DAFFODIL *is asleep in the small bedroom with* CROAKER *crouching beside her, eating a crust of bread.* RACHEL *and* JACKSON *are discovered coming out of the kitchen towards the*

stairs. JACKSON *is nervous and trying to hide it by being boisterous.* RACHEL *is quiet and saturnine.*

JACKSON (*in the middle of a story*). Well, of course, I could see he wor pulling his rank on me, and that, you know. Coming it proper strong he wor – bags of bull. I said, 'Sergeant Hipkinson,' I said. 'You may be carrying more of it up here (*He touches his upper sleeve.*) but there's other places,' I said where us Privates carry' – No; no, that's not right, I said it sharper than that – By, I told him proper – I said, 'There's other private places,' I said, 'where some of us carry' – Nay that's not it neither. Eh, I've forgot what I *did* say, now; but By, it wor strong, any road. And you know what he did? – He said, 'Fetch me a bucket,' he said, 'I'm going to be sick!' He said, 'Fetch me a bucket.' In that French tart's room and all. She wor just sat there on the bed, you know, humped up like a hedgehog and looking at him. He said, 'Fetch me a bucket,' he said – Eh –

He laughs uproariously, holding on the stair-rail for support. CROAKER *comes out of the bedroom.*

CROAKER. Ssh-ssh-ssh, ssh-ssh! She's asleep!

She pops inside again.

JACKSON (*alarmed*). Who's that?
RACHEL. That's the Old Croaker, that is.
JACKSON. You said there warn't anybody in.
RACHEL. No more there is, mister. Only her and her Daffodil.
JACKSON. Her what?
RACHEL. Christ, don't be feared, man. Who cares at all? One of 'em's daft and other's asleep. Come on, come on, man.

She goes upstairs and he follows apprehensively. She leads him into the big bedroom and sprawls out on the bedding.

JACKSON. I hope nobody saw me at your kitchen door. If I'd known you wor going to bring me back to this house I'd not have come. I mean it's damn dangerous – of course my job on the van, she doesn't know where I've got to all day, and of course she's out this afternoon, but –

RACHEL. Let's have a fag.

JACKSON (*finding one for her*). Here. (*She takes it and he lights it for her clumsily. She sticks it in the corner of her mouth and drags at it crudely. He watches her and his excitement begins to grow again.*) By, you're a right strider, I'll bet you are – I could tell it as soon as I saw you. Like this bint I knew in Naples – I wor in the old Headquarters Group in them days – ah we had some times there. She used to wear this red dress, you know, busting out at the corners of it like a pan of milk boiling over –

CROAKER *suddenly cackles with laughter.*

JACKSON. What's that!

RACHEL. That's the Old Croaker, that is.

JACKSON (*relieved*). Oh aye, so it is . . . Ah, the old H.Q. in Naples. We had a time there. By, you're a right strider, you are, lovely ripe and striding – By!

Scene Eight

Interior. Afternoon.
RACHEL, *half-dressed, sprawls on the bedding in the big bedroom. She is smoking the butt of a cigarette.* DAFFODIL *is asleep in the small bedroom.* CROAKER *is in the living room tearing up some paper.*

CROAKER (*sings – the tune is the same as the link songs between scenes*):

When I was a girl to dance and sing
Little I thought upon
How soon my youth be rooted out
And my pleasuring all torn down.

There is the noise of a lavatory chain being ineffectually pulled once or twice. JACKSON *comes out of the bathroom, buttoning his jacket.*

JACKSON. Fair shocking disgusting.

He starts to go down the stairs.

RACHEL. Hey! Come here, mister.

He halts and goes in the bedroom reluctantly.

You just walk out on me like that? Why, Johnny Jackson, you've got a sauce, eh?

JACKSON (*sourly*). How much do you want?

RACHEL. You tell me, you tell me, mister. Put a value on it. I'll wait.

JACKSON (*bitterly*). Value. You're a beauty, aren't you? I didn't come up here, you know, to be – What the hell you think you are, anyroad? Bloody animal, I'd call it.

RACHEL. You don't find much o' my sort of loving up and down *this* town, likely?

JACKSON (*in outrage*). No and it's a damn good thing we don't – what you want a lump of raw meat shoved in the bars of the cage to tear at, *you* want. By, I've never met the like. You bloody animal. What do you want to carry on like that for? We could have had us a right nice time this afternoon if you'd only – Well I didn't expect it like that, I can tell you.

RACHEL *laughs nastily.*

It's all right laughing. All right. But if I want a tart again –
it's the last time I come to *this* house. I've had my lot of
you, and that's for truth. I'd sooner spend my afternoons
rolling in a muck tip! It'd smell a bit sweeter, anyroad.
. . . Three quid. That do you? It'd better bloody do you.

RACHEL. You make it five, mister. And we'll not let on to
your wife.

JACKSON. You'll not *what*?

RACHEL *laughs*.

(*Very angry.*) Oh none o' that, you know, none o' that.
You'd better watch it. I'll have the police after you.
There's more than the police I could have, and all. I could
call this house a Public Nuisance, you know. I could tell
the Sanitary Department a thing or two about this house.
Aye and I could tell . . . I'll make it four pound ten and
there you are. I want nowt more to do with you. I'm fair
bloody disgusted.

*He thrusts the money at her and goes downstairs. She spits
after him. He turns angrily back at her, but then thinks better
and carries on down. As he reaches the bottom the* OLD
CROAKER *appears at the living-room door. He turns on her
with a snarl.*

And you. You mind to your own affairs. Keep yer old nose
out, aye.

He goes out furiously through the kitchen. DAFFODIL, *awake,
sticks her head out of her room.*

DAFFODIL. Is that Blackmouth downstairs?

RACHEL. No, it's not and bedamned.

DAFFODIL (*querulously*). It's time he wor back. Why don't he
come back? Eh I do feel bad. Why don't he come back, the
dirty devil?

She goes back to her bed. CROAKER *tears up paper and hums her song.*

Scene Nine

SONG

Oh why does he laugh and why does he cry
And why does he walk alone
Along the roof and over the wall
And underneath the moon?

Exterior. Evening.

MRS JACKSON *appears on her doorstep with a saucer of milk.*

MRS JACKSON (*calling*). Choo-choo choo-choo choo, puss puss puss! Choo-choo-choo! Pussy! Pussy! Tea time!

CROAKER *comes out from the Sawneys' door and watches her.*

CROAKER (*mimicking*). Choo-choo choo-choo-choo, choo-choo choo-choo-choo. Come for his milk. He likes his sup of milk.

MRS JACKSON (*taking no notice of her*). Choo-choo-choo, pussy-pussy, where are you! Where are you . . . ? (*She at length agrees to notice* CROAKER; *and speaks to her coldly.*) You've not seen our little cat, I suppose.

CROAKER. Eh, nay, I don't know. He's a strong tom, I'll bet he is, eh; makes 'em spring and yo-ow-owl-

MRS JACKSON (*sharply*). She's not a tom, she's a tabby. I said have you seen her?

CROAKER. Them tom-cats they know how to lead their jolly lives, they do. (*Beckoning mysteriously.*) Here, come here. Ssh-ssh. Come here, lady. You don't take to our Rachel, do you? I know. She tells you the dirty road to go. But I tell her, and I tell her, and –

MRS JACKSON (*interrupts in vain*). Look, I've not got all evening . . .

CROAKER. – do you know what they're at? Them Sawneys? They want to put, us, on, the road. Put-us-on-the-road!

MRS JACKSON. Yes, well, I dare say –

CROAKER (*detaining her*). My pretty girl, proper poorly, grudged her the drops of water for her thirst, they took the very shoes off her feet. There's more nor that they've took, ooh – don't go, don't go yet, gentle lady, lovely lady – you see, Old Croaker knows where your tom-cat went up this afternoon!

MRS JACKSON (*startled*). What! Where?

CROAKER. Ssh-ssh, they'll hear us . . .

MRS JACKSON. She's not a tom: she's a tabby. I knew it. That woman took her.

CROAKER. He was strong and squalling, but he ran away from her. Hoho yai! Down the stairs and out.

MRS JACKSON. Where is she now?

CROAKER. Nay nay nay, lady. How could Old Croaker tell you that?

(*She sings.*)
>   Come all you little black cats.
>   He chases the dirty rat
>   The rat is sharper than the cat
>   And fetches the blood right out of his back . . .

I'd sooner love a biting rat, I would, than any day with our Rachel; ee-ay-yai –

COL *enters from the street and goes towards the Sawney door. He has his haversack on his shoulder and is eating fish and chips out of the paper.*

COL (*to* CROAKER). What you gabbing over the fence, you old haystack? How's our chirping Daffodil today?

CROAKER (*in a sort of trance*). Eh? Who is it? Col?

COL. You know me as well as your own toe nails, you do. Where's Blackmouth?

MRS JACKSON (*to* CROAKER). I asked you where's my cat gone.

CROAKER (*hopelessly*). Miaow, miaow? Croaker doesn't see no cats, no more tom-cats now . . .

MRS JACKSON. But you just said –

CROAKER. Oh no no, all tore to little bits and gone.

MRS JACKSON *goes into her house in disgust.*

She's proper poorly.

COL. What?

CROAKER. My girl is. Aye-yai.

COL. I says where's Blackmouth?

CROAKER (*shakes her head*). Ooh, chips, eh?

COL (*crossly*). Ach – where is he? I've a thing for him to see.

CROAKER (*chants*). Old Sailor turns him out
                            turns him out
                            turns him out
                       Old Sailor turns him –

You haven't got a bit of fish, have you? Like, with the chips?

COL. Achtcha to that, you know: there's no man to turn *Blackmouth* out . . . Our Rosie, hey?

CROAKER *laughs.*

Ahahaha. Aye . . . Hoy there – (*He is looking down the street*) – Sally! Here –

He tosses the remnant of his fish and chips to CROAKER, *as* SALLY *comes running in from the street excitedly.*

SALLY. Col! Col! I done it, Col. I done it like you told me, Col.

COL. You give them tools to Charlie?

SALLY. Snotty Charlie.

COL. You give 'em?

SALLY. He warn't going to let me have more nor a quid, Col;

but I says to him, I says: 'Col says my dad Blackmouth's
home and he did a Screw right dead and if you don't give
me more nor two quid he'll do you too, good and proper,' I
tell him. So he give me thirty bob for 'em. Here, see. (*She
gives him the money.*)

COL (*vexed*) T't' t't – not much, wor it? O.K. kid, you buy
you some spice. O.K. (*He gives her a couple of coins back.*)

SALLY (*in delight*). Eee Col! . . . Is my dad back?

CROAKER *laughs and shakes her head several times. Having
finished the fish and chips she is now tearing up the paper.*

Ent he coming back, Col?

COL (*carelessly*). Aye, he'll be coming.

CROAKER. I tear it all up, don't I? (*She laughs again and goes
into the house.*)

COL. Hey, Sally, you go to Charlie, next time; you take him
this.

*He produces an electrically powered carpenter's drill from his
haversack.*

SALLY (*her eyes wide*). Oooh.

COL. There's all of ten quid here. (*He runs around with the
drill, presenting it like a Tommy Gun.*) Brrr-brrr-brrr . . .

SALLY. Brrrr-brrrr . . .

COL (*seeing the Jacksons' front door opening*). Oy-oy. Here,
kid, fetch it inside. Quick.

He thrusts the drill back in the haversack and SALLY *runs
indoors with it.* DOREEN *leaves her house, calling back.*

DOREEN. 'Bye mum.

COL (*slyly, to her*). Hey – *up!*

JACKSON *has entered from the street and meets his daughter –
who, watching* COL, *does not at first see him.* JACKSON *looks
at* COL.

JACKSON (*sourly*). You calling me?

COL (*taken aback*). Eh?

JACKSON. You calling me?

COL (*recovering himself, continues to call, but looking upwards*).
Hey – *up!* . . . No: I warn't. Calling the birds.

JACKSON. Birds.

COL. Give 'em a holler, down they swing down; sit on your
head. Hey – up! tweet-tweet.

He turns his back on JACKSON *and walks about pretending to
signal to birds.*

DOREEN. You're a bit late tonight, dad?

JACKSON (*in a foul temper all round*). Shut up, can't you? I've
had a bad day. Where are you off to, anyroad?

DOREEN. Going dancing. With Sheila.

JACKSON. Oh are you? Well you watch yourself. Them
young Teds at the Pally . . .

DOREEN. Oh, dad –

JACKSON. All right. I'm telling you.

DOREEN. 'Bye, dad.

JACKSON *snorts and goes in to the house.* DOREEN *glances at*
COL, *who does not appear to notice her, and then hurries off
down the street.*

DOREEN (*offstage*). 'Byee.

COL (*looking after her*). Hey-*up!* Sally!

SALLY *appears at ground floor window.* DAFFODIL *at the
same time looks out of an upper one.*

COL (*to* SALLY). I'm off out away. You take care of what I
have given you, while morning. O.K.?

SALLY *nods.*

COL. O.K.

SALLY *goes away from the window.*

DAFFODIL (*plaintive*). Col. Col. He run out when I wor
   sleeping, Col.

COL. He'll be back, eh.

DAFFODIL. Don't you go too, boy. You come up here.

COL. See you, my lovely . . . Hey-*up*.

He goes out down the street in the same direction as DOREEN.
DAFFODIL shuts the window and retires inside. JACKSON
comes out of his house, shouting back at his wife.

JACKSON. All right. All right. If I can't get a civil word in my
   own house, 'Cat's lost, cat's lost' – all you can say. I told
   you before what you could do with that cat. I'll be back
   while closing-time and you'll be lucky if it's no later.

He stamps off down the street.

Scene Ten

                    SONG
         At half past ten they turn you out
         And bar the bar-room door.
         The night is dark and the road is cold
         But why should you despair?
         For if you have no home to go
         Nor wife to hold you dear
         Then draw your sweet and naked knife
         And murder all your fear.

Interior. Night.
In the living-room ROSIE *and* SALLY *are sitting making clothes-*
pegs. The baby sleeps in the pram. In the small bedroom
DAFFODIL lies sleeping and CROAKER squats in the corner. COL
comes in through the front door in a bad temper, slams the door,
and starts upstairs.

SALLY (*running out of the living-room*). You back from dancing, Col, already?

COL. Aye, I'm back.

SALLY. You warn't at it long, wor you?

COL. No I bloody warn't.

He goes into the small bedroom and slams the door behind him. The OLD CROAKER *starts up. He stands looking at* DAFFODIL *while* CROAKER *makes signs to him to be quiet.*

SALLY (*going back into living-room*). He warn't at it long, wor he, mam? I say, mam, eh, he warn't at it long –

ROSIE. Get making them pegs and shut your noise.

SALLY (*rudely*). Owowow –

CROAKER. Don't wake her up, Eee. She do sleep beautiful, oh look at her, tender, tender my little duckey.

DAFFODIL (*waking*). Who is it? Blackmouth? . . . Oh. (*She lies back disappointed.*)

COL (*with a quiet smile*). No it's not. It's me. You says: come up. Well: I come.

He flicks his fingers towards the door and looks at CROAKER. *She giggles. He gestures again, more imperiously, and she hurries obediently out and downstairs. As she passes the living-room door, she pops her head in and says 'clothes-pegs!' – then she goes out into the kitchen.*

DAFFODIL (*putting on a seductive languor*). Oh sure you come climbing. Col . . . You seen Blackmouth out in the town, did you?

COL (*coming closer to her*). Na.

DAFFODIL (*mockingly*). Eh you'd never see him. All you'd be seeing's that daisy from next house, ent it? Ent it?

COL (*in a practised insinuating voice*). I know *you*, Daffodil, don't I? Heard of you, you see, all of us heard. Old Croaker's little Daffodil. Kind and right to the boys. Takes 'em and gentles 'em. Is truth of life is that. Why, you'd never be like – this dancing-and-warm the one way, knives-in-the-eyes the next, crying-and-scared the third – that's never *you*, is it? You tell me it's not you. (*He strokes her body and she relaxes to him as if of old habit.*)

DAFFODIL. No. Oh no. Not me.

COL (*suddenly*). What the hell is Blackmouth anyroad? Old Sailor Sawney, *he* throws that boy. A limping sailor throws him.

They embrace. BLACKMOUTH *comes quietly in through the front door. He looks white and haggard and is talking mechanically to himself in a low mutter, maudlin.*

BLACKMOUTH. Hey killer, are you at home? No, he's not at home. Who's at home? No one's bloody home. Home of friends gentle and kind. But for Blackmouth, but for Blackmouth – only one killer in Sawney's house allowed. Poor devil Blackmouth, let *him* try to set up his horn – where's the friends gone then?

He has been rummaging vaguely around in the rubbish in the hall, and picked up one or two possessions of his. Now he goes upstairs.

SALLY. (*in a whisper*). It's my dad.

ROSIE (*holding her*). Ssh.

BLACKMOUTH *goes into the small bedroom and continues to rummage, without taking the slightest notice of the two sitting on the bed.*

BLACKMOUTH. I left my bundle, so. (*He picks up his bundle from the floor and collects other oddments.*) Poor Blackmouth, on the road. Set up his horn in Scunthorpe, aye or Doncaster. No killers hold the road in Nottingham. Why not Nottingham? I never see Sheffield a long time. All right: Sheffield. (*He moves to the door. For the first time he appears to understand what* COL *and* DAFFODIL *are doing.*

They have lain petrified since his entry.) In her bed. In her bed. Ss ss ss. (*He picks out a flick-knife and jerks it open.*)

COL (*leaping to his feet*). Oh-oh. Knives.

He has no weapon, so he snatches up a garment and hangs it over his forearms as a shield. He and BLACKMOUTH *revolve slowly round each other,* COL *looking desperately for something to fight with. He sees a frying pan and grabs it just in time to parry a dangerous thrust by his enemy.*

DAFFODIL (*sitting against the wall*). Kill him, Col; kill him, Col, kill him, Col Col Col Col Col. (*She suddenly starts to scream like a lunatic, without moving her body.*)

BLACKMOUTH (*hissing at her*). Shut up!

Distracted by the noise, he relaxes his guard sufficiently to permit COL *to jump past him and so down the stairs. At the bottom of these* ROSIE, SALLY, *and the* CROAKER *have collected fearfully.*

COL (*pushing past them*). Get out of it!

He goes into the living-room, drops the pan, picks up a large clasp knife ROSIE *ws using for the clothes-pegs, and backs to the farthest wall of the room.* BLACKMOUTH *has stopped halfway down the stairs, undecided.* DAFFODIL *comes out into the landing. She has stopped her screams.*

COL (*taunting*). Are ye coming, Blackmouth? Are ye coming down? I'm not Old Sailor, ye know: *I* never killed no witches at sea – oho no, but I'll do *you*, Blackmouth, any man can do *you*, a limping sailor can do *you* – you fox-tailed Romany. Hey ey they can smell you to the top of Halifax, they can!

BLACKMOUTH *gives a moan of despair and rage and comes down the last stairs with a run. He trips over* SALLY *at the foot, raises his knife as though to strike her; and then stands looking at her with a silly smile.*

SALLY. Eh dad –

BLACKMOUTH. Sally. My Sally.

SALLY. Eh dad, what are you doing to Col –

BLACKMOUTH. Ss ss. Come on, kid. Come with your dad. Get ye some spice, eh? Right spice for you to suck, just like you like it, eh?

He backs to the front door, still holding his knife at the ready. COL *cautiously advances to the door of the living-room.*

ROSIE (*as* SALLY *seems to be about to go with* BLACKMOUTH). Sally, you stay here.

BLACKMOUTH. Are ye coming, Sally?

COL. You not take the kid, Blackmouth. Don't you go with him, kid. I'm *telling* you, Blackmouth.

ROSIE. Sally.

SALLY *stands a moment irresolute. Then she makes up her mind and runs to* ROSIE. BLACKMOUTH *moans again, makes a hopeless gesture, and ducks backwards out of the front door, moaning, and still holding the knife ready. Outside his voice rises to a howl like a dog's; and then dies away.*

COL. Ach, it's always the same, ye match yourself again a Romany man, and he runs out of the door! Don't he, Daffodilly?

DAFFODIL. Fast as a ferret, Col boy.

COL. Hey ey, let's have the old gramophone. *I* showed him where.

He goes into the living-room again, winds the gramophone, and puts on the 'Cigareets, etc.' record.

SALLY. My dad's gone all runny, ent he, mam? Eh with his knife and all?

CROAKER *laughs.* COL *mounts the stairs carrying the gramo-phone, with the record playing and he singing along with it. As he reaches the landing,* BLACKMOUTH *howls again outside. He pauses; then goes into the small bedroom with* DAFFODIL.

ROSIE (*weeping*). Now you've gone and woke up Geordie.

She goes back into the living-room and rocks the pram. SALLY *and* CROAKER *dance in the hall to the music.* SAILOR *and* RACHEL *enter through the front door.*

SAILOR (*imperiously*). Col! Col!
COL (*in the bedroom*). Oh-oy?
SAILOR. Cut that music off and come down here.
COL (*coming out on to the stairs*). What's for yelling about, ye old –
SAILOR. I said cut that music off, or I'll bloody cut *you*. D'ye hear me?

DAFFODIL *stops the music.*

Now then. There's that bloody Blackmouth raging in the street. Has he been here, has he?
COL (*sulkily*). He came and he went. *I* showed him where.
SALLY. He wor going for Col with a knife, you know – ooh.
SAILOR. What did he want?
COL (*shrugs*). Said he wor after his bundle. Took it with him, O.K.
ROSIE (*shouting from the living-room*). He tried for to take my Sally, that's what. I'll *kill* him, he does that again. Oh, oh, I will so.

CROAKER *is edging slyly to the kitchen door.*

SAILOR (*seeing her*). Don't you try to slip it out the road – I see you. Now is that smarty lass o' yourn better, or ent she? Hey?
CROAKER. Oh my Daffodil –
SAILOR. Hey?

CROAKER. Proper poorly. She takes it terrible hard. Sailor. She takes it —

SAILOR. She takes it nothing. I know 'em poorly, I know 'em dying, she ain't neither. Daffodil! (*He climbs the stair.*)

COL. Now wait, Sailor —

SAILOR (*pushing past him into the bedroom*). Daffodil! Let's have a look at ye. (*He seizes her by the wrist and holds her at arm's length, looking her up and down. Then he bites her on the forearm. She gives a yelp and aims a furious swipe at his head.*) Aye aye, there's nowt the matter with you. So away out on the road; and take your Croaker with you. And that's the lot and the last.

COL. You're not turning her off, you know.

SAILOR. Ah?

COL (*backing down the stair as* SAILOR *comes down*). Na na, Sailor. I'm telling her, she can bide.

DAFFODIL (*bitchily*). He likes me, don't you, Col? He wants I should bide.

SAILOR. Oh I know two o' that.

He pulls a beer bottle out of his pocket and offers to hit COL. COL *presents the knife which he is still holding.*

RACHEL. Let him be, Sailor. He wants his tart — he can have his tart, why shouldn't he? He's my lad, he's a mind and rights of his own.

SAILOR (*after a pause, lowering the bottle*). Ah, so. The young man cries for his rights and the old man carries the load. Well, live and let live. I'm asking nowt more nor that for *me* — so I'm as well to serve it to *you*, I dare say. Go on, Daffy, you bide. Till he breaks your neck. Heh heh. (*He comes downstairs, with sardonic resignation, and* COL *goes up. At the bottom,* SAILOR *turns and calls jeeringly.*) I say, Col!

COL (*on the landing*). What, then?

SAILOR. You're a quick-change dancer, aren't ye? Call it the

April weather. I thought your tart she lives in *next* house. Pally of dance and oho the right young lady! What happened to *her* tonight?

COL (*a little abashed*). Aye, well . . .

RACHEL. Aye well what? Did you do her?

COL (*defiant*). No, I didn't. (RACHEL *laughs*. COL, *no longer abashed, continues.*) All right and be damned. There's some windows have glass in, and there's others as don't.

He goes back into the bedroom with DAFFODIL *and puts on the gramophone.*

SAILOR. Sally, go to your mam.

SALLY *goes into the living-room.* CROAKER *starts dancing again to the music.* SAILOR *turns to her.*

Ah yah, dance away, dance the bloody roof down. (*He sits and drinks from his bottle.*) Ye know what, Rachel? They used to call me a killer. When I sailed the water, they would put that name on me. Ye know what, Rachel –

BLACKMOUTH *howls outside, and they all freeze, listening.*

Scene Eleven

Exterior. Night.

BLACKMOUTH *howls in the distance.* MRS JACKSON *comes to her door.*

MRS JACKSON. Ben, Ben, is that you, Ben? . . . Eh dear, I wish you'd come home. (*She picks up the cat's saucer of milk and puts it down again, then calls without much hope.*) Puss puss puss? (BLACKMOUTH *howls. She shudders and clutches herself with worry.*) Doreen? Doreen?

BLACKMOUTH (*quite close offstage*). Ow – yow, friends, good, good, good, friends to all –

MRS JACKSON (*to herself, in great fear*). Oh listen to it, it's been going for hours . . . What's that?

JACKSON *enters from the street, surly*.

JACKSON. *I'm* that. Me. Mister, the Boss, Lord and Gaffer, ha-ha. What are you talking about – 'what's that'?

BLACKMOUTH *howls*.

MRS JACKSON. That. I mean *that*.

JACKSON (*vaguely and with irritation*). Oh. It's the rising moon, the wolves of Russia – I dunno what it is; what the hell do you *want* to know for?

MRS JACKSON (*angrily*). Ben, where have you been? Do you know what the time is?

JACKSON (*savagely satirical*). Aye, I know what the time is. It's time your cat came home . . . oh such a, such a sweet companion, and pretty little feet, and, and –

MRS JACKSON. I've nowt to say to you! Come home in this state. It's not like you, Ben!

BLACKMOUTH *howls*.

Listen. Ben, oh *listen*.

JACKSON (*sobered with alarm*). That's not the moon . . .

MRS JACKSON. I'm frightened, frightened to death.

BLACKMOUTH *howls*.

JACKSON (*sharply*). Get in the house. Godsake, what are we doing here listening to a –

MRS JACKSON. Doreen.

JACKSON. Eh? (*Pulled up short.*) Eh?

MRS JACKSON. Doreen, Ben. She went out dancing. She's not back yet.

JACKSON. She'll be all right. Some young lad'll be bringing her home.

MRS JACKSON. I don't know as she's got a young lad though

. . . Of course, there's Sheila . . . Ben, please, will you go and find her?

JACKSON. Eh don't be daft . . .

MRS JACKSON (*grimly*). Then *I'll* go.

JACKSON (*futile protest*). Go, go where?

BLACKMOUTH (*in the distance*). I'll tear it in strips out of your bellies, I'll tear the yellow stripes out of you –

MRS JACKSON. Ben, I've got to go . . .

DOREEN enters from the street.

Doreen! Oh, *Doreen*! You get straight upstairs, young lady, how *dare* you come in all hours of the night out of our *wits* with worry –

DOREEN (*in a sob*). Mum. Oh mum . . . (*She pushes past them both and goes into the house.*)

JACKSON. What, what's she –

MRS JACKSON. You stay down.

She goes into the house. BLACKMOUTH *howls.* JACKSON *kicks over the cat's saucer, on purpose, and leans glowering against the porch.*

JACKSON. Cat's milk. Huh. Little pitter-pat feet. Huh. *Claws.*

He growls unintelligible profanity and kicks away at the doorstep. Sawneys' door opens and SALLY peeps out, with ROSIE behind her.

ROSIE. Lovey, you get in and sleep.

SALLY (*as BLACKMOUTH howls*). He's still out there in the streets, do you think he's come back, mam, eh?

ROSIE (*shrugs*). He might, maybe.

SALLY. He went off though, right off, didn't he, eh?

ROSIE. He did.

SALLY. He said he'd do us all with his knife, he reckoned. Ooh. Will he, mam, eh?

ROSIE. No, lovey, no. Now shut it, can't ye. Sleep.

BLACKMOUTH (*offstage, beginning quite close, then fading away*). You didn't ought to talk like that, oh no, not where Blackmouth shows his horn. Poor Blackmouth on the road. He knows his friends. Ow-yow . . .

ROSIE. There, he's going. Lovey, lovey – (*She beckons* SALLY *in and closes the door on them.*)

MRS JACKSON (*inside the house*). Ben!

JACKSON. What is it?

MRS JACKSON (*inside*). Ben! (*She comes out.*) Do you know what's happened to our Doreen? It was Mrs Atkins's Len, he found her and gave her a lift to the end of the road. Do you know where he found her, Ben? She wor up by the allotments at the corner of Honeywell Lane, and that young lad was with her.

JACKSON. Len Atkins?

MRS JACKSON. No. Them ruffians, *there*. The young one.

JACKSON (*ominously*). Eh?

MRS JACKSON. He'd been trying to interfere with her, Ben!

JACKSON. Wait while I get up to her!

MRS JACKSON. *Ben!* She's all right. She's a bit shook-up, and of course, her blouse and that are all torn, but she's *all right*. Len Atkins brought her home. He's a good boy, Len is.

JACKSON. Wait while I get up –

MRS JACKSON. Leave her till morning, Ben. It's not her fault at all. It's a matter for the Police. Come on in. (*She goes into the house.*)

JACKSON (*in alarm*). What, Police! Now wait, wait – eh, Police – (*He follows her, protesting.*)

BLACKMOUTH (*far away*). He knows his friends. He knows his friends. Oh Blackmouth knows his friends . . .

Scene Twelve

SONG
O Sailor Sailor love me close
I don't know where you go:
You set your foot on the gangway plank
So long long time ago.

Interior. Night.
The household are all in bed and asleep, so in each room nothing
is to be seen except shapeless huddles under the bedding. In the
big bedroom SAILOR *and* RACHEL *lie snoring.* SAILOR *tosses*
and groans.

SAILOR (*talking in his sleep*). Stand by to cast off!

RACHEL *grunts.*

Cast off forrard!

RACHEL (*aroused and irritable*). Oh shut up.

SAILOR (*loud and emphatic*). Cast off astern! What's fouling
her up? Will ye get them moorings sorted or have I got to –
wah wah wah . . . I'll bloody learn you gawp at *me*!

RACHEL (*shaking him*). Hey, Sailor, hey –

SAILOR (*still asleep, but quieter*). All cast off forrard and stern.
Half-speed ahead both engines. Port five. Mid-ships. Mid-
ships! Wah wah wah, mid-ships . . .

RACHEL (*shakes him again*). Hey, wake up, you old –

SAILOR (*waking*). Ah, huh, ah – what's the – what – what are
ye at?

RACHEL. You're gabbing in your sleep again.

SAILOR. Oh no I warn't.

RACHEL. Oh aye you was and I don't stand it. Ach, if I've
not got enough to do with you on a day without you're to
holler out like a foghorn half the night. What's the matter
with you?

SAILOR (*grumpily*). It's my bad leg.

RACHEL. What is?

SAILOR. It's bad. It hurts: so. Night-times, it hurts me.

RACHEL. It's been better all of six month. Why don't you get some work?

SAILOR. What likes of work?

RACHEL. Ah you tell me. You do most likes o' work, don't you? Digging, building, drive horses. What else? Why don't you go back to the sea, you growl about it all night?

SAILOR. I don't go to sea no more. You know that.

RACHEL. That was your Rosie's man fetched you from the sea.

SAILOR. Well?

RACHEL. Why don't your Rachel send you back, then? What do you do for me? What do you do for *me*?

SAILOR. Is it work? *I* can work. But what for, work? I've had my glories. On the sea. Aye aye. I've seen the lands of glory, and the gold and the fishes and the beasts. And the brown women, so.

RACHEL *laughs*.

SAILOR. More nor that, I've seen. New York. Archangel. Hard iron towns and they kill men in them towns. Oh aye I've seen 'em die . . . A man can work and he gets glory, right?

RACHEL. He gets the lolly too, boy.

SAILOR. But after that – but after that – where is it, his glory? It's in the folk around him and his sweet liberty to hold *their* lives and glory, and stand no man's work against it. So Sawney holds the road; and he takes his woman and he takes her boy, and he takes his daughter and hers.

RACHEL. Ah go to sleep.

SAILOR. I can't now. You've woke me up: and my bad leg.

RACHEL (*mockingly*). Your bad leg. Cut it off and get a new one. Chair-leg, table-leg – serve you better. Cut it off of a telegraph pole. Strength there, boy . . . Go on, now, go to sleep.

SAILOR *hunches himself up to sleep.*

SAILOR (*muttering*). Aye, it's always how it runs. Talk till your mouth breaks out to your lugs, and she says go to sleep. Uh. She says go to sleep. Uh.

He snores. RACHEL *continues sitting up and talking aloud to herself.*

RACHEL. Glory . . . *I* got glory . . . Like, glory of choice. Take: when I want. Choose one, choose 'em all. And the last one is the old one with the bad leg, and what'll *he* do?

SAILOR (*from the bedclothes*). He'll last you out, that's what. *And* he'll have his laugh at it, bad leg for ever!

RACHEL (*still apparently to herself.*) Then that's my glory too . . . Oh, work, has he had? Folk around him, has he got? Then let him have his laugh. I can carry up with it, marry along with the broke ghost of some tattery ship full of brown women. Or stuck in the ice. Or a sinking ship? Ah, sunk, and all . . . There's choices I've had. I've made 'em. They've gone. Like, nowt. But all *mine*. Take that little bastard at Northampton. Blue eyes. Yellow hair. No nose on his face. What about *him*? Hoopla stall at the fair he had. Choose your prize and toss your silver ring:
(*She sings.*)
    Oh who's throwing my way
    Or who's throwing yours
    Or who'll throw the other way
    And crawl out on all fours?
What does it matter which way, so you make your true own choice of it? Hey?

SAILOR (*stirs round and looks at her*). True choice at Northampton got you a dandy job, I don't think. Under the skirts of Tony Piazza's roundabout, warn't it?

RACHEL. Ah so, he shaped his little time, and I gave him glory for it.

SAILOR. He gave you more than glory, dearie.

RACHEL (*fiercely*). *And* I'd sooner take that from some than I'd take bloody fish and chips from others, I would: in cartloads and all. Hot. Aye, and with a sink-full of red sauce and that's the truth. For all the trouble and pain, and death. If I took it, I took it.

  (*She sings.*)

    Oh had he but warned me before he disordered me,
    Had he but warned me of it in time –

I'd have pulled him down to me there in the mud, just same like I did . . .

There's other words to the tune and all:

  (*She sings.*)

    For I was as free as a bird on the mountain,
    For I was as free as a swallow so high.

And that time I made it his time. For a while. Or –

  (*She sings.*)

    I was as free as a bloody great eagle –

Biting out me dinners for anyone's paunch as comes. From all of them. Biting and biting. Left tooth, right tooth. And what do I bite out of *you*? Hey?

SAILOR (*snapping his jaws at her*). Ah-arrh.

RACHEL (*triumphantly*). Ah, spite and warfare! *There's* the meat to feed: cos when you've et that, so you can sick it back again; yet always you're in liberty! Which I've *got* to be, boy. *Got*. Northampton wept and cried when I left him. I know well *you'd* not do that. And that's good.

  SAILOR *laughs*.

RACHEL. You'd never, would you? Northampton ran around his wagon, bawling for me: 'Bide wi' me, Rachel!' Just like lovely Blackmouth. But I went from him, so. To an old raving ghost with a warp in his keel and a half of a

split mast, voyaging God knows where. Where is it,
Archangel? God knows, you see. Cos Rachel don't.
And red eyes: and a bad leg, too . . . Hey then, hold it out.
I'll rub it till it's better. Oh me poor old horse. (*She
massages his leg, singing.*)

> Poor old horse, poor old horse.

SAILOR (*sings*).

> Poor old horse, poor old horse.

COL (*waking up in the small bedroom and shouting*). Shut the
bloody row!

SAILOR. } (*sing together*). Poor old horse, poor old horse,
RACHEL. }   etc.

> COL *beats on the wall.*

Scene Thirteen

> SONG
> You angry man, you rage away
> Against the women's game:
> But you served them your best part of you
> Without a wink of shame.

Exterior. Morning.
MRS JACKSON *is on her doorstep, sweeping it.* JACKSON *comes
out of the house.*

MRS JACKSON. Not a sign of her, Ben. I've called and I've
called.

JACKSON. Ah. She's run off on you. Gobbling food, stinking
out the kitchen, they fill your upholstery with fleas. So
who cares? *They* don't. Puss puss puss. Where's Doreen?

MRS JACKSON. Doreen! Hurry up then. Your dad's wanting
to be off to his work. You'll make him late.

DOREEN (*appearing at an upper window*). Well, all right, let
him go. I can get to the shop by myself.

MRS JACKSON (*angrily*). I'm not having you walking out alone, my girl, not after last night! Now don't argue.

JACKSON. Come on. I'm telling you.

DOREEN. All *right*, dad. I've got to go to the bathroom yet.

She shuts the window.

MRS JACKSON. It wouldn't surprise me if they'd not eaten her, the poor little thing.

JACKSON. Now who'd eat a cat? You're talking soft.

MRS JACKSON. *They'd* eat a cat. We wor better off with them black Americans in the war and that's no story . . . Yelling in the streets twelve o'clock at night. And besides – I think we ought to go to the police.

JACKSON (*angrily*). Now look. We had all that out.

MRS JACKSON. Well I'm not convinced. If our girl can't even –

JACKSON (*violently*). Do you want the police? Do you really want the police?

MRS JACKSON. It's not what I *want*, Ben –

JACKSON. Cos look: how long have we been on this Housing Scheme?

MRS JACKSON. Two year.

JACKSON. Well! Where did we live afore that?

MRS JACKSON. You know where we lived.

JACKSON. Then you don't need me to tell you. Balaclava Row, a lovely place *warn't* it? I'd enough of it at work, I can tell you. 'Hello Ben, how's the thieves' kitchen this morning?' 'I see there wor another Grievous Bodily Harm up your way last night, Ben – ooh you'll have to watch it, Ben – yer getting too well known to the coppers!' Ha ha. Funny jokers. Huh.

MRS JACKSON. Well. It wor as bad for me.

JACKSON. Aye. And when at last Corporation's good enough to let us get out up here and *get* a new house, what then? 'I think it's perfectly disgraceful the way they put those people from Balaclava Row into such nice new places. They tell me they even use the toilet seats for framing pictures with' – *and* the rest of it. Blah blah blah. You want to start all that again?

MRS JACKSON. No Ben.

JACKSON. *Well!* If you fetch the coppers up, you *will*. Doreen!

MRS JACKSON. Doreen! Whatever are you at up there?

She goes into the house. JACKSON *hangs moodily about on the doorstep.*

JACKSON. *And* it's washing day. God help us. Cold meat for us dinners and bloody underwear all over the kitchen.

RACHEL *comes out of her house to throw a pan of bones out on the garden. They look at each other.* RACHEL *spits on the ground and then laughs.*

JACKSON (*ominously*). All right. But I'm warning you.

RACHEL. Warning us what, mister?

JACKSON (*going towards her and lowering his voice*). It's one thing wi' *me*, you know: but I'm not standing your games with my lass.

RACHEL. Games?

JACKSON. Aye, games. There's a young lad in your house, you ask *him* what games.

RACHEL. Col, is it?

JACKSON. Is that what he's called? Well you tell him he'd best not walk where I walk, that's all.

RACHEL. And what'd you do if he did?

JACKSON. I'm not that old I couldn't learn him summat – *oh no* – it's a fair while sin I last took my jacket off, but by God if I –

RACHEL. He's *my* boy, is Col.

JACKSON. Eh? Oh, he is, is he? Well that just about caps it. That just about sets the blasted roof on it, that does. Your boy. I might have known. Well, I can't say I'm surprised neither. It's clear to see what nasty puddles he sucked *his* manners out of. Huh. Your boy!

RACHEL. So? There's not only my boy's manners sucks out of them puddles, is there, mister?

JACKSON. What do you mean?

RACHEL. You like to have your lick at a puddle or two, yourself, now and again, don't you? Johnny Jackson, Johnny Jackson – you ought to take better care of yourself when you wander the stairs of the town without a guard or guide, boy. You don't know *what* you're going to pick up, do you?

JACKSON (*taken aback*). Pick up?

RACHEL (*enjoying herself*). You see, now; take puddles. There's all sorts of feet can tread in the puddles, you know. Some clean, some mucky. Didn't they learn ye *nowt* in the Army, Johnny, all them foreign tarts you had?

JACKSON (*terrified*). Here, what are you getting at –

RACHEL (*sings*).

Oh had she but warned me before she disordered me – and all for lovely Rachel's love. Oh Johnny Jackson, you poor bloody animal, you . . .

She goes into her house again, laughing.

JACKSON (*frantic*). Hey, hey, wait a minute, wait a minute –

DOREEN *hurries cheerfully out to him.*

DOREEN. Hello dad, here I am ready at last. Eh! I *am* a slowcoach.

JACKSON (*turning on her in his terror*). Eh? What? Wait half the bloody morning for you: what d'you think you're playing at?

DOREEN (*dashed*). Dad!

JACKSON. Blah blah blah, you stupid –

RACHEL comes out again, carrying a lump of dripping on a bit of newspaper.

RACHEL. And another thing, mister. You tell them pair o' bitches of yourn to stop squealing in the streets at night. Driving our sleep away – what kind of way to live is that?

MRS JACKSON comes out. RACHEL hands the dripping to JACKSON and, as tho' in a trance, he takes it.

Here, I've brought you a bit of dripping. Cool and soothe you. I say I've brought him a bit of dripping missus. Good for him, ent it? Like, soo-oothing . . . Howl about the bloody streets all night . . .

She goes inside and slams her door.

MRS JACKSON. What did she want, Ben?

JACKSON. Eh?

MRS JACKSON. What did she want?

JACKSON. I don't know.

MRS JACKSON. Did you speak to her about Doreen?

JACKSON. Oh – like, like kind of.

MRS JACKSON. Well what did she say?

JACKSON (*violently*). Well you heard what she said! You've got a pair of ears, haven't you? She said you wor howling in the street last night.

MRS JACKSON (*in bewilderment*). Me?

JACKSON (*turning on his daughter*). Or you were: *I* don't know – I – what's *this*?

DOREEN. Dripping.

JACKSON (*stupidly*). She give me dripping.

MRS JACKSON. Why?

JACKSON (*throwing it down*). Tach! It's time you started on your wash-day!

MRS JACKSON (*firing up also*). And it's time *you* started on your road. What's the matter with you?

DOREEN. What *is* it, dad?

JACKSON. What's what? Bloody women.

MRS JACKSON. You'd best take Doreen to the bus-stop, hadn't you?

She goes indoors.

DOREEN. Look, dad, you don't have to come with me, you know.

JACKSON. Well I'm coming.

DOREEN. You don't really mean to meet me off the bus this evening, do you, like me mum said? You don't *need* to, dad; and look, I'll be with Shiela.

JACKSON. You were supposed to be with Shiela last night – ah find your own road. I'm sick and tired.

DOREEN. Well, I'll go with you to the bus-stop now.

JACKSON. Come on then. Why you didn't let that lad lay you, while he was about it, and make a proper job of it; instead of just –

DOREEN (*appalled*). Dad!

JACKSON. (*confused*). Oh you know what I mean. Or *I* know what I mean. Or, God, I don't know; who knows what, anyroad? Come on. I'm late.

They go off down the road.

Scene Fourteen

SONG

It's whether you come or whether you go
Or whether you bide at home:
They're always right behind you, Jack,
And never leave you alone.

In your footsteps they will plant their feet
For every step you tread,
They trample on your shadow, Jack
They trample on your head.

Interior. Afternoon.
The stage is empty. Two letters fall through the letterbox in the front door, and there is a pair of raps on the knocker.

RACHEL (*from the kitchen*). What d'ye want then?

She comes out of the kitchen, eating. She picks up the letters and looks at them dubiously.

SAILOR (*from in the kitchen*). Who is it? What's he after?
RACHEL. It's more of them letters.
SAILOR. Oh?

He appears in the kitchen doorway. SALLY *runs out into the hall underneath his arm.*

SALLY. Is it letters, is it? Who's sending us letters, eh? Eh? Eh?
RACHEL. Get out of it.

SAILOR *takes the letters and looks at them.* ROSIE *comes out of the kitchen.*

ROSIE. Sally, come here.
SALLY. Who sends us letters, mam?
ROSIE. I don't know, lovey. It's not so good, whoever it is. Now you bide quiet and don't make Sailor mad while he's thinking on what to do.
SAILOR. It's second lot this week.
RACHEL. Maybe we ought to open *these*, y'know.
SAILOR. Why?
RACHEL. I don't like to burn things always. Jocky Faa once tell'd me he burned a whole quid in a letter one time.
SAILOR. Aye, aye. But what a daft bloody trick that, put a quid in a letter. Am I opening these, or not?
RACHEL (*uneasily*). It'd be better so.
SAILOR. All right then. Let's have a look. (*He opens the letter and looks at them uncomprehending.*) There's one is printed

and there's this other is type-wrote. I don't like it. Read 'em. (*He hands the letters to* RACHEL.) What do they say?

RACHEL. This printed one. It's a form. For filling-in, see.

SAILOR. Then burn it. We've never had it.

RACHEL. Ach, I dunno. It's the National Insurance.

SAILOR. What about it? Those bastards'd chase ye from Newcastle to Cornwall. They're worse nor the bloody Peelers.

RACHEL. There might be an Entitlement, though. Like, you and your bad leg.

SAILOR. Na na. I said burn it . . . What's the typewriting all about?

RACHEL. I can't make it clear yet. It's from the Corporation.

SAILOR (*in alarm*). Oh . . . It is, eh? That's not so good, neither. Go on read it.

RACHEL. He says, 'Complaints relating to condition of – of aforesaid residence. And gardens appertaining.' Ach, all that it is – words.

ROSIE. They send these words at us under the door all the time. It's not right. What can *we* do when we get them? They put us, it's like a dog in a box, you can stick spikes through every corner at him and he's no place to turn at all.

There is a knock on the door. They look at one another. There is another knock. RACHEL *opens the door. The* OFFICIAL *from the Housing Department comes in.*

OFFICIAL. Good afternoon, Mrs Sawney . . . Mr Sawney . . . er, Mrs er . . . Hello love . . . I dare say you remember me, eh? aye, well . . . You had a letter last week from the Department, didn't you? And you should have had another today. Aye there it is, you've got it, I can see. Have you read it yet?

RACHEL. We've opened it. So what?

OFFICIAL (*embarrassed*). It's a bit awkward for me, is this, missus; you see, after all, I'm only the bottle-washer in the department – I mean.

SAILOR. What have you come for, mister?

OFFICIAL. The fact is, Mr Sawney, you've hardly been in this house two months, have you? And it's in a shocking state. I mean, look at it . . . Eh dear. There's been complaints, that's all. And what are we going to do about it, eh?

SAILOR. Aye. What *are* we going to do about it?

OFFICIAL. Well. My instructions, Mr Sawney, are to tell you that unless something *is* done, steps will be taken, Mr Sawney, by the Department, to put you out; and that's that. I'm sorry. There it is.

SAILOR. And where will we go? The institutions, isn't it? Cos you've burnt the tram-car we used to live in. We can't go on the road, we've two little kids with us. We've not got money for a wagon. So what do we do?

OFFICIAL. If you take my advice, you'll clean the house. Hang some curtains up. Tidy the garden. And get rid of your lodgers.

RACHEL. We ain't got no lodgers.

OFFICIAL. No?

RACHEL. No.

She has moved round behind him till she is standing between him and the closed front door. The others close in on him a little. He looks round nervously. A car is heard driving up outside.

OFFICIAL. It's no use you trying to intimidate me. I told you before, *I'm* not responsible. If you lot get evicted, you've only yourselves to thank –

There is a sharp double knock on the door. They look at one another.

OFFICIAL. Aren't you going to see who it is?

The knock is repeated, very loudly, and a voice shouts:
'Police!' The POLICE SERGEANT *opens the door and comes*
in abruptly.

SERGEANT. You're very ready to answer, aren't you? Sawney's house?

SAILOR. It is.

SERGEANT. Are you Sawney?

SAILOR *shrugs.*

SERGEANT. Proper mucky hole you've got here, and all . . .
(*He sees the* OFFICIAL.) Who are you?

OFFICIAL. Oh I'm from the Town Hall, Officer. Housing
Department.

SERGEANT. Ah . . . Sawney's, eh? You were down on the
old caravan site, weren't you; before they sorted you out?

SAILOR. We were.

SERGEANT. They were none too soon in shifting you,
neither.

He is wandering about the ground floor of the house, looking at
everything, and throwing his comments over his shoulder at
them.

There was a Police Constable wounded last night. At
approximately twelve forty-five a.m. Near the junction of
Market Hill and Princes Adelaide Street. Know anything
about it? Nasty dark place, that, middle of the night. So,
you see, he couldn't see who stabbed him. Could he?

SAILOR. It wasn't none of us, now.

SERGEANT. Not? You see, our lad couldn't see who stabbed
him, but he could hear. It was a man, probably drunk,
shouting out the name of Sawney. Shouting out your
name. There aren't many Sawneys are there, in this town;
specially ones as go stabbing policemen. Come on, then.
Who was it?

SAILOR. It wasn't none of us.

ROSIE. We was all in the house, middle of the night. *You* can't prove no different. No.

SERGEANT. You know who did it. I been fifteen year at this game. You can't play it clever with *me*, so don't think you can. Very well. We'll try it another way. (*He picks up the gramophone from the living-room floor.*) Where did you get this?

RACHEL. That's mine. I bought it fair. *You* can't prove no different.

SERGEANT. Not? You've got a receipt for it, have you?

RACHEL (*taken aback*). A what?

SERGEANT. A receipt. I'll bet you haven't. Now an instrument like this seems to me an unlikely item for folk in your sort of circumstances to possess. Don't it? So I am now going to Take you In – suspected In Possession of Stolen Property. Come on. And you – Sawney – you can come too. You live with her, don't you? Aiding and Abetting. Come on.

SAILOR. Wait a minute; you can't go taking us like this –

SERGEANT. Not? Who are you to tell me what I can do? (*He puts his whistle to his mouth.*)

DAFFODIL *comes in through the kitchen. When she sees the* SERGEANT *she recoils in terror.*

SERGEANT (*sprinting at her*). And who are *you*, young lady? . . . Well? Another Sawney? Are you?

RACHEL. She's with us. So?

SERGEANT (*pinning* DAFFODIL *in a corner*). What's your name? . . . Eh? What? Can't hear you!

DAFFODIL. What – what –

SERGEANT. Now then. *You* tell me. Who knifed the Constable last night down Adelaide Street, shouting the name of Sawney?

DAFFODIL. Why Blackmouth did. Least, I suppose, he did –

SERGEANT. Who's Blackmouth?

DAFFODIL (*now recovering herself*). Oh don't you know who Blackmouth is? Ooh, you want to go for *him*, Captain. He'll give you promotion, he will!

SERGEANT. Blackmouth? . . . *I* know. Wait a moment . . . (*He takes a notebook out and thumbs through the pages.*) Blackmouth . . . Aha! What about this: William Lewis, otherwise known as Blackmouth. Escaped from Strangeways Gaol, thirteenth of last month, after severe assault upon Prison Officer. Age twenty-eight, five foot ten tall, black hair, swarthy features, general gipsy-like appearance. That the lad, is it?

DAFFODIL *nods and smiles*.

SERGEANT. Where is he?

DAFFODIL. Sheffield.

SERGEANT. How do you know?

DAFFODIL. He said he wor going. He went, see. Last night. You catch him, Captain. Ah.

SERGEANT. All right, I will. (*He goes to the door.*) Now you behave yourselves. I'm warning.

OFFICIAL. Er – Officer. I wonder could you give me a lift to the Town Hall, if you're going that way.

SERGEANT. Oh, I don't mind, sir. I'll take you as far as the Station, anyroad . . . I'm warning. (*He goes out.*)

OFFICIAL. And bear in mind what *I* said, too. And *don't* let's be finding you've got lodgers here. I know. (*He goes out · with a meaning look at* DAFFODIL.)

ROSIE (*furiously, to* DAFFODIL). What you tell him that for?

DAFFODIL. Why should'nt I tell him? What's Blackmouth done for *me* I shouldn't tell him? Or you neither?

SAILOR. Shut up. He's no loss, is Blackmouth. But it's a fool's lark telling owt to them devils. You ought to know it be now.

SALLY *has collected* COL's *haversack (with the drill in it) from the living-room floor, and is on her way out of the house with it.*

RACHEL. What you got there, kid?

ROSIE. You leave her alone . . . Come here, lovey. Where are you off to?

SALLY. Taking it to Charlie's. Col said.

SAILOR. Na na. We're none on us walking the town with that like o'load for a day or two. Put it back where you found it. I'll talk to Col.

DAFFODIL. It's nowt to do wi' you what Col does with his work. You let the kid sell it for him, if he wants.

SAILOR *turns angrily on her. She retreats backwards up the stair.*

(*Childishly rude*) Ah wah wah – (*she pulls her tongue out and, going up the stairs, sings.*)
>The dirty old man
>Fell into the river
>The dirty fishes ate his liver
>Quack quack a dirty duck
>Bit the end off his dirty –

Angry knocking at the back door in the kitchen.

MRS JACKSON (*off*). Let me in. Let me in. (*She storms into the hall through the kitchen, very angry indeed.*) The last straw. Oh I've stood enough. Stood enough. But By, I'm not taking this. Where are they?

SAILOR. What the hell are you on about?

MRS JACKSON. My washing. All my washing hanging out on the line in the back garden and it's gone! I want it back, I tell you, I want it back!

SAILOR. We don't have your bloody washing. Now you get out o' here and keep out. It's not your place, no, and never will.

MRS JACKSON. I'm going to find my washing. And my little

cat. My little cat. Took her and eaten her. Took her and eaten her. . . . (*She hurries about the ground floor rooms, routing about in the piles of junk.*) You'll not stop me. I'll find my washing. I know you've got it here.

RACHEL *tries to stop her, with an angry shout; but* SAILOR *holds her.*

SAILOR (*restraining* RACHEL). Let her rummage if she wants. We've nowt o' hers. Can't ye sees she's – (*He taps his forehead.*) Let her be. She'll soon be tired of it.

MRS JACKSON. Where is it? Where is it? (*She goes upstairs into the big bedroom.*)

RACHEL. You keep out o' there!

SAILOR. Let her be. We're wanting no more trouble *this* day.

MRS JACKSON *goes into the small bedroom.* DAFFODIL *follows her in.*

DAFFODIL (*quietly*). My room, this is.

MRS JACKSON. I don't care.

DAFFODIL. Is it your husband: red face, hairy legs? Eh?

MRS JACKSON (*briskly*). Don't you talk about my husband's legs. There's enough and all to talk about without that like o' rudeness. I want my washing!

DAFFODIL. My mam the Croaker, she saw his legs when he wor with Big Rachel. She says, hairy.

MRS JACKSON (*taking it in*). Eh? . . . When he wor with –

DAFFODIL. Big Rachel? Oh aye. (*She giggles.*) Last afternoon. In *there*. Croaker knows what they did. I wor asleep though. I thought he wor Blackmouth, but he warn't.

MRS JACKSON (*stunned*). With Big Rachel . . .

DAFFODIL. In that room: *there*. They lay down. Lovely.

MRS JACKSON. That's not true.

DAFFODIL. Ent it?

MRS JACKSON. You're wanting to frighten me.

DAFFODIL *grins.*

MRS JACKSON (*in a whisper*). Oh no. It's not right. Ben wouldn't do that. Never. No. (*She comes down the stairs, and meets* RACHEL *in the hall.*) Are you – are you – you're Rachel.

RACHEL (*nods*). Have you found your washing yet, missus?

MRS JACKSON. He wouldn't do that? Would he? Would he?

She looks at RACHEL, *then turns and runs out of the house, through the kitchen door.*

RACHEL *laughs.*

DAFFODIL (*laughs*). That sent her, didn't it? Oh –
　　(*She sings.*)
　　　　Up and down the road we go
　　　　He comes fast and she comes slow
　　　　Slowly slowly wait for me –
　　　　Oh – I'm so blind that I can't see.
　　What can't you see?
　　　　Twenty fingers holding tight
　　　　Twenty toes in the middle of the night
　　　　Four lips, Four eyes. Four ears.
　　　　And all the rest as goes
　　SALLY. With his long red nose.
DAFFODIL. With his long red nose.
SALLY
DAFFODIL　} . With his long red *nose!*

The OLD CROAKER *cautiously puts her head in at the front door.*

CROAKER. I tear them all up, don't I?

She comes inside. She has her arms full of washing, all in rags and tatters, and streamers of it are trailing behind her. She continues to rip the fabrics up.

SAILOR (*strides furiously towards her*). Why, you old –
CROAKER (*terrified*). Oh *no.* Sailor, don't.

She throws the washing at his feet and cowers away. He looks at it and her, then bursts into laughter.

SAILOR. By God. Her bloody washing! Let 'em all come. We've got the washing –

They all start in, tearing the washing up and shouting: 'We've got the washing.' Up and down the house they dance throwing the washing all round and over each other.

Scene Fifteen

SONG

The rage of angry wives awaits
No trumpet-call nor drum:
When once it breaks, like thunder it breaks
And they run around the town.

For their hearts are hurt and their houses hurt.
Their houses are their heart.
And those within their houses are
The least important part.

At their left-hand lip they hang out their tongues,
Their teeth hang out at the right:
Their fingers' nails are red-hot coals
And their nostrils flaring white.

Exterior. Afternoon.
DOREEN *comes home from work, goes up to her door, and takes her key out to let herself in. As she prepares to do so, she looks off-stage along the street, and quickly drops her key back into her handbag.* COL *comes in from his work, and goes to the Sawney door without more than the merest glance at* DOREEN. *He sits before the door.*

DOREEN. Eh, I've gone and I've lost my key again.

COL (*casually wounding*). Hello there, hinny. So they're letting ye out alone in the street again, are they? Phoo – they didn't ought to do that, y'know.

DOREEN. I'm not having anything to say to you – you know why . . . What do you mean: they didn't ought to let me out alone?

COL. Ach, just what I said, so. Dancing and laughing, you. But let a man stand at ye just one half minute, and ye're off hollering like one o' they curlews; playing at the broken-wing game, isn't it, so?

DOREEN. Col, I don't know what you mean. Last night I was enjoying it all honest, until you began trying to –

COL. I warn't trying no more than what you'd like it from me; least, I'd *say* you'd like . . . You're not telling me you never wanted it, now. I mean, are you, hinny?

DOREEN. Well, of course, Col, I suppose all girls would like –

COL (*abruptly*). Ah so, then! . . . Well, come away round the wall there, and I'll give it you now. What d'ye wait for?

DOREEN (*on the verge of tears*). Oh but, but, Col –

COL (*disgusted*). Ach, ye're still the same, and it's all true I said it: y're not fit to be loosed outside of houses alone. (*He goes to the Jacksons' door and beats on it.*) Hey, missus, hey hey missus, come here!

MRS JACKSON *opens her door in amazement.* COL *jumps back a few paces into the garden, behind* DOREEN.

MRS JACKSON. What's all this about? What do you want?

COL (*pushing* DOREEN *forward*). She's yourn, ent she? Your little daisy flower? Then take her and water her and keep her away from beehives. Bzzzz. (*He goes back to the Sawneys' door and sits down before it again, ignoring and others.*)

MRS JACKSON. Doreen! Why aren't you with your – with your dad, Doreen?

DOREEN *bursts into tears and hurries away from the house.*

Doreen. Doreen. Where are you off to? Lovey! Lovey! Come here – (*She runs after* DOREEN *and catches hold of her arm imploringly.*)

DOREEN (*with passion*). Always on to me. You're always on to me. I never had a chance –

JACKSON *enters from the street; and intercepts his daughter as she breaks clear again of* MRS JACKSON. MRS JACKSON, *at the sight of her husband, withdraws a little.*

JACKSON. Here, what is it now? (*He sees* COL.) Has *he* been up to his fancy larks again, has he?

DOREEN. No, he's not. And what if he has, anyroad? I'm old enough. I can take care of myself, can't I? Can't I?

JACKSON. No!

DOREEN. Well I'm going to have a try. I don't want to stay in this house any longer. I – I mum, I'm *going* –

MRS JACKSON. Doreen, lovey, *where* are you going?

DOREEN. I'm going to Sheila's. That's what. And don't try and stop me. I'm going to Sheila's house. *Her* mum doesn't treat her like a, like a daisy flower! Nor beehives, beehives, neither! (*She runs off weeping.*)

MRS JACKSON (*trying to follow*). But lovey –

JACKSON (*checking her*). Eh, don't chase her now . . . Or she might go somewhere worse nor Sheila. Now take it easy.

MRS JACKSON (*looking at him for the first time*). Take it easy . . . So you thought you'd come home, did you?

JACKSON (*puzzled*). Eh? Why shouldn't I come home? It's tea-time, ent it?

MRS JACKSON (*bleak and deadly*). You can get your tea where you got your dripping. *And* the rest of what you got. (*She goes in and slams the door.*)

JACKSON (*astonished*). Here, Emmy! What's wrong?

The bolt is heard drawn on the inside of the door. JACKSON *becomes frightened.*

Emmy! I say Emmy, let me in! (*He beats on the door.*)

COL *laughs, and opens the Sawney door.*

COL (*calling indoors*). Hey, Daff!

DAFFODIL *comes to the threshold.*

DAFFODIL. Ai-oo?

COL. Locked out. Look at him.

DAFFODIL. Ooh.

JACKSON (*frantic*). Emmy, look. I don't know what you've heard, but it's not true . . . I mean, Emmy, you can't believe what folk like that'd tell you – I mean . . . Emmy, *will* you let me in?

COL. She won't let him in, y'see, till the milkman's got hisself dressed and away out the back . . . Ach, who's for the boozer? Come on.

He and DAFFODIL *come downstage and walk across past* JACKSON, *who ignores them and bangs on his door.*

(*Shouts*). Let him in, missus, he's clamming up wi' cold!

He makes a snatch at DAFFODIL's *haunches. She shrieks and runs off. With a roar he follows her. Offstage, she gives a yelp as he catches her, and then a soft giggle.*

JACKSON. Emmy! . . . (*He suddenly stands away from the door and shouts.*) All right, then, if that's how you're going to take it, you might as well have the lot and be damned. Tell 'em *all* about it! Let the whole Housing Scheme hear! Aye, I did go with that bloody tart next door, and a *right* time I had of it and all! Do you want to know what she did and how?

MRS JACKSON *opens the door again in horror.*

MRS JACKSON. *Ben!* Ben! *Shut up*, Ben!

A WOMAN'S VOICE (*offstage, calling*). Mrs Jackson, Mrs Jackson!

MRS JACKSON (*calling back*). Hello! Is that you, Mrs Atkins!

WOMAN'S VOICE (*off*). Is all your washing all right, love?

MRS JACKSON (*surprised*). No, it's not.

WOMAN'S VOICE (*off*). I thought not. She's been up and down all the gardens tearing it to shreds and all.

MRS JACKSON. Who has?

WOMAN'S VOICE (*off*). It's her, the old crooked devil out o' next door to you!

MRS JACKSON. No!

ANOTHER WOMAN'S VOICE. It's true.

MRS JACKSON (*leaning against the doorpost as though faint*). Then that's the lot. That's it. That's it. My cat, my Doreen, fat as a pig they called me – he said a right time he had of it and all, do you know that the bloody bitch she ate my little cat . . .

Her voice trails away and she stands in a sort of trance, gasping. JACKSON *looks at her in concern.* DAFFODIL, *offstage, giggles and squeals.* MRS JACKSON *stares after* COL *and* DAFFODIL, *breathes heavily, talks in gasps.*

There's a pair of them *now*, it's time we showed 'em what we thought of 'em in this town. (*Suddenly she roars in her throat like a bull and sets off at a run down the street after* COL *and* DAFFODIL.)

1ST WOMAN'S VOICE (*off*). That's it. That's it. Right.
Right.
2ND WOMAN'S VOICE (*off*). Right. Right.

There is sudden yelping, offstage, as of hounds worrying.
JACKSON *backs into his doorway, staring after his wife in the*
direction of the noise. His eyes are wide and horrified, and he
shakes his head.

Scene Sixteen

Interior. Evening (immediately after Scene Fifteen).
DAFFODIL *bursts through the front door, shouting:* 'Sailor,
Sailor!' *She is hysterical. She hangs on to the stair-rail and*
screams. SAILOR, RACHEL, ROSIE, SALLY, *and* CROAKER
crowd into the hall.

DAFFODIL. Sailor, they're tearing him to bits, they've all set
on to him, they've all set on to him, listen!

Shouting and screaming can be heard from outside.

RACHEL. Col?
DAFFODIL. They're tearing him to bits –
RACHEL (*setting to rush out of the door*). Let me get at 'em!
Sailor –
SAILOR (*catching her back and slamming the door*). It's his own
bloody lookout. Now you bide in here, ye great crocodile,
and use your bloody top. You know who was at this house
today and you know what they said. If Col and her want to
dance yelping on the doorsteps of the street, then they can
look to the cows in the street to trap them and be damned.
We start killing 'em for it, and we get the Peelers in again,
we're really for the nick, girl, I ent joking.

SALLY (*looking out of the hall window*). Col's coming, Col's coming, Col, Col, Col.

The shouts outside grow louder. COL *bursts in.* RACHEL *flings the door open for him and shuts it smartly behind him.* COL *is in an alarming state. His clothes are half torn off his back, and his face and body (where it shows through the ripped garments) are clawed and streaked with blood. He leans against the wall panting.*

COL. By – by – I got away.

RACHEL *seizes him and shakes and slaps him.*

RACHEL. You got away. Oh you got away. But not from me you don't get away, bringing 'em all on to us, you blasted young –

COL (*breaking away from her*). Hey, hey on, now. What have *I* done, you set on me like that?

RACHEL. They've been here today. Coppers –

COL (*stupidly*). Coppers?

ROSIE. Aye, and they're turning us out of the house and all, they said they give us warning, Col, they said –

SAILOR (*dominating*). Now wait, the lot of ye. Be easy . . . What did they do to ye, boy?

COL. Well look at me, for God sake . . . Women are they? I'll tell you, Daffy. They've near finished Col for *your* pleasuring, the next half-year.

SAILOR. How many were there?

COL. Twelve, fifteen, I dunno – three of 'em begin it, then they run out of every doorway at me . . . Women? Bloody leopards!

SALLY (*at the window*). They're all outside the garden fence.

SAILOR (*sharply*). Come away from that window, kid.

He pulls her away, just as a brick crashes through the hall window.

A WOMAN'S VOICE (*outside*). *And* any more of you, we'll serve 'em the same!

Outside is a constant noise of voices – not too many; there are only a score of women at most, at this stage.

SAILOR. See what I mean? (*To* RACHEL *who has her hand on the latch.*) *Don't* open the door.

RACHEL. I'm going to –

SAILOR. I said: wait. They'll clear away soon. Most likely they will. There aren't that many.

COL. Teeth, nails, feet, everything. Half a bloody brick. Look at my fingers. They held 'em flat on the causeway and – there wor three of 'em got me down and the rest they – I tell ye, they're –

Another brick is thrown at the window.

A WOMAN'S VOICE (*outside*). Come on out of it, we'll show you!

RACHEL (*furiously*). I'm going to talk! (*She flings open the door; and, standing on the threshold, screams out her defiance. As she goes on, she seems to become possessed by her rage, and her words are interspersed with sheer animal noises.*) You want us out o' here? I tell you, you want more'n you know you want, you darling lovely girls! We'll come out, oh we'll come out, you'll not forget us when we come. I tell you: we live like bloody animals, you don't know what animals are! You hide in your hutches in your good warm straw and you think you got thirty-two teeth in your heads; but we carry fifty three, ohoho-rho – and there's blood for each one of 'em between the leg and the neck, when *we* come, when *we* come blooding, ohoho-*rho* – who wants us now? (*She steps back, foaming at the mouth. Then she starts laughing quietly to herself, and says:* 'Ohoho-rho,' *to herself and shuts the door. The voices outside are silent.*)

SALLY (*at the window again*). They're going off. You've *feard* 'em, Rachel, ooh, terrible feared.

SAILOR. Are they going? (*He goes to the window*.) Looks like it, so.

RACHEL (*quietly*). Why not? They know I tell 'em true. I say it: and they run.

SAILOR. Aye aye. But it's not the first time.

RACHEL. What?

SAILOR. You been telling 'em it since we come here, right?

RACHEL. All right.

SAILOR. Each time you tell 'em louder. So each time they run not so far. And each time after, they get madder. Eh? The loudest time you tell 'em, they don't run at all.

RACHEL (*scornfully*). Don't give me that.

SAILOR (*he sounds depressed*). I'm giving you what I can see. You don't know this bastardy-like of folk like I do. I've lived longer, girl, so listen. Aye, aye, they belong inside their hutches, their houses and all. And they don't fight strong. But when they're out and calling *you* out, they don't run home soon, neither. They're in their crowd and they'll swarm you and you'll drown. Live and let live, I say. But that's been broke into two by this lot and we don't know where we are. They maybe look like they've run. I'd say different.

ROSIE (*frightened*). Then what'll happen, Sailor?

SAILOR (*shrugs*). Huh . . . There's just us, and there's *all* o' them. That's what'll happen. They're feared o' Big Rachel, O.K. Begod they're that feard of her, they'll kill her. All of us. Just cos we live.

ROSIE. What are we going to do?

SAILOR (*shrugs*). I'll tell you what *I'll* do now. I'll get out the back door of the house, over through the gardens, see are we clear that road. If we are, I'll stop in at the Beer-off, get us some bottles; give you the whistle; then we can *all* go.

RACHEL. Go where?

SAILOR. You tell me. Or if you're right, and they've run, we can bide. But I'll have to see, first.

RACHEL. I'm coming, too.

SAILOR. Na na. You can wait. And one of you go out. D'ye hear me?

They grunt assent.

Right then: I'm off. Lock the doors till you hear me give the whistle. I'll take some o' the empties while I'm on the job. There's money on 'em (*He gathers up some bottles and goes out through the kitchen.*)

RACHEL. You heard what he said. Col, go lock that door behind him.

DAFFODIL (*piteously*). No Col, you stay wi' me.

ROSIE. I'll do it.

She goes with SALLY *into the kitchen.* RACHEL *bolts and chains the front door.*

ROSIE (*from the kitchen, in fear*). Rachel!

RACHEL. What is it?

ROSIE. I can't lock this door!

RACHEL. Why not?

ROSIE. Old Croaker took the bolt off of it, Tuesday, and there's one of the hinges broke!

RACHEL. Oh God, I'd forgot. There is and all! Well, shove summat again it. The gas-stove, that. Wait, I'll help you. (*She goes into the kitchen. Then calls from thence.*) Col!

COL. Ah?

RACHEL. See, all them windows is fast for God-sake. We don't want 'em climbing –

COL. O.K. You done yet, have you – (*to* DAFFODIL.)

DAFFODIL (*who has been wrapping a rag round his injured hand*). Oh it's not tight, Col, it'll come off you again –

COL. Ah, leave it so.

The OLD CROAKER *suddenly comes running down the stairs, at the top of which she has been sitting throughout the scene.*

COL. Where d'you think you're off to, you silly old tortoise?

CROAKER. Fish-and-chip shop!

COL (*angrily*). Fish-and-chip – You heard what Sailor said, din't you? Din't you?

CROAKER. Sailor. Ooh, Sailor's all afeared.

COL. Aye and so am I. And so ought you, you old –

CROAKER. Oh, *I'm* afeared. Ooh. Daffy. Where's my girl? Daffy?

DAFFODIL (*impatient*). What is it she wants now?

CROAKER. Ah, Daffodil. She's my girl, she is. Daffy, are they coming for us – what he said?

COL. Coming, is it? They've bloody *come*!

DAFFODIL. Near tore him in bits, they did.

RACHEL, ROSIE *and* SALLY *come in from the kitchen.*

RACHEL. That's the door done. What about the windows?

COL. Doing 'em now. (*He secures the windows, upstairs and down.*)

CROAKER. Will they come in through windows?

COL (*in disgust*). Will they come in through windows.

CROAKER (*as if remembering something with a great effort*). I know it – I know it –

DAFFODIL (*quickly*). Now you don't know nothing.

CROAKER (*stubbornly*). I know it how to do with windows. Close them up, fast. Feared of them, through the windows. Feared. Where's my Daffodil? You come do it with me.

DAFFODIL. No oh no, we're not having that. That's old rubbish, you don't want that.

CROAKER. Daffy, I'm feared. You do it with Croaker.

DAFFODIL. No, I'm not doing it with you. We're not having it.

RACHEL. Not having what?

DAFFODIL. All her old rubbish. Words and that. She says rhyming, see. It's not –

RACHEL. If she wants it, let her do it.

CROAKER. Who's do it with me? it's for two to do – one says, one follows – or it's not good.

RACHEL. Let the kid do it.

ROSIE. Hey no –

RACHEL. Ach, it's all right. Let her help her.

CROAKER (*taking* SALLY). Little Sally, eh? Little lovey, we go to the window. This keep them out, the time they come.

She flattens her palms on the glass of the hall window's unbroken pane. SALLY *copies her, standing beside.* CROAKER *recites.*

> Window close and window true
> In and out and who comes through?
> Mary and Jesus and the Twelve Tall Riders
> Nobody else nobody else nick nack noo!
> Now you say it:
> Nobody else –

SALLY. Nobody else nobody else nick nack noo!

COL (*laughs*). Eh that ought to hold 'em. If you'd told us that the first place, there'd have been no coppers here today!

DAFFODIL. It's all rubbish, I won't let her do it.

RACHEL. It don't do no harm. Go on, Croaker, do it all the windows, and the bloody doors and all, why not?

CROAKER *and* SALLY *go from window to window, reciting the rhyme.* ROSIE *goes into the living-room and rocks the baby in its pram. There is a knocking on the back door.*

SAILOR (*offstage*). Aaah!

They all look at each other in fear.

RACHEL. It's Sailor. Come and let him in.

She and ROSIE *hurry into the kitchen.*

SAILOR (*off*). Quick, quick, open up! Aaah. (*After a moment, he comes in through the kitchen door, staggering. He has a wound on the side of his head. He drops a number of new bottles on the floor.*) No good. No good at all.

RACHEL. What's no good?

SAILOR. They're in the streets still. I got as far as the Beer-off, come out with the bottles, they see me in the street.

RACHEL. Hey hold up, what's the matter?

SAILOR. Let fire a stone at me.

ROSIE. Who did?

SAILOR. Oh, one o' them – out o' the dark – God knows. Stones. Yelling at the corner. It's no good us to try to run out again. They're all round the streets.

ROSIE. But what'll we do?

SAILOR (*shrugs*). Huh . . . I know now what I'll do. (*He knocks the head off a bottle of spirit.*) All around in the streets. (*He swills a great gulp of the spirit; and then another.*) Ha ha, they don't know.

COL. Who don't know?

SAILOR. They don't know. That I'm a killer. *Do* they?

COL. Oh God, *that*.

SAILOR (*laughs bitterly*). Aye aye, that. (*He sees* SALLY *and* CROAKER *still reciting, at the living-room window.*) What's *she* doing?

DAFFODIL. (*nervously*). It's like rhyming-words, she says it at the windows, Sailor.

SAILOR (*starting up*). Ah na na, none o' that. Damned Finmark witching. That's the end of *that*, so leave it!

CROAKER (*as he drags her away from the window*). Oh no, no –

SAILOR. Ah, so. You're feared, eh? But never mind, though. I'm a killer. (*He passes the bottle around.*)

RACHEL (*drinking*). So we're in, and we wait.

SAILOR *laughs bitterly. The baby cries.* ROSIE *sits and rocks the pram. It is now dark.*

ROSIE (*sings*).
> Sleep, O sleepy babby, now
> They sow the corn is after the plough
> They reap the corn when it grows green
> And grind the corn to make the bread
> To grow the golden hair on your head,
> Sleep, O sleepy babby, now.

Scene Seventeen

SONG
> Afeared and waiting all the night
> And never go to bed.
> They've trampled on your shadow, Jack,
> They'll trample on your head.
>
> The morning comes, they all of them come,
> Now fight them for your life:
> They'll have you out and down and dead,
> So fight fight fight for your life.

Before the Scene is discovered, as the song is ending, we hear the sounds of the house being attacked – shouts of a mob (much larger than in the previous scene) composed of both men and women – broken windows, etc.

Interior. Morning.
All the Sawneys are clustered together in the hall. The gramophone is playing the ragtime record. RACHEL *is leaning against the wall in exhaustion.* SALLY *is clutching* ROSIE's *skirts, terrified.* ROSIE *holds the baby in her arms.* DAFFODIL *is huddled down in a corner beside the* OLD CROAKER, *whimper-*

ing. SAILOR *sits on the bottom of the stairs, holding his head in his hands.* COL *screams through the letter box.*

COL. What are you trying to do at us? What are you trying to do at us? What are you trying –

MAN'S VOICE (*outside*). We're going to get you out o' that house –

WOMAN'S VOICE (*outside*). We're going to show you, by God, we're going to show you! what are you trying –

MAN'S VOICE (*outside*). You bloody gipsies, we'll chuck you in the canal.

COL (*hopelessly*). He's calling us Romanies. (*He shouts.*) Look, there's kids in this house –

ANOTHER WOMAN'S VOICE (*outside*). Aye, and *we've* got kids and all. What about Mrs Jackson's lass?

There is an angry growl from the crowd outside.

COL. There's scores of 'em outside. We can't do nowt if they make a rush. (*He has a knife in his hand*). I've got this, though. *I'll* let 'em know aren't I better nor any Romany with it.

SAILOR. He comes to me and he says – 'Sawney, who killed that Finn? There's only one man on this ship,' he says, 'has the strength to strangle that one. And I'm glad,' he says. 'He was the death of this ship.' Aye aye. Sawney has the strength . . .

ROSIE. It's his head still, where the stone hit him. Hey Sailor, wake up, it's *Rosie* – don't you know me –

SAILOR (*vaguely*). Eh? What's that?

MAN'S VOICE (*outside*). Chuck 'em in the canal.

COL. I think they're coming.

RACHEL (*taking deep breaths like a tired runner*). Ah ah ah . . .

The noise outside grows, fitfully – as though the people were approaching the house a little, then withdrawing, then making a short rush – a gradual crescendo, cut into by the sound of the arrival of a Police-car with bell clanging.

COL (*runs from the letter box to window*). It's the coppers – look! The *coppers* coming –

RACHEL (*defiant*). Let 'em come.

COL. Hey but no, they're in among the crowd. Eh begod, boys, I never thought I'd be glad for no damn coppers. Heh, I say, it's the coppers, for *us* – they're saving *us*, they're chasing them off! Eh Daffy, they're chasing 'em off –

Loud knocking at the door.

SERGEANT (*outside*). Police!

COL *moves to unbolt the door.*

RACHEL (*checks him*). No.

More knocking.

COL. Come on come on, we *got* to let 'em in now.

He opens the door and the POLICE SERGEANT *comes in.* RACHEL *stops the gramophone.*

SERGEANT (*looking round grimly*). Well? . . . Once here, soon back again, eh? What's all this going on?

COL. They wor going to do us, that's what.

ROSIE. We're glad to see you, oh God, we're glad to see *you*, mister.

SERGEANT. Oh aye? They wor going to do you? And what were *you* going to do with that piece of ironmongery? Peeling onions I suppose. Were you?

COL *drops his knife.*

Aye. I should think so.

The SERGEANT *turns in the doorway and calls to the crowd.*

Go on, clear away now, get moving! Saunderson, go round
the back of the house and break up that mob in the garden.
I've got summonses, you know, for anyone obstructing
Officers! (*He turns back to the Sawneys.*) Now then. What's
it all about?

MAN'S VOICE (*outside*). They're bloody Gipsies, Sergeant.
They've been mucking about with our lasses –

SERGEANT (*to the crowd*). Go on. Go home!

He shuts the door.

Well?

SAILOR. Who is it? What does he want? . . . Why, he's a
Peeler, stood there; he's a tall Bobby Peeler inside of
Sawney's door! . . . (*He stands up, very tottery; but perti-
nacious.*) This is a house. They made me have a house and
they put a door on it, and you can't come past that door
without you're warranted. Right?

SERGEANT. Now don't you talk what you know nowt about,
Sawney. *I'm* the one to say who's warranted. There's been
a Breach of the Peace here this morning: I've reason to
believe you've provoked it. So let's have no back-answers.
You're now living in a law-abiding neighbourhood. Least,
it has been for the last year or two, once the folk got settled
down; and we don't want your lot stirring it up again.

RACHEL. Who stirs it up? They all but gelded my poor boy
last evening – you don't stand and tell us –

SERGEANT. That'll do, missus. I'm going to have a proper
look around this place for once. I ought to have done it
yesterday, but there was other things was more important.

He goes upstairs. SAILOR *follows him up.*

SAILOR. You're not warranted. You got no right for this.

SERGEANT. I know my rights, old man: I don't need you to
tell me.

COL goes into the living-room and starts hunting among the clutter.

COL. Here, where's my haversack – by –

SAILOR (*on stairs as the* SERGEANT *prowls in the bedrooms*). I've got rights. I've got a house and I've got rights. I say you can't come here without you're warranted.

SALLY runs out of the kitchen with COL's haversack containing the drill.

SALLY (*whispers*). Col, Col, here it is, Col.

COL (*runs out of living-room to her, whispering*). Get that out of here –

They involve themselves in an awkward little huddle and the haversack drops on the floor. The SERGEANT sees them over the banisters.

SERGEANT. Hey hey, lad, what are *you* up to? Stay where you are.

He starts coming downstairs, but SAILOR gets in his way.

Let me past, will you –

The SERGEANT pushes past; SAILOR falls back down the stairs and lands at the bottom with a cry of pain. ROSIE runs to him. DAFFODIL snatches up the haversack, thrusts it at COL.

DAFFODIL. Col, Col, run boy, run!

COL gives a yelp of excitement, runs through the living-room, flings open the window. DAFFODIL comes after him, having tripped up the SERGEANT, who is not fully disentangled from SAILOR. COL jumps through the window and pulls DAFFO-DIL after him. The SERGEANT, obstructed by RACHEL, follows as quick as he can. Instead of jumping out of the window, he leans out of it and blows his whistle, then calls to the Policeman in the back garden.

SERGEANT. Saunderson, hold that man! *Hold* him! Aah!
. . . Well, get after them then! (*He hurries through the house
and throws open the front door to call.*) Williams! There's a
couple got away across the gardens with some sort of swag.
Drive down to the main road. Try and cut 'em off.
Saunderson's after them.

POLICEMAN (*outside*). All right, Sergeant!

The Police-car is heard starting away. SAILOR *lies writhing
and groaning on the hall floor.*

ROSIE (*to* SERGEANT). You've killed him, you have.

SERGEANT. Eh, what? Rubbish. Now come on, Sawney,
stand up again, you're not hurt.

SAILOR (*hopelessly*). My bad leg, it's my bad leg, done for me
with my leg . . .

SERGEANT. Let's have a look at it. (*He handles* SAILOR's *leg.*
SAILOR *gasps and cries in agony. The* SERGEANT *seems
rather disconcerted.*) H'm. Ha-h'm. Aye, well. There does
seem to be some damage there. Your own fault, you know.

He goes to front door and calls out into the street.

SERGEANT. Hallo there, somebody! You, missus! Will you
go and ring for an ambulance, please? There's a police-box
on the corner. Say it's an old man with a broken leg. And
tell 'em to look sharp. Right. (*He comes in again.*) It'll not
be long. They'll have you in hospital, so lie still while it
comes.

SAILOR (*sobbing his heart out*). He's done for me. Rachel, he's
done it, he's broke my leg and he's broke my life. He's
broke my life, Rachel, it's all my glory, Rachel, it's all
drank up and dry, it's all dry, it's all dry. Oh – oh – oh . . .

SERGEANT (*in a tired voice*). I could take the lot of you in, you
know – Obstructing Police, Stolen Goods, Breach of the
Peace – but I doubt if it'd be worth while. You'll be getting
a summons on the last of them charges, anyroad.

CROAKER. Where's my girl?

SERGEANT. Why you people can't live decent, I can't think.

CROAKER. She went off out of window. *I* know. Old Croaker, she goes after . . . (*She giggles and moves towards the living-room.*)

SERGEANT. Oh shut up, mother, and stay put. She'll be fetched back soon enough.

CROAKER. Oh? Oooh. Copper.

RACHEL moves towards the front door and picks up a bundle from the floor.

SERGEANT. Where are you off to?

RACHEL. Northampton.

SERGEANT. Oh no you're not. I said there's summonses waiting.

RACHEL. Then they can chase me to Northampton, and that's all about it.

ROSIE (*fiercely*). You bloody bide with Sailor, you!

SAILOR (*imploringly*). Rachel –

RACHEL. Heh! An old man with a broken leg. He says 'Bide with me, Rachel!'

She laughs and goes out of the house. As she leaves she meets the OFFICIAL on the threshold.

Come on in, Mister, *I'm* just out!

She leaves, laughing.

SERGEANT (*to the OFFICIAL*). Good morning.

OFFICIAL (*who is carrying a little cat in his arms*). Oh hullo, Sergeant. What's been happening here, for goodness' sake?

SERGEANT. You might well ask. What can we do for you?

OFFICIAL. I, er, I'd come about this question of unauthorized lodgers, but –

SERGEANT. We're waiting for the ambulance.

OFFICIAL. Oh . . . You know, it's a nice little cat, isn't she?
I found her in the road outside, she wor frightened to
death by all of them stamping women. I wonder who she
belongs to? Timid, she is, eh? (*In a confidential tone, to the*
SERGEANT.) They'll *have* to go now, you know. I mean
it's not just a question of lodgers, is it?

SERGEANT. H'm.

OFFICIAL. We don't *like* doing it, but –

CROAKER *comes over to* SAILOR *and crouches down beside
his head.*

CROAKER (*chants*).
Old Sailor's fallen down
fallen down
fallen down –

ROSIE. You leave him alone.

CROAKER. Ah, it's you and me, Sailor, we're the old bones,
aren't we? They tear us all up, you see.
(*She sings.*)
Old, old and thrown on the road,
Washed away with the rain:
Dig a hole and put them in
And never come out again.

SALLY. Mary and Jesus and the Twelve Tall Riders.

CROAKER }. Nobody else nobody else nick nack noo.
SALLY

CROAKER *laughs. The ambulance bell is heard approaching.*

Serjeant Musgrave's Dance

An Un-historical Parable

To Margaret

Introductory Note

This is a realistic, but not a naturalistic, play. Therefore the design of the scenes and costumes must be in some sense stylised. The paintings of L. S. Lowry might suggest a suitable mood. Scenery must be sparing – only those pieces of architecture, furniture, and properties actually used in the action need be present: and they should be thoroughly realistic, so that the audience sees a selection from the details of everyday life rather than a generalised impression of the whole of it. A similar rule should also govern the direction and the acting. If this is done, the obvious difficulties, caused by the mixture of verse, prose, and song in the play, will be considerably lessened.

The exact date of the play is deliberately not given. In the London production, the details of costume covered approximately the years between 1860 and 1880. For instance, the soldiers wore the scarlet tunics and spiked helmets characteristic of the later (or 'Kipling') epoch, while the Constable was dressed in tall hat and tail coat as an early Peeler – his role in the play suggesting a rather primitive type of police organisation.

The songs should be sung to folk-song airs. There are many available tunes which equally well suit the various songs – perhaps these are as good as any:

Sparky's song (Act One, Scene 1): 'Six Jolly Wee Miners' – Scottish.

Sparky's song and chorus (Act Two, Scene 2): 'Blow away the Morning Dew' – English.

Sparky's song (Act Two, Scene 3): 'The Black Horse' – Irish.

Attercliffe's song (Act Three, Scene 2): First three stanzas – 'John Barleycorn' – English Air. Final stanza – 'John Barleycorn' – Irish Air.

Musgrave's song (Act Three, Scene 1) proved in production to be more satisfactory if the words were spoken against a background of drum rolls and recorded music.

The characters perhaps need a few notes of description:

The Soldiers: these are regulars and seasoned men. They should all have moustaches and an ingrained sense of discipline. Musgrave is aged between thirty and forty, tall, swart, commanding, sardonic but never humorous; he could well have served under Cromwell. Attercliffe is aged about fifty, grey-haired, melancholy, a little embittered. He is the senior O.R. of the party and conscious of his responsibility. Hurst, in his twenties, is bloody-minded, quick-tempered, handsome, cynical, tough, but not quite as intelligent as he thinks he is. Sparky, also in his twenties, is easily led, easily driven, inclined to hide from himself behind a screen of silly stories and irritating clownishness. The Dragoon Officer is little more than the deus-ex-machina at the end of the play. All he needs to be is tall, calm, cold, and commanding. His Trooper is a tough, reliable soldier.

The Townsmen: The Mayor is a bustling, shrewd, superficially jovial man with a coarse accent and an underlying inclination to bully. The Parson is very much a gentleman: he is conscious of the ungentlemanly nature of the community in which he lives. He must have the accent and manners of a balked aristocrat rather than a stage-clergyman. He too has some inclination to bully. The Constable has a continual inclination to bully, except when in the presence of his superiors. He is as inefficient as he is noisy. The Colliers are all embittered but not so as to make them unpleasant. Walsh is a strong man, physically and morally. He knows what he wants and is entirely impatient with those who are not so single-minded. The Slow Collier is not particularly intelligent but has a vacuous good humour. The Pugnacious Collier is pugnacious, and very quick to show it. The Bargee is something of a grotesque, a hunchback (though this should not be over-emphasised), very rapid in his movements, with a natural urge towards intrigue and mischief.

The Women: The Landlady is a large, immobile widow of about fifty. She sits behind her bar and watches everything that happens. She is clearly a woman of deep sympathies and intelligence, which she disguises with the normal north-country sombre pessimism. Annie is a big-boned girl, not particularly attractive, but in an aggressive sort of way she provokes the men. Her emotional confusion expresses itself in a deliberately enigmatic style of speech and behaviour. Her voice is harsh.

As for the 'Meaning of the Play': I do not think that an introductory note is a suitable place for a lengthy analysis of the work, but in view of the obvious puzzlement with which it was greeted by the critics, perhaps a few points may be made. This is not a nihilistic play. This is not (except perhaps unconsciously) a symbolist play. Nor does it advocate bloody revolution. I have endeavoured to write about the violence that is so evident in the world, and to do so through a story that is partly one of wish-fulfilment. I think that many of us must at some time have felt an overpowering urge to match some particularly outrageous piece of violence with an even greater and more outrageous retaliation. Musgrave tries to do this: and the fact that the sympathies of the play are clearly with him in his original horror, and then turn against him and his intended remedy, seems to have bewildered many people. I would suggest, however, that a study of the roles of the women, and of Private Attercliffe, should be sufficient to remove any doubts as to where the 'moral' of the play lies. Accusations of nihilism seem to derive from the scene where the Colliers turn away from Musgrave and join in the general dance around the beer barrel. Again, I would suggest, that an unwillingness to dwell upon unpleasant situations that do not immediately concern us is a general human trait, and recognition of it need imply neither cynicism nor despair. Complete pacifism is a very hard doctrine: and if this play appears to advocate it with perhaps some timidity, it is probably because I am naturally a timid man – and also because I know that if I am hit I very easily hit back: and I do not care to preach too confidently what I am not sure I can practise.

J.A.

Serjeant Musgrave's Dance was first performed at the Royal Court Theatre on 22 October 1959, with the following cast:

PRIVATE SPARKY	Donal Donnelly
PRIVATE HURST	Alan Dobie
PRIVATE ATTERCLIFFE	Frank Finlay
BLUDGEON, *a bargee*	James Bree
SERJEANT MUSGRAVE	Ian Bannen
THE PARSON	Richard Caldicot
MRS. HITCHCOCK	Freda Jackson
ANNIE	Patsy Byrne
THE CONSTABLE	Michael Hunt
THE MAYOR	Stratford Johns
A SLOW COLLIER	Jack Smethurst
A PUGNACIOUS COLLIER	Colin Blakely
WALSH, *an earnest collier*	Harry Gwynn Davies
A TROOPER OF DRAGOONS	Barry Wilsher
AN OFFICER OF DRAGOONS	Clinton Greyn

Produced by LINDSAY ANDERSON
Music by DUDLEY MOORE
Decor by JOCELYN HERBERT

The play is set in a mining town in the north of England eighty years ago. It is winter.

Act One

SCENE ONE

A canal wharf. Evening.

HURST *and* ATTERCLIFFE *are playing cards on the top of a side-drum. A few yards away* SPARKY *stands, as though on guard, clapping himself to keep warm. There is a pile of three or four heavy wooden boxes with the WD broad arrow stencilled on them, and a lantern set on top.*

SPARKY. Brr, oh a cold winter, snow, dark. We wait too long, that's the trouble. Once you've started, keep on travelling. No good sitting to wait in the middle of it. Only makes the cold night colder. (*He sings*):

> One day I was drunk, boys, on the Queen's Highway
> When a recruiting party come beating that way.
> I was enlisted and attested before I did know
> And to the Royal Barracks they forced me to go.

Brr! And they talk of the Crimea! Did I ever tell you that one about the field kitchens at Sebastopol? Well, there was this red-haired provost-sarnt, y'see . . . and then the corporal-cook – now *he'd* got no hair at all . . . now the Commissary in that Regiment was – oh . . . (*He finds no one paying attention.*) Who's winning?

HURST. I'm winning.

ATTERCLIFFE. Oho, no you're not. The black spades carry the day. Jack, King and Ace. *We* throw the red Queen over. That's another shilling, you know. Let's have it.

HURST. All right. Deal agen, boy. Or no, no, *my* deal, this game. Now let's see if I can't turn some good cards on to my side for a difference. Here: one, two, three, four . . . (*He deals the cards.*)

SPARKY. How much longer we got to wait, I'd like to know. I want to be off aboard that damned barge and away. What's happened to our Black Jack Musgrave, eh? Why don't he come and give us the word to get going?

ATTERCLIFFE. He'll come on the stroke, as he said. He works his life to bugle and drum, this serjeant. You ever seen him late?

SPARKY. No. (*He sings*):

When first I deserted I thought myself free
Till my cruel sweetheart informed upon me –

ATTERCLIFFE (*sharply*). I don't think you ought to sing *that* one.

SPARKY. Why not? It's true, isn't it? (*He sings*):

Court martial, court martial, they held upon me
And the sentence they passed was the high gallows tree.

HURST (*dropping cards and springing up in a rage*). Now shut it, will you! God-damned devil of a song to sing on this sort of a journey! He said you didn't ought to, so don't! (*He glances nervously around.*)

SPARKY. Ha, there's nobody to hear us. You're safe as a bloody blockhouse out here – I'm on the sentry, boy, *I'm* your protection.

ATTERCLIFFE (*irritably*). You make sure you are then. Go on: keep watching.

SPARKY (*returns to his guard*). Ah. Ha-ha . . . Or did you think *he* could hear you? (*He gestures towards the boxes.*) Maybe, maybe . . . *I* thought I heard him laugh.

ATTERCLIFFE. Steady, boy.

SPARKY (*a little wildly*). Steady yourself, you crumbling old cuckold. He might laugh, who knows? Well, make a rattling any road. Mightn't he, soldier boy?

HURST. Are you coming funny wi' me –

SPARKY. Funny? About *him*? You don't tell me he don't know what we're at. Why shouldn't he have a laugh at it, if that's how he feels?

HURST. Arrh, you're talking daft.

SPARKY. Now don't you be nervous, boy: not for *you* to be nervous. You're a man and a soldier! Or an old red rag stretched over four pair o' bones – well, what's the odds? Eh?

HURST (*after glaring angrily, sits down again*). *All right . . . All right, play.*

They play in silence. SPARKY *hums and blows his knuckles. Then he starts.*

SPARKY. Who goes there!

The BARGEE *enters with a lantern, whistling 'Michael Finnegan'.*

BARGEE. Hooroar, my jolly buckos! It's only old Joe Bludgeon, the Captain of the Lugger. Crooked old Joe. Heh heh. And what's the news with you? Are we ready yet, are we?

SPARKY. Ready for what?

BARGEE. Ready for off, of course, what do you think? Are we?

ATTERCLIFFE. No.

BARGEE. Why not, then?

ATTERCLIFFE. 'Cos it's not time, that's why not. Half-past seven, you was told.

BARGEE. Oh, it's as near as –

ATTERCLIFFE. No begod it's not, and he won't be here till it is.

BARGEE. Ah, the serjeant, eh?

ATTERCLIFFE. Aye, the serjeant. Is your barge up yet?

BARGEE. It's up. And the old horse waiting.

ATTERCLIFFE. Then we'll start to load.

HURST. Hey, we've not finished the game.

ATTERCLIFFE. Save it, mucker. You heard what Black Jack said.

HURST. All right. All right.

BARGEE. You can load these smaller cases 'side of the cabin. What you got in 'em, for Godsake? Ten ton and a half here.

SPARKY (*kicking one of them*). There's a Gatling gun in that one. You know what a Gatling gun is, friend?

BARGEE. I don't, and I don't care neither, tell you truth of it. By Lordy, what a life, the bloody Army. Do they still tie you fellers up and stripe you across with the cat-o'-nine-tails, eh?

HURST. No they don't.

ATTERCLIFFE *and* HURST *start carrying the cases out.*

BARGEE (*gloating*). Heheh, when I wor a young lad they told me, they did. Whack, whack, whack. Ooh, cruel it was. You know what they used to call 'em in them days – soldiers, I mean? Eh?

SPARKY. I know a lot o' names for calling soldiers.

BARGEE. I'll bet you don't know this one, though. Heh. Bloodred roses, that was it. What d'you think o' that, eh? Whack, whack, whack. Bloodred roses, eh? (*He calls off-stage.*) Not there, don't put it there, give me some room to swing me tiller, can't you! Soldiers. Get 'em aboard a barge, you'd be as well off wi' a row of deaf niggers from Peru. That's right, now leave it where you've dropped it, and come ashore before you capsize her—you bloodred bloody roses, you!

HURST *re-enters.*

HURST. That's enough of that, matey. Watch it.

MUSGRAVE *enters.*

MUSGRAVE (*to the* BARGEE). Aye, you watch it. Now I'll tell you just once, old man, and that's all. We travel on your barge, passengers: we pay our fare. So don't you talk to my men like they're deck-hands. Clear?

BARGEE. Oh it's clear, serjeant, I only wanted a little joke.

MUSGRAVE. Aye. And now you've had one. So be thankful.

ATTERCLIFFE *re-enters.*

ATTERCLIFFE (*as he and* HURST *pick up the remaining smaller boxes.*) We got the Gatling loaded on, serjeant, and we're fetching the rest of it. Then there's just the drum and the other box left. Any news?

MUSGRAVE (*quietly to him*). We're all all right. Don't worry.

ATTERCLIFFE *and* HURST *go out with their load.* MUS-GRAVE *taps the drum meditatively and turns to the* BARGEE.

I say, you, bargee. Is it going to snow again before to-morrow?

BARGEE. Likely. There's ice coming on the water too. Give her another day and this canal'll be closed. They say the road over the moors is fast already with the drifts. You've chose a merry time o' year beating up for recruities, haven't you? What you got in here? Another Gatling gun? (*He smacks the last box.*)

MUSGRAVE. Why not? Show 'em all the best equipment, glamourise 'em, man, fetch 'em in like conies ... Now get this last box loaded, and be careful. And then we're all ready. You can start.

ATTERCLIFFE *and* HURST, *having returned, pick up the box and carry it out,* SPARKY *going with them, the drum slung on his shoulder.* MUSGRAVE *takes the soldiers' lantern and makes a rapid circuit of the stage to see if anything is left. He stands for a moment looking out in the direction from which he has come in.*

BARGEE (*waiting for him*). This your first trip to the coal-mining towns, serjeant?

MUSGRAVE. It is.

BARGEE. Ooh, brr, bitter and bleak: hungry men for the Queen. If you're used to a full belly, you'll want it when you get there.

MUSGRAVE (*curtly*). It's not material. We have our duty. A soldier's duty is a soldier's life.

BARGEE. Ah, duty.

> The Empire wars are far away
> For duty's sake we sail away
> Me arms and legs is shot away
> And all for the wink of a shilling and a drink . . .

Come on, me cheery serjeant, you've not left nowt behind.

They go out after the soldiers.

SCENE TWO

The bar of a public house.

MRS. HITCHCOCK *is sitting in the body of the room, talking to the* PARSON, *who is very much at his ease, with a glass of brandy in his hand.* ANNIE *is polishing glasses etc. behind the bar.*

PARSON. No. No, madam, no. I cannot be seen to countenance idleness, pauperism, beggary. If no one comes to buy your drink, I am sorry for you. But the fact is, madam, a little less drunkenness and disorder will do this town no harm. The Church is not a speculative bank, you know, to subsidise pot-houses.

MRS. HITCHCOCK (*sulkily*). Always a respectable house.

PARSON. What?

MRS. HITCHCOCK. Always a respectable house, reverend. Aye. If not, why renew the licence? You're a magistrate, you know. You could have spoke agen me on me application. But you didn't.

PARSON. That is not to the purpose, Mrs. Hitchcock. The Bench allows that there have to be public houses to permit an outlet for the poorer sort of people, but in times of regrettable industrial conflict it is better that as many of them as possible remain empty. If the colliers cannot afford drink because of the strike – because of their own stupidity – then there is the less likelihood of their being inflamed to acts of violence. I am not at all certain that the Bench ought not to withdraw all licences altogether until the pits are working.

MRS. HITCHCOCK. That'd be grand. See half a dozen publicans going on the parish – beer-dregs from the workhouse served to the Trade – ooh, talk of arsy-versy! (*She laughs throatily*.)

PARSON. I'm quite sure that would not be necessary.

MRS. HITCHCOCK (*reasonably*). Now, look, reverend, you've been taking me crossroads since the minute I began. All I asked you in to say is this: this strike is bad for the town. Well, I mean, of course, that means me. But it means you too. *And* it means His Worship the Mayor: oh aye, aye:

> I am a proud coalowner
> And in scarlet here I stand.
> Who shall come or who shall go
> Through all my coal-black land?

(*She laughs again.*) Eh, if we can't have a laugh, we'll starve!

PARSON. You are impertinent. I have nothing more to say.

MRS. HITCHCOCK. Ah, but I come to you because you're Church, you're charity. Go on, reverend, you tell the Mayor to agree with his men and give them a good price, then they'll buy and sell in the town and they'll drink in this taproom, and – ho-hoo – who knows, they might even come to church! That'll be the day.

The PARSON *turns irritably from her and goes to the door.*
The BARGEE *enters and confronts him.*

BARGEE (*touching his cap mockingly*). Parson.

PARSON (*coldly*). Good afternoon.

BARGEE. Cold enough for you, eh?

PARSON (*trying to pass*). It is cold, yes.

BARGEE. How's the strike?

PARSON. It is not yet settled.

BARGEE. No, I bet it's not, and all. Hey missus!

MRS. HITCHCOCK. Hello.

BARGEE. A quart o' taddy. Best!

MRS. HITCHCOCK (*impassive*). Can you pay for it?

BARGEE. 'Course I can pay – wait a minute, Parson, just a
minute, all under control – I'm not one of your colliery
agitators, you know. *I'm* still in work. I've news for you.

MRS. HITCHCOCK (*to* ANNIE). He says he can pay. Draw him
his quart.

BARGEE (*to the* PARSON). I didn't think, like, to find you here,
but, eh, well, seeing as how here you are – canal's froze up,
you know.

PARSON. Well?

BARGEE. Well. Last barge come in this morning. *My* barge.
There was passengers.

PARSON. I am not really interested.

BARGEE (*significantly*). Four on 'em, Parson. Soldiers.

ANNIE *hands the* BARGEE *his tankard.*

PARSON (*in some alarm*). Soldiers! Already? Who sent for
them? Why was I not told? This could be very dangerous –

BARGEE. They're not here for what you think, you know. Not
yet, any road. You see, they've come recruiting.

PARSON (*relieved, but vexed*). Oh . . . Well, what if they have?
Why bother me with it? You're just wasting time, man.
Come on, get out of my way . . .

BARGEE (*still detaining him*). Eh, but, Parson, you're a magistrate.

PARSON. Of course I'm a magistrate.

BARGEE. You're a power, you are: in a town of trouble, in a place of danger. Yes. You're the word and the book, aren't you? Well then: soldiers. Recruiting. Useful?

PARSON (*beginning to follow his drift*). H'm. I do not think the Bench is in any real need of *your* suggestions. But I am obliged to you for the news. Thank you.

He gives the BARGEE *a coin and leaves.*

BARGEE (*flipping the coin*). Heh, heh, I said I could pay.

He gives it to ANNIE *and starts whistling 'Michael Finnegan'.* ANNIE *goes back to the bar.* MRS. HITCHCOCK *takes the coin from her and tests it between her teeth.*

MRS. HITCHCOCK. Soldiers. Annie, love, you could tell us what soldiers is good for.

ANNIE (*sullen*). Why should I tell you?

BARGEE (*gleefully*). Go on, go on, lassie, tell us about the soldiers. She knows the good red coat button-to-back, I'll bet. Go on, it's a cold day, warm it up for us. Heh, heh, our strong Annie's the champion, eh?

He smacks her on the bottom. She swerves angrily.

ANNIE. *When* I've given you leave: and not afore. You bloody dog, sit down.

BARGEE (*subsiding in mock terror*). Ooh, sharp, sharp.

MRS. HITCHCOCK. Aye, so sit down . . . Go on, Annie, tell us.

ANNIE. I'll tell you for what a soldier's good:

To march behind his roaring drum,
Shout to us all: 'Here I come
I've killed as many as I could –
I'm stamping into your fat town

From the war and to the war
And every girl can be my whore
Just watch me lay them squealing down.
And that's what he does and so do we.
Because we know he'll soon be dead
We strap our arms round the scarlet red
Then send him weeping over the sea.
Oh he will go and a long long way.
Before he goes we'll make him pay
Between the night and the next cold day –
By God there's a whole lot more I could say –

What good's a bloody soldier 'cept to be dropped into a slit in the ground like a letter in a box. How many did you bring with you – is it four?

BARGEE. Aye. Four.

ANNIE. That's four beds in this house?

MRS. HITCHCOCK. I should hope it's in this house. It's the best house in town.

ANNIE (*in a sudden outburst*). Then you'd do well to see they stay four nights because I'll not go with more nor one in one night, no, not for you nor for all of Egypt!

She lets out a howl and rushes out of the door behind the bar, clattering a tin tray full of tankards on to the floor.

BARGEE. Ooh, Lordy! Champion, strong, and sharp. Annie! Tell us some more!

MRS. HITCHCOCK (*crossly*). Let her alone. She's said enough for you, hasn't she? It's not right to set her off . . . I suppose they *are* coming to this house?

BARGEE. Oh surely, aye, surely. *I* told 'em : *I* took care.

A rat-tat-tat on the drum heard, off.

There, you see, they're coming.

SPARKY *enters magnificently, beating the drum.*

SPARKY. Ho-ho, atten-tion! Stand by your beds! Name of the Queen, missus – has he told you – there's four on us : we three, we'll settle for palliasses in the loft, but the serjeant he wants a big brass bed with knobs on, that's his fancy! Can you do it?

MRS. HITCHCOCK. So here they are, the gay recruiters. Aye, I can do it, young man. I've only one room in the house. The serjeant can have that. The three of you'll have to doss down in me old stable, out back, but there's a good stove, you'll be warm. Now, who's going to pay? You or the Queen?

SPARKY. Oh, Queen at end of it all, I suppose.

MRS. HITCHCOCK. But you at beginning, eh?

SPARKY. Oh-oh, chalk it up, you know . . . we've brought some gear with us too.

BARGEE. Ten and a half ton. Nigh foundered the old barge, it did, I can tell you.

SPARKY. But we got here, friend, didn't we? Like we get ourselves to everywhere we go, we do. No question o' that, y'see.

BARGEE. Heh, heh, none.

SPARKY (*calls to offstage*). Serjeant! We're fixed!

MUSGRAVE (*off*). And the equipment?

SPARKY. And the equipment, missus?

MRS. HITCHCOCK. There's a coach-house across the yard.

SPARKY (*calls to offstage*). Coach-house across the yard, serjeant! . . . While they're taking it round there, missus, let's have a pint apiece drawn ready. Like what *he* drinks, eh? Recommend it, friend?

BARGEE. You could stand your bayonet up in this, you could.

SPARKY. Right, then. And we'll give you another while we're at it. That's five on 'em, pints, unless *you're* drinking with us, too, are you?

MRS. HITCHCOCK. Why not, soldier? Queen as pays . . . Annie! Hey Annie!

As there is no reply, she goes herself behind the bar and starts filling the tankards. MUSGRAVE *enters.*

MUSGRAVE. Is the padlock on your coach-house door a strong one, ma'am?

MRS. HITCHCOCK. Likely so.

MUSGRAVE. Valuable equipment, y'see. Your window in there's barred, I notice.

MRS. HITCHCOCK. That's right.

MUSGRAVE (*picking up a tankard*). Good . . . This for me?

MRS. HITCHCOCK. If you want it.

The other two soldiers enter.

ATTERCLIFFE. The cases are all locked up and safe, serjeant.

MUSGRAVE (*indicates drinks*). Very good. Here you are.

HURST and ATTERCLIFFE. Thank you, serjeant.

BARGEE (*raising his drink*). Good health to Her Majesty; to Her Majesty's wars; to the girls we leave behind us. Drink!

They all drink.

MRS. HITCHCOCK (*raising her drink*):

> Into the river, out of the river
> Once I was dry, now I am wet
> But hunger and cold they hold me yet.

They drink again, with a certain puzzlement at the toast.

MRS. HITCHCOCK. They hold this town today, any road, serjeant; or had you been told?

MUSGRAVE. What's the matter?

MRS. HITCHCOCK. No work in the colliery. The owner calls it a strike, the men call it a lock-out, we call it starvation.

The CONSTABLE *enters violently.*

CONSTABLE. His Worship the Mayor.

MRS. HITCHCOCK. Eh?

CONSTABLE. I said, His Worship the Mayor!

BARGEE. Oho, *now*, me jolly buckos, give attention, stand-to, to the present!

CONSTABLE (*to the* BARGEE). Ssssh – ssh –

BARGEE. Heh, heh, heh –

The MAYOR *enters at speed, wearing his gold chain. After him comes the* PARSON. MUSGRAVE *calls his men to attention.*

MAYOR. Mrs. Hitchcock, I'm seeking the soldiers. Ah, here they are! Well, I'm the Mayor of this town, I own the colliery, I'm a worried man. So I come seeking you when I could send for you, what do you think to that? Let's have a look at you . . . Ah. Haha . . . Clear the snug a minute, missus. I want a private word with the Parson. Serjeant, be ready outside when I send for you.

MUSGRAVE. At your service, sir . . . Come on.

Beckoned by MRS. HITCHCOCK, *he leads his party out behind the bar.*

CONSTABLE (*propelling the* BARGEE *to the street door*). Go on, you, out this road.

BARGEE (*dodging him*). Oo-er –

> Constable Constable alive or dead
> His head is of leather and his belly's of lead.

Go – whoops . . . How are you, Parson?

He ducks out, whistling 'Michael Finnegan'.

MRS. HITCHCOCK (*sourly, to the* MAYOR). Do you want a drink?

MAYOR. No.

MRS. HITCHCOCK. At your service, when you do.

She curtsies and goes out behind the bar.

MAYOR. What do you think to 'em, Parson?

PARSON. Fine strong men. They make me proud of my country. Mr. Mayor, Britain depends upon these spirits. It is a great pity that their courage is betrayed at home by skulkers and shirkers. What do *you* think?

MAYOR (*looking at him sideways*). *I* think we'll use 'em, Parson. Temporary expedient, but it'll do. The price of coal has fell, I've had to cut me wages, I've had to turn men off. They say they'll strike, so I close me gates. We can't live like that for ever. There's two ways to solve this colliery – one is build the railway here and cut me costs of haulage, *that* takes two years and an Act of Parliament, though God knows I want to do it. The other is clear out half the population, stir up a diversion, turn their minds to summat else. The Queen's got wars, she's got rebellions. Over the sea. All right. Beat these fellers' drums high around the town, I'll put one pound down for every Royal Shilling the serjeant pays. Red coats and flags. Get rid o' the trouble-makers. Drums and fifes and glory.

PARSON (*severely*). The soldier's calling is one of honour.

MAYOR. It's more than that. It's bloody convenient. Town Constable, fetch that serjeant in!

CONSTABLE (*nervously*). Er, excuse me, Your Worship. A point. Soldiers, you see. Now, I've got a very small force in this town. Only one other regular officer, you know: the rest is them deputy-specials – I can't trust *that* lot to stand fast and fear nowt when the time comes.

PARSON. What time?

CONSTABLE. There's been stone-throwing this morning. Two of my office windows is broke. And I'm nervous—that's frank, you know – I *am*.

MAYOR. Well?

CONSTABLE. Your Worship. I want these soldiers added to my force. It's all right recruiting. But what we need's patrols.

MAYOR. Not yet.

CONSTABLE. Your Worship. I'm asking you formal. You've got agitators here, and they won't stop at throwing stones: that's frank.

MAYOR (*angrily*). I said not yet. We'll try it my road first. Godsake, man, what's four soldiers agen the lot of 'em? This town's wintered up, you'll get no more help till there's a thaw. So work on that. Call in the serjeant.

CONSTABLE. Right, Your Worship. Serjeant! Come in here!

MUSGRAVE *re-enters.*

MUSGRAVE. Sir?

MAYOR. Serjeant, we're very glad to have you. I speak for the Council, I speak for the magistrates. Now listen: there's loyal hearts and true here, and we're every man-jack of us keen to see our best lads flock to the colours. Isn't that so, Parson?

PARSON (*taken a little by surprise*). Ha-h'm – with great pride, yes.

MAYOR. Right. For every Queen's Shilling you give out, I give out a golden sovereign – no, two. One for the recruit, and one to be divided among you and your three good lads. What do you say to that?

MUSGRAVE. That's most handsome, sir.

MAYOR. I should damn well think it is. How do you propose to work?

MUSGRAVE. Sir?

MAYOR. Aye, I mean, d'you tramp around the streets drumming, or set on your fannies in a pub—or what?

MUSGRAVE. Depends what's most appropriate, sir, according to the type of town. I've not had time for a look at yours yet. But the pubs seem pretty empty, if this one's owt to go by.

PARSON. They *are* empty.

MUSGRAVE. Aye. Well, in that case, I'll have to make a reconnaissance, won't I? When I'm decided, I'll let you know.

CONSTABLE. And let me know, serjeant. I'll see you get facilities.

MUSGRAVE. Thank you, mister.

MAYOR. And while you're on about them facilities, constable, perhaps you might let in the serjeant on a few likely names for his list, eh? Could you pick him some passable strong-set men, could you?

CONSTABLE (*significantly*). I could have a try, Your Worship.

MAYOR. Right. Then if that's settled, I'll be off back to town hall. I've not got time to waste wi' nattering, snug and all though it is in here. Come along, Constable. I want a little word wi' you about them stones.

MAYOR *and* CONSTABLE *go out.*

PARSON (*severely*). I think I ought to make one thing clear, serjeant. I know that it is customary for recruiting-parties to impress themselves upon the young men of the district as dashingly as possible, and no doubt upon the young women also. Now I am not having any of that. There's enough trouble in the place as it is. So remember.

MUSGRAVE. Yes, sir. I'll remember.

PARSON. I want no drunkenness, and no fornication, from your soldiers. Need I speak plainer?

MUSGRAVE. No, sir. There will be none. I am a religious man.

PARSON. Very well. Good day to you.

MUSGRAVE. Good day, sir.

The PARSON *goes.* MUSGRAVE *sits down, takes out a small pocket bible and reads.* MRS. HITCHCOCK *enters.*

MRS. HITCHCOCK. What, they've not all gone, already?

MUSGRAVE. They have, ma'am.

MRS. HITCHCOCK. Just like, isn't it? Use my bar for a council-parlour, leave nowt behind 'em but bad breath and a shiny bench – *they* take care. I'm giving your three their dinners in back. You eating with 'em?

MUSGRAVE (*of-handed*). No. I'll have a hand of bread and cheese and eat it here.

MRS. HITCHCOCK. Drink with it?

MUSGRAVE (*still at his book*). No . . . Thanks, no. Just the cheese.

MRS. HITCHCOCK (*sourly*). H'm, another on 'em . . . Hey, Annie! Slice o' bread and a piece o' cheese in here for this one! Pickles?

MUSGRAVE. Eh?

MRS. HITCHCOCK (*annoyed*). Pickles!

MUSGRAVE. No . . . (*He looks up suddenly.*) Tell me, ma'am, is there many from this town lately have gone for a soldier?

MRS. HITCHCOCK. Some. It's not a common pleasure here – not as long as the coal wor right to sell, any road. But there was some. You'll know the sort o' reasons, I daresay?

> The yellow-haired boy lay in my bed
> A-kissing me up from me toes to me head.
> But when my apron it did grow too short
> He thought it good time to leave his sport.

Enter ANNIE *with the bread and cheese. She gives it to* MUS-GRAVE.

MUSGRAVE. Thank you.

ANNIE (*confronting him*). Serjeant you are.

MUSGRAVE. That's right.

ANNIE. You seem a piece stronger than the rest of 'em.

He nods.

And they call you Black Jack Musgrave?

He looks at her.

Well, I'm looking at your face, mister serjeant. Now do you know what I'd say?

MUSGRAVE. What?

ANNIE. The North Wind in a pair of millstones
    Was your father and your mother
    They got you in a cold grinding.
    God help us all if they get you a brother.

She looks at him another minute, then nods her head and goes out.

MUSGRAVE (*wryly*). She talks a kind of truth, that lassie. Is she daft?

MRS. HITCHCOCK. No, no, no, I wouldn't say daft. But there's not many would let her bide in their house.

MUSGRAVE. Tell me, ma'am. It sticks on my mind that I once had a sort of a comrade came from this town. . . Long, yellow-haired lad, like in your little verse. Name of, oh, Hickson, was it, Hickman?

MRS. HITCHCOCK (*astonished and disturbed*). Ey, ey –

MUSGRAVE. What was it now, his name – Billy – Billy –

MRS. HITCHCOCK (*very upset*). Billy Hicks. Hicks. Aye, oh, strange, serjeant, strange roads bringing you along, I'd not wonder.

MUSGRAVE. What do you mean? . . . It *was* Hicks – I remember.

MRS. HITCHCOCK (*reminiscently*). Not what you'd call a bad young feller, you know – but he weren't no good neither. He'd come in here pissed of a Sat'dy night – I'd tell him straight out, 'You needn't reckon on to get any more here.' But he'd lean on this bar and he'd look at me, and he'd sing. You know – *hymns* – 'Uplift your heads, you gates of brass' – church hymns, he'd sing. Like he'd say to me, 'I'll sing for me drinking, missus' . . . hymns . . .

She hums the tune of 'Uplift your heads' and breaks off sharply.

He gave her a baby, and he went straight off to the war. Or the rebellions, they called it. They told us he was killed.

MUSGRAVE (*without emotion*). Aye, he was killed. He was shot
dead last year . . . Gave a baby to who?

MRS. HITCHCOCK (*jerks her thumb to door behind bar*). Her.

MUSGRAVE (*truly surprised*). Go on?

MRS. HITCHCOCK. True. But when it wor born, it came a
kind of bad shape, pale, sick: it wor dead and in the ground
in no more nor two month. About the time they called
him dead, y'see. What d'you reckon to that?

MUSGRAVE (*carelessly*). It's not material. He was no great
friend to me. But maybe, as you said, strange. He did use
to sing. And yellow hair he had, didn't he? (*He goes to the
door behind the bar and calls.*) Have ye finished your dinners?
Because we'll take a look at the town before it gets dark.
(*Confidently to* MRS. HITCHCOCK) What you've just
been telling me, don't tell it to these. Dead men and dead
children should bide where they're put and not be rose up
to the thoughts of the living. It's bad for discipline ... (*He
calls again.*) Come on, let's be having you!

The SOLDIERS *come in.* MUSGRAVE *points to each one as they
enter.*

East; south; west; I'll go north; I'm told it suits my nature.
Then meet at the churchyard rail and tell me what you've
seen. Let's make it sharp.

They go out.

SCENE THREE

The churchyard.

Sunset. HURST *enters and walks about, whistling nervously. The*
SLOW COLLIER *enters and looks at him. They pass each other,
giving each other good hard stares. The* SLOW COLLIER *is about
to leave the stage when he turns round and calls.*

SLOW COLLIER. Hey! Soldier!

HURST. Aye?

SLOW COLLIER. How many on you is there?

HURST. Four.

SLOW COLLIER. Four . . . Four dead red rooks and be damned.

HURST. What? What's that?

SLOW COLLIER (*contemptuously*). Arrh . . .

He slouches out.

HURST *makes to follow, but decides not to, and continues walking about.*

MUSGRAVE *enters.*

MUSGRAVE. Coldest town I ever was in. What did you see?

HURST. Hardly a thing. Street empty, windows shut, two old wives on a doorstep go indoors the minute I come. Three men on one corner, two men on another, dirty looks and no words from any on 'em. There's one man swears a curse at me just now. That's all.

MUSGRAVE. H'm . . .

He calls to offstage.

Hello! We're over here!

ATTERCLIFFE *enters.*

What did you see?

ATTERCLIFFE. Hardly a thing. Street empty, doors locked, windows blind, shops cold and empty. A young lass calls her kids in from playing in the dirt—she sees me coming, so she calls 'em. There's someone throws a stone –

MUSGRAVE. A stone?

ATTERCLIFFE. Aye. I don't know who did it and it didn't hit me, but it was thrown.

HURST. It's a cold poor town, I'm telling you, serjeant.

MUSGRAVE. Coldest town I ever was in. And here's the fourth of us.

Enter SPARKY.

What did you see?

SPARKY. Hardly a thing. Street empty, no chimneys smoking, no horses, yesterday's horsedung frozen on the road. Three men at a corner-post, four men leaning on a wall. No words: but some chalked up on a closed door – they said: 'Soldiers go home'.

HURST. Go home?

SPARKY. That's it, boy: home. It's a place they think we have somewhere. And what did *you* see, serjeant?

MUSGRAVE. Nothing different from you . . . So, here is our town and here are we. All fit and appropriate.

HURST (*breaking out suddenly*). Appropriate? Serjeant, now we've come with you so far. And every day we're in great danger. We're on the run, in red uniforms, in a black-and-white coalfield; and it's cold; and the money's running out that you stole from the Company office; and we don't know who's heard of us or how much they've heard. Isn't it time you brought out clear just what you've got in mind?

MUSGRAVE (*ominously*). Aye? Is it? And any man else care to tell me what the time is?

ATTERCLIFFE (*reasonably*). Now serjeant, please, easy—we're all your men, and we agreed –

HURST. All right: if we *are* your men, we've rights.

MUSGRAVE (*savagely*). The only right *you* have is a rope around your throat and six foot six to drop from. On the run? Stolen money? I'm talking of a murdered officer, shot down in a street fight, shot down in one night's work. They put that to the rebels, but *I* know *you* were the man. We deserted, but you killed.

HURST. I'd a good reason . . .

MUSGRAVE. I know you had reason, else I'd not have left you alive to come with us. All I'm concerned about this minute is to tell you how you stand. And you stand in my power. But there's more to it than a bodily blackmail – isn't there? – because my power's the power of God, and that's what's brought me here and all three of you with me. You know my words and purposes – it's not just authority of the orderly room, it's not just three stripes, it's not just given to me by the reckoning of my mortal brain – well, *where* does it come from?

He flings this question fiercely at HURST.

HURST (*trying to avoid it*). All right, I'm not arguing –
MUSGRAVE. *Where!*
HURST (*frantically defensive*). I don't believe in God!
MUSGRAVE. You don't? Then what's this!

He jabs his thumb into HURST'S *cheek and appears to scrape something off it.*

HURST. Sweat.
MUSGRAVE. The coldest winter for I should think it's ten years, and the man sweats like a bird-bath!
HURST (*driven in a moral corner*). Well, why not, because –
MUSGRAVE (*relentless*). Go on – because?
HURST (*browbeaten into incoherence*). All right, because I'm afraid. 'Cos I thought when I met you, I thought we'd got the same motives. To get out, get shut o' the Army – with its 'treat-you-like-dirt-but-you-do-the-dirty-work' – 'kill *him*, kill *them*, they're all bloody rebels, State of Emergency, high standard of turnout, military bearin' – so *I* thought up some killing, I said I'll get me own in. I thought o' the Rights of Man. Rights o' the Rebels: that's *me*! Then I *went*. And here's a serjeant on the road, he's took two men, he's deserted same as me, he's got money, he can bribe a civvy skipper to carry us to England . . . It's nowt to do wi' *God*. I don't understand all that about God, why d'you bring God into it! You've come here to tell the people and then there'd be no more war –

MUSGRAVE (*taking him up with passionate affirmation*). Which *is* the word of God! Our message without God is a bad belch and a hiccup. You three of you, without me, are a bad belch and a hiccup. How d'you think you'd do it, if I wasn't here? Tell me, go on, tell me!

HURST (*still in his corner*). Why then I'd – I'd – I'd tell 'em, Sarnt Musgrave, I'd bloody stand, and tell 'em, and –

MUSGRAVE. Tell 'em *what*!

HURST (*made to appear more stupid than he really is*). All right: like, the war, the Army, colonial wars, we're treated like dirt, out there, and for to do the dirty work, and –

MUSGRAVE (*with withering scorn*). And they'd run you in and run you up afore the clock struck five! You don't understand about God! But you think, yourself, you, alone, stupid, without a gill of discipline, illiterate, ignorant of the Scriptures – you think you can make a whole town, a whole nation, understand the cruelty and greed of armies, what it means, and how to punish it! You hadn't even took the precaution to find the cash for your travel. I paid your fare!

HURST (*knuckling under*). All right. You paid . . . You're the Serjeant . . . All right. Tell us what to do.

MUSGRAVE (*the tension eased*). Then we'll sit down, and we'll be easy. It's cold atween these tombs, but its private. Sit down. Now: you can consider, and you can open your lugs and you can listen – ssh! Wait a minute . . .

The SLOW COLLIER *enters at one side, the* PUGNACIOUS *and* EARNEST COLLIERS *at the other. All three carry pick-hefts as clubs.*

SLOW COLLIER (*calls to the other two*). Four on 'em, you see. They're all here together.

PUGNACIOUS COLLIER. Setting in the graveyard, eh, like a coffin-load o' sick spooks.

EARNEST COLLIER (*coming towards the soldiers*). Which one's the Serjeant?

MUSGRAVE (*standing up*). Talk to me.

EARNEST COLLIER. Aye and I will too. There's a Union made at this colliery, and we're strong. When we say strike, we strike, all ends of us: that's fists, and it's pick-hefts and it's stones and it's feet. If you work in the coal-seam you carry iron on your clogs – see!

He thrusts up his foot menacingly.

PUGNACIOUS COLLIER. And you fight for your life when it's needed.

MUSGRAVE. So do some others of us.

EARNEST COLLIER. Ah, no, lobster, *you* fight for pay. You go sailing on what they call punitive expeditions, against what you call rebels, and you shoot men down in streets. But not here. These streets is *our* streets.

MUSGRAVE. Anything else?

EARNEST COLLIER. No. Not this evening. Just so as you know, that's all.

PUGNACIOUS COLLIER. Setting in the graveyard. Look at 'em, for Godsake. Waiting for a riot and then they'll have a murder. Why don't *we* have one *now*: it's dark enough, ent it?

EARNEST COLLIER. Shut up. It'll do when it's time. Just so as they know, that's all.

The COLLIERS *turn to go.*

MUSGRAVE. Wait a minute.

They pause.

Who told you we'd come to break the strike?

EARNEST COLLIER. Eh?

MUSGRAVE. Who told you?

EARNEST COLLIER. Nobody told us. We don't need to be told. You see a strike: you see soldiers: there's only one reason.

MUSGRAVE. Not this time there isn't. We haven't been sent for –

PUGNACIOUS COLLIER. Get away wi' that –

MUSGRAVE. And all soldiers aren't alike, you know. Some of us is human.

SLOW COLLIER }Arrh –
PUGNACIOUS COLLIER }(laughs)

MUSGRAVE. Now I'm in Mrs. Hitchcock's bar tonight until such time as she closes it. There'll be my money on the counter, and if you want to find what I'm doing here you can come along and see. I speak fair; you take it fair. Right?

EARNEST COLLIER. No it's not right, Johnny Clever. These streets is our streets, so you learn a warning . . . Come on, leave 'em be, *we* know what they're after. Come on . . .

The COLLIERS *go, growling threateningly.*

ATTERCLIFFE. They hate us, Serjeant, don't they? Wouldn't you say that's good?

MUSGRAVE. Because of the bad coal-trade they hate us; the rest just follows. True, there's one man talks of shooting rebels down in streets, but the others only think of bayonets turned on pitmen, and that's no good. At the present, they believe we've come to kill them. Soon they'll find we haven't, so they'll stop hating. Maybe even some o' them'll come and sign on. You'll see: His Worship's sovereigns – they'll fall too damned heavy into these boys' pockets. But we'll watch and take count, till we know the depth of the corruption. 'Cos all that we know now is that we've had to leave behind us a colonial war that is a war of sin and unjust blood.

ATTERCLIFFE (*sharply*). All wars is sin, serjeant . . .

MUSGRAVE (*impatient*). I'm not discussing that. Single purpose at a single time: your generalities aren't material: this is particular – one night's work in the streets of one city, and it damned all four of us and the war it was part of. We're each one guilty of particular blood. We've come to this town to work that guilt back to where it began.

He turns to SPARKY.

Why to this town? Say it, say it!

SPARKY (*as with a conditioned reflex*). Billy. Billy's dead. He wor my mucker, back end of the rear rank. He wor killed dead. He came from this town.

MUSGRAVE (*relentless*). Go on.

SPARKY (*appealing*). Serjeant –

MUSGRAVE. Use your clear brain, man, and tell me what you're doing here! Go on.

SPARKY (*incoherent with recollecting what he wants to forget*). I'm doing here? I'm doing . . . Serjeant, you know it. 'Cos he died. That wor Billy. I got drunk. Four days and four nights. After work of one night. Absent. Not sober. Improperly dressed.

He tries to turn it into one of his jokes.

> Stick me in a cell, boys,
> Pull the prison bell
> Black Jack Musgrave
> To call the prison roll –

Sarnt, no offence – 'First ye'll serve your punishment' he says. 'Then I'll show you how,' he says, the Serjeant. I says, 'You'll show me what?' He says, 'I'll show you how your Billy can be paid for.' . . . I didn't want to pay for him – what had I to care for a colonial war? . . .

He meets MUSGRAVE'S *eye and takes a grip on his motives.*

But I *did* want to pay for him, didn't I? 'Cos that's why I'm here. 'You go down, I'll follow' . . . You, Serjeant, ent it?

> Black Jack Musgrave
> He always calls the roll.

He says:

> Go down to Billy's town
> Tell 'em how he died.

And that's what I'm doing here. The Serjeant pays the fare. Here I am, I'm paid for. Next turn's for Billy. Or all that's left of Billy. Who'll give me an offer for his bones? Sixpence for a bone, for a bone of my dead mucker ...

He again avoids emotion by turning on HURST, *jeeringly.*

You didn't even know him when he lived, you weren't in his squad, what do *you* care that he's dead? To you he's like God, ent that the truth, you don't care and you're not bothered!

HURST (*angrily*). Hold your noise, you dirty turd! Who are you telling?

SPARKY. You. Oh you, me boy, you. A man and a soldier –

He meets MUSGRAVE'S *eye again, and his voice trails away.*

– a man and a soldier ...

MUSGRAVE (*emphatically*). Aye. And *you're* a soldier. Don't forget that. You're my man and you'll here me. You're not on any drunk now. Now you've got discipline. You've got grief, but good order, and it's turned to the works of God!

SPARKY (*submissively*). Yes, Sarnt.

MUSGRAVE (*to* HURST). Turned to the works of God!

HURST (*submissively*). Yes, Sarnt.

MUSGRAVE (*in a more encouraging voice*). There was talk about danger. Well, I never heard of no danger yet that wasn't comparative. Compare it against your purposes. And compare it against my strategy. Remember: the roads are closed, the water's frozen, the telegraph wires are weighted down with snow, they haven't *built* the railway. We came here safe, and here we are, safe here. The winter's giving us one day, two days, three days even – that's clear safe for us to hold our time, take count of the corruption, then stand before this people with our white shining word, and let it dance! It's a hot coal, this town, despite that it's freezing – choose your minute and blow: and whoosh, she's flamed your roof off! They're trembling already into the strikers' riots. Well, their riots and our war are the same one corruption. This town is ours, it's ready for us: and its people, when they've heard us, and the Word of God, crying the murders that we've done – I'll tell you they'll turn to us, and they'll turn against that war!

ATTERCLIFFE (*gravely*). All wars, Serjeant Musgrave. They've got to turn against all wars. Colonial war, do we say, no war of honour? I'm a private soldier, I never had no honour, I went killing for the Queen, I did it for me wages, that wor my life. But I've got a new life. There was one night's work, and I said: no more killing.

HURST (*with excitement*). It's time we did our *own* killing.

ATTERCLIFFE. No, boy, it isn't.

HURST. Aye, and I mean it. We're all on the run, and we're all of us deserters. We're wild-wood mad and raging. We caught it overseas and now we've got to run around the English streets biting every leg to give it *them* – that can't be done without –

MUSGRAVE (*interrupting*). Listen to me!

HURST (*subsiding*). Serjeant.

MUSGRAVE (*with angry articulation*). We are here with a word. That's all. That's particular. Let the word dance. That's all that's material, this day and for the next. What happens afterwards, the Lord God will provide. I am with you, He said. Abide with Me in Power. A Pillar of Flame before the people. What we show here'll lead forward forever, against dishonour, and greed, and murder-for-greed! There is our duty, the new, deserter's duty: God's dance on this earth: and all that we are is His four strong legs to dance it . . . Very well. That'll do. It's dark. We'll go in. Now we'll be likely buying drinks around and so on, in the public tonight.

I don't want to see any o' you with more nor you can hold. When there's danger, there's temptation. So keep it gay, but that's all. Off you go now! Take 'em in.

ATTERCLIFFE (*as the senior*). All right then, smartly now, walking up the street. Remember, we're recruiting. I'll give you the time – left right left right.

They walk out briskly, leaving MUSGRAVE *alone. As they go, the* BARGEE *enters, and gives them a parody salute in passing.* MUSGRAVE *doesn't see him, walks downstage, crosses his hands on his chest and stands to pray. The* BARGEE *parodies his attitude behind his back.*

MUSGRAVE. God, my Lord God. Have You or have You not delivered this town into my hands? All my life a soldier I've made You prayers and made them straight, I've reared my one true axe against the timber and I've launched it true. My regiment was my duty, and I called Death honest, killing by the book – but it all got scrawled and mucked about and I could not think clear . . . Now I have my duties different. I'm in this town to change all soldiers' duties. My prayer is: keep my mind clear so I can weigh Judgement against the Mercy and Judgement against the Blood, and make this Dance as terrible as You have put it into my brain. The Word alone is terrible: the Deed must be worse. But I know it is Your Logic, and You will provide.

He pauses for a moment, then turns sharply on his heel and strides away after the soldiers. He still fails to see the BARGEE. *The latter has whipped off his hat at the conclusion of* MUS-GRAVE'S *prayer, and now he stands looking solemnly up to Heaven. He gives a sanctimonious smirk and breathes: 'Amen'.*

Act Two

SCENE ONE

The bar of the public house.

 A scene of noise and conviviality, crowded confusion. MRS. HITCHCOCK *is seated behind the bar, drinking tea with brandy in it.* ANNIE *is going backwards and forwards in the room carrying drinks and empties.* MUSGRAVE *is sitting with a tankard, calmly watching.* SPARKY *is wearing his drum and alternately beating it and drinking and singing. The* SLOW *and* PUGNACIOUS COLLIERS, *well-oiled, are drinking and dancing. The* BARGEE *is drinking and dancing and playing a mouth-organ and beating time to the singing.* ATTERCLIFFE *is drinking and dancing and pinning cockades to the hats of the* COLLIERS. *At intervals one of the dancers grabs hold of* ANNIE *and swirls her around, but she retains a contemptuous aloofness and carries on with her work. As the scene opens the men (save* MUSGRAVE*) are all joining in the chorus:*

CHORUS. Blow your morning bugles
    Blow your calls ey-ho
    Form platoon and dress the ranks
    And blow, boys blow!

 This chorus is sung (with progressively less correctness) by most of the men at the end of each verse of the song.

SPARKY (*singing*).

    When first I came to the barracks
    My heart it grieved full sore
    For leaving of my old true love
    That I would see no more.

chorus

SLOW COLLIER (*to* MUSGRAVE, *who is studying a notebook*).
  I'm not signing nowt. Provisional, I said, provisional.
MUSGRAVE. Aye, aye, provisional. No one makes it different.
SPARKY (*sings*).

> They made us drill and muster
> And stand our sentries round
> And I never thought I'd lay again
> A girl upon the ground.

chorus

PUGNACIOUS COLLIER (*to* ATTERCLIFFE). That's *my* point,
  my point, too . . . all right enlisting, aye . . . but I'm a
  married man –
SPARKY (*sings*).

> But soon we were paraded
> And marching to the war
> And in every town the girls lay down
> And cried out loud for more.

chorus

PUGNACIOUS COLLIER (*to* ATTERCLIFFE). I'm not so sure I
  like your looks, aye, *you*!
SPARKY. Me?
PUGNACIOUS COLLIER (*pointing to* ATTERCLIFFE). You!
SPARKY (*sings*).

> And when we'd lodge in billets
> We'd beer in every can
> And the landlord's wife and daughters learnt
> Just how to love a man.

chorus

PUGNACIOUS COLLIER (*going at* SPARKY). I'm a married
  man, bedamn, I've got a wife, I've got a wife, a wife . . .

SPARKY. No one's taking her from you.

PUGNACIOUS COLLIER. Not you?

SPARKY. No.

MUSGRAVE (*interrupting*). All right, steady, friend, *no one*.

SLOW COLLIER. *I'll* take her from you when you go to the war,
  I'll take her –

PUGNACIOUS COLLIER. You?

SLOW COLLIER. Me! Or no, no, no: I'll make do with our
  Annie!

He makes a drunken lurch at her which she more or less evades.

Come on then, mucker!

Foiled by ANNIE, *he seizes the* PUGNACIOUS COLLIER *and
they do a clog dance together while the* BARGEE *plays.
Chorus while they dance, and general cheer.*

BARGEE. Bring 'em in some more, Annie, it's all on the Queen
  tonight – how many have you listed, serjeant!

MUSGRAVE. I'm not listing no one tonight. (*He bangs with
  his tankard for silence*). Now then, boys, everybody –

BARGEE (*officiously*). Everybody listen!

A roll on the drum.

BARGEE. Listen!

MUSGRAVE (*expansively*). This is Her Majesty's hospitality –
  that's *all* that it is, boys, on a soldier's honour, so! Any man
  that drinks tonight –

BARGEE. Any man that drinks tonight –

MUSGRAVE. He drinks at the Queen's pleasure, and none of
  you need fear to find a shilling in your mug at end of it –
  that like o' lark's finished and gone with the old days – the
  Army only wants good men, that's free men, of your own
  true will for the Empire – so drink and welcome: and all
  men in this town –

BARGEE. All men in this town –

MUSGRAVE. When we hold our meeting and the drum beats and we bring out our colours, then you can make your return in the signing of your names – but only those men willing! That's all : drink and away!

A roll on the drum.

BARGEE. Drink and away, me boys, hurray!

PUGNACIOUS COLLIER. Serjeant, you're a bleeding lobster, but you're a man! Shake me by the hand!

The BARGEE gives a whoop and starts to dance, playing a mouth-organ. He stumbles, and everybody laughs.

ANNIE (*scornfully*). And what regiment's *that* one, serjeant? The Backwards-Mounted-Foot?

BARGEE. I'll tell you, me lovely, why not? The Queen's Own Randy Chancers : or the Royal Facing-Both-Ways – hey, me clever monkeys :

> Old Joe looks out for Joe
> Plots and plans and who lies low?
> But the Lord provides, says Crooked Old Joe.

MUSGRAVE (*looking sharply at him*). Eh?

The BARGEE shrugs and grins. MUSGRAVE dismisses the question.

BARGEE. Just a little joke . . . little joke : little dog, I'll be with you . . .

He whistles 'Michael Finnegan' and ducks out of the pub. Meanwhile SPARKY has taken off his drum and come downstage to intercept ANNIE. ATTERCLIFFE is drinking with the COLLIERS and one or other of these plays the drum at intervals. The going of the BARGEE has made the room somewhat quieter for a while.

SPARKY (*to ANNIE*). Little dog – bow-wow, *I'm* a little dog, any trick for a bit of biscuit, Annie, bit o' meat – look :

He takes a pack of cards out of his pocket and presents it.

Take one, go on, take one.

She obeys.

Well?

ANNIE. Queen o' Spades.

SPARKY (*laughing*). That's a hell of a card to take: I think there's treacle on it, sticks to all fingers out o' this pack, I call her Grandma, makes her gentle, y'see – hope she'll kiss me whiskers and leave it at that.

He has replaced the card and shuffles.

Now then, take first four cards on top. Tell me what they are.

ANNIE (*obeying*). Eight Nine Ten Jack, all spades.

SPARKY (*triumphantly*). Right, right, calls the roll straight up to the one you took, the Queen, and where's the one you took? On the bottom – take it!

ANNIE (*obeying*). It is the Queen and all!

SPARKY. 'Course it is: I *told* you. That's what I call life – it all turns up in the expected order, but not when you expect it. And that's what sets your two teeth laughing, click-clack, doesn't it, ha ha ha! Oh I'm a clever lad, you see, they call me Sparky, lots o' games, lots o' jokes . . .

ANNIE (*not impressed*). Lots of liquor too. Now get out of me road while I fetch some more – *I've* got *work*, you know.

SPARKY (*going after her and again intercepting her*). Hey, but lovey, listen: there was an Englishman, a Welshman and a bloody great Irish – all three of 'em on Defaulters, y'see, for drunk. Now the Orderly Sarnt, he says, 'One, Two, Three, all we want's a Scotchman.' And a voice in the guardroom-yard says: 'Hoots awa', man, I'm taking back the empties fairst.'

She avoids him and goes away to the bar, thus ruining the

climax of his tale. He tries to follow her up, but this time he is intercepted by MUSGRAVE. HURST *appears in the doorway.* ANNIE *looks up at him and follows him with her eyes for the rest of this dialogue.*

MUSGRAVE (*to* SPARKY). You've had enough.

SPARKY. I'm not drunk.

MUSGRAVE. No and you won't be neither. This is no time.

SPARKY (*pointing to* HURST). No – and *here* he comes, look at him.

MUSGRAVE (*striding angrily over to* HURST). Where have you been?

HURST (*surlily*). Down by the canal.

MUSGRAVE. Why?

HURST. All right, I'd got things on my mind. And I'll tell you this, Serjeant, it isn't enough.

MUSGRAVE. What isn't enough?

HURST. What you and that old cuckold are reckoning to do. It's all soft, it's all flat, it's all – God and the Word! Tchah! What good's a word, what good's a bloody word, they can *all* talk bloody words – it isn't enough: we've got to be strong!

MUSGRAVE. Leave it alone, boy. *I* hold the logic. *You* hold some beer and get on with your work.

MUSGRAVE *walks away from* HURST.

HURST (*shouts after him*). It isn't enough!

He turns to find ANNIE *standing at his elbow, looking into his face and handing him a tankard of beer. He takes it and drinks it rapidly, without looking at her.*

MRS. HITCHCOCK (*calling from the bar*). The Queen's in debt, Serjeant!

MUSGRAVE. Hello, ma'am?

MRS. HITCHCOCK. I said the Queen's in debt!

MUSGRAVE. Chalk it up Ma'am, and another round for us all.

MRS. HITCHCOCK. No more chalk.
MUSGRAVE. Easily found though.

He plunges his hand in his pocket and pulls out a quantity of money. He does a rapid count, whistles in consternation, and selects a few coins.

ATTERCLIFFE (*watching him*). Not so much of it left, is there?
MUSGRAVE. Easy, easy.

He goes over to the bar and pays. SPARKY *is now showing his card tricks to the* COLLIERS. ANNIE *plucks at the sleeve of the pensive* HURST.

ANNIE (*simply*). You're the best to look at of all the four, aren't you?
HURST. Eh? What's that?
ANNIE. Tell you again? Why? You know it, don't you?
HURST (*preoccupied*). I'd forgot it. I'd other matter beyond wondering what you'd think to our looks.

He studies her closer, and snaps out of his gloomy mood into an attitude of lady-killing arrogance.

Why, I don't need to think o' women. I let them think of *me*. I've knocked greasier ones than you between me porridge and me bacon. Don't flatter yourself.
ANNIE. I'm not, soldier: I'm flattering you. I'll come to you tonight.
HURST (*pleased, though trying not to show it*). Will you? That's a good choice, you've got sense.
ANNIE (*meaningly*). But you forget them other matters, eh?
HURST (*decidedly warming to her*). I'll try . . . I'd rather. I hope I can . . . Stand straight: let's see . . . Gay and greasy, like I like 'em! You're big, and you're bonny. A good shape, I'd call it. And you've got good hair, but wants a comb in it. You ought to wash your face. And your neck smells of soot, don't it?

ANNIE (*accepting this in the spirit in which it's meant*). I've been blowing up the fire.

HURST (*boastfully*). Ah, the last I had was a major's daughter. I've got standards. Lovely.

ATTERCLIFFE *comes across to them.*

ATTERCLIFFE. You said he was the best looker. I heard you. But it's not true.

ANNIE. Then who is? You?

ATTERCLIFFE. I'll tell you a tale about that. That pitman over there – he said to me he thought I'd steal his wife. By God, I'd sooner steal his nightsoil . . . I've got a wife. Ask me to tell you one o' these days.– Sparky'd make a joke of it – wouldn't you, Sparky!

The last phrases are shouted across the room.

SPARKY (*shouts back*). Not any more – we're all going too fast.

He turns back to the COLLIERS

Down, down – any card, any card, mate – tell me its name – down.

PUGNACIOUS COLLIER. Six o' Hearts!

SPARKY. Right, right – *and* we shuffle and cut –

Enter the BARGEE.

BARGEE (*shouts*). Time, gennelmen please, everybody time, last orders everybody!

MRS. HITCHCOCK (*angrily*). Who's given *you* leave to do the calling here!

BARGEE (*singing*).

> Blow your morning bugles
> Blow your calls ey-ho –

If it's not me and it's not you, there'll be somebody else – *look!*

Enter CONSTABLE.

CONSTABLE. All right, Mrs. Hitchcock, it's time you closed your bar.

MRS. HITCHCOCK. What are you talking about!

CONSTABLE. Magistrates' orders, missus. All public houses to close at nine o'clock sharp, pending settlement of colliery dispute.

MRS. HITCHCOCK. It's the first I've heard of it.

SLOW COLLIER (*to the* CONSTABLE). Get out of it.

PUGNACIOUS COLLIER (*ditto*). Go home, you closhy blue-bottle, and sweep your bloody chimney.

CONSTABLE. That'll do there.

MUSGRAVE. That'll do, lads, keep it easy.

PUGNACIOUS COLLIER (*to* MUSGRAVE). We're not in the Army yet, y'know!

ATTERCLIFFE. Steady, matey, steady. All friends, y'know: married men together.

PUGNACIOUS COLLIER. But, Serjeant, you're a man, and I'll *shake* you by the hand.

CONSTABLE (*now things seem quiet again.*). Magistrates issued the order only this evening, missus. I've let you stay open a lot longer than the others – it's nigh on a quarter to ten already – and I'm in my rights to allow an exception for this house, on account of the Army. Question of facilities. I trust you've made good use of the extra time, Sarnt Musgrave?

MUSGRAVE. H'm.

PUGNACIOUS COLLIER (*with great friendliness*). Have the last drink on me, bluebottle!

CONSTABLE (*curtly*). The last drink's been had already. Close your bar, please, missus.

PUGNACIOUS COLLIER (*an angry idea occurring to him*). Wait a minute . . . Suppose I join your Army. Suppose I bloody 'list. What does my wife do?

BARGEE. Cock-a-doodle-do!

PUGNACIOUS COLLIER (*finding his own answer*). She goes to bed with the Peeler! I'll break his wooden head off.

He goes for the CONSTABLE *with a tankard, the* CONSTABLE *staggers backwards and falls, the* COLLIER *raises his tankard to smash it into his face.* ATTERCLIFFE *and* MUSGRAVE, *being nearest, jump to prevent him.*

ATTERCLIFFE (*pulling the* COLLIER *fiercely back*). Hey, ey, ey, ey-ey, hold it there, boy, hold it there! My God, you might ha' killed him. No . . .

ATTERCLIFFE *is trembling all over.*

SLOW COLLIER. Why shouldn't he if he wants to?

ATTERCLIFFE (*with great passion*). We've had enough o' that already – no more, no more, no more of it.

MUSGRAVE (*holding* ATTERCLIFFE *to quiet him*). Stop it there!

CONSTABLE (*getting up slowly*). Stand back, stand back. By God, it's *time* this place was closed. Turn out into the street, go on with you, get home. D'ye want me to whistle up me specials? Go on.

He hurls the COLLIERS *and* BARGEE *out of the pub.*

ATTERCLIFFE. He was going to, Serjeant. He would have, he'd have killed him. It's always here. Kill him. Kill.

MUSGRAVE (*roughly*). That'll do . . . We've all had enough, Mr. Constable. I'll get this lot to bed.

CONSTABLE. All right then. And try and keep folk quiet. I know you've got to buy 'em drink and that – but . . . *you* know – easy?

MUSGRAVE. Aye aye, easy. We know the trends. Don't you worry : *we* stand for law-and-order too, don't we?

CONSTABLE. Well, I hope so –

He goes to the door and calls into the street.

I said home, no loitering, go on, go on, or I'll run you in!

He comes back to MUSGRAVE *in a confidential conspiratorial sort of way.*

It's a sort of curfew, you see. I told His Worship: 'If there's trouble at night, you can't hold *me* responsible. I've done my best,' I said – I told him frank . . . Oh, and while we're on about His Worship, Serjeant, I might as well take occasion to discuss some names with you. There's a few like I could tell you as'd look very convenient on a regimental muster.

MUSGRAVE (*coldly*). I'm here for volunteers only, you know.

CONSTABLE (*insinuatingly*). Ah well, what's a volunteer? You, you, and you – the old Army custom – eh, Serjeant? Mrs. Hitchcock! A couple o' pints o' taddy for me and the Serjeant.

MRS. HITCHCOCK. We're closed.

CONSTABLE (*broad-mindedly*). That's all right, missus. Serve to the Serjeant: hotel-resident. All above the board.

MRS. HITCHCOCK (*to* ANNIE). So take 'em their drinks. Queen as pays.

She pours herself out another cup of tea. ANNIE *prepares the drinks and brings them to* MUSGRAVE *and the* CONSTABLE, *who gets into a huddle over a list the latter produces.*

SPARKY (*to the other two* SOLDIERS). Very commodious Queen. I say, a very commodious Queen, ha ha, if she'd drank all she paid for tonight, heh, Sponge By Appointment, they could swab out the Windsor Castle Guardhouse, ha ha, who'd be a Coldstream! I say, they could swab out –

ATTERCLIFFE. Oh shut up, man, for God's sake. We've had all we can take of your stinking patter.

SPARKY (*aggrieved*). Ey-ey, matey – ey-ey.

He withdraws, hurt.

HURST (*to* ATTERCLIFFE). Shut up yourself – what's got into you?

ATTERCLIFFE. Why, *you* were making enough carry-on earlier, weren't you? Are you so daft or so drunk you didn't see what just happened?

HURST. There was nowt happened. Couple o' pitmen three parts pissed? What's the matter wi' that? You were near as bad yourself – don't tell *me*. *You* were on about your *wife!*

ATTERCLIFFE. There was all but a man killed. We've come to stop it, not to start it – go on, sing to us.

He sings, with savage emphasis.

> Who'll give a penny to the poor blind man
> Holds out his hand with an old tin can.

– 'Cos that's all you are and it curdles up my bowels. I'm going to the coach-house.

HURST. The coach-house! What for?

ATTERCLIFFE. Where there's a man to talk to who don't talk like a fool.

He goes out of the door behind the bar.

SPARKY. Here, what d'you think to *him*? What sort o' talk does he reckon he'll get.

HURST. Keep your mind off that!

SPARKY (*wildly*). Rattling, clattering, old bones in a box? Billy used to sing, d'you think he'll have a sing-song?

HURST. I don't understand you. This don't make *me* laugh. It fair makes me sick.

SPARKY (*jeeringly*). Sick and bloody scared. Hey-ey, that's you, that's you truly.

HURST. Well, I've got things on my mind. If you can call it scared –

SPARKY. You and me, we're a pair, boy.

HURST (*savagely*). All right. But you'll learn. All *right*.

He turns abruptly away, and broods.

SPARKY (*beckoning* ANNIE, *who comes unenthusiastically*). I say, Annie – oh I'll tell you what, Annie, I don't know what I'm doing here.

She looks at him questioningly; he waves the point aside.

Aha, for that . . . Look, we've made us our beds up in the stables – ha, loose-box for every man, but the serjeant in the house.

ANNIE. Aye, I know.

SPARKY. We call it the Discipline, y'see. Yes-sarnt-no-sarnt, three-bags-full-sarnt – that's our merry lives. Ha ha. Third box from the end tonight, the fastest racehorse of 'em all. Oaks, Derby, I carry 'em away, boy: but I'm best at a steeple-chase – *hup* and *hover*, hedge and ditch, dear, and not by soldiers' numbers neither . . . Come for a gallop.

It is clear from the tone of the last phrase he is not joking.

ANNIE (*unemotionally*). Not tonight.

SPARKY. Oh . . . Go on, tonight.

ANNIE (*with something of a sneer*). Maybe next I will. I can't tell from day to day.

SPARKY. No more can I. You know, you've not yet give me one little laugh . . . But I'll contrive it: now y'see, there was a butcher, a baker, and a cats'-meat-man, all on the edge of the river. And down this river comes this dead dog, floating.

HURST (*whose head has dropped, suddenly jerks himself up again*). God, I was near asleep! I started a bad dream and it woke me.

MUSGRAVE (*to the* CONSTABLE). No, mister, it won't wash. We can't play pressgangs these days. If a man gets drunk and then signs, all right: but otherwise –

CONSTABLE (*vexed*). You're not over-co-operative, are you?

MUSGRAVE. I'm sorry. Oh, I'll see what I can do: but I won't promise more. Besides, agitators is agitators, in or out the Army. I'm not sure we want 'em. But I'll think. Good night.

He goes with the CONSTABLE *to the street door.*

CONSTABLE. Good night. Good night, missus.

Exit the CONSTABLE. MUSGRAVE *comes down to the* SOLDIERS.

MUSGRAVE (*calling* ANNIE). Lassie.

ANNIE. Hello.

MUSGRAVE. These are my men. They're here with their work to do. You will not distract them.

ANNIE. I won't?

MUSGRAVE. No. Because *they* know, whether you know it or not, that there's work is for women and there's work is for men : and let the two get mixed, you've anarchy.

ANNIE (*rather taken aback*). Oh? And what's anarchy? You, you clever grinder – words and three stripes –

MUSGRAVE. Look, lassie, anarchy : now, we're soldiers. Our work isn't easy, no and it's not soft : it's got a strong name – duty. And it's drawn out straight and black for us, a clear plan. But if you come to us with what you call your life or love – *I'd* call it your indulgence – and you scribble all over that plan, you make it crooked, dirty, idle, untidy, *bad* – there's anarchy. I'm a religious man. I know words, and I know deeds, and I know how to be strong. So do these men. You will not stand between them and their strength! Go on now : take yourself off.

ANNIE. A little bit of wind and a little bit of water –

MRS. HITCHCOCK. Annie –

ANNIE. But it drowned three score of sailors, and the King of Norway's daughter. (*She smiles for the first time in the play.*)

She sings:

> O mother O mother
> It hurts me so sore
> Sing dody-eye-dodo
> Then ye daft little bitch

> Ye should do it no more
> For you've never left off
> Since we sailed from the shore.

MRS. HITCHCOCK (*sharply*). Annie, get to bed.

MUSGRAVE (*to the* SOLDIERS). You two, get to bed. And pay heed to what I say.

ANNIE *goes out behind the bar, with a satirical curtsy.* MUSGRAVE *goes out by the street door.* HURST *makes a move as though to speak to him, but is too late. He stands reflective.*

SPARKY.

> To bed to bed says Sleepy-head
> Tarry a while says Slow
> Open the book, says the wise old Rook
> We'll have prayers before we go.

He sways a little tipsily, and laughs.

SCENE TWO

A street. Night.

The PUGNACIOUS *and* SLOW COLLIERS *enter, drunk and marching, the* BARGEE *drilling them. (This is a kind of 'Fred Karno' sequence which must be kept completely under control. At each command each of the three carries out, smartly, a drill-movement; but each drill movement is different for each man, and none of them performs the movement shouted. They must not be so drunk that they cannot appear erect and alertly jerking. The effect should be, not so much of three incompetents pretending to be soldiers, but of three trained soldiers gone mad.) The* COLLIERS *carry pickhefts as rifles, and the* BARGEE *an oar.*

MUSGRAVE *enters, and stands quietly watching.*

BARGEE. Right turn. Forward march. Left right left right left right left.

PUGNACIOUS COLLIER. To the front present. Halt.

BARGEE. About turn.

SLOW COLLIER. One two three four.

BARGEE. Order arms.

PUGNACIOUS COLLIER. Present and correct. By the right, number.

SLOW COLLIER. One two three four.

They are now at attention, together.

PUGNACIOUS COLLIER. Present and correct.

BARGEE (*this order is properly obeyed*). Stand-at-ease. Easy . . .

PUGNACIOUS COLLIER (*breaking the spell*). I'll tell you what, we're bloody good.

BARGEE (*with enthusiasm*). Eh. Lordy, mucker – good! By, I've never seen the like – y'know, if you signed on they'd excuse you three weeks' drill on the spot. You make that serjeant look like Old-Mother-Bunch-in-the-Popshop, alongside o' you – love you, mucker, you're *born* to it!

PUGNACIOUS COLLIER. Well, why didn't I think on it afore?

SLOW COLLIER (*still on parade*). One two three four.

PUGNACIOUS COLLIER. I'd not ha' got wed if I'd known!

SLOW COLLIER (*suddenly coming to attention and starting off*). Quick march. One two three –

He bumps against WALSH, *who has just entered.*

Arh and be damned.

WALSH. Where the hell are you going to?

MUSGRAVE *starts to go out. He passes* WALSH, *who stops him with a hand on his chest.*

WALSH. So we was mistook, eh? You're not here for no riots after all, but catching up men: that's it, in'it? Guineas?

MUSGRAVE. Sovereigns.

PUGNACIOUS COLLIER (*suddenly indicating* MUSGRAVE *to* WALSH). Here. This one: three stripes, but he's a man.

WALSH. Aye? And what are you? Drunk on *his* money: marching and drilling like a pack o' nit-headed kids at a barrack-gate!

PUGNACIOUS COLLIER. Better nor bloody starve for no coal-owners, any road!

WALSH (*with passion*). I'll tell you, I'm that ashamed, I could spew.

MUSGRAVE (*gripping* WALSH *by the lapel and drawing him away*). Now listen here. I can see you, and see *you* what you are. I wasn't given these – (*he touches his stripes*) – for not knowing men from ninepins. Now I'm telling you one word and I'm telling you two, and that's all. (*He lowers his voice.*) You and me is brothers –

WALSH (*in high irony*). Eh begod! A Radical Socialist! Careful, soldier, careful. D'ye want to be hanged?

MUSGRAVE (*very seriously*). No jokes. I mean this. I mean it. Brothers in God –

WALSH (*even more scornful*). Oh, hoho, *that* –

MUSGRAVE. – And brothers in truth. So watch. And wait. I said, *wait*.

WALSH (*jeering*). Brothers in God.

> Gentle Jesus send us rest
> Surely the bosses knows what's best!

Get along with yer –

MUSGRAVE (*calmly*). Well: I said, wait. You'll see.

Exit MUSGRAVE.

SLOW COLLIER (*who has been marking time since his collision, now mutters*).

> One two three four
> Where's the man as lives next door?
> Five six seven eight
> Come on in, he's working late.

WALSH (*looking at him in disgust*). Holy God, I'd never ha' dreamt it.

SLOW COLLIER (*his muttering rising in volume*).

> Nine ten eleven twelve
> Take his place and help yourself,
> Thirteen fourteen fifteen sixteen –

PUGNACIOUS COLLIER (*with a stupid laugh*). He's talking about my wife.

SLOW COLLIER (*annoyed at being interrupted*).

> Thirteen fourteen fifteen sixteen
> Into the bed and there we'll fix him!

PUGNACIOUS COLLIER (*in rising rage*). I couldn't do it to the soldiers, I couldn't do it to the Peeler, but by, I'll do it to you! I'll break your bloody head.

He goes for SLOW COLLIER, *who hits him in the belly, lets off a yell and runs out.* PUGNACIOUS COLLIER *follows with a roar.*

BARGEE (*calling after them in glee*). Watch out for the Constable! Heh heh heh.

WALSH. Holy God! My mates! My brothers!

BARGEE (*kindly*). Ah well, they're drunk.

WALSH. I know they're drunk, and I know who's helped 'em to it.

BARGEE. I could help *you* to summat, and all.

WALSH. What's that?

BARGEE. They won't stay drunk all week. Oh the soldiers gives 'em sport, they *need* a bit o' sport, cold, hungry . . . When you want 'em, they'll be there. Crooked Joe, he's *here*.

WALSH. Aye?

BARGEE. Could you shoot a Gatling gun?

WALSH (*looking at him sideways*). I don't know.

BARGEE. If you really want a riot, why don't you go at it

proper? Come on, I'll tell you . . . (*He hops out, whistling 'Michael Finnegan' and looking back invitingly.*)

WALSH (*considering*). Aye, aye? Crooked clever keelman, eh? . . . Well – all right – then *tell* me!

He hurries after him.

SCENE THREE

Interior of the pub (stable and bedroom).

Night. The stage is divided into two distinct acting-areas. The downstage area represents the stable, and is supposed to be divided into three loose boxes. If it is not practicable for the partitions between these to be built, it should be sufficient to suggest them by the three mattresses which are laid parallel, feet to the audience. The actors must not appear to be able to see each other from box to box. The forestage represents the central passage of the stable and is the only access to the boxes. Entry to the forestage can be from both wings (one side leads to the house, the other to the yard and coach-house).

The upstage area, raised up at least a couple of feet, represents a bedroom in the house. It is only large enough to contain a brass-knobbed bedstead with a small table or other support for a candle. The two areas must be treated as completely separate. Access to the bedroom area should be from the rear, and the audience must not be allowed to think that the actors can see from one area to the other (except as regards the light in the window, which is supposed to be seen as if from across the yard).

MUSGRAVE, *in shirt and trousers, is sitting on the bed, reading by candlelight. His tunic etc. lies folded beside the bed.*

HURST *and* SPARKY *come into the stable from the house carrying palliasses and blankets. They proceed to make up their beds (in the two end boxes, leaving the middle one empty. SPARKY is at the house end,* HURST *next to the yard). They also undress to their shirts (of grey flannel) and their (long woollen) underpants and socks. Their clothes are laid out neatly beside the beds.*

SPARKY (*as he prepares for bed*). I say . . . I say, can you hear me?

HURST (*uninterested*). I can.

SPARKY. You know, I'll tell you: I'm a bit pissed tonight.

HURST. Uh. What of it?

SPARKY. What's that?

HURST. I said what of it? We all are, aren't we? *I* want an hour or two's sleep, I don't know about *you*, so let's have less o' your gab.

SPARKY. I say, there's a light on still in Black Jack's window.

HURST grunts.

MUSGRAVE *has now lain down on top of his blanket, but has not taken off his trousers, or put out his candle.*

SPARKY. Aye, aye. God's awake. Ha, Ha! Not only God neither. Y'know, I think there might be some of us mortal, even yet . . . I said God's awake!

HURST. I *heard* you, and be damned.

A pause.

SPARKY. Hour or two's sleep . . . What do you want to *sleep* for, and a fine fat tart all promised and ready!

HURST (*who has got undressed and under his blanket*). That'll do. Now shut your row, can't ye, when you're asked! I said I wanted to sleep, so let me.

SPARKY. Why, it's you she's promised, y'see – *you*, not me – wake up, mucker, wake up. She'll soon be here, y'see. She'll soon be here! (*He blows 'reveille' with his lips, then gets under his blanket.*) You, boy, *you*, not me! . . . Shall I sing you a song?

HURST (*almost asleep, and woken again*). Eh, what? Are you going to shut up, or aren't you!

SPARKY. Well, are *you* going to shut up or aren't you, when she comes? It's all right the best-looker loving the girl, but his two mates along the row wi' nowt but a bit o' wainscot atween – hey-ey-ey, it'll be agony for *us* tonight, y'know – so keep it quiet.

A pause.

(*He starts to sing, softly*).

> She came to me at midnight
> With the moonshine on her arms
> And I told her not to make no noise
> Nor cause no wild alarms.
> But her savage husband he awoke
> And up the stairs did climb
> To catch her in her very deed:
> So fell my fatal crime . . .

While he is singing, ANNIE *enters from the house, carrying a candle. She goes gently to* HURST'S *box and stands looking down at him. When she speaks, he sticks his head out of the bedclothes and looks at her.*
In the bedroom, MUSGRAVE *sits up, blows out his light, and goes to sleep.*

ANNIE (*with tender humour*). Here I come. Hello. I'm cold. I'm a blue ghost come to haunt you. Brr. Come on, boy, warm me up. You'll not catch cold off *me*.
HURST (*getting up*). No . . . I daresay not . . .

They put their arms round each other.

But what about the morning?
ANNIE. Ah, the morning's different, ent it? I'll not say nowt about mornings, 'cos then we'll *all* be cold. Cold and alone. Like, stand in a crowd but every one alone. One thousand men makes a regiment, you'd say?
HURST. Near enough.

ANNIE. But for all that, when you're with them, you're still alone. Ent that right? So huggle me into the warm, boy, now. Keep out the wind. It's late. Dark.

HURST (*suddenly breaking away from her*). No, I won't. I don't care what I said afore, it's all done, ended, capped – get away. Go on. Leave me be.

ANNIE (*astonished and hurt*). What is it? What's the matter? Lovey –

HURST (*with violence*). Go on. As far as *my* mind goes, it's morning already. Every one alone – that's all. You want me to lose my life inside of you –

ANNIE. No. No. But just for five hours, boy, six –

HURST. You heard Black Jack say what's right. Straight, clear, dark strokes, no scrawling, I was wrong afore, I didn't trust him. He talked about God, so I thought he wor just nowt. But what he said about *you*: there, that was truth. He's going to be *strong!*

ANNIE (*scornfully*). So *you* take note of Black Jack, do you?

HURST. Aye, and I do. It's too late tonight for anything else. He's got to be trusted, got to be strong, we've got no alternative!

ANNIE (*standing a little away from him*). My Christ then, they *have* found him a brother! It was only this evening, warn't it, *I* saw you, down by the canal, all alone and wretched –

She sings with fierce emphasis:

All round his hat he wore the green willow – !

HURST. All right.

ANNIE (*not letting him off*). But it can't have been you, can it? 'Cos now you're just the same as the rest of 'em – the Hungry Army! You eat and you drink and you go. Though *you* won't even eat when it's offered, will you? So *sprawl* yourself on the straw without me, get up to your work tomorrow, drum 'em in and write 'em down, infect 'em all and bury 'em! I don't care.

HURST. What are you on about, what's the matter, why don't you go when you're told? Godsake, Godsake, leave a man to his sleep!

ANNIE. You know what they call me?

HURST. I'd call you a bloody whoor –

ANNIE (*savagely ironical*). Oh, not just a whoor – *I'm* a whoor-to-the-soldiers – it's a class by itself.

ATTERCLIFFE *has entered from the yard with his bedding. They do not notice him yet.* ANNIE *turns to pleading again.*

ANNIE. Christ, let me stay with you. He called me life and love, boy, just you think on *that* a little.

HURST *pushes her away with a cry. She falls against* ATTERCLIFFE.

ATTERCLIFFE (*holding her up*). Life and love, is it? I'm an old soldier, girly, a dirty old bastard, me, and *I've* seen it all. Here.

He grips her and kisses her violently all over face and neck. He sneers at HURST.

Hey-up there, son, get in your manger and sleep, and leave this to the men.

HURST. All right . . . and you're welcome.

He goes to his box and lies down again, huffily, trying to sleep.

ATTERCLIFFE (*still holding* ANNIE, *with a sort of tenderness*). Now then, what'll I do to you, eh? How d'you reckon you're going to quench *me*? Good strong girly with a heart like a horsecollar, open it up and let 'em all in. And it still wouldn't do no good.

ANNIE (*hard and hostile*). Wouldn't it? Try.

ATTERCLIFFE. Ah, no. Not tonight. What would *you* know of soldiers?

ANNIE. More'n you'd think I'd know, maybe.

ATTERCLIFFE. I doubt it. Our Black Jack'd say it's not material. He'd say there's blood on these two hands. (*He looks at his hands with distaste.*) You can wipe 'em as often as you want on a bit o' yellow hair, but it still comes blood the next time so why bother, *he'd* say. And *I'd* say it too. Here. (*He kisses her again and lets her go.*) There you are, girly: I've given you all you should get from a soldier. Say 'Thank you, boy', and that's that.

ANNIE (*still hard*). Thank you boy . . . You know it, don't you? All I should get. All I ever have got. Why should I want more? You stand up honest, you do, and it's a good thing too, 'cos you're old enough.

ATTERCLIFFE (*with a wry smile*). H'm. I am and all. Good night.

He starts making up his bed and undressing. SPARKY *has sat up and is listening. As* ANNIE *is standing still,* ATTERCLIFFE *starts talking to her again.*

ATTERCLIFFE. Girly. When I was a young lad I got married to a wife. And she slept with a greengrocer. He was the best looker (like *he's* the best looker) – (*he points towards* HURST'S *box*) – or any road that's what *she* said. *I* saw him four foot ten inch tall and he looked like a rat grinning through a brush; but he sold good green apples and he fed the people and he fed my wife. I didn't do neither. So now I'm a dirty old bastard in a red coat and blue breeches and that's all about it. Blood, y'see : killing. Good night.

He has now undressed and lies down to sleep immediately.
ANNIE *stands for a minute, then subsides to a crouching position, in tears.*
SPARKY *creeps out of his box.*

SPARKY. Tst tst tst, Annie. Stop crying : come here.
ANNIE. Don't talk to me, go to bed, I can't bear wi' no more of you.

SPARKY. Annie, Annie, look now, I want to talk. I'm not deaf, y'know, and I'm not that drunk, I mean I've been drunker, I mean I can stand, ha ha, one foot and all, I'm a stork, look at me – (*He tries to balance on one foot*). Him at the far end – don't you worry for *him*, Annie – why, he's not mortal any more, he's like God, ent he? And God – (*He looks towards* MUSGRAVE'S *light*) – hello, God's asleep.

ANNIE. God?

SPARKY. He's put his light out. Look,

ANNIE. That's where the serjeant is.

SPARKY. That's right. I never thought he'd sleep. *I* can't sleep . . . what have you got against me?

ANNIE (*surprised*). Nowt that I know.

SPARKY. But you didn't come to me, did you? I mean, you asked *him* and he said no, I asked *you* and you said no. That's all wrong. I mean, you know what the Black Musgrave'd call that, don't you – *he'd* say anarchy!

ANNIE. *He'd say?* He?

MUSGRAVE *groans in his bed.*

Every one of you swaggering lobsters, that serjeant squats in your gobs like an old wife stuck in a fireplace. What's the matter with you all!

SPARKY. Ssh ssh, keep it quiet. Come down here . . .

He leads her as far as possible from the other two.

Listen.

ANNIE. What for?

SPARKY. Snoring. Him? Him? Good, two snorings. They're asleep . . . I told you in the bar, y'know, they call me Sparky – name and nature – Sparky has his laugh. . . . A man can laugh, because or else he might well howl – and howling's not for men but for dogs, wolves, seagulls – like o' that, ent it?

ANNIE. You mean that you're frightened?

SPARKY (*with a sort of nervous self-realisation*). Aye, begod, d'you know: I am. God's not here, he's put his light out: so I can tell you, love: I *am*. Hey, not of the war, bullets in the far Empire, that's not the reason, don't think it. They even give me a medal, silver, to prove so. But I'll tell you, I'm – here, kiss me, will you, quickly, I oughtn't to be talking . . . I think I've gone daft.

ANNIE (*who is looking at him curiously but fascinated*). All right, I will . . .

She kisses him, and he holds her.

MUSGRAVE (*in clear categorical tones, though in his sleep*). Twenty-five men. Nine women. Twenty-five men. No children. No.

ANNIE (*in a sudden uprush*). Look, boy, there was a time *I* had a soldier, he made jokes, he sang songs and all – ah, *he* lived yes-sarnt no-sarnt three-bags-full-serjeant, but he called it one damned joke. God damn you, he was killed! Aye, and in your desert Empire – so what did *that* make?

SPARKY. I don't know . . .

ANNIE. It made a twisted little thing dead that nobody laughed at. A little withered clover – three in one it made. There was me, and there was him: and a baby in the ground. Bad shape. Dead.

She can say nothing more and he comforts her silently a moment.

SPARKY (*his mind working*). Why, Annie . . . Annie . . . you as well: another one not paid for . . . O, I wish *I* could pay. Say, suppose I paid for yours; why, maybe you could pay for mine.

ANNIE. I don't understand.

SPARKY (*following his thought in great disturbance of mind*). It *wouldn't* be anarchy, you know; he can't be right there! All it would be, is: *you* live and *I* live – we don't need his duty, we don't need his Word – a dead man's a dead man! We could call it *all* paid for! Your life and my life – make our *own* road, we don't follow nobody.

ANNIE. What are you talking about?

SPARKY (*relapsing into his despair again*). Oh God, I don't know. God's gone to sleep, but when he wakes up again –

ANNIE (*bewildered but compassionate*). Oh quiet, boy, be quiet, easy, easy.

She stoops over him, where he has crumpled into a corner, and they embrace again with passion.

MUSGRAVE (*now shouting in his sleep*). Fire, fire! Fire, fire, London's burning, London's burning!

MRS. HITCHCOCK, in a nightdress and robe, and carrying a tumbler, hurries into his bedroom.

MRS. HITCHCOCK. What's the matter?

She lights his candle.

MUSGRAVE (*sitting up and talking very clearly as if it made sense*). Burning. Burning. One minute from now, and you carry out your orders – get *that* one! *Get* her! Who says she's a child! We've got her in the book, she's old enough to kill! You will carry out your orders. Thirty seconds. Count the time. (*He is looking at his watch.*) Twenty-six . . . twenty-three . . .

MRS. HITCHCOCK (*very alarmed*). Serjeant – Serjeant –

MUSGRAVE. Be quiet. Twenty . . . Eighteen . . . I'm on duty, woman. I'm timing the end of the world. Ten more seconds, sir . . . Five . . . three . . . two . . . one.

He lets out a great cry of agony and falls back on the bed. All in the stable hear and take notice. ATTERCLIFFE turns over again to sleep. HURST sits up in alarm. ANNIE and SPARKY stand apart from each other in surprise.

ANNIE. Sparky, it's your God. He's hurt.

SPARKY *sits staring and gasping, till* ANNIE *pulls him to her again.*

MRS. HITCHCOCK. What are you playing at – you'll wake up the town!

MUSGRAVE *shivers and moans.*

MRS. HITCHCOCK (*shaking him gently*). Come on – it's a nightmare. Wake up and let's get rid of it. Come on, come on.

MUSGRAVE. Leave me alone. I wasn't asleep.

MRS. HITCHCOCK. You warn't awake, any road.

MUSGRAVE. Mind your own business.

MRS. HITCHCOCK. I thought you might be poorly.

MUSGRAVE. No . . . No . . . (*Suddenly*) But it *will* come, won't it?

MRS. HITCHCOCK. What will?

MUSGRAVE. The end of the world? You'll tell me it's not material, but if you could come to it, in control; I mean, numbers and order, like so many ranks this side, so many that, properly dressed, steadiness on parade, so that whether you knew you was right, or you knew you was wrong – you'd know it, and you'd stand. (*He shivers.*) Get me summat to eat.

MRS. HITCHCOCK. I got you a hot grog. Here. (*She gives him a tumbler.*)

MUSGRAVE. What – what . . . ?

MRS. HITCHCOCK. I take it at nights for me bad back. I heard you calling so I brought it in. Have a biscuit.

She gives him a biscuit from her dressing gown pocket.

MUSGRAVE. Aye, I will . . . (*He eats and drinks.*) That's better . . . You *do* understand me, don't you? Look, if you're the right-marker to the Company and you're marching to the right, you can't see the others, so you follow the orders you can hear and hope you hear them true. When I was a recruit

I found myself once half across the square alone – *they'd* marched the other way and I'd never heard the word!

MRS. HITCHCOCK. You ought to lie down. You *are* poorly, I can tell. Easy, Serjeant, easy.

MUSGRAVE (*relaxing again*). Easy . . . easy . . .

She draws the blanket over him and sits soothing him to sleep.

SPARKY (*with a sudden access of resolution*). Annie, I don't care. Let him wake when he wants to. All I'll do this time is to stand and *really* laugh. Listen to this one, because here's what I'll be laughing at. There was these four lads, y'see, and they made it out they'd have a strong night all night in the town, each boozer in turn, pay-day. And the first one in the first boozer, he says : 'Each man drinks my choice,' he says. 'One sup of arsenic to every man's glass' – and *that's* what they've to drink. Well, one of them, he drinks and he dies, next man drinks and *he* dies, what about the third? Has he to drink to that rule? 'Cos they'd *made* it a rule – each man to the first man's choice.

HURST *has left his box and crept up and is now listening to this.*

ANNIE. I don't know –

SPARKY. Neither do I. But I can tell you what *I'd* do.

ANNIE. What?

SPARKY (*with a switch to hard seriousness*). I'd get out of it, quick. Aye, and with you. Look, love, its snowing, we can't leave the town now. But you could bed me down somewheres, I mean, like, hide; bide *with* me while it's all over, and then get me some clothes and we'd go – I mean, like, go to London? What about London? You've never been to London?

ANNIE. Bide hid while *what's* all over? What's going to happen?

SPARKY. Eh, that's the question. I wish I could tell you. It's Black Jack's work, not mine.

ANNIE. Bad work, likely?

SPARKY. Likely . . . I don't know. D'you know, I never *asked!* You see, he's like God, and it's as if *we* were like angels – *angels*, ha, ha! But that's no joke no more for me. This is funnier nor *I* can laugh at, Annie, and if I bide longer here, I'm *really* wild-wood mad. So get me out of it, quick!

ANNIE (*decisively*). I will. I'm frightened. Pull your clothes on, Sparky. I'll hide you.

SPARKY. Good love, good –

ANNIE. But you'll not leave me behind?

He has started dressing, very confusedly, putting his tunic on first.

SPARKY. No.

ANNIE. Swear it.

He has his trousers ready to step into. He lets them fall while he takes her for a moment in his arms:

SPARKY. Sworn.

HURST *nips in and seizes the trousers.*

(*Releasing* ANNIE) Now then, sharp. Hey, where's me trousers?

HURST. Here!

SPARKY. What's the goddamn – give 'em back, you dirty –

HURST (*triumphantly*). Come and get 'em, Sparky! Heh, you'll be the grand deserter, won't you, running bare-arsed over the moor in six-foot drifts of snow!

SPARKY. Give me them!

He grabs one end of the trousers and a farcical tug-o'-war begins.

HURST (*in high malice*). A man and a soldier! Jump, natter, twitch, like a clockwork puppet for three parts of the night, but the last night of all, you *run*! You little closhy coward.

ATTERCLIFFE *has woken and tries to intervene.*

ATTERCLIFFE. What the hell's the row – easy, easy, *hold* it!
SPARKY. He's got my bloody trousers!

He gives a great tug on the trousers and pulls them away,
HURST *falling down.*

HURST. I'm going to *do* you, Sparky.

His hand falls on SPARKY'S *belt, with bayonet scabbard
attached, which is lying on the floor. He gets up, drawing the
bayonet.*

ANNIE. No, no, stop him!
ATTERCLIFFE. Drop that bayonet!

ANNIE *mixes in, seizing* HURST'S *wrist and biting it. The
bayonet drops to the floor.* ATTERCLIFFE *snatches it and*
HURST *jumps upon him. Together they fall against* SPARKY
and all three crash to the floor. SPARKY *gives a terrifying,
choking cry.*
MUSGRAVE *leaps up in the bedroom. Those on the forestage
all draw back, appalled, from* SPARKY'S *dead body.*

MUSGRAVE (*to* MRS. HITCHCOCK). Stay where you are.

He leaves the bedroom.

HURST. He's dead. He's dead. *I* didn't do it. Not me. No.
ATTERCLIFFE. Dead?
HURST. Of course he's dead. He's stuck in the gut. That's you.
   Your hand. You killed him.
ATTERCLIFFE. I can't have.
HURST. You did.
ATTERCLIFFE (*stupidly*). I've got the bayonet.
HURST. Aye, and you've killed him.
ATTERCLIFFE. O Holy God!

MUSGRAVE *enters from the house.* MRS. HITCHCOCK *has left the bedroom.*

MUSGRAVE. What going on?

HURST. Sparky's been killed.

MUSGRAVE. *What!* How?

HURST. His own bayonet. He was deserting. I tried to stop him. Then *he* –

He points to ATTERCLIFFE.

MUSGRAVE (*to* ATTERCLIFFE). Well?

ATTERCLIFFE (*hopelessly*). Here's the bayonet. I got holding it, Serjeant. I did. It's always me. You can call it an accident. But *I* know what that means, it means that it –

MUSGRAVE. Shut up. You said deserting?

HURST *nods.*

What's *she* doing here? Was she with him?

HURST *nods.*

Aye, aye . . . Desertion. Fornication. It's not material. He's dead. Hide him away.

HURST. Where?

MUSGRAVE. In the midden at back of the yard. And don't show no lights while you're doing it. Hurry.

HURST (*to* ATTERCLIFFE). Come on.

ATTERCLIFFE. Holy God, Holy God!

They carry the body out.

MUSGRAVE (*to* ANNIE, *unpleasantly*). Oh, you can shake, you can quiver, you can open your mouth like a quicksand and all – blubbering and trouble – but *I've* got to think, and *I've* got to do.

MRS. HITCHCOCK *enters from the house. She is carrying* MUSGRAVE'S *tunic, hat, and boots, which she puts down.*

Missus, come here. There's things going wrong, but don't ask me what. Will you trust me?

She looks at him searchingly and gives a short nod.

Get hold of this lassie, take her upstairs, lock her in a cupboard, and keep quiet about it. I've got a right reason : you'll know it in good time. Do as I tell you and you won't take no harm.

MRS. HITCHCOCK. The end of the world, already.

MUSGRAVE. What's that? D'ye hear what I say?

MRS. HITCHCOCK. Oh aye, I heard you.

She takes the shuddering ANNIE *by the hand, and then looks sharply at her fingers.*

Hey-ey-ey, this here, it's blood.

MUSGRAVE. I know. I repeat it : don't ask me.

ANNIE *looks at* MUSGRAVE *and at* MRS. HITCHCOCK, *then licks her hand, laughing in a childish fashion.*

MRS. HITCHCOCK. Come away in, Annie . . . Aye, I'll go and lock her up . . . It might be the best thing. I've got to trust you, haven't I? I've always praised religion.

She takes ANNIE *away, into the house.* MUSGRAVE *sits down suddenly, with his head in his hands. The* BARGEE *creeps in from the yard and sits beside him, in a similar attitude.*

BARGEE (*singing softly*).

> Here we set like birds in the wilderness,
>   birds in the –

MUSGRAVE *sits up, looks at him, realises who it is, and grabs him by the throat.*

BARGEE (*struggling free*). It's all right, bully, it's only Old Joe.

MUSGRAVE (*relaxing, but still menacing*). Oh it is, is it? Well?

BARGEE (*significantly*). I was thinking, like, if I wor you, *I* wouldn't just set down in a stable, not now I wouldn't, no.

MUSGRAVE. Why not?

BARGEE. *I* see your jolly muckers, over there, mucking in the muck-pile, eh? But if they turned theirselves around and looked at the coach-house –

MUSGRAVE leaps up in alarm.

MUSGRAVE. What about the coach-house?

BARGEE. There's bars at its windows : and there's a crowbar at the bars – listen!

A crash of glass offstage from the yard.

That's the glass gone now! If you're quick, you can catch 'em!

MUSGRAVE has run to the yard side of the stage.

MUSGRAVE (*calling to offstage*). Get to the coach-house, get round the back! Quick! Quick!

He runs off in great excitement.
More crashes of glass, shouting and banging.
The BARGEE watches what is happening in the yard, leaping up and down in high delight.

BARGEE. Go on, catch 'em, two to the back and the serjeant to the door, open the padlock, swing back the wicket – one little laddie, he's trapped in the window – head in, feet out – pull him down, Serjeant, pull him down, soldiers – boot up, fist down, tie him in a bundle – oh me pretty roses, oh me blood-red flowers o' beauty!

The two SOLDIERS hurry back, with WALSH frogmarched between them, his hands bunched up and tied behind his back. MUSGRAVE follows. All are panting. They throw WALSH down.

MUSGRAVE. What about the others?

HURST. Run away, Serjeant.

ATTERCLIFFE. Nigh on a dozen of 'em.

HURST. Ran down the alley.

MUSGRAVE. Let's have a look at this one! Oho, so it's *you!* What were you after?

WALSH (*grinning*). What d'you think, lobster?

MUSGRAVE. Our little Gatling? Isn't that right?

WALSH. That's right, boy, you're sharp.

MUSGRAVE (*quieter*). But *you're* not sharp, brother, and I'm going to tell you why.

Shouting and shrill whistles, off.

HURST. It's that Constable's out, and his Specials and all – listen! Hey, we'd better get dressed.

He starts huddling on his tunic and trousers.

MUSGRAVE (*to* WALSH). Chasing your friends. He'll be coming here, shortly.

Whistles again.

CONSTABLE (*offstage, in the house*). Open up, Mrs. Hitchcock, open up – name of the Law!

MUSGRAVE. Ah, here he is. Now he asked me this evening to kidnap you for the Army. But *I* told you we was brothers, didn't I? So watch while I prove it. (*To* HURST.) Take him out and hide him.

HURST (*taken aback*). Him in the midden too?

MUSGRAVE. Don't be a fool. Do as you're told.

WALSH. Wait – wait a minute.

MUSGRAVE (*furiously*). Go with him, you damned nignog. Would ye rather trust the Constable?

WALSH (*very puzzled*). What are you on, for God's sake?

MUSGRAVE. Don't waste time! (*He pushes* WALSH *and barks*

at HURST.) Get him in that woodshed. God, what a shower o' tortoises!

HURST *hustles* WALSH *out to the yard.* MUSGRAVE *turns on* ATTERCLIFFE.

You get your trousers on.

ATTERCLIFFE *obeys.* MRS. HITCHCOCK *comes in, very agitated.*

MRS. HITCHCOCK. The Constable's here, he's running through the house.
MUSGRAVE. Then send him to me! It's in control, in control, woman. I *know* all about it!

MRS. HITCHCOCK *goes back into the house.*

ATTERCLIFFE. Musgrave, what are you doing?
MUSGRAVE. I'm doing what comes next and that's all I've got time for.
ATTERCLIFFE (*in a gush of despair*). But he was killed, you see, killed. Musgrave, don't you see, that wipes the whole thing out, wiped out, washed out, finished.
MUSGRAVE. *No!*

MRS. HITCHCOCK *and the* CONSTABLE *hurry in from the house.*

CONSTABLE. Ah, Serjeant, what's happened? Saw a gang breaking in at the back of this coach-house. What's kept in the coach-house? (*To* MRS. HITCHCOCK.)
MRS. HITCHCOCK. The Serjeant's got his –
MUSGRAVE. I've got my gear.
MRS. HITCHCOCK. Hello, here's the Parson.

The PARSON *hurries in from the house.*

PARSON. Constable, what's going on?
CONSTABLE. I think it's beginning, sir. I think it's the riots.

PARSON. At this hour of the morning?

CONSTABLE. I've sent word to the Mayor.

He starts making a rapid report to the PARSON. *The* BARGEE *sidles up to* MUSGRAVE.

BARGEE. Don't forget Old Joe. I brought the warning. Let me in on a share of it, go on, there's a bully.

MUSGRAVE. Get out, or you'll get hurt!

The MAYOR *hurries in from the house.*

MAYOR. This is bad, it's bloody bad. How did it start? Never mind that now. What steps have you taken?

CONSTABLE. Me Deputy-Specials all around the streets, but I've not got enough of 'em and they're frightened – that's frank. I *warned* you, Your Worship.

MAYOR. Question is this: can you hold the town safe while twelve o'clock mid-day?

CONSTABLE. Nay I don't know.

MAYOR. The telegraph's working.

MUSGRAVE. The telegraph!

MAYOR. Aye, there's a thaw begun. Thank God for that: they've mended the broken wire on top of the moor. So I sent word for the Dragoons. They'll come as fast as they can, but not afore twelve I shouldn't think, so we've *got* to hold this town!

MUSGRAVE. Six hours, thereabouts. Keep 'em quiet now, they may bide. Mr. Mayor, I'll do it for you.

MAYOR. How?

MUSGRAVE. I'll do what I'm paid for : start a recruiting-meeting. Look, we had 'em last night as merry as Christmas in here, why not this morning? Flags, drums, shillings, sovereigns – hey, start the drum! Top o' the market-place, make a jolly speech to 'em!

MAYOR. Me?

HURST *begins beating the drum outside in the yard.*

MUSGRAVE. You! You, Parson, too. Mrs. Hitchcock, free beer to the crowd!

PARSON. No!

MAYOR (*catching the idea*). *Aye*, missus, bring it! *I'll* pay for it and all!

MUSGRAVE (*to the* BARGEE). *You*, if you want to help, you can carry a flag. (*To* ATTERCLIFFE.) Get him a flag!

Exit ATTERCLIFFE. *Enter* HURST, *drumming furiously.*

We'll *all* carry flags. Fetch me me tunic.

MRS. HITCHCOCK. Here it is, I brought it.

MUSGRAVE (*quite wild with excitement*). Flags, ribbons, bunches o' ribbons, glamourise 'em, glory!

ATTERCLIFFE *hurries in from the yard, with his arms full of colours. He hands these out all round.*

BARGEE. Rosebuds of Old England!

MAYOR. Loyal hearts and true!

PARSON. The Lord mighty in battle!

MUSGRAVE. GOD SAVE THE QUEEN!

General noise, bustle and confusion.

Act Three

SCENE ONE

The market-place.

Early morning. In the centre of the stage is a practicable feature – the centre-piece of the market-place. It is a sort of Victorian clock-tower-cum-lamppost-cum-market-cross, and stands on a raised plinth. There is a ladder leaning against it. On the plinth are the soldiers' boxes and a coil of rope. The front of the plinth is draped with bunting, and other colours are leaning against the centre-piece in an impressive disposition.

When the scene opens, the stage is filled with noise and movement HURST *is beating his drum, the* MAYOR, *the* PARSON *and* MUSGRAVE *are mounting the plinth, and* ATTERCLIFFE *is up already, making the last arrangements. The* CONSTABLE *takes up his stand beside the centre-piece, as does* HURST. *The* BARGEE *is hopping about on the forestage.*

The SOLDIERS *are all now properly dressed, the* MAYOR *has put on his cocked hat and red robe and chain, and the* PARSON *his gown and bands, and carries a Bible. They are all wearing bright cockades.*

The role of the BARGEE *in this scene is important. As there is no crowd, the speeches are delivered straight out to the audience, and the* BARGEE *acts as a kind of fugleman to create the crowd-reactions. Noises-off indicated in the dialogue are rather unrealistic – as it were, token-noises only.*

At one side of the stage there is an upper-storey window.

BARGEE (*casting his cap*).
>Hip hip hooroar
>Hark hark the drums do bark
>The Hungry Army's coming to town
>Lead 'em in with a Holy Book
>A golden chain and a scarlet gown.

Here they are on a winter's morning, you've got six kids at home crying out for bread, you've got a sour cold wife and no fire and no breakfast : and you're too damn miserable even to fight – if there's owt else at all to take your mind off it – so here you are, you lucky people, in your own old market-place, a real live lovely circus, with real live golden sovereigns in somebody's pocket and real live taddy ale to be doled out to the bunch of you!

MRS. HITCHCOCK *enters, trundling a beer-barrel.*

Oh, it's for free, you can be certain o' that, there's no strings to this packet – let's lend you a hand wi' that, missus!

He helps her roll the barrel to one side of the centre-piece, where she chocks it level and sits down on it. She also has a hand-basket full of tankards. The BARGEE *comes back downstage.*

There we are, then. And here *you* are, the streets is filling, roll up, roll up, and wallow in the lot! I'll tell you the word when to cheer.

The platform party is now all in place. The drum gives a final roll. The MAYOR *steps forward.*

CONSTABLE. Silence for the Mayor!
BARGEE. Long live His Worship, who gives us food and clothing and never spares to meet the people with a smile! Hooroar!

Three boos, off.

Boo, boo, boo? Don't be so previous, now; he'll surprise us

all yet, boys. Benevolence and responsibility. Silence for the Mayor!

MAYOR. All right. Now then. It's been a hard winter. I know there's a bit of a thaw this morning, but it's not over yet, there may be worse to come. Although you might not think it, I'm as keen and eager as any o' you to get the pits working again, so we can all settle down in peace to a good roast and baked 'taters and a good pudding and the rest of it. But I'm not here to talk strikes today.

A noise off.

BARGEE (*interpreting*). He says: 'Who says strikes, it's a bloody lockout.'

CONSTABLE. Silence for the Mayor!

BARGEE. Silence for His Worship!

MAYOR. I said I'm not up here to talk on that today. Serjeant Musgrave, on my right, has come to town to find men for the Queen. Now that's a good opportunity – it's a *grand* opportunity. It's up to you to take it. By God, if I was a young lad in a town without work, you'd not catch me thinking twice –

BARGEE. He says: 'There's only one man drives the work away in this town.'

The CONSTABLE *steps forward, but the* BARGEE *forestalls him.*

Silence for the Mayor!

MAYOR. All right. You think I'm playing it crooked all the time – *I* know.

A cheer off.

But listen to this: (*He holds up a jingling money-bag.*) Here's real gold. It rings true to me, it rings true to you, and there's one o' these for every lad as volunteers. That's straight. It's from the shoulder. It pulls no punches. Take

it or throw it away – I'm set up here and waiting. (Parson,
tell 'em *your* piece now.) And keep quiet while the Rector's
at you : he talks good sense and you need it. If you can't give
me credit, at least you can give *him* some, for considering
what's best for the community. Go on, Parson : tell 'em.

He retires and the PARSON *steps forward.*

PARSON. 'And Jesus said, I come not to bring peace but a
sword.' I know very well that the times are difficult. As your
minister of religion, and as a magistrate, it is my business to
be aware of these matters. But we must remember that this
town is only one very small locality in our great country.

BARGEE. Very true, very true.

Two cheers, off.

PARSON. And if our country is great, and I for one am sure
that it *is* great, it is great because of the greatness of its
responsibilities. They are world wide. They are noble. They
are the responsibilities of a first-class power.

BARGEE. Keep 'em there, Reverend! First-class for ever! Give
a cheer, you boys!

Three cheers, very perfunctory.

And the crowd roars! Every hat in the air, you've struck 'em
in the running nerve, hooroar!

PARSON. Therefore, I say, therefore : when called to shoulder
our country's burdens we should do it with a glancing eye
and a leaping heart, to draw the sword with gladness, thinking nothing of our petty differences and grievances – but all
united under one brave flag, going forth in Christian resolution, and showing a manly spirit! The Empire calls! Greatness is at hand! Serjeant Musgrave will take down the names
of any men willing, if you'll file on to the platform in an
orderly fashion, in the name of the Father, the Son and
mumble mumble mumble . . .

He retires. There is a pause.

MUSGRAVE. Perhaps, Mr. Mayor, before we start enrolling names, it might be as well if I was to say a few words first, like, outlining the type of service the lads is likely to find, overseas, and so forth?

The SLOW COLLIER *slouches in, and up to the base of the plinth.*

SLOW COLLIER. Have you got my name down?

MUSGRAVE. No. Not yet.

SLOW COLLIER. Are you sure of that ?

MUSGRAVE. Aye, I'm sure. D'you want me to take it?

SLOW COLLIER. Some of us was a bit full, like, last night in the boozer.

MUSGRAVE. A man's pleasuring, friend, that's all. No harm in that?

SLOW COLLIER (*thrusting forward his hat with the cockade in it*). Then what's this? Eh? Someone gave me this.

MUSGRAVE (*laughs*). Oh I'll tell you what that means : you drank along of me – that's all that it means – and you promised you'd come and hear me this morning. Well, here you are.

SLOW COLLIER. Ah. Provisional. Aye. I thought that's what it was. Provisional.

The PUGNACIOUS COLLIER *slouches in.*

PUGNACIOUS COLLIER. Provisional or not, we're not signing nowt without we've heard more. So go on then, soldier, tell us. Prove it's better to be shot nor starve, *we'll* listen to you, man, 'cos we're ready to believe. And more of us and all.

CRIES OFF. Aye. Aye. Aye. Tell us.

BARGEE. Go on, Serjeant, tell us. It's a long strong tale, quiet while he tells it – quiet!

MUSGRAVE. Now there's more tales than one about the Army,

and a lot of funny jokers to run around and spread 'em, too. Aye, aye, we've all heard of 'em, we know all about 'em, and it's not my job this morning to swear to you what's true and what's not true. O' *course* you'll find there's an RSM here or a Provost-sarnt there what makes you cut the grass wi' nail-scissors, or dust the parade-ground with a toothbrush. It's all the bull, it's all in the game – but it's not what sends me here and it's not what put *these* on my arm, and it's nowt at all to do with *my* life, or these two with me, or any o' yours. So easy, me boys, don't think it. (*To the* COLLIERS.) There was another lad wi' *you*, in and out last night. He ought to be here. (*To the* BARGEE.) Go and fetch him, will you? You know where he is.

BARGEE (*finger to nose*). Ah. Ha ha. Aye aye.

He slips out conspiratorily.

MUSGRAVE (*continues his speech*). I said, easy me boys, and don't think it. Because there's *work* in the Army, and bull's not right work, you can believe me on that – it's just foolery – any smart squaddy can carry it away like a tuppenny-ha'penny jam jar. So I'll tell you what the *work* is – open it up!

ATTERCLIFFE *flings open one of the boxes. It is packed with rifles. He takes one out and tosses it to* MUSGRAVE.

MUSGRAVE. Now this is the rifle. This is what we term the butt of the rifle. This is the barrel. This here's the magazine. And this – (*he indicates the trigger*) – you should know what *this is*, you should know what it does . . . Well, the rifle's a good weapon, it's new, quick, accurate. This is the bayonet – (*he fixes his bayonet*) – it kills men smart, it's good and it's beautiful. But I've more to show than a rifle. Open it up!

ATTERCLIFFE *opens a second case. It contains a Gatling gun and tripod mounting.*

This is the newest, this is the smartest, call it the most beautiful. It's a Gatling gun, this. Watch how it works!

ATTERCLIFFE secures the gun to its mounting.

ATTERCLIFFE. The rounds are fed to the chambers, which are arranged in a radial fashion, by means of a hopper-shaped aperture, *here*. Now pay attention while I go through the preliminary process of loading.

He goes through the preliminary process of loading.

MUSGRAVE (*his urgency increasing all the time*). The point being that here we've got a gun that doesn't shoot like: *Bang*, rattle-click-up-the-spout-what're-we-waiting-for, *bang!* But: Bang-bang-bang-bang-bang-bang-bang-bang-*bang* – and there's not a man alive in the whole of this market-place. Modern times. Progress. Three hundred and fifty rounds in one minute – *flat!*

The BARGEE re-enters, soft-footed.

MUSGRAVE (*quickly to him*). Is he coming?

The BARGEE nods, finger to lips.

ATTERCLIFFE. Now then, you see, the gun's loaded.
MUSGRAVE. It didn't take long, you see.
ATTERCLIFFE. No.

HURST gives a roll on the drums.
ATTERCLIFFE swivels the gun to face out into the audience.
MUSGRAVE loads his rifle with a clip of cartridges.

MUSGRAVE (*his voice very taut and hard*). The question remains as to the *use* of these weapons! (*He pushes his rifle-bolt home.*) You'll ask me: what's their purpose? Seeing we've beat the Russians in the Crimea, there's no war with France (there *may* be, but there isn't yet), and Germany's our friend, who do we have to fight? *Well*, the Reverend answered *that* for you, in his good short words. Me and my three lads – two lads, I'd say rather – we belong to a regiment is a few thousand miles from here, in a little country without much importance except from the point of view that there's a Union Jack flies over it and the people of that country can write British Subject after their names. And that makes us proud!

ATTERCLIFFE. I tell you it makes us proud!

HURST. We live in tattered tents in the rain, we eat rotten food, there's knives in the dark streets and blood on the floors of the hospitals, but we stand tall and proud: because of why we are there.

ATTERCLIFFE. Because we're there to serve our duty.

MUSGRAVE. A soldier's duty is a soldier's life.

WALSH *enters at the extreme rear of the stage and walks slowly up behind the others and listens.*
A roll on the drum.

MUSGRAVE. A soldier's life is to lay it down, against the enemies of his Queen,

A roll on the drum.

against the invaders of his home,

A roll on the drum.

against slavery, cruelty, tyrants.

A roll on the drum.

HURST. You put on the uniform and you give your life away, and who do you give it to?

ATTERCLIFFE. You give it to your duty.

MUSGRAVE. And you give it to your people, for peace, and for honesty.

A roll on the drum.

MUSGRAVE. That's *my* book. (*He turns on the* MAYOR.) What's *yours?*

MAYOR (*very taken aback*). Eh? What? I'm not a reading man, but it *sounds* all right . . . strong. Strong . . .

MUSGRAVE (*to the* PARSON). What about *yours?*

PARSON (*dubiously*). You speak with enthusiasm, yes. I hope you'll be listened to.

MUSGRAVE (*at the top of his passion*). By God, I hope I am! D'ye hear me, d'ye hear me, d'ye hear me – I'm the Queen of England's man, and I'm wearing her coat and I know her Book backwards. I'm Black Jack Musgrave, me, the hardest serjeant of the line – I work my life to bugle and drum, for eighteen years I fought for one flag only, salute it in the morning, can you haul it down at dark? The Last Post of a living life? Look – I'll show it to you all. And I'll *dance* for you beneath it – hoist up the flag, boy – up, up, *up!*

ATTERCLIFFE *has nipped up the ladder, holding the rope. He loops the rope over the cross-bar of the lamp-bracket, drops to the plinth again, flings open the lid of the big box, and hauls on the rope.*

HURST *beats frantically on his drum. The rope is attached to the contents of the box, and these are jerked up to the cross-bar and reveal themselves as an articulated skeleton dressed in a soldier's tunic and trousers, the rope noosed round the neck. The* PEOPLE *draw back in horror.* MUSGRAVE *begins to dance, waving his rifle, his face contorted with demoniac fury.*

MUSGRAVE (*as he dances, sings, with mounting emphasis*).

> Up he goes and no one knows
> How to bring him downwards
> Dead man's feet
> Over the street
> Riding the roofs
> And crying down your chimneys

Up he goes and no one knows
Who it was that rose him
But white and red
He waves his head
He sits on your back
And you'll never never lose him
Up he goes and no one knows
How to bring him downwards.

He breaks off at the climax of the song, and stands panting. The drum stops.

That'll do. That'll do for *that*. (*He beckons gently to the* PEOPLE.) You can come back. Come back. Come back. We're all quiet now. But nobody move out of this market-place. You saw the gun loaded. Well, it's on a very quick swivel and the man behind it's well trained. (*He gestures with his rifle towards the platform party.*) And I've won a regimental cup four year running for small-arms marksmanship. So be good, and be gentle, *all* of you.

That checks the BARGEE, *who made a move. The* MAYOR *seems to be about to speak.*

Right, Mr. Mayor – I'll explain the whole business.

PARSON (*in a smaller voice than usual*). Business? What business, sir? Do you intend to imply you are *threatening* us with these weapons?

MAYOR. The man's gone balmy. Constable, do summat, grab him, quick!

The CONSTABLE *makes an indecisive move.*

MUSGRAVE. Be *quiet*. I shan't warn agen. (*To the* MAYOR *and the* PARSON.) You two. Get down there! Constable, *there!*

He gestures peremptorily and the three of them obey him, moving downstage to stand facing the platform and covered by the gun.

Now I said I'll explain. So listen. (*He points to the skeleton.*)
This, up here, was a comrade of mine – of ours. At least, he
was till a few months since. He was killed, being there for
his duty, in the country I was telling you about, where the
regiment is stationed. It's not right a colony, you know, it's
a sort of Protectorate, but British, y'know, British. This, up
here, he was walking down a street latish at night, he'd
been to the opera – *you've* got a choral society in this town, I
daresay – well, he was only a soldier, but North Country, he
was full of music, so he goes to the opera. And on his way
again to camp he was shot in the back. And it's not surprising, neither : there was patriots abroad, anti-British,
subversive ; like they didn't dare to shoot him to his face. He
was daft to be out alone, wasn't he? Out of bounds, after
curfew.

ATTERCLIFFE (*with suppressed frenzy*). Get on to the words as
matter, serjeant!

MUSGRAVE (*turning on him fiercely*). *I'm* talking now ; you wait
your turn! . . . So we *come* to the words as matter. He was the
third to be shot that week. He was the fifteenth that month.
In the back and all. Add to which he was young, he was
liked, he sang songs, they say, and he joked and he laughed
– he was a good soldier, too, else *I'd* not have bothered (we'll
leave out his sliding off to the opera WOL, but by and large
good, and I've got standards). So at twelve o'clock at night
they beat up the drums and sounded the calls and called
out the guard and the guard calls us *all* out, and the road
is red and slippery, and every soldier in the camp no longer
in the camp but in the streets of that city, rifle-butts,
bayonets, every street cut off for eight blocks north and west
the opera-house. And that's how it began.

HURST (*the frenzy rising*). The streets is empty, but the houses
is full. He says, 'no undue measures, minimum violence', he
says. 'But bring in the killers.'

ATTERCLIFFE.The killers are gone, they've gone miles off in

that time – *sporting* away, right up in the mountains, I told you at the time.

MUSGRAVE. That's not material, there's one man is dead, but there's *everyone's* responsible.

HURST. So bring the *lot* in! It's easy, they're all in bed, kick the front doors down, knock 'em on the head, boys, chuck 'em in the wagons.

ATTERCLIFFE. I didn't know she was only a little kid, there was scores of 'em on that staircase, pitch-dark, trampling, screaming, they're all of 'em screaming, what are we to do?

HURST. Knock 'em on the head, boy, chuck 'em in the wagons.

ATTERCLIFFE. How was I to tell she was only a little kid?

MUSGRAVE (*bringing it to an end*). THAT'S NOT MATERIAL! You were told to bring 'em in. If you killed her, you killed her! She was just one, and who cares a damn for that! Stay in your place and keep your hands on that Gatling. We've got to have order here, whatever there was *there;* and I can tell you it wasn't order . . . (*To* HURST.) You, take a rifle. Leave your drum down.

HURST *jumps on the plinth, takes a rifle and loads.*

We've *got* to have order. So I'll just tell you quietly how many there were was put down as injured – that's badly hurt, hospital, we don't count knocks and bruises, any o' that. Twenty-five men. Nine women. *No* children, whatever *he* says. She was a fully grown girl, and she had a known record as an associate of terrorists. That was her. Then four men, one of them elderly, turned out to have died too. Making five. Not so very many. Dark streets. Natural surge of rage.

HURST. We didn't find the killers.

MUSGRAVE. Of course we didn't find 'em. Not *then* we didn't, any road. We didn't even know 'em. But *I* know 'em, now.

(*He turns on* WALSH.) So what's *your* opinion?

MAYOR. He's not balmy, he's mad, he's stark off his nut.

PARSON. Why doesn't somebody do something? Constable?

Noises off.

MUSGRAVE (*indicates* WALSH). I'm talking to *him*.

CONSTABLE (*very shakily*). I shall have to ask you to – to come down off this platform, Sarnt Musgrave. It looks to me like your – your meeting's got out of hand.

HURST (*covering the* CONSTABLE). Aye, it has.

MUSGRAVE (*to* WALSH). Go on, brother. Tell us.

WALSH *climbs up at the back of the plinth.*

WALSH (*with a certain levity*). *My* opinion, eh? I don't know why you need it. You've got *him*, haven't you? (*He waggles the skeleton's foot familiarly.*) What more d'you want? (*He comes forward and sits on the front of the plinth, looking at the other two* COLLIERS.) Aye, or you too, with your natty little nosegays dandled in your hatbands. Take 'em out, sharp! He's learnt you the truth, hasn't he?

They remove their cockades, shamefacedly.

PUGNACIOUS COLLIER. All right, *that'll* do.

WALSH. Will it, matey, will it? If it helps you to remember what we've been fighting for, I daresay it will. Trade Unions aren't formed, you know, so we can all have beer-ups on the Army.

SLOW COLLIER. He said that'll do. I'm sick and bloody tired – I don't know *what* it's all about.

WALSH (*drops down to the forestage*). Come home and I'll tell you. The circus is over. Come on.

MUSGRAVE. Oh no it's not. Just bide still a while. There's more to be said yet. When I asked you your opinion I meant about them we was talking about – them as did *this*, up here.

WALSH. Well, *what* about them – brother? Clear enough to me. You go for a soldier, you find yourself in someone else's country, you deserve all you get. *I'd* say it stands to reason.

MUSGRAVE. And that's *all* you would say? I'd thought better of you.

WALSH (*irritated*). Now look, look here, what *are* you trying to get? You come to this place all hollering for sympathy, oh you've been beating and murdering and following your trade boo-hoo: but we're not bloody interested! You mend your own heartache and leave us to sort with ours – we've enough and to spare!

MUSGRAVE (*very intensely*). This *is* for your heart. Take another look at *him*. (*Points to skeleton.*) Go on, man, both eyes, and carefully. Because you all used to know him: or most of you did. Private Billy Hicks, late of this parish, welcome him back from the wars, he's bronzed and he's fit, with many a tall tale of distant campaigning to spin round the fireside – ah, *you* used to know him, *didn't* you, Mrs. Hitchcock!

MRS. HITCHCOCK *has risen in great alarm.*

SLOW COLLIER. That's never Billy Hicks, ye dirty liar.

PUGNACIOUS COLLIER. He wor my putter for two year, when I hewed coal in number five – he hewed there hisself for nigh on a year alongside o' my brother.

SLOW COLLIER. He left his clogs to me when he went to join up – that's never our Billy.

NOISES OFF. Never Billy. Never Billy.

BARGEE. 'Never Billy Hicks' – 'Never Billy Hicks' – they don't dare believe it. You've knocked 'em to the root, boy. Oh the white faces!

MRS. HITCHCOCK. She ought to be told. She's got a right to know.

MUSGRAVE. Go along then and tell her.

HURST (*to* MUSGRAVE). You letting her go?

MUSGRAVE. Yes.

HURST. But –

MUSGRAVE (*curtly*). Attend to your orders.

MRS. HITCHCOCK *goes out*.

When I say it's Billy Hicks, you can believe me it's true.

WALSH. Aye, I'll believe you. And you know what I think – it's downright indecent!

MUSGRAVE. Aye, aye? But wait. Because here is the reason. I'm a religious man, and I see the causes of the Almighty in every human work.

PARSON. That is absolute blasphemy!

MAYOR. This won't do you a pennorth o' good, you know.

MUSGRAVE. Not to me, no. But maybe to you? Now as I understand the workings of God, through greed and the world, this man didn't die because he went alone to the opera, he was killed because he had to be – it being decided ; that now the people in that city was worked right up to killing soldiers, then more and more soldiers should be sent for them to kill, and the soldiers in turn should kill the people in that city, more and more, always – that's what I said to you : four men, one girl, then the twenty-five and the nine – *and* it'll go on, there or elsewhere, and it can't be stopped neither, except there's someone finds out Logic and brings the wheel round. You see, the Queen's Book, which eighteen years I've lived, it's turned inside out for *me*. There used to be my duty: now there's a disease –

HURST. Wild-wood mad.

MUSGRAVE. Wild-wood mad we are ; and so we've fetched it home. You've had Moses and the Prophets – that's *him* – (*He points at* WALSH.) – 'cos he told you. But you were all for enlisting, it'd still have gone on. Moses and the Prophets, what good did they do?

He sits down and broods. There is a pause.

WALSH (*awkwardly*). There's no one from this town be over

keen to join up now. You've preached your little gospel: I
daresay we can go home?

MUSGRAVE *makes no reply. The* SOLDIERS *look at one another
doubtfully.*

HURST. What do we do now?
ATTERCLIFFE. Wait.
HURST. Serjeant –
ATTERCLIFFE (*shushing him*). Ssh-ssh!

A pause. Restive noises, off.

HURST. Serjeant –
ATTERCLIFFE. Serjeant – they've heard your message, they'll
none of them forget it. Haven't we done what we came for?
HURST (*astonished, to* ATTERCLIFFE). Done what we came
for?

ATTERCLIFFE *shushes him again as* MUSGRAVE *stirs.*

MUSGRAVE (*as though to himself*). One man, and for him five.
Therefore, for five of them we multiply out, *and* we find it
five-and-twenty. . . . So, as I understand Logic and Logic to
me is the mechanism of God – that means that today there's
twenty-five persons will have to be –

ATTERCLIFFE *jumps up in horror.* ANNIE *and* MRS. HITCH-
COCK *appear at the upper window. When she sees the skeleton*
ANNIE *gasps and seems about to scream.*

MUSGRAVE (*cutting her short*). It's true. It's him. You don't
need to cry out; you knew it when he left you.
ANNIE. Take him down. Let me have him. I'll come down for
him now.
BARGEE. Away down, me strong Annie. I'll carry you a golden
staircase – aha, she's the royal champion, stand by as she
comes down.
*As he speaks he jumps on to the plinth, takes away the ladder,
nips across the stage and props it under the window.*

MUSGRAVE. No! Let her wait up there. I said: wait! . . . Now
then, who's with me! Twenty-five to die and the Logic is
worked out. Who'll help me? You? (*He points to* WALSH.)
I made sure that you would: you're a man like the Black
Musgrave, you: you have purposes, and you can lead. Join
along with my madness, friend. I brought it back to England
but I've brought the cure too – to turn it on to them that
sent it out of this country – way-out-ay they sent it, where
they hoped that only soldiers could catch it and rave! Well
here's three redcoat ravers on their own kitchen hearthstone!
Who do we start with? These? (*He turns on the* MAYOR.)
'Loyal hearts and true, every man jack of us.' (*To the*
PARSON.) 'Draw the sword with gladness.' Why, *swords* is
for honour, carry 'em on church parade, a *sword'll* never
offer you three hundred and fifty bullets in a minute – and it
was no bright sword neither finished *his* life in a back street!
(*He points to* BILLY, *and then at the* CONSTABLE.) Or what
about the Peeler? If we'd left it to *him, you'd* ha' been boxed
away to barracks six or eight hours ago! Come on now, let's
have you, you know I'm telling you truth!

WALSH. Nay: it won't do.

HURST. It won't do? Why not?

WALSH. I'm not over clear why not. Last night there was
me and some others tried to whip away that Gatling. And
we'd ha' used it and all: by God, there was need. But that's
one thing, y'see, and this is another – ent it, you tell me?

He appeals to the COLLIERS.

PUGNACIOUS COLLIER. Nay, I don't know.

SLOW COLLIER. I think they're all balmy, the whole damn
capful's arse-over-tip –

WALSH. No it's not. *I'm* not. And it comes to this wi' me: *he's*
still in uniform, and he's still got his Book. He's doing his
duty. Well, I take no duties from no bloody lobsters. This
town lives by collieries. That's coal-owners and it's pitmen

– aye, and they battle, and the pitmen'll win. But not wi' no soldier-boys to order our fight for us. Remember their trade: you give 'em one smell of a broken town, you'll never get 'em out!

MUSGRAVE (*with growing desperation*). But you don't understand me – all of you, listen! I told you we could *cure* –

ATTERCLIFFE. I don't think you can.

MUSGRAVE (*flabbergasted*). Eh? What's that? Stay by your weapon!

ATTERCLIFFE. No. (*He stands away from the gun.*)

HURST *rapidly takes his place.*

HURST (*to the crowd*). Keep still, the lot of you!

ATTERCLIFFE. It won't do, Black Jack. You swore there'd be no killing.

MUSGRAVE. No I did not.

ATTERCLIFFE. You gave us to believe. We've done what we came for, and it's there we should have ended. *I've* ended. No killing.

He deliberately gets down from the platform, and squats on the ground. MUSGRAVE *looks around him, appealing and appalled.*

BARGEE. I'm with you, general!

MUSGRAVE. You?

BARGEE. Nobody else! I'll serve you a lovely gun! Rapine and riot! (*He scrambles on to the plinth, picks up a rifle from the box and loads it.*) When do we start breaking open the boozers? Or the pawnshops and all – who's for a loot?

MUSGRAVE. None of you at all? Come on, come on, why, he was your Billy, wasn't he? That you knew and you worked with – don't you want to revenge him?

ANNIE. Somebody hold the ladder. I'm going to come down.

The SLOW COLLIER *does so.*

MUSGRAVE (*urgently, to her*). Billy Hicks, lassie: here: he used to be yours! Tell them what they've got to do : tell them the truth!

ANNIE *has started to come down the ladder. When she is down, the* COLLIER *lowers it to the ground.*

HURST. Wait a minute, serjeant, leave me to talk to them! We've not got time bothering wi' no squalling tarts.

MUSGRAVE. Keep you your place.

HURST (*furiously*). I'm in my bloody place! And I'll tell you this straight, if we lose this crowd now, we've lost all the work, for ever! And remember summat else. There's Dragoons on the road!

General sensation. Shouts off: 'Dragoons'.

HURST (*to the crowd*). So you've just got five minutes to make up your minds.

He grabs his rifle up, and motions the BARGEE *violently to the Gatling. The* BARGEE *takes over, and* HURST *leaps off the plinth and talks straight into the* COLLIERS' *faces and at the audience.*

We've earned our living by beating and killing folk like yourselves in the streets of their own city. Well, it's drove us mad – and so we come back here to tell you how and to show you what it's like. The ones we want to deal with aren't, for a change, you and your mates, but a bit higher up. The ones as never get hurt. (*He points at the* MAYOR, PARSON *and* CONSTABLE.) Him. Him. Him. You hurt them hard, and they'll not hurt you again. And they'll not send *us* to hurt you neither. But if you let 'em be, then us three'll be killed – aye and worse, we'll be forgotten – and the whole bloody lot'll start all over again!

He climbs back and takes over the gun.

MUSGRAVE. For God's sake stand with us. We've *got* to be remembered!

SLOW COLLIER. We ought to, you know. He might be right.

WALSH. I don't know. I don't trust it.

PUGNACIOUS COLLIER. Ahr and be damned, these are just like the same as us. Why don't we stand with 'em?

WALSH (*obstinately*). I've not yet got this clear.

ANNIE. To me it's quite clear. He asked me to tell you the truth. My truth's an easy tale, it's old true-love gone twisted, like they called it 'malformed'– they put part in the ground, and hang the rest on a pillar here, and expect me to sit under it making up song-ballads. All right.

> My true love is a scarecrow
> Of rotted rag and bone
> Ask him : where are the birds, Billy?
> Where have they all gone?

He says: Unbutton my jacket, and they'll all fly out of the ribs – oh, oh, I'm not mad, though you told us that *you* were – let's have that bundle!

MRS. HITCHCOCK *throws down a bundle.* ANNIE *shakes it out, revealing* SPARKY'S *tunic.*

Take a sight o' this, you hearty colliers : see what they've brought you. You can match it up with Billy's. Last night there were four o' these walking, weren't there? Well, this morning there's three. They buried the other one in Ma Hitchcock's midden. Go on, ask 'em why!

HURST. He's a deserter, is why!

ANNIE (*holding up the tunic*). Hey, here's the little hole where they let in the bayonet. Eee, aie, easily in. His blood's on my tongue, so hear what it says. A bayonet is a raven's beak. This tunic's a collier's jacket. That scarecrow's a birdcage. What more do you want!

WALSH. Is this what she says true? Where *is* he, the fourth of you?

MUSGRAVE. He was killed, and that's all. By an accident
killed. It's barely materi –

ATTERCLIFFE. Oh, it's material. And no goddamned accident.
I said it to you, Musgrave, it washes it all out.

WALSH. It bloody does and all, as far as I go. (*He turns to the
other* COLLIERS.) If you want to stand by 'em when they've
done for their own mucker and not one of the bastards can
tell ye the same tale, well, you're at your damned liberty and
take it and go!

The COLLIERS *murmur dubiously.*

HURST (*frantic*). I'm going to start shooting!

General reaction of fear: he clearly means it. He spits at
MUSGRAVE.

You and your everlasting Word – you've pulled your own
roof down! But *I'll* prop your timber for you – I'll give a
One, Two, and a Three : and I'm opening fire!

ATTERCLIFFE. No.

*He jumps up and stands on the step of the plinth, below the gun
and facing it, with his arms spread out so that the muzzle is
against his breast.*

HURST (*distorted with rage*). Get down! Get down off it, you old
cuckold, I don't care who you are. I'll put the first one
through you! I *swear* it, I will! One! Two! . . .

MAYOR (*to the* CONSTABLE). Go for that gun.

The CONSTABLE *is making a cautious move towards the gun,
but he is forestalled by* MUSGRAVE, *who flings himself at*
HURST *and knocks him away from the breach. There is a
moment's tense struggle behind the gun.*

MUSGRAVE (*as he struggles*). The wrong way. The wrong way.
You're trying to do it without Logic.

Then HURST *gives way and falls back down the steps of the plinth. He recovers himself.*

HURST (*panting with excitement*). All right then, Black Jack. All right, it's finished. The lot. You've lost it. I'm off!

MUSGRAVE (*stunned*). Come back here. You'll come back, you'll obey orders.

HURST *makes a grab forward, snatches his rifle from the platform and jumps back clear.*

HURST (*to the crowd*). Get out o' my road!

At the very instant he turns towards the wings to run away, a shot is fired offstage. His quick turn changes into a grotesque leap as the bullet hits him, and he collapses on the stage. A bugle blares from offstage.

VOICES OFF. Dragoons!

Orders shouted and general noise of cavalry coming to a halt and dismounting.

MAYOR ⎫ (*one after another, rapidly.*)
CONSTABLE ⎬ The Dragoons! The Dragoons!
PARSON ⎭ Saved! Saved! Saved!
VOICES OFF. Saved! Saved! Saved!

MUSGRAVE *is standing beside the gun, temporarily at a loss.* ATTERCLIFFE *has jumped down beside* HURST *and lifted his head. Everyone else stands amazed.*
Suddenly MUSGRAVE *swings the gun to point toward the Dragoons. The* BARGEE *ups with his rifle and sticks it into* MUSGRAVE'S *back.*

BARGEE. Serjeant, put your hands up!

MUSGRAVE *is pushed forward by the rifle, but he does not obey. The* TROOPER *enters, clicking the bolt of his smoking carbine, and shouting.*

TROOPER. Everybody stand where you are! You, put your hands up!

MUSGRAVE *does so.*

BARGEE. I've got him, soldier! I've got him! Crooked Joe's got him, Mr. Mayor.

The OFFICER *strides in, drawing his sabre.*

Give a cheer – hooroar!

Cheers off.
The OFFICER *comes to attention before the* MAYOR *and salutes with his sabre.*

OFFICER. Mr. Mayor, are we in time?
MAYOR. Aye, you're in time. You're *just* in bloody time.
OFFICER (*seeing* MUSGRAVE). 22128480 Serjeant Musgrave, J.?
MUSGRAVE. My name.
OFFICER. We heard word you'd come here. You are under arrest. Robbery and desertion. There were *three* who came with you.
ATTERCLIFFE (*getting up from* HURST, *whose head falls back.*) You can count me for one of them. One other's dead already. Here's the third.
OFFICER. You're under arrest.
CONSTABLE. Hold out your hands.

He takes out two pairs of handcuffs and fetters them.

OFFICER. Mr. Mayor, my troopers are at your disposal. What do you require of us?
MAYOR. Well, I'd say it was about all over by now, young man – wouldn't you?
OFFICER. Law and order is established?
PARSON. Wiser counsels have prevailed, Captain.
BARGEE. *I* caught him, *I* caught him, *I* used me strategy!

OFFICER. My congratulations, all.

WALSH (*with great bitterness*). The community's been saved. Peace and prosperity rules. We're all friends and neighbours for the rest of today. We're all sorted out. We're back where we were. So what do we do?

BARGEE.

Free beer. It's still here.
No more thinking. Easy drinking.
End of a bad bad dream. Gush forth the foaming stream.

He takes the bung out of the barrel and starts filling tankards.

OFFICER. The winter's broken up. Let normal life begin again.

BARGEE. Aye, aye, *begin* again!

He is handing the mugs to the people. He starts singing, and they all join in, by degrees.

There was an old man called Michael Finnegan
He had whiskers on his chin-egan
The wind came out and blew them in agen
Poor old Michael Finnegan –
Begin agen –

There was an old man etcetera . . .

He gives out mugs in the following order: the MAYOR, *the* PARSON, *the* SLOW COLLIER, *the* PUGNACIOUS COLLIER, *the* CONSTABLE. *Each man takes his drink, swigs a large gulp, then links wrists with the previous one, until all are dancing round the centre-piece in a chain, singing.*
ANNIE *has climbed the plinth and lowers the skeleton. She sits with it on her knees. The* DRAGOONS *remain standing at the side of the stage.* MUSGRAVE *and* ATTERCLIFFE *come slowly downstage. The* BARGEE *fills the last two tankards and hands one to* WALSH, *who turns his back angrily. The* BARGEE *empties one mug, and joins the tail of the dance, still holding the*

other. After one more round he again beckons WALSH. *This time the latter thinks for a moment, then bitterly throws his hat on the ground, snarls into the impassive face of the* DRAGOON, *and joins in the dance, taking the beer.*

The scene closes, leaving MUSGRAVE *and* ATTERCLIFFE *on the forestage.* MRS. HITCHCOCK *retires from the window.*

SCENE TWO

A prison cell.

This scene is achieved by a barred wall descending in front of the dancers of the previous scene. After a while the sound dies away, and the lights change so that we can no longer see past the bars.

MUSGRAVE *remains standing, looking into the distance with his back to the audience.* ATTERCLIFFE *sighs and sits down gingerly on the floor.*

ATTERCLIFFE. Sit down and rest yourself, serjeant. That's all there is left ... Go on, man, sit down ... Then stand and the devil take you! It's *your* legs, not mine. It's my *hands* is what matters. They finished Sparky and that finished me, and Sparky finished you. Holy God save us, why warn't I a greengrocer, then I'd never ha' been cuckolded, never gone for no soldier, never no dead Sparky, and never none of this. Go on, serjeant, talk to me. I'm an old old stupid bastard and I've nowt to do now but fret out the runs of the consequence; and the whole croaking work it's finished and done. Go on, serjeant, talk.

MUSGRAVE *does not move.*

A pause.

MRS. HITCHCOCK *enters, carrying a glass.*

MRS. HITCHCOCK (*to* MUSGRAVE). It's port with a bit o'

lemon. I often take it of a morning; like it settles me stummick for the day. The officer said I could see you, if I warn't no more nor five minutes. Sit down and I'll give it to your mouth – them wrist-irons makes it difficult, I daresay.

MUSGRAVE (*without looking at her*). Give it to him. I don't want it.

MRS. HITCHCOCK. He can have half of it. You take a sup first.

MUSGRAVE *shakes his head.*

All right. How you like.

She goes to ATTERCLIFFE *and puts the glass to his mouth.*

ATTERCLIFFE. I'm obliged to you, missus.

MRS. HITCHCOCK. It's on the house, this one. Change from the Queen, ent it?

MUSGRAVE. Numbers and order. According to Logic. I had worked it out for months.

He swings round to MRS. HITCHCOCK.

What made it break down!

MRS. HITCHCOCK. Ah, there's the moral of it. You ask our Annie.

MUSGRAVE (*furiously*). He was killed by pure accident! It had nothing to do –

ATTERCLIFFE. Oh by God, it had.

MRS. HITCHCOCK. The noisy one, warn't he? Pack o' cards and all the patter. You asked me to trust you – (*her voice rises with rage and emotion*) – he was only a young lad, for gracious goodness Christ, he'd a voice like a sawmill – what did you want to do it for, you gormless great gawk!

ATTERCLIFFE. *He* didn't do it.

MRS. HITCHCOCK. He did, oh he did! And he broke his own neck.

MUSGRAVE. What's the matter with you, woman!

MRS. HITCHCOCK. All wrong, you poured it out all wrong! I

could ha' told you last night if only I'd known – the end of
the world and you thought you could call a parade. In control – *you!*

MUSGRAVE (*very agitated*). Don't talk like that. You're talking
about my duty. Good order and the discipline : it's the only
road I know. Why can't you see it?

MRS. HITCHCOCK. All I can see is Crooked Joe Bludgeon
having his dance out in the middle of fifty Dragoons! It's
time you learnt your life, you big proud serjeant. Listen : last
evening you told all about this anarchy and where it came
from – like, scribble all over with life or love, and that makes
anarchy. Right?

MUSGRAVE. Go on.

MRS. HITCHCOCK. Then *use* your Logic – if you can. Look at
it this road : here we are, and we'd got life and love. Then
you came in and you did your scribbling where nobody
asked you. Aye, it's arsy-versey to what you said, but it's
still an anarchy, isn't it? And it's all your work.

MUSGRAVE. Don't tell me there was life or love in this town.

MRS. HITCHCOCK. There was. There was hungry men, too –
fighting for their food. But *you* brought in a different war.

MUSGRAVE. I brought it in to end it.

ATTERCLIFFE. To end it by its own rules: no bloody good.
She's right, you're wrong. You can't cure the pox by further
whoring. Sparky died of those damned rules. And so did the
other one.

MUSGRAVE. That's not the truth. (*He looks at them both in
appeal, but they nod.*) That's not the truth. God was with
me . . . God . . . (*He makes a strange animal noise of despair,
a sort of sob that is choked off suddenly, before it can develop
into a full howl.*) – and all they dancing – all of them – there.

MRS. HITCHCOCK. Ah, not for long. And it's not a dance of
joy. Those men are hungry, so they've got no time for *you.*
One day they'll be full, though, and the Dragoons'll be gone,
and then they'll remember.

MUSGRAVE (*shaking his head*). No.

MRS. HITCHCOCK. Let's hope it, any road, Eh?

She presents the glass to his lips. This time he accepts it and drinks, and remains silent.

ATTERCLIFFE (*melancholy but quiet*). That running tyke of a Sparky, he reckoned he wor the only bastard in the barracks had a voice. Well, he warn't. There's other men can sing when he's not here. So listen at this.

He sings.

> I plucked a blood-red rose-flower down
> And gave it to my dear.
> I set my foot out across the sea
> And she never wept a tear.
>
> I came back home as gay as a bird
> I sought her out and in :
> And I found her at last in a little attic room
> With a napkin round her chin.

At her dinner, you see. Very neat and convenient.

He sings.

> Oh are you eating meat, I said,
> Or are you eating fish?
> I'm eating an apple was given me today,
> The sweetest I could wish.

So I asked her where she got it, and by God the tune changed then. Listen at what she told me.

He sings to a more heavily accented version of the tune.

> Your blood-red rose is withered and gone
> And fallen on the floor :
> And he who brought the apple down
> Shall be my darling dear.

For the apple holds a seed will grow
In live and lengthy joy
To raise a flourishing tree of fruit
For ever and a day.
With fal-la-la-the-dee, toor-a-ley,
For ever and a day.

They're going to hang us up a length higher nor most apple-trees grow, Serjeant. D'you reckon we can start an orchard?

The Happy Haven

Written in collaboration with
Margaretta D'Arcy

Introductory Note

The play is intended to be given a formalized presentation. This involves the use of masks, which are worn as follows – the Five Old People wear character masks of the *commedia dell'arte* type, covering the upper part of their faces only. The Doctor does not wear a mask, except at the very end, when he is shown in one that covers his whole face, and represents himself as a child. The Nurses and Orderlies have their mouths and noses covered by hospital antiseptic masks.* The Distinguished Visitors wear masks similar to those of the Old People, but less individualized.

The Setting should suggest a Hospital atmosphere, not too clinical and rectilinear. The scenes are not localized to any particular rooms.

The Dog is to be imagined by the audience, but must be understood to be seen by all the characters on the stage – it is not a 'delusion'.

The stage directions are those used for the original production at Bristol University, when the play was presented on an open stage, following roughly the Elizabethan model. There were two doors opening from the back wall of the stage, with between them a recess closed by sliding doors, which accommodated the Doctor's laboratory equipment. Above this recess was a small upper stage. At the Royal Court, the play had of necessity to be played within the proscenium arch. This is a necessity that will doubtless be imposed upon most productions of *The Happy Haven* in this country, but it is none the less a regrettable one. The unsatisfactory organization of the English theatre in general

* It may be found more convenient if they only wear these in specifically 'clinical' scenes: otherwise, they are bare-faced.

and the archaic design of its buildings continually hamstring any attempts on the part of dramatists and directors to open out the conventions of the drama; and I must record my gratitude to Bristol University and its Department of Drama for making it possible to prove to myself that the leanings I have long had towards the open stage and its disciplines were justifiable in practice as well as in theory. I would urge anyone who wishes to produce this play to do so, if at all possible, on an Open Stage. Structural limitations may prevent the use of the upper stage: but it is not an essential part of the setting, and the scenes set on it may be brought down to the main acting level without undue difficulty.

The Happy Haven

First produced at the Royal Court Theatre, London, on 14
September 1960, with the following cast:

DR COPPERTHWAITE	Peter Bowles
MRS PHINEUS	Susan Engel
MRS LETOUZEL	Rachel Roberts
MR GOLIGHTLY	Barrie Ingham
MR HARDRADER	Nicholas Selby
MR CRAPE	Frank Finlay
ROBINSON } LORD MAYOR }	James Bolam
SMITH } SIR FREDERICK HAPGOOD }	Edward Fox
NURSE JONES } LADY MAYORESS }	Mary Watson
NURSE BROWN } LADY FROM THE MINISTRY }	Rosalind Knight

Directed by WILLIAM GASKILL

ACT ONE

Scene One

DOCTOR COPPERTHWAITE *enters on upper stage and addresses the audience directly.*

DOCTOR. Ah-hum. Good evening, ladies and gentlemen. First, let me say how glad I am to see you here and to extend a cordial welcome to the Happy Haven. We are, as you know, as yet only a small institution and our grant from the revenues of the National Health Service is alas not as generous as it might be – but, well, I dare say you'll know the old proverb – Time Mends All. I'd like you to meet some of the old people who are in our care. As the phrase is, the evening of their lives – well, I've more to say about that later – but at present sufficient to indicate that this hospital for the amelioration of the lot of the aged is situated in pleasant rural surroundings, almost self-supporting – own produce, eggs, butter, and so on – within easy reach of London, and, I am happy to say, the most up-to-date facilities for both medical treatment and – most important of all from my point of view – research. I'm the Superintendent, my name's Copperthwaite, I've been here five years, and – er, yes, well, you want to meet the patients, don't you? Nurse Brown, Nurse Jones. We're ready to meet the patients.

The NURSES *enter and remove a screen on the main stage, which reveals the* OLD PEOPLE *all enjoying their party. The Old People have entered through the doors of the recess, which are closed before the screen is taken away.*

We call them patients, but you'll understand they're not really ill, they're just old, you know, the passage of time, the gradual declension – it's a physical fact, you look at it scientifically, it all fits the picture – above all things in an establishment of this nature, *must* preserve the clinical approach: can't be too often stressed. We might say today is really an auspicious occasion for meeting these five old people. You see, the old lady in the middle is enjoying her ninetieth birthday, and, of course, there's a bit of a celebration. Shouldn't there be a cake, Nurse?

NURSE BROWN *exits*.

Right. Well, she's going to cut the cake and they'll congratulate her. She's our oldest, Mrs Phineus her name is, and she's been a widow for twenty years.

Enter NURSE BROWN *with cake. She carries it to* MRS PHINEUS, *and puts the knife into her hand.*

Now here's the cake, and here's the knife to cut it: and Mrs Phineus is just about to cut it; and she's *cut* it!

As MRS PHINEUS *cuts the cake, the* NURSES *and* OLD PEOPLE *all clap.*

Now they're all about to congratulate Mrs Phineus in the traditional fashion.

OLD PEOPLE (*sing*).
    Happy birthday to you
    Happy birthday to you
    Happy birthday, Mrs Phineus,
    Happy birthday to you.

The cake is cut up by NURSE BROWN *and a piece handed to each patient.*

DOCTOR. And the party is in full swing. While they're all enjoying themselves, it would perhaps be appropriate if I were to give a brief resumé of their names, ages, and case histories.

He refers to a sheaf of notes.

We'll start with Mrs Phineus – not much to be said about her, general condition remarkably promising considering her years. Some obstruction recorded in the condensers, sandbox apertures require occasional overhaul, but by and large answers very well to her regulator. Now then: number two. On Mrs Phineus's right we have Mr Golightly, seventy-five years old, bachelor, very good state of preservation. Fitted six years ago with improved Walschaerts valve-gear replacing original Stephenson's link motion, and injectors also recently renewed. Latent procreative impulses require damping down on the firebox, but less so than formerly. Next one, number three, on Mrs Phineus's left, you will observe the only other female member, Mrs Letouzel. Aged seventy, all moving parts in good condition, cross-head pins perhaps slightly deteriorated, and occasional trouble from over-heated bearings when financial gain is in question. General report, extremely favourable. Now next to her we have Mr Hardrader, number four, our best running specimen. Very firm original design in smokebox and blast pipe has resulted in continual first-class steaming conditions. Age eighty-eight on the thirteenth of next month. Finally, on the extreme left, you will see Mr Crape. There has been here an unfortunate case history of overall deterioration, but last year was given a complete refit, including enlongated smokebox, revised cylinder-head design, and replacement of obsolete perforated splashers. Age is now seventy-nine. There is still a tendency to overexceed the power-potential beyond nominal capacity, but provided this can be overcome – well, I think we can say, further outlook quite hopeful. This is about all I can usefully tell you at the moment. Their little party is well under way, though they mustn't be allowed to get too excited –

OLD PEOPLE (*sing*).

> Knees up, mother Brown
> Knees up, mother Brown
> Knees up, knees up, don't get the breeze up,
> Knees up, mother Brown.

DOCTOR. I think we'd better tactfully put an end to the evening now, a little kicking over the traces goes a long way at this age.

OLD PEOPLE's *song repeated.*

Ye-es, I think so. Nurse. I think that had better be all, Nurse. Off to bed, boys and girls, you're half an hour late as it is, burning the candle at both ends, y'know, have to go easy, don't we, that's the way, off to bed now, Nurse. Good night, good night, boys and girls. If you've not ate your cake yet, you can take it to bed and finish it there. That's right.

OLD PEOPLE. Good night, Doctor.

DOCTOR. Good night.

Exeunt NURSES, *taking in* OLD PEOPLE – *each one holding half-eaten slice of cake.*

And for the time being, that's that. Now the next thing, ladies and gentlemen, is my laboratory. I dare say it would be of interest if I were to give you some short exposition of the type of research I'm at present engaged in? Smith, Robinson.

ORDERLIES *enter on main stage.*

Get the lab ready, will you? Thank you very much.

Exeunt ORDERLIES, *into recess.*

If you'll just wait one moment, ladies and gentlemen – I'll be with you directly.

Exit DOCTOR. ORDERLIES *re-enter on main stage, wheeling out from the recess the lab bench with its equipment. As they place it in position, the* DOCTOR *enters on the main stage.*

We can call it the next morning now, and this is my morning routine – every morning, very early, before the patients have their breakfast, just about the time they're beginning to be washed. This is also, I suppose, how shall I call it, well, you will no doubt best understand me if I say, that this is the one true 'Ratio Operandi', the 'Reductio ad Quem', the – oh I don't know – the overriding purpose and ambition of my work in this hospital. My research. My project. My daily work for the full five years I've been Superintendent here. To quote, somewhat tentatively, a literary example as being perhaps most appropriate for this audience, you can call me if you like, a Doctor Faustus of the present generation. It's not an exact parallel – Faustus sold his soul to the devil, I believe. I'm selling mine to nobody. But what I have here or what I shall have here, ladies and gentlemen, is nothing less, or will be nothing less, than the Elixir of Life – of Life, and of Youth. I haven't got it yet. Now I'm near, I'm extremely near, oh I can tell you that, in certainty. Perhaps this very morning will prove the last of all the mornings I've had to stand in this lab, and calculate, and attempt, and slowly progress, experiment by experiment, formula by formula. Those five old people you saw go to bed last night are to be the raw material upon which I shall work. They don't know it yet, but they are. If I am successful, and the Elixir is found – *Copperthwaite's Elixir* – or might I call it the Happy Haven Elixir – the institution is greater than the man – *if* I am successful; then those five old people will not be at the end of their established term of years, but at the beginning! They will be able, they will be able, to be completely reborn! To any age we may see fit to lead them. Think of that. Think of that! . . . But let us preserve our professional detachment. The experiment, ladies and gentlemen, is by no means over yet. (*He turns to his bench.*) We'll have a look at it now. Notebooks please.

ORDERLY SMITH *hands him books as he names them.*

Number thirty-two, thirty-three, thirty-five-A, and the current one. Thank you. Experiment Number One; two-eight-six, Stage Four. Are you all paying attention, I want you to take particular note of the equipment mounted here, and containing, in the vessel, the solution derived from yesterday's work, reading nine-by-three by four-and-a-half scantlings, ledged braced battened and primed. The solution is now cool, yes, it's cool, and it has been allowed to stand for twenty-two hours. I term this the secondary or tensile state of loading. To it I am about to add nought point three-double-six degrees of *this* (*He holds up a second retort, also with liquid in it.*) – which is a five-eighth screed, three parts three-sixteenth aggregate, one-and-a-half parts plastic terrazzo. The resulting precipitate will then be heated for three hundred and twelve seconds, all headers, stretchers, and squints removed by oxidization: and then I – and *then*, why perhaps *then* – ah, well, we'd better take it as it comes, hadn't we? (*He pours the second liquid into the first.*) Bunsen burner, please.

ORDERLY ROBINSON *lights the burner.*

I want absolute quiet. This is very tense, very delicate. Thank you. Before heating I add the necessary trimmers and binding members. Number four.

ORDERLY ROBINSON *hands him a test-tube of liquid which he pours into retort.*

DOCTOR. Number eight.

Similar business.

Twelve-B.

Similar business.

Eighteen. Eighteen . . . where's number eighteen? Come on, come on! God's sake, Robinson, have these things ready —

Similar business, rather flurried.

Now then, timing dial. Thank you.

ORDERLY SMITH *hands him large stop-watch.*

DOCTOR (*reads the seconds off stop-watch*). Three-twelve. Three-ten. Three-eight. Six. Four. Two, one, three hundred.

ORDERLY ROBINSON *has taken the retort and is holding it over bunsen while* DOCTOR *calls the time. Every twelve seconds — indicated by* DOCTOR *jerking up his arm — he whips retort away from flame and agitates rapidly in the air, then holds it back again above bunsen.*

This is done every twelve seconds exactly, to prevent coagulation of sediment. After the first hundred seconds, we do it every five. Two-nine-four. Two-nine-two. Two-ninety. Two eighty-*eight.*

Mixture agitated again.

All right so far. Seems to be all right. This is the most dangerous part though. . . . Two eighty-four. Two-eight-two. Two hundred and eighty —

CRAPE *enters.*

CRAPE. Er, excuse me, Dr Copperthwaite –

DOCTOR (*whirling round, startled*). Eh, *what*! What is it, what are you doing here –

CRAPE. Excuse me if I interrupted. Doctor –

DOCTOR. *Interrupted!* You bloody dog, get out! (*He looks at the retort.*) Oh my God: coagulated. The whole damn thing's coagulated. It's no damn good at all. Clear it out, clear away, it's three weeks' consolidated work, oh no, it's nothing, no – it's all the luck of the game, *isn't* it, you interfering old – (*He pulls himself together.*) Eh, what's the use. I'm sorry, ladies and gentlemen. I'm afraid you're disappointed. We didn't reach it after all. But we will. Very shortly. It's a long road that has no turning, as they say. We all find these little setbacks. Don't we?

The ORDERLIES *have wheeled away the bench, etc., into the recess.*

Cleared away, Smith? Good. I'm not doing any more this morning. Tomorrow we'll start again at Number One-two-eight-one, Stage two. All right? And tell Sister that I want all male patients to be given an enema before this evening. I'm a little alarmed about the state of their blood-streams. There seem to be symptoms of mortification. . . . Thank you.

Exeunt ORDERLIES.

You know very well I am never available to patients when I am working in the laboratory, Mr Crape. So what do you want?

CRAPE. I do beg your pardon, Doctor, if I in any way intruded – of course we're all of us aware how important your work is –

DOCTOR. Are you? There are rules in this hospital, you know, and they're meant to be obeyed –

CRAPE. Oh naturally, naturally, Doctor, I do indeed apologize yes – but this is as you might say special, as a matter of fact, a delicate question, you see –

DOCTOR. And why can't it wait till a more normal time? There are stated hours for making complaints about the other patients, as you know perfectly well, Mr Crape – you take advantage of them often enough.

CRAPE. But Doctor, in these cases, one is often impelled to, well, like, to break with decorum, on account of the importance of imperceptibility – I mean, I don't want to be seen here, do I? I mean, bad for the value of our little talks, Doctor – after all it *is* only out of loyalty to the hospital, eh?

DOCTOR. All right, all right . . . So what has Mrs Letouzel been up to this time? I hope it isn't more pilfering. I told them to see that the collecting box for the spastic children had a padlock put on to it. Hasn't it been done?

CRAPE. Oh yes, yes, I think so, Doctor, yes – it's not about Mrs Letouzel really this morning. Mr Hardrader.

DOCTOR. Well?

CRAPE. He's still got it, you know. He takes it for walks.

DOCTOR. In the hospital?

CRAPE. Not exactly, no . . . but –

DOCTOR. In the grounds then?

CRAPE. Well to be quite frank, Doctor, I am not entirely sure –

DOCTOR. Mr Crape, I see nothing whatever to prevent Mr Hardrader possessing a bull-terrier or any other sort of dog, provided he does not infringe my regulations by keeping it on the premises. If you can't bring evidence to show that that *is* what he's doing, then you can please stop wasting my valuable time! Is there nothing else? Are they satisfied with their diet? There's far too much of a tendency for grumblings and grumblings and nobody ever tells me – one has to know these things – Well?

CRAPE. I think Mrs Phineus sometimes gets into the larders when there's no one about – Mrs Letouzel said she keeps a pot of strawberry jam under her bedclothes, but I don't think it can be very likely –

DOCTOR. I suppose a pot of jam won't do her any harm: but it could be a dangerous precedent . . . all right, Mr Crape. That'll do for now. Off you go to breakfast.

CRAPE. Oh, but Doctor, I've just thought –

DOCTOR. Off to breakfast, Mr Crape, I've a great deal to attend to this morning –

CRAPE. You asked about Mrs Letouzel. There *is* something, you know. It's about what she is, Doctor. That old woman – she's a Spy.

DOCTOR. Spy?

CRAPE. That's right.

    Ooh, Doctor, she's a greedy Spy

    Ooh, Doctor, she's so sharp and sly!

And what she wants to find out, Doctor, find out, here . . .

He makes a series of gestures around him and towards where the bench, etc., have been taken out.

DOCTOR. Now please, let's have it in English.

CRAPE. Sh-ssh . . . I'll whisper it. She wants, to find out, what it is, you're at!

DOCTOR. I dare say she does. Anything else?

CRAPE. Isn't that enough? Of course we all know the importance of your work –

DOCTOR. How?

CRAPE. How?

DOCTOR. Yes, Mr Crape. *How* do you know my work is so important?

CRAPE. Why . . . it stands to reason, Doctor. I was saying to Mr Golightly only the other day – 'Dr Copperthwaite, Mr Golightly, is what they term an Intellectual – he's a real scientist,' I said. 'And what he does in his Laboratory, I'll wager you nor I couldn't come near comprehending it, not if we tried for twenty years.' Could we, Doctor? It stands to reason.

DOCTOR. H'm.

CRAPE. Now you and me, Doctor –

DOCTOR. Mr Crape, you have been talking for nearly ten minutes, you have told me absolutely nothing: and you *ruined* my experiment! I don't want to see you again for a very long time.

Exit DOCTOR.

CRAPE. Ah, disappointing. What we might term a disappointing devolution? But they aren't all, you know – oho no. There's times when I've been able to learn that Doctor some most remarkable things, yes: *he* knows my value. (*He sings.*)

> The darkening age of James J. Crape
> Yet burns with one surviving fire:
> To see the old fools all a-shiver and a-quiver
> At the secret probings of my power!

Oi-oi, what's this? (*His eye falls on a loose leaf which has fallen from the* DOCTOR'*s notebook at the time of the interruption, and has lain unnoticed on the floor. He picks it up.*) The Doctor's dropped his – hey, Doctor! Doctor! Doctor, you've dropped your – he doesn't hear me, I'm too late. Good. (*He has called in a careful diminuendo, ending in a whisper.*) Not but what there's much advantage to be gained out o' *this*, I don't imagine. Signs, calculations, arithmetics, algebras, squared paper, crossing out – real Doctor's handwriting, too – I can't hardly read it. . . . 'Optimum ages and reduced minimum of estimated reductions – thirty years, forty years, fifty –' A list of names – oho . . . 'Letouzel, Phineus, Hardrader, Golightly – *Crape*.' Well: I don't know what it is, and I don't like it. But it's got *their* names on, as well as mine. Forewarned is forearmed. I'd call it worth preserving.

ORDERLY ROBINSON *enters.* CRAPE *whips the paper into his coat.*

Oh, Mr Robinson, er, looking for something? Left something behind? No . . . no, nothing here . . . but I'll keep a sharp eye – ha ha, good morning . . .

Exit ORDERLY.

This place isn't safe. I'd better make meself scarce. I'll go and find Letouzel – see what the old nutmeg-grater's plotting today. Maybe something there to advantage? Ha ha . . . maybe . . . (*He goes out singing.*)
    All a-quiver and a-shiver
    At the secret probings of my power . . .

Scene Two

A VOICE *over the loudspeaker.*

VOICE. Mr Golightly, please, Mr Golightly to report to Sister's office. Mr Golightly, if you please.

Enter MRS LETOUZEL *pushing* MRS PHINEUS *in her wheelchair.*

PHINEUS. Yes . . . I think I do, yes.
LETOUZEL. No, dear, no.
PHINEUS. Yes.
LETOUZEL. It comes more expensive.
PHINEUS. No.
LETOUZEL. Oh yes it does, dear, much more expensive. Besides, it's better to drink Indian. Not so much tannin.
PHINEUS. I beg your pardon, Mrs Letouzel?

LETOUZEL. I said Indian tea, dear, does not contain so much tannin. The China tea is very corrosive, you see.

PHINEUS. Corrosive?

LETOUZEL. To the intestines, dear. It corrodes them.

PHINEUS. Yes . . . I spoke to Dr Copperthwaite. He said I could have China tea if I asked for it. He said so. I want it.

LETOUZEL. It's much more expensive.

PHINEUS. Yes.

LETOUZEL. I'll see about it. Next week. . . . Oh, by the way, dear, I wonder if you wouldn't mind putting your name on this. (*She produces a document and a fountain-pen.*)

PHINEUS. Oh dear . . . what?

LETOUZEL. Your usual signature, you just write it *here*. We have to make sure that your Anglo-Ethiopian Copper Shares remain well consolidated, don't we?

PHINEUS. I don't quite understand . . .

LETOUZEL. Consolidated, dear. If we are to spend so much more on having China tea, we must preserve for our investments a degree of consolidation, you know. Sign here, dear.

PHINEUS (*signing*). Yes . . . yes . . .

LETOUZEL (*sings to the audience*).

> One thousand pounds she thought that she could save.
> For no true need, you see:
> Indeed for naked greed.
> The State will pay to dig her narrow grave.

(*She takes the document back.*) That's right, dear . . . thank you. I shall send it to the Solicitor's by the afternoon post. Here is the letter to go with it. (*She produces a letter.*) Would you like to read it over? It refers to your quarterly payments to Dr Copperthwaite, you know he has put his fees up this summer, don't you?

PHINEUS. Has he? Oh dear. I expect it will be because of the extra cost of the tea . . . No, no, I don't want to read it, Mrs Letouzel, I'm afraid it might perturb me . . . must I put my name?

LETOUZEL. If you don't mind, dear. Here.

PHINEUS (*signing*). Yes . . . yes . . .

LETOUZEL (*sings as before*).

> One thousand pounds she thought that she could save.
> For no true need, you see:
> Indeed for China tea.
> A marble teapot should adorn her grave.

She takes the letter back and puts it together with the other document into an envelope, closes it, but does not seal.

PHINEUS. Is Mr Golightly coming to see me this afternoon, do you imagine?

LETOUZEL. I've no idea, I'm sure. He usually contrives to. So I expect he will today. . . . Oh by the way, dear, you've forgotten your contribution for the Spastic Children Fund, haven't you? Dr Copperthwaite wants all of us to be regular contributors, you know. (*She produces from the recesses of her clothing a small oblong collection box which she presents.*) Half a crown, dear.

MRS PHINEUS *finds a coin after much fumbling in her huge knitting bag.*

LETOUZEL (*sings to the audience during the fumbling*).

> One thousand pounds she thought that she could save.
> The children's need, you see,
> To me is dear indeed.
> This narrow box more fruitful than the grave.

Thank you, dear. Tired? Yes. Why don't we have a nice

rest, that's right, close your eyes, dear, a nice rest . . . yes . . .

She wheels her away.

Scene Three

Enter GOLIGHTLY.

GOLIGHTLY. Ah, well, thank goodness that's over for today. Undignified, yes, but alas, you will tell me, necessary. Dr Copperthwaite says necessary, a good working bowel is the foundation of a good working life. Even in the evening of our days the heart may – may it not? – beat its wings a little, unencumbered by the more brutish obstructions. It will shortly be time for my cup of tea with Mrs Phineus. You understand that most days she condescends to receive me, and – a cup of tea, a Bath-bun, or Eccles-cake, a few mild words of tender and respectful intercourse, and if she is so minded – a little sport or game, a gay twenty minutes. Sometimes dominoes, sometimes spillikins, sometimes halma – *today* – ha ha – (*He produces a small dartboard from under his coat.*) I have obtained permission, with some difficulty, for this. Darts, in a hospital, may be said to be hazardous. But I pressed the point. I emphasized to the Doctor that my skill was considerable and there would be no damage. Mrs Phineus can't play darts. But if I can teach her, shall I not in some manner be putting her in my debt, and is not that an enviable state for a yearning heart? Hey? Let's hang it up. (*He hangs the board on the rear wall of the stage.*) Now then: three darts – let's see what we can score. (*He throws the darts. They all miss the board.*) Oh.

Never mind. Practice makes perfect. Try, try again. (*He throws them again. They all hit the board but with a very low score. He quickly takes the two worst and improves their position.*) Ye-es. Well, we'll call that one bull, one twenty – oh, we'll allow this one, a five – not so good, but it *got* there. (*He now pretends to talk to his opponent.*) Your turn, Mrs Phineus – no, no, dear lady, hold it so, the helping hand, the tenative touch on the shoulder – ah dear, dear dear, balance, above all, *balance*! Splendid! Splendid! Next time they'll *all* be on the board. Remarkable progress for such a beginner. . . . Perhaps we're a little tired? Tea? Oh, *tea*, Mrs Phineus – how very kind, certainly, dear lady, or may I use a more familiar name? This tender moment, Margaret, this – oh Margaret, all my life, all my life I have waited for such a – Margaret, I melt, I weep, forgive me, my presumption, so sweet, so tender, oh so very vulnerable and in need of my protection, dearest love, my heart, my chick, my chuck, princess of pulchritude – oh love, dear love –

In his emotion he is now kneeling at an imaginary pair of feet. MRS LETOUZEL *enters wheeling* MRS PHINEUS *in her chair.* MRS PHINEUS *is asleep.*

GOLIGHTLY. Oh, good gracious, how do you do, dear lady – Mrs Letouzel – I seemed to have broken a shoelace. Careless, but undaunted, I should wear elastic-sided boots, should I not?

LETOUZEL. Ssh, she's asleep.

GOLIGHTLY. Oh.

LETOUZEL. Do you think I could have a word with you, Mr Golightly? Now, quickly, before she wakes up? She'll be asking for her tea.

GOLIGHTLY. Ah, yes, her tea –

LETOUZEL. How does it go?

GOLIGHTLY. I beg your pardon?

LETOUZEL. You: her: how does it go? Let's play the Truth
game – we're old enough, aren't we?

> Truth or Lie, till the day I die
> Strike you dead if you tell me a lie.

Come on, Mr Golightly, oho come on, rogue, *I* know the
tickling heart. Who's the discreet one – you or me? Who
sends her tea in every day and always asks the nurse for
two cups? Who contrives the Eccles-cakes or Bath-buns
on her plate and sees that always there's an *even* number?
Who's your fairy-godmother, Mr Golightly? Dr Copperthwaite – or me? Oh come on – come on, you rogue –

GOLIGHTLY. You put me to a confusion, Mrs Letouzel, I
had not realized that I was so apparent. . . .

LETOUZEL. The tender heart calls to the tender heart, you
know. Yes: but: ah no: no, no: yet, but: I *do* wonder . . .

GOLIGHTLY. You wonder?

LETOUZEL. If perhaps I haven't been a half-inch stupid, a
quarter-inch too easily swung, by sentiment maybe – she
will eat you up.

GOLIGHTLY. Eat me?

LETOUZEL. What happened to *Mister* Phineus?

GOLIGHTLY. Mister? Why, post-operative complications
following an appendicectomy, I understood.

LETOUZEL. Yes. But complications; not always organic, are
they?

GOLIGHTLY. What? but –

LETOUZEL. I am saying not a thing. Only reflecting. I see
you: and I see her, and ah, it's not always so good to be too
warm and trusting. The trusting heart, the fallen fled-
gling.

GOLIGHTLY. Mrs Letouzel, really, I must protest. These
are insinuations, yes, that is what they are, dear lady, I'm
sorry, but there is no other word. And in fairness to Mrs
Phineus I must ask you either to keep them to yourself, or
at least not behind her back, or in the long run to establish

evidence, madam, but not just to *toss* – this broadcasting, this subversive, this cruel undermining – I must insist, madam: *no!*

MRS PHINEUS *wakes.*

LETOUZEL. Ssh, she's awake.

PHINEUS. It is now half past four.

LETOUZEL. Not quite yet, my dear. Twenty past.

PHINEUS. Eh.

LETOUZEL. Twenty past. Twenty past four, dear.

PHINEUS. No. Half past. I never make a mistake about the time. When I wake up I know to the moment the exact hour of the day. Your watch must be slow, dear Mrs Letouzel. Ten minutes. Yes.

GOLIGHTLY. You are quite right, Mrs Phineus. It *is* half past four.

PHINEUS. I beg your pardon – I am a little hard of hearing – ah, Mr Golightly, how very agreeable to see you this afternoon and what a pleasant surprise. Yes. You're quite right, it is half past. Dear Mrs Letouzel, as you go out, perhaps you would be so kind as to ask nurse to bring in my tea. Mr Golightly, will you join me? I do hope so. Two cups, my dear. You just ask the nurse. Yes.

Exit MRS LETOUZEL.

PHINEUS. Sit beside me, Mr Golightly.

GOLIGHTLY. Shall we have our little game, before tea, my dear lady.

PHINEUS. I beg your pardon? I'm a little hard of –

GOLIGHTLY. I said would you like to play our –

PHINEUS. Oh no, I don't think so today, I am very tired of dominoes. Dr Copperthwaite says that the black and white, so often repeated, must eventually affect my eyes. Yes.

GOLIGHTLY. Not dominoes today.

PHINEUS. No, no, not dominoes. Dear Mrs Letouzel will send in the nurse and she shall bring us tea.

GOLIGHTLY. I thought you might prefer to play –

PHINEUS. I have asked this week for neither Bath-buns nor Eccles-cake, but a small tomato sandwich. One has to consider the intake of protein. Dr Copperthwaite does not seem very aware of the danger of starch in my diet. I have spoken to him about it. Yes. Twice.

GOLIGHTLY. To play *darts*?

PHINEUS. I beg your pardon?

GOLIGHTLY. Darts? You see, there is the board all ready for us. Three darts and they're very light and easy to throw. Perhaps if I could demonstrate –

PHINEUS. No no. Not dominoes today. Hopscotch.

GOLIGHTLY. Hopscotch?

PHINEUS. Yes. You see, you must mark out the floor – and then – oh we're neither of us too old to jump here – and then there. Are we? No. Dr Copperthwaite says I must leave my chair for a good half hour every day. Give me a piece of chalk.

GOLIGHTLY. Oh, chalk? Well I should have a piece –

PHINEUS. I have a piece. (*She takes a huge piece of chalk out of her enormous reticule.*) Mark out the squares.

GOLIGHTLY. I don't think I quite remember how –

PHINEUS. I do. (*She jumps out of her wheel-chair and points out the position of the squares on the stage for him, moving with surprising agility, and always being a couple of moves in front of him.*) One there.

GOLIGHTLY (*drawing hastily*). Here?

PHINEUS. Then two. Here.

GOLIGHTLY. Here?

PHINEUS. There.

GOLIGHTLY. Oh. Here.

PHINEUS. Then three. Three there.

GOLIGHTLY. Here.

PHINEUS. Three more. More.

GOLIGHTLY. Yes.

PHINEUS. Two.

GOLIGHTLY (*puffed*). Oh ha hoo – Two.

PHINEUS. And one. And one. And one, here. Here. Here. One there. There.

GOLIGHTLY. And one and one and one . . . would you like first turn?

PHINEUS. No, you.

GOLIGHTLY. Are you quite sure you wouldn't –

PHINEUS. Go on. Go on. Hop!

GOLIGHTLY. But shouldn't there be a stone, or a tin, to – to kick?

PHINEUS. What have you got?

GOLIGHTLY (*produces a matchbox*). This?

PHINEUS. No.

GOLIGHTLY (*produces spectacle-case*). This?

PHINEUS. No. No.

GOLIGHTLY (*produces gold cigarette-case*). Well, all I have left is –

PHINEUS. That one. Yes.

GOLIGHTLY. But, dear lady, it's real gold –

PHINEUS. Very pretty. That one. Yes. Now hop.

GOLIGHTLY (*hopping with difficulty*). One: and two: and –

He rests on both feet.

PHINEUS. No no no! Not to rest yet. One foot, only. *This* square, you can rest.

GOLIGHTLY. Oh dear. Yes. Ah . . . Ah . . . Oh dear. (*He falls down.*) I don't think I can quite –

PHINEUS. My turn. The rules are strict, you see. Not to rest except in the outside square. *My* turn now. (*She hops.*) One. Two. Oh . . . Oh . . . Three! I'm allowed a rest. (*She rests.*)

GOLIGHTLY. No.

PHINEUS. Yes. The second time, you see. This is the *second* hop. So we have extra rests. Yours was the *first* hop, wasn't it?

GOLIGHTLY. But this is the first hop *you've* had.

PHINEUS. No. In the whole game: the *second* hop. Now then: (*She hops farther.*) One two three. Ah . . . Ah . . . A little rest, here. Yes. Now then: one two three. I'm allowed another rest. Here. Yes. This is the second hop. Now then: one two three – (*She accidentally kicks the cigarette-case out of play: but picks it up and puts it in the final square.*) *Home! I* won. *I* won. *I* won. *I* won. Yes. *I* won. *I* won. Yes. *I* won. *I* won. *I* won. Yes. *I* won. *I* won. *I* won.

GOLIGHTLY. No!

PHINEUS. I *won*.

GOLIGHTLY. But you used your fingers. Picked it up with your fingers. It has to be *kicked*.

PHINEUS. No. No. The second hop: you see. Those are the rules.

GOLIGHTLY. Oh? Are they? Oh. I didn't quite remember them like that, I must say, but –

PHINEUS. Shall we have tea? Yes.

Enter NURSE JONES *with tea-things*.

Here it is. I thought it would come now. Thank you so much, Nurse. So very kind.

NURSE JONES *helps her back into her chair, and then leaves*.

I'm mother, am I not? Yes. So while I pour the tea, dear Mr Golightly, perhaps you would sing to me? It would be so kind. Yes. The melancholy song, perhaps.

GOLIGHTLY. Oh, please, not that one – I had really rather not . . .

PHINEUS. The melancholy one. It begins, you know how it begins – about the Sea Captain who steers his ship in vain,

and then about the whales. You remember, don't you?
Sing it. Yes.

She attends to the tea-things.

GOLIGHTLY. As you wish, dear lady – (*He sings.*)
        It is in vain the bold sea-captain
        Steers his ship toward a star
        The world turns round, the star is turning,
        His voyage wanders wide and far.

        He cannot mark the course he's taking
        His eyes are blind with salty scale.
        The storm destroys his very heart root
        As tears the harpoon through the whale.

        The whalefish dies in a bloodred whirlpool
        The sailor dies on the frozen strand.
        Washed up by waves for years that drove him
        Brought him at last to an unknown land.

        The life of man is lost and lonely,
        Whereas the porpoise and the whale
        They both have meaning and conclusion –

The song loses coherence.

        But he finds no meaning nor conclusion
        He finds no meaning nor –
        Whereas the porpoise and the whale –
I don't believe it! have always said love, Mrs Phineus, I
have always believed it, I must still believe it, you cannot
but credit that I have always certainly held to it, and even
if without true experience, look, I have never really been
able to put it to the proof – oh my dear, dear Mrs Phineus,
I have never killed a whale, I have never *seen* a whale, nor
yet travelled on a ship, except to the Isle of Wight when
my sister lived in Shanklin – but, Love, it must surely be
Love, *there* is a star that will not turn, I have had faith in

this, for years, years, please, it must be true, *Love* is the meaning, say it is the conclusion – say it say it – *please!* . . . Why, you've finished up all the tea, Mrs Phineus.

PHINEUS. Oh no, not all of it. Surely not.

GOLIGHTLY. But then, I suppose, I suppose, why not? Is it not your prerogative? Indeed, dear lady, are you not fully entitled – perhaps there is just a little bit left at the bottom of the pot? Oh dear, oh dear. Well then . . . And after all she brought very few sandwiches, and small ones, small . . . Perhaps I may have eaten one without actually noticing? I *do* feel quite full, as though I *had* had tea. I am quite absent-minded. Yes.

PHINEUS. Yes.

GOLIGHTLY. Yes?

PHINEUS. I am particularly partial to tomato sandwiches. I am so glad that you are as well.

Enter NURSES *and* MRS LETOUZEL.

LETOUZEL. Time for your bath, dear. Isn't it, Nurse? Half past five, dear.

PHINEUS. No. Five and twenty to six. I always know the time. I always know the time. I don't think I wish to have my bath tonight. No bath tonight, no bath tonight. No –

LETOUZEL. Oh but you must, dear, you must have your bath –

PHINEUS. No, no, no, no, no bath tonight –

Protesting in panic, she is wheeled out by the NURSES.

GOLIGHTLY. Give her a bath. Give her a bath. Hot, seething, pitch and brimstone. That's what she deserves. Cruel. Oh: here, here, there's a fish hook, here – (*He touches his throat.*) She's jerking it, tugs at it! Cruel!

LETOUZEL. It's true what I said then?

GOLIGHTLY. I would ask you not to concern yourself,

madam, with what is not your concern. Permit me, if you please, to confine my misery to my own private bosom.

Exit. MRS LETOUZEL *then sits down and takes out her collection box and documents. She starts looking over these, making ticks with a pen, etc.*

LETOUZEL (*as* GOLIGHTLY *leaves*). Ye-es, well, now that the interference seems to be at least temporarily eliminated, perhaps we'd better check our current totals, h'm? . . . 'One thousand pounds she thought that she could save . . .'

Enter CRAPE *creeping up behind her. He starts singing, and she jumps to her feet, whipping the documents, etc., out of sight.*

CRAPE (*sings*).
> There was an old woman in our town
> In our town did dwell
> And she grafted in a thousand pounds
> But she wanted more as well.

LETOUZEL. Highly diverting, Mr Crape, but it would be more to your credit if –

CRAPE (*laughing fit to split*).
> Whip she larey tidifoo larey
> Whip she larey oh
> She grafted in a thousand pounds
> But she –

LETOUZEL. I said I had no doubt it is highly diverting, but you don't astonish me, Mr Crape: and particularly I am not astonished to find you creeping about, behind a lady's back, in carpet slippers. It's all of a piece. Go to the devil.

CRAPE. That's a very disagreeable sentiment, Mrs Letouzel. I prefer to ignore it. . . . Heh, ha ha, I see you sent off our little Golightly with a good sharp nip to his backend. Crabs' claws or lobsters', eh? (*He picks up her hand and examines her fingers.*) They look a bit blue, dear. I'd call it lobsters. . . . Let's play the Truth Game. Old Mrs Phineus's thousand pounds isn't as easy to get at as you thought it ought to be? A snippet here, a snippet there, but no real achievement – true?

    Truth or Lie: till the day you die

    Strike you dead if you tell me a lie.

Go on . . . true? All right. *Your* turn. You ask me.

LETOUZEL. I have no intention of being so childish.

CRAPE. As you like then. I'm only playing fair.

LETOUZEL. Wait a minute. Wait: I *will* take a turn.

    Truth or Lie: till the day you die

    Strike you dead if you tell me a lie.

CRAPE. Granted.

LETOUZEL. You have little talks with the Doctor, don't you, two or three times a week?

CRAPE. Eh? Now, now look here, old woman –

LETOUZEL. Truth or lie?

CRAPE. Uh . . . true. But don't you go thinking –

LETOUZEL. I know the sort of thing you trot along to tell him, Mr Crape, make no mistake about *that*! But I'm really far more interested in what *he* tells to you.

CRAPE. He doesn't tell me anything – or anyway, if he does, it is under the seal of confidence. I wouldn't dream of infringing it.

LETOUZEL. What about this Bounty?

CRAPE. Bounty? What Bounty?

LETOUZEL. I know because he said so. I went to see him on Friday to make a very justified complaint. I said to him: 'Dr Copperthwaite, the present-day cost of living is very very hard upon we older people who have lived through two world wars.' And he said to me –

CRAPE. 'Bah wah wah wah-wah, Robinson, Smith, clear it up, sweep it away, that's all for this morning!'

LETOUZEL. And I said to him –

CRAPE. 'But for we *older* people, Dr Copperthwaite, who have lived through two world wars, the Old Age Pension is scandalous, the National Assistance gives us nothing –'

LETOUZEL. 'The Socialist Party in 1947 quite deliberately stole my savings.'

CRAPE. 'There are those of us, Dr Copperthwaite, who have lived through two world wars!'

LETOUZEL. And he said to me –

CRAPE. 'Bah wah wah wah-wah, Nurse Brown, Nurse Jones, swabs, basins, towels, liniment, ointment –'

They both dissolve into excessive laughter. CRAPE *emerges from it first.*

'Mrs Letouzel, you cantankerous old bag, what d'you mean, by complaining about your money! Your board and lodging and medical treatment in this benighted Bridewell is free! It's paid for by the voluntary contributions of our worshipful Patrons, and also, in part, by the Government. All *you* are asked to provide, God damn your eyes, are those few small comforts which –'

LETOUZEL. Which – ?

CRAPE. '*Which* in the fullness of time will be rendered unnecessary by –'

LETOUZEL. 'By the Bounty paid out by the Ministry of Health.'

CRAPE. That's not what I was going to say.

LETOUZEL. No. But it *is* what *he* said. I'm afraid he had lost control. He was most ill-tempered and abusive. But that was what he said.

CRAPE. I've never heard of no Ministerial Bounty.

LETOUZEL. No more had I, Mr Crape. And the doctor made it perfectly clear that I was not supposed to have done, either. He turned red in the face and went stamping and bumbling away. A slip of the tongue, you see: but what did it signify?

CRAPE. Steady, steady – here comes the Heavy Brigade –
'The Colonel said, die hard my boys. And by God they
died hard. . . .'

HARDRADER *enters. He looks around for his dog, sees it is not
with him, then goes back to the door, opens it, calls 'Hector,
Hector'. The dog (imaginary of course) comes apparently
running in and leaps up at* CRAPE. *He and* MRS LETOUZEL
react in a panic. The dog barks.

HARDRADER. No no, down boy, down – go to heel, Hector,
heel, boy, *heel!*

LETOUZEL. Must you bring that dog in here, Mr Hardrader?

CRAPE. Hey, hey, down you devil, down!

HARDRADER. Down, boy, down, leave him alone, he's all
right, Crape, don't be frightened, he's a gentle as a
goldfish. If you show him you're afraid of him, of course
he comes round on you. Now Hector, sit down. Behave
yourself. I shan't tell you twice. That's better. There, you
see: perfectly disciplined – the word of command. He was
only having his fun. Do you know, we've made a splendid
walk this afternoon, Hector and me – eight miles out,
eight and a half miles in again, over the hill past the
housing estate, along the arterial road, railway line,
gasworks – out into the fresh air, beautiful. I composed
two verses in praise of nature – then sharp about turn at
the bridge over the motorway, back we came, eight miles,
half a mile detour at the cemetery corner to visit Mrs
Hardrader's grave, flowers on the grave, a few words,
composed a verse in praise of the departed, Hector gives
her a howl too in commemoration – oh he remembers,
don't you, boy? Then home again for tea, fit, tired,
splendid.

LETOUZEL. You ought to see he stays in his kennel. It's not
fair on other people. Good boy, then, good boy . . . er

Hector, there you are now, Hector – keep him away, man, keep him away for heaven's sake!

HARDRADER. Hector, I said *sit!*

LETOUZEL. It is quite wrong to bring a dog that size into the hospital, Mr Hardrader. I'm surprised Dr Copperthwaite –

HARDRADER. Nonsense, Mrs Letouzel. Best friend a man ever had. Why, he used to live in my own room when I first came here, but some busybody made a complaint. Do you know this, Mrs Letouzel: I'm not an unsociable man, but I can only claim to have had two real friends in the whole of my life. That's Mrs Hardrader, and Hector. And Hector is the better of the two. Aha, boy, aha, nearly time for your biscuits. . . . What *you* need, y'know, Crape, is a bit more physical exercise. Nothing else necessary. A few strong walks, ride a tricycle, up and down with the dumb-bells! I tell you what, when the equipment arrives for the Doctor's new Gymnasium, I'll give you two afternoons a week on the parallel bars and the climbing ropes. I'll put something like a framework back inside *you*, man: completely rejuvenate you in less than a month!

CRAPE. *Parallel bars!* What are you talking about? He's not going to waste his money getting us parallel bars at *our* age! Why, I couldn't *possibly* –

HARDRADER. Maybe not now, but I think you'll find you will. Astonishing what a man can do with a bit of training. The equipment certainly has been ordered, y'know. The storekeeper told me himself. *He* was a bit surprised, as well . . . H'm, yes . . . Oh it'll do us a power of good! You can give me ten years, I suppose, Crape: but you take a look at me. There's good fresh air in here – (*Thumping his chest.*) What have you got? What have you got there? Smog.

VOICE (*over the loudspeaker*). Mr Golightly, please. Mr

Golightly to report to Sister's Office. Mr Golightly, if you please.

HARDRADER. Ha! Sounds like the silly pansy's got to have another enema! Hope he enjoys it. Ha ha.

VOICE. Correction to the last announcement. Correction. Mr *Hardrader* to report to Sister's Office, *not* Mr Golightly. Mr Hardrader, if you please.

HARDRADER. Indeed I shall do nothing of the sort! I have no use at all for that sort of treatment. It's merely pandering to one's natural sluggishness. No good. No good. (*He sings, with gestures that alarm* CRAPE *and* MRS LETOUZEL.)

> I will not stoop, I will not bend,
> I live my life to the uttermost end.
> And when they come to drag me in –
> Ho! Left, right, straight to the chin!
> Bang, crash, ho, ooh, wallop, out –
> Take him away!
> Hardrader, Hardrader,
> Hardrader wins the day.

What do *you* say, Hector?

> Ho! Grab him, get him, sick him, go for his throat –
> Take him away!
> Bold Hector, Bold Hector,
> Bold Hector wins the day –

Enter NURSE BROWN. HARDRADER *nervously tries to escape the other way.*

Yes, Nurse, right away. Yes . . .

He tries to drive the dog out the far side.

Go away boy, go on, go – you're not wanted, no. Get rid of him, Crape. Go on, be off! . . . (*The dog is pushed out by* CRAPE *and* LETOUZEL.) Oh, yes, Nurse. Yes. Indeed, yes: Sister's Office, I was just on my way – yes.

HARDRADER *goes out with the nurse.*

LETOUZEL. I shall speak to Dr Copperthwaite. That abominable dog. It's entirely ridiculous.

CRAPE. He says to me rejuvenated? *That* old man – rejuvenated!

LETOUZEL. Rowdiness and rhodomontade, dogs and smells and great muddy boots –

CRAPE. What possible good can any of us get from wanting to be young again? It's only when you're old that you can see how it all sets up – you need experience, you need wisdom – you're not kidding me I'm sorry for my age!

LETOUZEL. Oh? Now you don't believe that, do you, Mr Crape?

CRAPE. Eh?

LETOUZEL. Do you mean to say that there's any sort of value in knowing how to get, when you've no time left you to *spend*? Here we are, look at us, dried up in this Institution, the only things we know how to do are the worst things we ever learned – plotting and planning, avarice and spite. Well, why not? We have no opportunity for anything different. . . . *We* should stop quarrelling: we ought to be friends.

CRAPE. Ah yes, we ought. . . . Oh that stupid Copperbottom, he's wasting his time. What he needs to be working on, if he wants to be worth while, is a *real* rejuvenation! If he could discover a drug that'd make us all young again, yet not destroy our memories – eh? *There* there'd be some value.

LETOUZEL. Who knows? Perhaps he is.

CRAPE. Wait a minute –

LETOUZEL. What d'you mean, wait a minute –

CRAPE. Oh wait a minute . . . we're talking flat rubbish. It's too much to hope for . . . *He* said: Gymnasium. Why build a Gymnasium? Right?

LETOUZEL. I suppose so –

CRAPE. Wait a minute. *You* said: Ministerial Bounty. Why

give us a Bounty? It's not been provided for in any Act of Parliament so far as *I* know. Right?

LETOUZEL. No, you're right, it hasn't . . .

CRAPE. But supposing –

LETOUZEL. Supposing –

CRAPE. Supposing *you* were a mermaid, you'd have a lovely silver tail – right? And you'd need water to swim in!

LETOUZEL. Right!

CRAPE. But supposing, supposing, instead of a mermaid, you was a young woman! You'd need some sort of dowry to start you out in life! And if *I* was a young man – parallel bars! I could *swing* on the parallel bars! Oh my good Lord, I'd be jumping like a monkey!

LETOUZEL. It isn't very likely.

CRAPE. Not? Is it not? (*He pulls out the paper he found in* SCENE ONE.) Now take a look at this. Disregard the mathematics. Look at these names. Optimum ages, estimated reductions, here we are, months, years, you see! He's *doing* it!

LETOUZEL. He must be!

CRAPE. That's what he's doing!

BOTH TOGETHER. He's going to *rejuvenate* us!

Startled by a sudden noise, they go rigid, saying: 'Ssh!'

CRAPE. It's all right: it's nothing. Someone slammed a door. . . .

LETOUZEL. When will it happen?

CRAPE. I was in with him this morning. There was a sort of an accident. Bound to hold things up a little. We've got time to reflect.

LETOUZEL. Ye-es. . . . How dare he? How *dare* he? Without one word to us!

CRAPE. Quite right – how dare he. . . . But it stands to reason, after all, he's got to keep it secret till he's worked out his formulas. What *you* want to fix your mind on, y'know, is this question of the Bounty.

LETOUZEL. H'm, yes, of course. There is that point of view . . . ah, it's bound to be inadequate. Public funds, bureaucratic parsimony – and just when I was really reaching my nose into the true fat meat of her savings. . . . I have it! I shall go into partnership with her.

CRAPE. Partnership in what?

LETOUZEL. In a little Agency, Mr Crape. She'll still have what I've left her out of her thousand, we'll invest it intelligently according to my system. All my life, I have been waiting for this. Scheme after scheme, absolutely foolproof, has been baulked from the beginning by my never having quite enough capital to carry it through. In 1945 everything was set for such a speculation in transport shares that – oh, that shameful General Election! The black ingratitude of the British public. . . . Enough of this. I shall set up my Agency.

CRAPE. What sort of Agency?

LETOUZEL. A general Agency. No staff. Just myself (and of course, the sleeping partner, dear Mrs P – oh yes, and she will sleep!). Our clients will write in and I shall conduct their business for them entirely through correspondence. The letters come, the transaction is performed, the letters go out again, and the percentages accrue. Each profit invested, and investment profitable! Life, Mr Crape: *life*, to be relived once more. I can't wait for the day!

CRAPE. *I'm* going into business, and all. I'm going to open a warehouse. Export-Import. Y'know. packing-cases, oil-drums, boxes of porridge-oats – there are going to be *men* working for *me* – fifteen of 'em, in green aprons and a cap with a leather peak. 'Three more lorries to be unloaded, hurry it up, ah, Parkinson, how's the kiddies? And the missus? Good . . . Hardrader! Get them iron girders to the other end of the shed before lunch-time and when you've done that you can carry them big bales right up into the loft.'

LETOUZEL. You're not going to employ *him*!

CRAPE. Ho ho, I am so – you see him young again and out into the world – he'll be as helpless as a babe! He was put in here in the first place by some of his own family. Too hearty about their house by far, he was. They lived in a semi, y'know, only about a mile away, and he brought all the half-timbering down one night sleep-walking – he strides into a bow window and he carries it straight out into the garden with him! But when he's thirty-five and I'm twenty-six, I'll have that physical phenomenon working for me till the floor-joists rock beneath him! Bow wow, bow wow, down, ye devil, *down*! What about Golightly?

LETOUZEL. What about him?

CRAPE. If he marries Ma Phineus, and he might very well – you won't find much partnership left, will you? A bit of rejuvenation could make a great deal of difference.

LETOUZEL. Then I'd better go and court him myself, I suppose, and you'd better court Hardrader, if you want to make sure of him before he gets his own ideas. But for God's sake keep it secret!

CRAPE. Strike me dead if I utter a word! *We* know, don't we, and nobody else! We're on a stance of power, *we* are – like, hand in hand, aren't we? . . . We ought to get wed! Why, who knows *what* we're going to turn out like? We might be like *Gods*!

LETOUZEL. Ah no, Mr Crape. It's Business is our business, that's all.

CRAPE. Oh, but I used to be handsome – you know, they called me Dandy Jimmy! You wait and see! (*He sings.*)

> To be born into this world again
> As a little child to grow
> Where the young need the old

For to show them the road –
LETOUZEL (*sings*). And the old need the young to go.

They sing the song through, once more together, and dance out.

VOICE (*over the loudspeaker*). Mr Crape, please. Mr Crape to report to Sister's Office. Mr Crape, if you please.

ACT TWO

Scene One

DOCTOR (*offstage*). Robinson! Mr Robinson! Mr Smith! Mr Smith!

Enter DOCTOR, *followed by* ORDERLY ROBINSON *who carries a retort full of liquid.* ORDERLY SMITH *enters by other door and meets them. He carries notebooks.*

DOCTOR. Notebooks? Have you got the retort? Let's have a look at it . . . Ah, aha, ha. You see, you see – dark blue, dark blue, look at it, and it shades into black down at the bottom. Black sediment: blue: just as I thought. It came in a flash. I never even dreamt – I'll tell you, by God, I think this is it! What a devil of a good chance that damfool patient interrupted us when he did! He doesn't know it, no, but he's speeded up his own chances by a third, by a half, I should think by *three-quarters* – you see what he's done? The very fact it coagulated, may be the one clue we need! I must have been blind. This is one of those discoveries in the history of science that –

He leafs through his notebooks.

Yes, yes – here we are – ha: six point eight-six-nine, seventy-two, four by three by two, *divide*, cross the co-ordinates, bending-moment, bending-moment – quick –

ORDERLY SMITH *finds a place for him in a log-table and does a quick calculation in the margin with a biro.*

Good boy, good: right, right – and by the power of three – and there we are! So. Twenty-four hours more: there should be one more change in the colour. I'm certain there will be. Then we'll try it again over the bunsen, add in your accotile and heraclith solution – half-quantities, make a note – and if it turns green, we've got it! A short cut at last. It's more than a short cut – it's much more than that – I hardly dare say it but it's opening out a whole new field of development. This means, this means that I'm going to be able to put this Elixir straight into full production, straight on the world market! Robinson, I want you to get a draft report made out, as soon as you have time. We must tell the Ministry. It alters our whole timetable. An agonizing – a *wonderfully* agonizing reappraisal of the entire Copperthwaite Project! You know, I'm going to have those five young again by the end of next week. I tell you they're going to skip like mountain bloody goats! All right, Robinson. Take it away. Put it back in the rack. And make sure you check that temperature. Twenty-four hours more. How on earth am I going to live through it? Go on, boy, go on . . .

Exit ORDERLY ROBINSON *with retort.*

Get me the telephone. I want to talk to Charlie Sanderson. You know his number, don't you?

ORDERLY SMITH *fetches from the recess a telephone on a lead. He rapidly dials a number, then hands receiver to* DOCTOR.

Hello – Charlie? . . . Jack. How are you, sport? Ha ha, go on, go on, you don't tell me, he he, watch it, Charlie, watch it, she'll have you at the altar before you've buttoned your breeches. . . . Now seriously, Charlie, look, I'm going to have to scratch from the match on Saturday. . . . No no, of course it isn't because of last week, of course I don't bear a grudge, boy. I was off form and I knew it, you were quite right what you said to me,

I'd have told you the same. . . . All right, sport, all right. Forgiven and forgotten. But the fact of the matter is, there's something big coming up at the hospital. . . . Oh the usual line, you know, nothing earth-shaking, bedpans and thermometers – but it may be important and I just daren't commit myself, I'm sorry. . . . Well what about Jimmy Ricketts, then, can't you play him in the second row, make that new type with the big 'tache your hooker – what's his name – Hawkins? – and then swop your scrum-half with – take it easy, Charlie, I know you're the Captain, I know it's short notice. And I may be damn good, boy, but I'm not indispensable – in any case, we're only playing a Teachers' Training College, they'll be outclassed, sport, no question – you'll never even notice I'm not there. . . . Oh, good. Well that's damned accommodating of you, Charlie, I'm bloody grateful, really . . . what? . . . Ho, ho, no! Oh, you look out for *her*, chum – and make sure you know where you've hidden your bedroom key. . . . All right Charlie, I'll remember. I'll put 'em in the post for you. Medical goods, a plain envelope – *I* know the drill. We'll keep you a bachelor yet. . . . Yes, on the Health Service. Taxpayers for ever! So long, sport, so long. And best of luck on Saturday. I'll be round for the beer in the evening. . . . So long. (*He rings off.*) Thank you Mr Smith. Put it away, please.

ORDERLY SMITH *removes telephone.*

Oh, while I've got it in my mind – I want you to take a letter – I heard a dog bark in the corridor this afternoon. Before we know where we are, we'll have old Crape along with more of his eternal complaints: so I'm damn well putting a stop to it, *now*.

ORDERLY SMITH *prepares to take dictation in one of the notebooks.*

To Mr Hardrader. Dear Mr Hardrader, it has been brought to my notice that in defiance of the permanent regulations of this hospital, you persist in retaining your pet animal on the premises. I would be glad if you would arrange to have the dog removed within thirty-six hours or else I shall have no option but to give instructions to have it destroyed. Yours, etcetera, etcetera, J. Copperthwaite, Superintendent. Sign it p.p. me and see he gets it at once. . . . That ought to make the place a little more hygienic. I don't like dogs anyway. . . . Dogs . . . I may need that dog. Cancel the letter. Write it like this: 'The dog must be delivered to my Office within thirty-six hours or else.' Then get someone who knows about these things to put a value on the beast. I think it's only a mongrel: but I wouldn't want to take it from the old fellow without paying him something. . . . That'll do for this afternoon. Will you attend to it directly? Thank you.

Exeunt severally.

Scene Two

MRS LETOUZEL *enters cautiously. She creeps across the stage to the opposite door, peeps through it, and then flattens herself against the doorpost as* GOLIGHTLY *enters, slowly. He does not see her, nor the mitten which she has taken off and dropped in his path.*

LETOUZEL. Ha h'm. (*He turns round, sees her, inclines his head, coldly but politely, and continues on his way.*)

LETOUZEL. Mr Golightly! I'm afraid I've dropped my mitten.

GOLIGHTLY. I beg your pardon, Mrs Letouzel. I was in a

brown study. Pray forgive me. (*He hands her the mitten and leaves her.*) Good evening . . .

She gives an exasperated exclamation, and dodges out of the door by which he has entered. He sits down dejectedly. She reenters by the door of her original entry: or rather, peeps round it to see what he is doing. He gets up and starts towards her, but without realizing she is there. She retreats behind the door, and when he reaches it, pops out at him with a startled little squeak.

LETOUZEL. Oh! Mr Golightly, really! . . . We seem to be running into each other everywhere! I was just on my way to – well, I didn't expect to meet any gentlemen in *this* corridor, Mr Golightly!

GOLIGHTLY. Good gracious, madam, I really *do* beg your pardon! Excuse me! I will return to my quarters at once.

LETOUZEL (*detaining him*). Mr Golightly.

GOLIGHTLY. Madam?

LETOUZEL. I am truly sorry for you, Mr Golightly. Please believe me when I tell you that. I know what you came here for, you see.

GOLIGHTLY. You do? Oh . . .

LETOUZEL. You hoped to catch some fleeting glimpse, did you not? One last appeal to her implacable divinity, as she is swept from room to room – but it wouldn't be any use. She will never change, never. . . . Dear friend, I beg you: put her out of your mind!

GOLIGHTLY. No. . . . No. . . . I cannot. . . . And you are as bad, you know! Oh yes you are! You gloat and look on. I know what they think – namby-pamby little Golightly, tripping about, ogling, smirking, ha ha, yes, the lady-killer: but all that he's fit for is the queen-bee's dirty work! But I can tell you: when I was a young man I was most certainly admired! It was not considered disgraceful, in those days, to appear spruce and to behave with chivalry. If I could be young – for just one evening, Mrs Letouzel,

I'd show up the crudities, the brutalities of this age! There are young women who would be *astonished*! And that is no fable!

LETOUZEL. Suppose – why not suppose – suppose that you *were* young. Suppose *she* was too. You'd still allow it to go on, just as it goes on now.

GOLIGHTLY. Oh no I would not.

LETOUZEL. Ah, you would not? You'd tear her right out of you, leap away like a rattlesnake, and ravage alone through the hips and the hearts of innumerable others! Oh you promiscuous, you uncontrolled, you terrible danger!

GOLIGHTLY. I don't mean that either. All I intended to say was that I should be able for once to pay my court where my inclinations have dictated, without prejudice from my old age and my concomitant ridiculous appearance.

LETOUZEL. But I told you: she will eat you up.

GOLIGHTLY. Only because of my age.

LETOUZEL. No! If you were no more than eighteen years old tomorrow, and she no more than – you stupid little man, do you not understand that that's all you are going to be! And she, she, she, will already be more than *thirty*! Mr Golightly, what you need is a *friend*: a loving, loyal, and vigilant friend. (*To the audience*.) I have said too much. (*To* GOLIGHTLY.) I should not have told you. (*To audience*.) I should not have told him. Business is business. Business isn't passion. But if passion does occur – ? To me, that *must* be business. I have let myself go. I think I am an idiot. But let's look for advantage. (*To* GOLIGHTLY.) I'll accept it: I've told you. I'd better tell you more. Tell you the lot. Come on.

Exeunt.

Scene Three

Enter HARDRADER *with a piece of paper, pursuing two nurses.*
CRAPE *follows him.*

HARDRADER (*trapping the Nurses in a corner*). Excuse me,
excuse me, Nurses, I won't keep you a moment. Don't be
in such hurry to get away – I may be an old man, but I'm
not an old ghost, y'know. I can assure you, if you listen,
you'll find yourself edified. There now, sit down, sit
down. Nurse Brown –

The NURSES *reluctantly do so.*

Ha ha, Brown, down, what do we make out of that?
    I watch Nurse Brown
    As she sits down
    On the seat beside Nurse Jones.
    Two diamond stones
    Upon one golden ring.
    To view them both,
    Sets my old heart to sing.
    Hey ding-a-ding, ding.
Only an improvisation, of course. Rough, rough. I know.
But what about this? This one's *considered*, this is what I
want you to hear: (*He reads.*) To Hector – that's my dog.
    Old fellow. You and I through life
    Have wandered without hurt or strife
    Between us, man and dog. How few
    Of humankind can say so too!
    How few can say, that with a wife
    The years have passed so freely, as with you!
    Alas, how few!
Well, there you are? There's the Sentiment: is it the
Truth? Oh, come on, young ladies, don't be bashful. A
poem must be true or else it's no good – so tell me, be
honest. . . .

LOUDSPEAKER. Nurse Jones, Nurse Brown, to report at
once to Sterilization Room. Nurse Jones, Nurse Brown,
please. Sterilization.

Exeunt NURSES.

HARDRADER. Oh. Thoroughly disheartening. Every time I
try to teach these young women something, there's
something else calls them away. Always the same. They
never seem to allow them any free time.

CRAPE. They're supposed to be on duty. Stands to reason
they're going to be called for.

HARDRADER. But if they were *off* duty, d'you imagine
they'd stay and listen to me for more than two minutes?
All they want to do is to jig around with yellow-faced
young doctors at these, at these I think they call them
'boogie-woogie' parties, far too late at night. It's not as if
they even took any sensible interest in a few out-of-door
activities. Look at Dr Copperthwaite, certainly he plays a
very respectable game of Rugger every Saturday: but who
bothers to support him? No one from this hospital. Except
me. No one at all.

Enter ORDERLY SMITH *with letter*.

Ah Mr Smith? A letter? For me? For me! What's the
matter? Er, wait a moment – Mr Smith, I say, I say,
please –

Exit ORDERLY SMITH.

What d'you imagine this is?

CRAPE. I should expect it's from the Superintendent.

HARDRADER. I hope nothing's wrong.

CRAPE. It's just the usual routine bureaucracy – you've been
here long enough to know about *that*.

HARDRADER. Dr Copperthwaite only sends notes if there's

something wrong. D'you imagine there could be a – a serious discovery, I mean, for instance, my last X-ray? Cancer? TB?

CRAPE. At your age?

HARDRADER. Why not?

CRAPE. Well at your age, why worry? We're all waiting for it, aren't we?

HARDRADER. I have always prided myself on my continued robust condition. I have always been happy to think that when I go, I shall go – straight: suddenly: upright to the end. I have never a cold, never a cough – which is more than can be said for you –

CRAPE (*with a snuffle*). Colds and coughs are nothing –

HARDRADER. Yes they are, they're symptoms. If there is one thing I have dreaded, it is that something might come – say, cancer, without warning, without warning, without *any* symptoms. Every time the Doctor examines us, I say to myself – 'Not this time, oh my God, not this time.'

CRAPE. Why don't you open it?

HARDRADER. Open it. . . . Goddamit, who's afraid? Who cares a brassnuckle for any blasted young sawbones! Ha – (*He tears the letter open and reads it to himself.*) Good heavens. . . . Oh good heavens. . . . Oh . . . Crape: are you a man?

CRAPE. What sort of a man?

HARDRADER. Breathing. Feeling. Living. That sort. Well, are you?

CRAPE. What's the matter?

HARDRADER. Read it. The man who wrote this letter was not a man. Even if this letter is a joke, if it is mistimed pleasantry in a juvenile bad taste, it was written by no man. Because it is an inhuman letter: and I can tell you Crape, it has made me wish to die.

CRAPE (*having read the letter*). Oh dear dear dear, Mr Hardrader, summon our spirits, man, come on, old chap, cheer up cheer up, rally round the flag, boys. You've still got the dog, I take it?

HARDRADER. I suppose so. I keep him in a potting-shed to the north of the tennis courts. I feed him every day under cover of going to examine the hardcore and the greensward. They all know I like to inspect the sports grounds regularly, and I thought I had been taken for granted down there. Some of the nurses are in the secret, of course. But I said to them: please turn a blind eye. And they are good girls, loyal. They did so. But now – Crape, Crape, what on earth am I going to do?

CRAPE. Give me the dog.

HARDRADER. Give you the –

CRAPE. Get him out of that shed. Let me take him. And don't ask me where. When they come to tell you to hand him over: why, you deny all knowledge. Tell 'em he's run away. What could be easier?

HARDRADER. But what will happen then? Hector can't live without me, why, he –

CRAPE. Of course you'll get him back, old chap, old chap. When the hunt's died down. But don't put him in the potting-shed again. No. Now see: what about the old greenhouse among the rhododendrons west of the cricket pavilion? You go up there to inspect the state of the wicket, don't you? get it . . . eh?

HARDRADER. I would never have trusted Hector to anyone, before, ever. And then, there's another thing. How can I repay you? I am not a man to stand in debt to anyone, ever. You see, I don't even know that I can manage to survive this business. I have not admitted this very often, but I *am* old, Crape, an old man, older than you. And the shock of the separation may –

CRAPE. Temporary separation.

HARDRADER. It is still a separation, and an unendurable one.

CRAPE. It's true you haven't very long to live –

HARDRADER. No. I haven't, now. Under no circumstances, now. Today I know this: I am altogether too old for all those things that I have lived for. Energy. Vigour. Strength of the body. Comradeship. Hector. What does it matter if Hector is destroyed. I am a dead man too. I was a big strong man. Yes, Crape, I was. But it is finished, you see. This letter –

CRAPE. Oh, no, old chap.

HARDRADER. What do you mean?

CRAPE. I wasn't going to tell you – (*To audience.*) I wasn't going to tell him. (*To* HARDRADER.) But you're so down in the dumps, it looks as if I'll have to. (*To audience.*) I don't give a damn for *her*: do I? And do you? No, you don't because I'm the quicker of the two of us: you know it – and whatever she plans, I'll be the paymaster at the end of it all. (*To* HARDRADER.) Old chap, we're going to save Hector. And you're going to understand how very very much it is going to be worth it. You talk of repayment? Aha, you'll have your chance. Come on, and I'll tell you. And then we'll find the dog. Come on, come on. Old chap. Old chap.

Exeunt.

Scene Four

The telephone rings in the recess. ORDERLY SMITH *hurries in, brings out the apparatus, at the same time answering it. Before he has time to speak, the* DOCTOR *enters and takes it from him.*

DOCTOR. All right, Mr Smith, all right – I hear him, I'll take it. Hello, Superintendent here . . . Eh? What? I didn't catch it. Hello! . . . Damn nuisance, they've disappeared. You pick up the phone, there's some silly chicken on the other end, she says 'burble burble' will you hang on for one moment please, I'll put you right through! – and I'm damned if I know who she's putting me through to. Buckingham Palace for all I'm informed. Hello, yes, your Majesty, how simply super of you to call! Yes, of course, Your Majesty, five o'clock would be splendid – shall we wear court dress or is it going to be formal? Eh, hello, yes? . . . Yes, yes, of *course* I'm Copperthwaite. . . . What? (Oh my God, it *is* the Queen – or next best anyway.) Good morning, Sir Frederick – I'm really sorry, I didn't quite recognize . . . Eh, dear dear dear, no no no no, Sir Frederick, *any* time of the day is a convenient time except when I'm . . . Oh. Sunday. I see. . . . Of course, I can't very well say no. But it *would* be a bit happier for me if you could see your way, sir, to deferring it a week. You see, I have to . . . why, if you put it like that, Sir Frederick, of course. Yes. . . . Sunday. Very well sir. . . . No question, no. No no no. *Quite* all right, Sir Frederick. Very happy. Very proud to see you here. Yes. . . . And good-bye to *you*, sir. (*He rings off.*) And good-bye to you, sir. And sir to you, sir. And good-bye, good-bye, good-bye. I'm talking to my peace of mind, that's all. To my careless existence. Good-bye! . . . There, Smith, it's gone! Look at it disappearing. Flight of a swallow. D'you want to know the reason? Sir Frederick, no less. The Lord Mayor and the Bishop. The Mayoress and Mrs Bishop. The Town Clerk and Mrs Clerk, I dare say. Half the bloody Ministry straight down from Whitehall. They're coming, on Sunday. A ceremonial visit. We'd better buy a flag. Get a carpet. Scarlet. Buns, tea, cream in the buns. But I'm not giving 'em drinks. This is a hospital, not a country club. No drinks, no cinema shows, no dancing, no billiards. . . . This is Robinson's report, y'know – too damn keen by far, that chap – I *told* him not to make it so melodramatic. They want to see the Elixir, and they want to see it at work. I'm not ready for an audience! Who do they think I am? They'll be asking for a sputnik or a descent in a bathyscaphe before we know where we are. . . . Well: let's have it organized. Shoulder to the wheel, boy, your back to the wall. They're coming on Sunday. Dial me 36786 will you. And then go away. I want this one private.

ORDERLY SMITH *dials the number, hands back the phone to doctor and exits.*

Hello, is that you, mother? Jack here. . . . Yes, I'm very well indeed, mother – now, look – . . . Just a minute, mother, I'm trying to tell you – . . . I'm *telling* you, mother, I can't come on Sunday. Well of course I hadn't let you know: I'm letting you know now. Look, I can't come on Sunday because there's a man from the Ministry of Health and a whole lot more of the nobs and they're coming down to look at the hospital and I have to be here. . . . No, mother, you *can't* meet them. It's not social, it's official, and . . . now, look, love, I'm sorry: I like to come home as much as you like me to come . . . oh, *was* she? Did I ask her . . . ? For God's sake let me invite my own girls to tea. . . . I *know* Joyce is a nice girl, I'm sure she's a lovely girl, she'll make a positively splendid wife for some stupid . . . All right, mother. I'm sorry. The tongue is sharper than the sword, or the thought is slower than the knife, or whatever they say. I didn't mean to be rude. Make my excuses, tell Joyce I'm sorry. If you must have her to tea, she can come the weekend after –

Barking heard. DOCTOR *becomes aware of dog on stage.*

What's that! Get out of it! Get down there! Down! Smith – I say Smith.

Enter ORDERLY SMITH.

Get this damned dog out! Who let it in? There's a dog in the room, I shall have to ring off. . . . No mother, no,

there's a bloody great dog. . . . I'm sorry, mother . . .
NO! You can ring me next week! (*He rings off and thrusts
telephone at* ORDERLY SMITH.) Where's it gone? Here!
No, no, stop it! Here!

They pursue the dog round the stage in a flurry.

Lord help us, use your sense man, get it to the door – go
on, now, go on, don't be afraid of it, it isn't going to bite
you –

ORDERLY SMITH, *bitten, screams.*

Get it out of the door!

*The dog is got out of the door and they slam the door behind it,
and take breath in relief. The barking starts again at the other
side of the stage.* CRAPE *enters, struggling with the dog at that
side.*

CRAPE. Down, boy, down – go to heel, good boy, good dog,
Hector, Hector – no . . . Doctor, I'm sorry, it's nothing to
do with me – he seemed to run away, I was trying to catch
him –

DOCTOR. Robinson – Where's Robinson?

Enter ORDERLY ROBINSON *above.*

Who let this dog in?

ORDERLY ROBINSON *shrugs and shakes his head helplessly.*

Well, we've got to get it out. Entice it, entice it. Get some
food for it – *quickly* – How should I know what food –
meat, eggs, fish, hurry!

Exit ORDERLY ROBINSON *right.*

CRAPE. Watch him, Doctor, he's beginning to snarl. I think
you've got him vexed.

DOCTOR. Keep still. Just keep still. Smith, I said *still!*
Robinson, where are you?

ORDERLY ROBINSON *enters on main stage with a plate of food.*

What have you got there? Stew? All right, I dare say it eats stew, now attract him, attract him; lead him along with it – gently, gently – look dog, there's a plate of stew, look at the bloody stew, will you – good dog, good dog – rattle the eating irons, Robinson, make some effort to attract him, man – dinner, dinner, dinner – what do they call him?

CRAPE. Hector.

DOCTOR. Hector, boy, Hector, dinner for Hector, that's right, boy, that's right, come to the Doctor – give me the dinner – (*He takes the plate of stew.*) Doctor's got dinner, dinner for Hector, Doctor for Hector, Hector for Doctor, Doctor, Doctor, Hector, Doctor, dinner, dinner, dinner – (*He has worked his way backwards to the recess and quickly lays the plate down inside, clapping the screen closed behind him as he comes out. The barking is heard muffled.*) Three brass balls and be damned for his dinner. Where did he come from? Hardrader? Is it?

CRAPE. Now, doctor, all I was doing was –

DOCTOR. Poking your nose in, that's all you always do – red nose, Mr Crape, thick nose, carbuncles. Too much blood, Mr Crape. Too much. A nose like that needs a good blistering poultice. I shall bear it in mind. Get out of my sight.

Exit CRAPE.

Now then, the dog: go in after him – *carefully* – put him in a basket, strap down the basket, come out again, *carefully* – lock the door behind you. Look sharp.

Exit ORDERLY ROBINSON *into recess.*

So we're all set for Sunday. There's nothing now I need worry about. The Elixir is fermenting all according to plan, Sir Frederick and his friends are all fermenting

according to plan, the dog's in a box according to plan –
my God, the patients. I hadn't given them a thought. They
might none of them be fit – snap check-up, all five, lay it
on. X-rays, all the rest of the business. Robinson!

Enter ORDERLY ROBINSON *from recess, carrying empty
plate.* MRS LETOUZEL *enters.*

All fixed? Then get ready. Snap check-up. All five X-rays,
all the rest of the business. Smith, do you hear me . . .

LETOUZEL. Dr Copperthwaite, if you please, I maintain that
it will not do. This sort of rudeness, simply snatched from
my hands, I shall report it to the governors –

DOCTOR. Nurse, Nurse, Nurse Brown, Nurse Jones – All
five, snap check-up, get ready, lay it on –

DOCTOR *and* ORDERLIES *exeunt severally.* NURSES *cross
the stage busily.*

LETOUZEL. They may have given me the wrong diet, I
wouldn't know, I wasn't told, but to serve me a dinner,
and then to come immediately, simply to snatch it away –

DOCTOR *crosses the stage, meeting* ORDERLIES *who cross in
opposite direction.*

DOCTOR (*en passant*). Report cards, temperature charts,
blood pressures, quick quick quick; Nurse Brown, Nurse
Jones, where have you gone to?

LETOUZEL. I didn't even have time to see what was on the
plate. I thought steak and kidney. But what was there with
it? Pie crust – suet crust, steamed gravy, potatoes, why, I
don't know – I'm not at all fond of steamed suet pudding.
. . . But I should have liked to have known . . .

Enter NURSE JONES.

I tell you, I should like to have known . . .

Exit MRS LETOUZEL *with the* NURSE.

Scene Five

LOUDSPEAKER. Attention, please. Attention, please. This is important. This is urgent. This is extra, unusual, a breach in routine. Mr Crape, Mr Hardrader, Mr Golightly, Mrs Phineus, Mrs Letouzel, will you all report, please, at once, to the X-ray department for immediate examination. The Superintendent's instructions. Will Orderlies and Nurses please ensure, at once, that Mrs Letouzel, Mrs Phineus, Mr Golightly, Mr Hardrader, Mr Crape, all report, at once, for immediate examination. Important. Urgent. Attention. Attention. Nurses and Orderlies, please, attention, attention . . .

OLD PEOPLE (*except* MRS PHINEUS) *run across the upper stage, accompanied by* NURSES. *Then they enter on main stage and cross it going out at opposite side.* ORDERLIES *cross the main stage in the other direction, passing them in the middle. Then the four* OLD PEOPLE *and* NURSE BROWN *reappear on upper stage and sit down in a row. The* ORDERLIES *re-enter on lower stage, as does the* DOCTOR.

DOCTOR. Is everybody there? One, two, three, four –

MRS PHINEUS *is wheeled on to main stage by* NURSE JONES.

– *And* Mrs Phineus. Right. Nurse Brown, I want to make a complete examination of each patient with as few delays as possible – time's as short as patience, remember that, so have everybody undressed and ready to come in, in turn, the minute I give the word. Right? Mr Robinson, Mr Smith, attend to the X-ray equipment inside and let's have the negatives on the dot, in my hand, the minute I give the word. Nurse Jones, you stay down here in the consulting room, please. Right. Speed it up. I'll start with Mrs Phineus in precisely one minute.

The ORDERLIES *go into the recess.* MRS PHINEUS *is taken out of her wheel chair by* NURSE JONES *and led out of one door. The* DOCTOR *goes out of the other.*

CRAPE (*sings*).

> There were five green bottles
> A-hanging on the wall
> Five green bottles a-hanging on the wall
> But one green bottle has obeyed the Doctor's call
> So there's four green bottles a-hanging on the wall,
> Why we're here a-hanging
> We haven't yet been told
> There's an extra-urgent reason that shortly will
>   unfold
> But one green bottle has suddenly gone cold –

At a possible explanation on which his mind takes hold – As he sits here imagining all sorts of explanations and emergencies and urgencies and all manner of unforeseen contingencies, disorders, alarms, provoked or otherwise called into being by the dark hand or instrumentality of chance –

He sneezes, coughs, and splutters.

– Doctor Copperthwaite's examining our health – how is our health? Mrs Letouzel?

LETOUZEL. Good.

CRAPE. Mr Golightly?

GOLIGHTLY. Good. Except for pains about my heart.

CRAPE. Mr Hardrader? Mr Hardrader? Oh tell me an answer – you can tell *me* an answer – (*In a whisper.*) I've got him away, bow-wow, bow-wow, away, away, O.K. *away* –

HARDRADER *brightens up.*

Now, how's your health?

HARDRADER. Oh by jove, by *jove* –

LETOUZEL. Mr Crape, how's yours?

CRAPE. Do you know, I think I've caught a cold – I don't believe it's serious, but you never know, do you, and at this time of year –

LETOUZEL. Don't be alarmed. I'm not alarmed. I'm relaxed: and I'm *silent*.

HARDRADER. Crape, you don't imagine –

GOLIGHTLY. Dear lady, you don't imagine –

HARDRADER *and* GOLIGHTLY. That today is the Day!

LETOUZEL. I said relaxed, and I said I was *silent*.

GOLIGHTLY. Ah, yes, the word. Ssh ssh, quite right.

He puts his finger to his lips, and looks significantly at her. CRAPE *puts his finger to his lips and looks at* HARDRADER, *who puts his finger to his lips and looks at* CRAPE. *On the main stage,* MRS PHINEUS, *wearing a sort of white nightshirt, is brought in by* NURSE JONES. *The* DOCTOR *enters from opposite door.*

DOCTOR. Ah, Mrs Phineus. And how are we today? In good shape, are we? Are the X-rays taken, Mr Robinson?

ORDERLY ROBINSON *looks out of recess and nods.*

Now there's no need to worry, Mrs Phineus, about all this bustling about and medical business. I just want a small routine check-up, nothing to it, nothing to it specially, my dear, as you might say, a brief once-over – say Ah.

PHINEUS. Ah.

DOCTOR. Ninety-nine.

PHINEUS. Doctor, if you please – what is the meaning of all this commotion – ?

DOCTOR. Ninety-nine.

PHINEUS. But. Doctor, we are not dangerously ill. No, I am

in excellent health, Doctor, why do you wish to – ninety-nine.

DOCTOR (*at her knees with little hammer*). One, two, three, *hup*. (*Calls to upper stage*.) Will you get Mrs Letouzel ready please.

NURSE BROWN *leads* MRS LETOUZEL *off upper stage*.

PHINEUS. Please what is the meaning –

DOCTOR. One, two, three, *hup*. Good. Good. Waterworks all right?

PHINEUS. I beg your pardon, Doctor? Oh yes, yes, I suppose, I think –

DOCTOR. Yes. I think they are, me dear. Thank you. That'll do. . . . Now then, generally speaking, would you say you're in good shape, Mrs Phineus? I'd say you were, I'd say you were never better, I'd say I was very pleased with you – I'd say many more years, we can give you many more years. All right, me dear, off you go. Nurse.

NURSE JONES *takes* MRS PHINEUS *out*.

X-rays ready, Robinson?

ORDERLY ROBINSON *enters from recess and hands X-rays to* DOCTOR.

DOCTOR. Good. Good. Nothing wrong here that the odd dab of iodine won't cure. She'll do. A positive report on Mrs Phineus. Write it down.

ORDERLY ROBINSON *writes it down*.

Now for the next, Mrs Letouzel. X-rays taken, Smith?

ORDERLY SMITH *puts his head out of recess and shakes it*.

Hurry up about it then and send her in when it is.

ORDERLY ROBINSON *goes back into recess.* NURSE
BROWN *reappears on upper stage.*

CRAPE (*sings*).

> There was four green bottles
> A-waiting in a row
> The next green bottle was fetched to go below
> So there's three green bottles a-sweating at every pore
> Three poor soldiers conscripted for the war
> For death or glory or to hear the cannons roar –

I was at Passchendaele, I was, oh what a terrible mess,
terrible, four years in the Service Corps issuing new socks
to men with trench feet, I can tell you it was a terrible
bloody mess, oh God I was fair terrified.

He coughs, snuffles, and sneezes. NURSE JONES *brings* MRS
LETOUZEL, *in her white robe, to see the doctor.*

LETOUZEL. Dr Cooperthwaite, this is not the usual routine
of the hospital. Now I would like to know, Doctor,
because it is only fair to us older people who have been
through two world wars –

DOCTOR. Now there's no need to worry, Mrs Letouzel, just
medical business, a small routine check-up, me dear – say
Ah.

LETOUZEL. Ah.

DOCTOR. Ninety-nine.

LETOUZEL. But, Doctor.

DOCTOR. Ninety-nine.

LETOUZEL. Ninety-nine.

DOCTOR. That sounds all right.

LETOUZEL. It does?

DOCTOR. Oh yes . . . One, two, three, *hup*.

LETOUZEL. Hup.

DOCTOR. One, two, three – hello?

LETOUZEL. Doctor, what's the matter?

388 THE HAPPY HAVEN

DOCTOR. Again. One, two, three, *hup*. *Hup*. I dare say it's
only local. Clear up by Sunday. Now don't you be
worried, me dear, no need to worry. (*Calls to upper stage.*)
Mr Hardrader, get him ready, please.

NURSE BROWN *leads* HARDRADER *off upper stage.*

How are you generally, I mean, walking, talking, reading
the papers? Waterworks?

LETOUZEL. Oh I'm sure, sure, why quite sure, not a particle
of doubt –

DOCTOR. Good, good, you're sure? Waterworks?

LETOUZEL. Oh, yes, I am quite sure, Doctor, really, I am
perfectly –

DOCTOR. Let's have the X-rays.

Enter ORDERLY ROBINSON *with them.*

Ye'es . . . well . . . I think so. This is only routine, me
dear – but, yes, many more years for you. Splendid form,
splendid. Off you go.

NURSE JONES *takes her out.*

She'll do. Positive. Make a note, not too heavy a dose. I
don't think we'd better have her going any farther back
than, say, thirty-five, thirty. I doubt if she's ever been that
far back ever. I doubt if she could do it now. Mr
Hardrader, when he's ready – I've no worries about him,
nor yet for Mr Golightly. But Crape? We-e'll, we'll see . . .

ORDERLY ROBINSON *goes back into recess.*

CRAPE. Two green bottles a-hanging on the wall. Two green
bottles. A-hanging on –

GOLIGHTLY. Don't be nervous.

CRAPE. I'm not nervous.

GOLIGHTLY. I'm never nervous. Why should we be nervous?

CRAPE. I think I've got a cold. Why should that matter?

GOLIGHTLY. Not to me, no.

CRAPE. Nor to me neither. Anyone can have colds.

GOLIGHTLY. Seasonable. Rain. Snow, Sleet. Draughts from the windows.

CRAPE. Anyone can have a cold! (*He coughs.*) Or a cough?

NURSE BROWN *re-enters on upper stage.* HARDRADER *in his robe is brought in to the* DOCTOR *by* NURSE JONES.

DOCTOR. Aha, Mr Hardrader. (*Calls to upper stage.*) Mr Golightly, please!

NURSE BROWN *leads* GOLIGHTLY *off upper stage.*

Had your X-rays taken? Good. Now don't you bother your head about all this medical business. A routine check-up, nothing to it – say Ah . . . Ninety-nine . . . One, two, three, *hup* . . . Next one, one, two, three, *hup* . . . waterworks, waterworks, ye-es . . . walking, talking, reading the papers? Good, good.

HARDRADER. Doctor, about Hector. You wrote me a letter –

DOCTOR. Don't you be worrying about that, old boy, all the best and the best of all possible worlds.

HARDRADER. You see, I was looking for him and he seems to be lost. Lost, Doctor, yes, I was trying to find him, I was doing my best –

DOCTOR. We mustn't delay the progress of science, I'm quite sure you understand, that these little sentiments, of no avail really, when looked at in proportion, as we say, the greatest good for the greatest possible number – waterworks all right?

HARDRADER. Why, yes, they're all right . . .

DOCTOR. Mr Golightly ready yet?

NURSE JONES *brings* GOLIGHTLY *in, in his robe.* NURSE BROWN *re-appears on upper stage.*

Now don't you get flustered, Mr Golightly, old chap, about all this medical business, just a brief once-over, routine, routine. Had your X-rays taken? Hurry up with those – Robinson, X-rays, bring both lots in. Ah. Ninety-nine. One, two, three, *hup* – next one, one, two, three, *hup* good, good, waterworks, read the papers do you, good –

HARDRADER. Doctor, I suppose –

DOCTOR. Least said, soonest mended, that's the way, stiff upper lip – where are those X-rays?

ORDERLY ROBINSON *enters with two sets of X-rays.*

Let's have a look. (*Calls to upper stage.*) Mr Crape, please!

NURSE BROWN *leads* CRAPE *off upper stage.*

Both sets, are they? Good. Nothing wrong here we can't set up with a couple of stitches. Right you are then, positive, positive – many happy years for the pair of you, eh? Don't you worry at all. That'll do, Nurse, take 'em away.

NURSE JONES *takes* GOLIGHTLY *and* HARDRADER *out as* NURSE BROWN *brings in* CRAPE *at the same door, in his robe.* NURSE JONES *re-enters.*

X-rays taken, Mr Crape? Now this is just the usual medical business, no need to get flustered. Waterworks all right?

ORDERLY ROBINSON *goes back into recess.*

CRAPE. Oh yes, Doctor. Never any trouble. Clockwork. One green bottle a-hanging on the wall.

DOCTOR. Eh, what? Say Ah.

CRAPE. Ah.

DOCTOR. Say it again.

CRAPE. Ah.

DOCTOR. H'm . . . Go on, again.

CRAPE. Ah. Ah . . . Ah . . .

DOCTOR. Hoarse . . . a bit hoarse, aren't we? Ninety-nine.

CRAPE. Ninety-nine.

DOCTOR. Say ninety-nine.

CRAPE. I said it.

DOCTOR. I didn't hear you. Say it again.

CRAPE. Ninety-nine.

DOCTOR. Louder. Like this: ninety-nine.

CRAPE. Ninety-nine.

DOCTOR. What's the matter with you?

CRAPE. Nothing! Nothing's the matter, Doctor, I'm splendid, I'm on the top of the form –

DOCTOR. Bad throat, haven't you? Bronchial.

CRAPE. No –

DOCTOR. Oh yes you are. X-rays ready on Mr Crape yet? Come on, slap it about! I'm a bit worried about you. You're not all you ought to be.

CRAPE. Oh, Doctor, don't say that. No, Doctor, please don't. If it's anything at all it could be a little piece of a chronic condition I got, back in 1917, y'know. The wet trenches you see, it gave the boys trench feet and they'd bring in their socks to my stores to be changed, and it was the constant humidity in there, all hanging round the walls – but it hasn't troubled me serious, not for thirty years, Doctor, no Doctor, please Doctor, really it hasn't –

The ORDERLIES *come in with his X-rays.*

DOCTOR. Ah . . . good, aha . . . H'm, h'm, ye-es . . . say ninety-nine.

CRAPE. Oh, Doctor, please – if it's because of the business with the dog, I assure you –

DOCTOR. Mr Crape: ninety-nine!

CRAPE. Ninety-nine.

DOCTOR. No. It won't do. Put him down provisionally negative and mark it with a query – maybe six months' time . . . but not now, no. We can't have you prejudice yourself with a suppurated larynx, can we?

CRAPE. Negative –

DOCTOR. But don't you worry, old fellow, it's only routine. Usual medical once-over, checkups, nothing at all to be flustered about. All right, that'll do. Come.

Exeunt DOCTOR *with* NURSES *and* ORDERLIES. *Exit* CRAPE, *separately*.

ACT THREE

Scene One

Enter HARDRADER *and* CRAPE, *severally.*

HARDRADER. I'm passed. He's passed me. He told me I was positive. He's even passed Golightly. Though goodness knows I've no particular wish to meet *him* thirty years ago . . . Hoorah! I say hoorah! – oh, what you told me, bow wow, you know? It *was* true, wasn't it – you *did* do it – got him away?

CRAPE. Eh? Oh that, the dog? Oh, yes, he's away, yes, quite away, don't worry . . .

HARDRADER. When do you think we are going to be given it? Will it be a jab, or a pill, or something in a glass? God knows, I don't know, I'd never have dreamt it possible – you know, I asked Copperthwaite, you know I asked him straight out –

CRAPE. You asked him *what*?

HARDRADER. About the dog. I told him, I said: Hector seems to be lost. I said: well, Doctor, what about it? But it didn't seem to register.

CRAPE. I don't suppose it would.

HARDRADER. What's the matter?

CRAPE. I've got a cold.

HARDRADER. Oh dear. Take my handkerchief. Clean.

CRAPE. Damn your bloody handkerchief.

HARDRADER. Steady, Crape, steady. Be a man. Stand up to your new life. It's bound to be a shock, of course, but –

Enter GOLIGHTLY.

GOLIGHTLY. He passed me, he told me I was positive, absolutely passed! Hoorah! I say Hardrader, hoorah!

HARDRADER. You're very cheerful. Why? Have you heard something?

GOLIGHTLY. Me? Heard? Oh no, no. It's just that I'm – I'm passed, I'm passed, my physical condition –
(*He sings.*)
> O I am a man and a very healthy man
> I'm a racehorse in my prime
> Ten thousand fields of the brilliant green
> For my pleasuring they all are mine.

But you are cheerful too, yes I can see that – there's somebody knows something – do they? Don't they?

HARDRADER. Oh no, no no, no significance, no. But health and strength and life, man –
(*He sings.*)
> O I am a man and a very healthy man
> A porpoise upon the storm
> I leap and leap ten thousand miles
> From Australia to Cape Horn.

Enter MRS LETOUZEL.

GOLIGHTLY. Passed? Are you passed? Yes, of course, you are passed, dear lady, oh your features without doubt declare it, bright eyes, glowing cheeks, aha, aha, I shall give you a kiss –

He does so, spontaneously.

HARDRADER. You too, you too, we all know, don't we, Mrs Letouzel, no question of secrecy now: we've all found out, somehow – we're all passed fit for life –

HARDRADER *and* GOLIGHTLY (*sing*).
> Boys and girls come out to play
> The moon doth shine as bright as day –

LETOUZEL (*while* HARDRADER *and* GOLIGHTLY *dance round and round*). Who's been talking? Crape?

CRAPE. Leave me alone.

LETOUZEL (*hissing at him*). You swore you'd keep it secret.

CRAPE. And so did you, you old scragged rabbit, but *Golightly's* been told –

LETOUZEL. Not by me –

CRAPE. Oh yes he has.

LETOUZEL. And what does it matter? The question is this: everything's moving too fast. The Doctor said to me something about Sunday. Now that can only mean –

CRAPE. It means I'm left out.

LETOUZEL. Out?

CRAPE. I have a cold. I have a cold. Hoarse in my throat. It only began this morning. He said I wasn't positive. But my waterworks are perfect. Ears, eyesight, lungs, bowels, there's nothing wrong at all. Cruelty, damnable, why me? You, you're nothing but a galvanized tin money box on two jerking legs with the slit choked up – (*To* HAR-DRADER.) You're a lost dog looking for a lost dog, all you can do is howl in the gutter – (*To* GOLIGHTLY.) You, you stale doughnut oozing mouldy jam, if they put the drug into you, there's only one part of you they'll ever rejuvenate and then the police will run you in for a permanent obscenity. Who wants to be young again? What'll you find to do when you are? All the things you want to do – why, you'll bloody well have to set to and *do* them! So how will you like *that*?

HARDRADER. I shall like it very much indeed, and I'd remind you, Crape, that you are in mixed company.

GOLIGHTLY. Your own disappointment is no excuse for abusing others. Mr Crape, I think you are very rude.

LETOUZEL. Go on, get lost.

CRAPE. Why don't all of you leave me alone?

He goes to a far corner of the stage and sits down to sulk, with his back to the others. NURSE BROWN *leads in* MRS PHINEUS *and puts her in her wheel-chair.*

PHINEUS. Thank you, Nurse, thank you. Yes, I'll be easy. Yes.

Exit NURSE BROWN.

I asked the Nurse to bring me to you, because I wanted to know about what has been happening. All this excitement in the hospital, commotion, disturbances, they're all so abrupt: I don't like it! No! There's no more routine. Mr Golightly, I'm frightened, whatever is the matter? What? What?

GOLIGHTLY. I don't know quite how to express it to you, dear Mrs Phineus, but –

PHINEUS (*jumping out of her chair*). Tell me. Tell me. Mr Hardrader: are we all going to be killed?

HARDRADER. Killed – good heavens, no –

PHINEUS. I think we are. Yes. They are tired of us, they don't want to feed us any more. Mrs Letouzel: he's decided to get rid of us, that is the truth and you are hiding it from me!

LETOUZEL. No. Oh, no –

PHINEUS. Yes it is, yes it is. Yes. Mr Crape – *he* knows, look at him! There he sits, yes, and with no doubts at all. *He* turns his back and he cries.

CRAPE (*turning round*). What do you want to know, old lady – hey?

LETOUZEL. Oh leave her alone, she's no idea what she's talking about. She's not right in the head.

CRAPE. Be quiet. Now the lot of you, shut up!

HARDRADER. Crape, nobody is talking except yourself.

CRAPE. I'm going to play a jolly game with old Mrs Phineus: she'll excuse me – won't you, me old love – if I step for a pair of minutes into Mr Golightly's slippery shoes –

> Truth or lie till the day you die
> Strike you dead if you tell us a lie.

PHINEUS. No. No. I won't have you doing it, you must not make me frightened, Dr Copperthwaite says –

CRAPE. Truth or lie till the day you die
Strike you dead if you tell us a lie.

PHINEUS. Why should I play your games? I don't like you, I don't want to play with you – Mr Golightly, tell him I don't want to –

She falls back into her wheel-chair.

GOLIGHTLY. Mr Crape, please, this old lady doesn't want to –

CRAPE. Oh yes, she does. When she plays with *me* she plays my game, don't you, you dear old thing, you sweet old sweetheart you –

HARDRADER. I say there, steady, Crape, really –

LETOUZEL. Let him be. Just for a little. See how far he goes. (*To audience.*) I may use this, you know. I couldn't conquer her, but if he can, and I can conquer *him* – more use than Golightly, wouldn't you say? Watch him, watch him, he's beating her down –

CRAPE. After we've played, I'll get you your tea, how would you like that? I'll feed you your tea, everything you want, scones, and crumpets and tarts and Eccles-cakes galore, oh delicious, delicious – come on, come on, me lovely –
Truth or lie till the day you die
Strike you dead if you tell us a lie –

PHINEUS. Truth or lie –

CRAPE. Yes?

PHINEUS. Truth or lie till the day I –

CRAPE. Till the day you –?

PHINEUS. No. No.

CRAPE. Come on, come on, yes! Splendid, you're doing it beautifully – come on –

PHINEUS. Truth or lie till the day I die
Strike me dead if I tell you a lie . . .

CRAPE. That's right, you've got it! Now we're really playing.
Aren't we? I shall give you a kiss. (*He does so.*) There.
That's for being a jolly sporting girl! I'll start. Supposing I
told you the Doctor *was* going to have us all killed –

PHINEUS. Oh . . . Oh . . .

CRAPE. Supposing he was. What would you think of it?
What would you truly think?

PHINEUS. I don't want to have to die.

CRAPE. Why not?

PHINEUS. I don't want to.

CRAPE. Margaret, *why not?*

PHINEUS.

> I'm an old old lady
> And I don't have long to live.
> I am only strong enough to take
> Not to give. No time left to give.
> I want to drink, I want to eat,
> I want my shoes taken off my feet.
> I want to talk but not to walk.
> Because if I walk, I have to know
> Where it is I want to go.
> I want to sleep but not to dream
> I want to play and win every game
> To live with love but not to love
> The world to move but me not move
> I want I want for ever and ever.
> The world to work, the world to be clever.
> Leave me be, but don't leave me alone.
> That's that I want. I'm a big round stone
> Sitting in the middle of a thunderstorm.
> There you are: that's true.
> That's me. Now: you.

CRAPE. No, no. Not yet. My turn soon. I'm playing to
different rules. I play the *second* time, you see. Yes . . .
Now answer me this one. Supposing you died. Today.

Here. Now. Just supposing. And then you were born again. Young. Strong. Not beautiful. You never were beautiful until you were old – I've seen your wedding photograph, so I know what you were like, apple-duff and custard, that was you: and your poor little Phineus-man, the pudding-cloth you were wrapped in, he was boiled all to shreds in the water! Suppose you were born again –

PHINEUS. I don't know –

CRAPE. I do. You wouldn't dare to face it. Oh Lord, it would be far too much like hard work . . . Truth or lie? Truth or lie?

PHINEUS. Truth. Truth. But I'd like to be a baby, be born again to be a little baby . . .

CRAPE. Teething, wetting your nappy, teething, struggling to crawl when you've barely learned the strength to move a knee or an elbow, teething, safety-pins stuck into you, squalling, teething, scalded with your bath-water, losing your rattle over the side of the pram –

PHINEUS. No, no.

CRAPE. No! now you've said it. No. Anyone else say 'yes'?

GOLIGHTLY. I said 'yes'.

CRAPE. Did you? For *her*? Now you've heard what she's just told you. She was your only reason. Do you still want to do it; for *her*?

GOLIGHTLY. Others – there are plenty of others.

CRAPE. There always were plenty of others. How many of them did you get?

GOLIGHTLY. Never mind, Mr Crape.

CRAPE. I'll tell you what they used to call me. They used to call me Dandy Jim! The only name anybody ever had for you was Little-Wet-Willy-in-a-Half-Pint-Pot. Now isn't that the truth? (*To* HARDRADER.) Old chap. Old chap Hardrader. Big strong games and sports, boxing and cricket, badminton and the high-jump, Egyptian P.T. Only two friends and one of them's in her grave – you couldn't make her love you, so you went toughing it on the greensward and bellowing at your dirty dog. If you were to start again, what would *you* find?

HARDRADER. I hope I would find a healthy humane existence.

GOLIGHTLY. No no, excuse me, no: Mr Hardrader. You would be as lonely as ever you were. I know, because *I* would be, too. Isn't it terrifying?

CRAPE. Isn't it?

HARDRADER. I do not understand you, sir. You seem to have changed your mind entirely. But why should you try to change ours?

CRAPE. I'm playing the game of Truth, old fellow. It's three points wilder than a bracing set of hockey –

HARDRADER. Set of tennis.

CRAPE. Hockey, chum, hockey. When *I* call the rules.

LETOUZEL. Crape. Play with me.
> Truth or lie till the day I die
> Strike me dead if I tell a lie.

CRAPE. Truth or lie, ta tum tum-tum, – ah we know the rest of it – you start first!

LETOUZEL. No. You.

PHINEUS. These are the two stout players. Mr Golightly, Mr Hardrader, sit by me and we will watch them play.

They do so.

CRAPE. You don't want rejuvenation. There's nothing different between you and him, and him and her. All your life you've burrowed for the money: and you haven't got a red ha'penny.

LETOUZEL. Ho ho, have I not?

CRAPE. Mrs Phineus's thousand pounds – you don't have much of that, old woman, and you never really did, 'cos she hasn't got it. It's all in the air, ticker-tape, bog-bumph, Dr Copperbox holds the lot, he gives you pocket money for your China tea and your hair-dyes. All right, she made it over to you, put her scratching old fist on fifty-five miles of stored affidavits – how much of that money have you actually seen? Cash? Coin of the realm? Paid on the Bristol nail?

LETOUZEL. You don't understand the principles of finance. You uneducated old man, what should you know of the poetry and dreams of organized paper? Kleenex to wipe your nose with, that's about your sum.

CRAPE. I've got a cold. I can't help that. It's my bloody curse. Every damned project gets drowned in catarrh. It's a neurotic disability, it's not my fault. Don't you dare mock me with it! But you've told me the truth. You don't want the money: all you want's the notion of it. Here, in here, at your age – that's your luxury. But outside – in the world, between the bus-stops and the supermarkets and the no-parking areas, you've got to have hands on the real jingling metal: or the only place you'll find yourself is back in the Happy Haven, in seventy years' time. What happened to Mister Letouzel?

LETOUZEL. Eh? Keep to the point. What's that to do with it?

CRAPE. We're playing the game. You have to tell me. All right, I'll tell *you*. He didn't exist. You lived all your life a spinster on a little bit of a railway share, and when those rats nationalized, you found you'd no alternative but to give yourself to Copperthwaite.

GOLIGHTLY. Just the same as us.

CRAPE. Poor dears. Poor old dears. Your only safe investment disappeared in the night and if you had any bolder gambles –

LETOUZEL. They were not successful. That was my misfortune. It wasn't my fault. Don't you dare to mock me with it.

GOLIGHTLY. I'm sure if she wishes to call herself Mrs
Letouzel she has a perfect right. If she thinks it suits her.
It is what we term a courtesy title. You wouldn't be
expected to understand that, Mr Crape.

CRAPE. Oh skip it, skip it . . . I think I've made my point. Is
there one person here has any single motive for wanting to
be young again?

LETOUZEL. Truth or lie. What about you?

CRAPE. I thought that was obvious. I've been rejected.

LETOUZEL. Why, so you have. And don't you enjoy it too,
you abominable coffin-carrier. You turn us against our
own selves and you disgust us to the very gorge of our
throat with what we've all been for the whole of our lives.
It's quite made your day, hasn't it? You've never been so
happy since the time you were weaned. Ah my goodness
gracious me, Mr Crape, at last you've found yourself in
power!

CRAPE. Truth or lie, I have.

LETOUZEL. No. Truth or lie, you have not! Now you think,
because you snarl and grin and run around between our
ankles, that we've all changed our minds and that we'll all
stay with you at your term of years and we'll all die
together a-keeping you company? Maybe we will. But for
a different reason . . . We heard everything you said –
good, good, it worked. Yes, we're humiliated. You've
made us afraid, you see. Here we are, worms. Old ones.
We don't want to die, but we none of us dare state that we
want any more life. Let's look around us! Now then, who
cares?

CRAPE. I don't know what you're talking about, but I'd say
nobody cares.

LETOUZEL. And you would be right. Nobody, not even the
Doctor. Not even him, call him our Lord, Priest, and
Superintendent, great Guardian of the Mysteries – (*She
sings.*)

Take off your hats, bow down:
The High King wears the crown,
He lays out his land with a long directing hand
And the measurements all written down.

The measure of you and of me
In numbers so clearly told –
Say you are a field and I am a tree
And you are a house or a road.

If he wants to root out or rebuild,
Raise up or lay level or burn,
He draws his new line, we obey in his good time:
We suffer, we praise him, we learn.

We learn how to love and submit,
To lie down like a frightened new wife.
Each day and each hour we have given to his power
To the end and beyond of our life –

That's immortality: he grants it to us and then we hand it
back. He's the undisputed custodian of everything that's
good for us. Security. Reliability. Though some people
have said he failed to save the score the other Saturday at
football –

HARDRADER. Why – yes –

LETOUZEL. They relied on him to stop the goals; when he
came back from the match he was swearing, frustrated – I
know because I heard him. He'd let them all through, he
had to apologize, I tell you I heard him –

HARDRADER. Quite right, so did I!

LETOUZEL. Apologized – Copperthwaite – in his humility,
to the Captain of the Team . . . but despite that, you silly
children, we are all his worms. And he says 'Turn, worms,
turn,' and he thinks we have got no choice!

GOLIGHTLY. I am not a worm. I am not a worm. My name is Henry Golightly and I walk upon legs.

HARDRADER. Two legs. Ten toes. Two arms. Ten fingers. Ribs. Shoulders. Backbone. Backbone. If my backbone *does* bend, it still belongs to *me*.

PHINEUS. Mr Crape.

CRAPE. I read my Bible. God said, he said it to the snake, I remember, he said: 'Because thou hast done this,' he said –

PHINEUS. Mr Crape.

CRAPE. 'Thou art cursed above all cattle, and above every beast of the field. Upon thy belly shalt thou go, and dust shalt thou eat all the –'

PHINEUS. Mr Crape.

CRAPE. 'All the days of thy life. Because thou has done this.' There, that's your true fortunes. Don't talk to me about bones.

PHINEUS. Mr Crape. Please. Please. What is the Doctor going to do? You haven't told us yet.

CRAPE. 'Because thou hast done this,' he said. Done what? Grown old. That's what we've done . . . And the doctor – oh, the doctor? He's going to give us medicine, dear, to make us all young again. It's not of importance. You wouldn't like it. Don't bother . . .

PHINEUS. But he never told me.

LETOUZEL. Why should he? He's a professional man, dear, he works to the rules.

PHINEUS. I call it very unfair. Very, very unfair. Yes.

HARDRADER. I don't want his Elixir now. You've confused me so much with all of your reasons. But if my backbone bends, it's mine.

CRAPE. Old chap. Old chap. You're the Doctor's patient. You have to do what he says.

HARDRADER. I shall ask to leave the Haven.

GOLIGHTLY. But where would you go?

HARDRADER. Find another Nursing Home.

LETOUZEL. And another Copperthwaite.

HARDRADER. Not necessarily.

GOLIGHTLY. But are you willing to take the risk?

HARDRADER. I don't know . . . We can refuse to accept the Elixir. Obviously we can. Free country. Citizens. Voters.

LETOUZEL. He's worked on this for years. Weighed us and dieted us and taken our temperatures.

GOLIGHTLY. Humiliating forms of treatment, with, with rubber pipes and so forth: when I haven't even been ill.

LETOUZEL. He's not likely to let us ruin the masterpiece of his life, is he?

HARDRADER. But what can he do?

LETOUZEL. Turn us out, that's what.

CRAPE (to HARDRADER). Or worse, worse. Supposing he told you you'd got cancer in your lungs. Would you believe him?

HARDRADER. Oh my God, I don't know.

CRAPE. But he could, and it might be a lie – how would you know? He'd terrify you to death. Look what he wanted to do to your dog!

HARDRADER. You mean – vivisection?

CRAPE. What else?

HARDRADER. For a man who'd do that to a poor dumb animal – no punishment could be sufficiently severe.

LETOUZEL. Then why don't we punish him?

HARDRADER. By God, I wish I could . . . Oh I would do . . . this, and I'd do – that, and I'd do – oh, this, this, that, that –

PHINEUS. I once said to Mr Phineus. 'Why don't we have a little baby, I would so love a little baby to hold and to enclose and to have.' Some women say, oh the trouble and the worry and the noisiness and the naughtiness and the mess – but I said, 'I don't care about that. Mr Phineus shall pay for a good sensible old-fashioned girl to be his

Nanny, and later he can go to boarding-school. All I want to do is to hold him and to have him and to enclose him.' I said it to Mr Phineus. And he tried. Yes. He tried to pleasure me and he tried to give me my baby, so many times, oh so often and so many times to no purpose. He was no good. No. No courage in him at all. So he died and there was no succession. I had expected a baby. I had bought all his little clothes and his toys and everything right up to when he would go to the boarding-school, where I suppose they would want him to wear uniform, so I couldn't get that for him in advance. But I bought all the rest and I kept them and I have them all here in my room, locked in my big box. I would so like to have a little baby.

Pause.

CRAPE. Somebody said he was talking about Sunday. There's something going to happen on Sunday. He hasn't got his drug ready yet, or I'm sure we'd have heard about it. But we have to find out the moment he *does* get it. To find out before Sunday. We must spy on his Laboratory.

GOLIGHTLY. How can we do that?

LETOUZEL. Oh we'll find a way. Use your little brains, you silly little fellow, or else shut your mouth while the rest of us use ours.

The DOCTOR *enters on the upper stage.*

DOCTOR. Off to bed, now, boys and girls, you're half an hour late as it is – burning the candle at both ends, you know, have to go easy, don't we? That's the way, off to bed, now – Nurse!

NURSE BROWN *enters on main stage.*

Good night. Good night, boys and girls.

OLD PEOPLE. Good night, Doctor.

DOCTOR. Good night.

Exeunt – NURSE *wheels* MRS PHINEUS *out. The* DOCTOR *remains above.*

Scene Two

The DOCTOR *is on the upper stage.*

DOCTOR. Ladies and gentlemen. Twenty-four hours; and now I'm going to see if it works! In my Laboratory, as you know, the retort with the solution in it – is it or is it not going to turn green? Bear with me a few moments. I'll just make the arrangements, and hey presto, open sesame, abracadabra – I'll tell you confidentially, it is going to turn green. *This* time, I'm right. Mr Smith, Mr Robinson, Lab ready if you please!

He enters the upper stage. GOLIGHTLY *enters cautiously on the main stage, in pyjamas.*

GOLIGHTLY. Why me, why me, why should I have to do it? Why not somebody else?

MRS LETOUZEL *enters cautiously after him in nightgown and hair net.*

LETOUZEL. Because you're the smallest, that's why. We've told you that ten times –

GOLIGHTLY. But, personally speaking, I have nothing against Dr Copperthwaite – Mr Hardrader has been the worst done by, surely *he* should –

HARDRADER *enters cautiously at the opposite door in pyjamas.*

HARDRADER. Golightly, pull yourself together, man. If you've any chivalry at all, remember Mrs Phineus. The man who would deny a woman the child she has craved for is an unmitigated scoundrel.

GOLIGHTLY. Quite right, Mr Hardrader. You have put me to shame, sir, I will do what I am asked. (*He goes into the recess, and we hear him blundering about in there, out of sight.*) The door is locked!

Enter CRAPE *cautiously, in pyjamas, holding a burglar's jemmy.*

CRAPE. Of course it's locked, you dithering old nightingale — I told you you'd not get in till you'd waited for me! Let me have a look at it.

DOCTOR (*offstage*). Smith!

HARDRADER. Cave!

ORDERLY SMITH *enters from the opposite side to the* DOCTOR's *shout, carrying a tray of test tubes, etc.*

CRAPE. Freeze where you are!

They all crouch down like hares. ORDERLY SMITH *crosses the stage and goes out without seeing them.*

That's the way to do it. You stand stark still and they think you're a bush — I learnt that in France! Now, where's this locked door?

He goes into the recess. GOLIGHTLY *comes out of it.*

Aha . . . Ha . . . clickety-clock, clock-clock!

He reappears.

Dandy Jimmy and his jemmy
Save us all a pretty penny!

Mr Golightly, in you go lightly! (*He pushes* GOLIGHTLY *in again.*) Ha ha, he's in.

DOCTOR (*offstage*). Robinson!

HARDRADER. Cave!

CRAPE. Freeze.

ORDERLY ROBINSON *crosses the stage with tray, same business as before.*

Safe again. I told you. Come on.

Exeunt. COOPERTHWAITE *and* ORDERLIES *enter.*

DOCTOR. Let's have it, let's have it.

ORDERLIES *open the recess and bring out the Lab bench.* GOLIGHTLY *is crouched underneath it, and is pulled out unobserved.*

Bunsen Burner. Right. Now let's see the retort . . . H'm ha. H'm . . . Looks promising, ladies and gentlemen. Sediment developed *just* as I forecast, and the whole thing is approximately the consistency of – of water. Good. Boil it.

It is held over the flame.

Accotile and heraclith solution? Good. You see what I'm doing? Watch for the change of colour . . . That hot enough yet? Come on, come on, come on –

> Put another nickel in
> In the nickelodeon
> All I want is loving you
> And boil it boil it boil it –

Right! She's boiled. Give it to me. *I'll* pour. (*He pours in the contents of a second retort. It turns green.*) Beautiful. Oh my beautiful. Oh my lovely girl. Green as the leaves on the weeping willow tree, where my true love lies sleeping. I've done it. I've done it. Gentlemen, you may smoke. One of mine? One of mine?

They stand side by side. The ORDERLIES *remove their masks and all three take a few formal puffs at cigarettes. Then they drop their butts, grind them into the floor, and turn back to the work.* ORDERLIES *replace masks.*

Stage Two. A Practical Test. Go and fetch the dog.

ORDERLY ROBINSON *goes into the recess. The dog is heard barking.*

Taking a common-sense point of view, ladies and gentlemen, scientific detachment – I know that this green liquid is the Elixir of Youth, but I can't go administering it to my patients without some further evidence, can I? Besides, how would I know how much I ought to give them, unless we'd some sort of a preliminary run-through, eh?

ORDERLY ROBINSON *re-enters with a large basket, fastened up.*

Is the dog all right in there?

Dog barks.

Seems to be. Put two ounces of the Elixir into a saucer.

ORDERLY ROBINSON *does so.*

If anybody in the audience is a little worried at my giving this admittedly unproven drug to an unfortunate dumb animal: there's a lot of silly nonsense talked by so-called humanitarians – would any one of those ladies like to step up here to me and take the place of the dog? . . . NO? I didn't think that you would. You look altogether too sensible. Open the box, please.

ORDERLY ROBINSON *does so. Dog barks.*

Take him out – *gently.*

ORDERLY ROBINSON *takes the dog out in his arms – cradling quite a large-sized beast. Dog continues to bark.*

Saucer on the floor. Dog by the saucer. Let him drink.

The dog is set down. More barking. The men watch closely.

Doesn't seem very thirsty. You haven't given him any-thing to drink already, have you? Robinson? Smith? H'm. Come on, come on, doggie, good boy, good boy, drinky, drinky, drinky. Lap lap lap. Oh for Godsake . . . Go on, *drink*! I'm sorry, but it looks like a long wait. We might as well sit down . . .

They sit.

　　　Put another nickel in, in the nickleodeon –
Where's he going? He can't leave the room, can he? You've shut all the doors? . . . Oi, oi . . . Keep still, Smith. You can clean that up later, don't distract him, he's looking for the saucer . . . steady, steady, quiet every-body, absolute quiet – he's drinking, he's drinking – he's *drunk* it! Good dog, good dog, good, good –

Dog barks.

Now then we shouldn't have to wait long, any minute now, we're going to see – yes – yes –

The barks become shriller.

Yes! It's worked! It *really* has worked! Oh my God, I'm a famous man.

The bark is now a high-pitched squeal.

Don't let the dog get out – catch him, catch him, Robinson quick! Oh, the sweet little fellow –

ORDERLY ROBINSON *is now holding a very small bundle.*

Oh, the dear little puppy, oh, the little chick, there, there, there, did the horrid Doctor givums nasty green water forums dinners, didums didums? Put him inside and give him something to chew – he seems to be teething. That's right.

ORDERLY ROBINSON *takes the dog out.*

Now we'll take in my notebooks and the Elixir, please, for safety: and we'll make a proper coordinated report upon the whole business, without any flights of poetic fancy. And let's not get so excited either that we forget the formalities – oh, but this is epoch-making, this is scarcely believable unless you'd been told, this is the greatest experience of your lives and I hope you'll not forget it . . . Come on.

Exeunt, ORDERLY SMITH *carrying the retort and the notebooks.* GOLIGHTLY *emerges from under the bench.*

GOLIGHTLY. Poor Mr Hardrader. However can I break it to him? Still, a little puppy, very tender, very winsome, perhaps he won't be altogether so completely cast-down? There seems to be quite a lot left – now then, a test-tube – quickness of the hand deceives the eye, oh dear, I've spilt a bit, now then – there we are, and there's enough left in the saucer to –

He has poured some of the contents of the saucer into a test-tube.

DOCTOR (*offstage*). You've forgotten the saucer!
GOLIGHTLY. Only just in time! My goodness, aren't I brave?

He nips off, as ORDERLIES *come on again from opposite sides. They clear away the bench into recess and go out, taking the saucer with them.*

Scene Three

The sound of church bells. Enter COPPERTHWAITE *in a hurry.*

DOCTOR. Excuse me, it's Sunday morning already, listen! I'm in a tearing hurry, the whole place is upside down, nothing prepared, and they'll be here in ten minutes. Who will? I can just spare sixty seconds to tell you. First of all: Sir Frederick Hapgood, makes cars, makes money, and a good deal of the money he makes he puts into this hospital – no question, I've got to impress him. Then, second: a lady from the Ministry of Health – there's a lot of government money put into this, and all – to be quite frank, they pay my salary – so I've got to impress *her*. Then thirdly and fourthly: our own local Mayor, and his good wife the Mayoress. They sit on the committee of this hospital, carry a deal of influence in this district – socially speaking, they *are* this district – county society, very conservative, very well worth keeping in with. And to keep in with them: impress them. There was to have been a bishop, but he's not coming now, thank goodness. I think he's had to go off somewhere to kick a High-church Vicar out of some parish or other . . . But there's enough of 'em, I say, there's enough. And, by God, I can tell you, they're going to be impressed. Because what they're going to see is my Elixir at work. The World Premiere, that's what. After they've all had coffee, I shall try it on Mrs Phineus.

Sound of arrival of motor-cars, horns blow, doors slam, etc.

And here comes the Establishment. Dead on time. I'd better go and meet them. Do I look sufficiently impressive? Ah well, we're all as God made us, so to speak. The Institution is greater than the Man.

Exit. Enter MRS LETOUZEL *and* GOLIGHTLY, *coffee pots, cups, etc. (In this scene the* OLD PEOPLE *are all in their best clothes.)*

LETOUZEL. Aren't there supposed to be biscuits?

GOLIGHTLY. Mr Hardrader is bringing the biscuits.

LETOUZEL. Good. Everything else all right? Coffee, cream-jug, sugar-bowl, cups, one, two, three, four, and one for the Doctor, spoons, one, two, three, four, and one for the Doctor.

GOLIGHTLY (*producing his test-tube*). Shall I put it in now?

LETOUZEL. Put it in where?

GOLIGHTLY. I thought we were going to pour out the – (*He waves at the coffee-pot.*)

LETOUZEL. Not till they come in! Now take it easy, Henry, don't be in a hurry, all the time in the world.

GOLIGHTLY. I don't like having to put it in when they're all in the room – one of them might notice –

LETOUZEL. The quickness of the hand deceives the eye.

GOLIGHTLY. Yes, but I wish it didn't have to be *my* hand – Mrs Letouzel, I think I've done sufficient, cannot somebody else –

Enter HARDRADER *with a plate of biscuits.*

HARDRADER. Here are the biscuits. You have it on you?

GOLIGHTLY *shows him the test-tube.*

I'd be obliged if you'd give it to me.

LETOUZEL. Why?

HARDRADER. Dear lady, if you please. *I* should be the one to put it in. Hector would have wished it so. Would he not, Golightly?

GOLIGHTLY. Oh, I'm sure that he would, sir. Here you are.

He hands him the tube.

HARDRADER. Thank you.

GOLIGHTLY. But you know, Hector isn't dead.

HARDRADER. To me he is dead. My Hector is dead. Whatever is alive, it's – it's some other dog. Where the devil is Crape?

LETOUZEL. He's gone to make sure we shan't be disturbed. No nurses, nor orderlies, nobody here except for ourselves, and our visitors, and our leader and teacher.

> Take off your hats, bow down.
> The High King wears the Crown.

HARDRADER. Cave: Here they come.

The DOCTOR *enters with the four* VISITORS. *He leads them round the stage as though showing them round the hospital.*

DOCTOR. The Convalescent Wing, as you see, to our left, facing the sun, big balconies, very airy, very spacious. To the right, my Operating Theatre, and ancillary departments, as you might say, perfection of function is in itself beautiful – but of course, Sir Frederick, *you* know all this already – Mr Mayor and ladies, we see over there the Sir Frederick Hapgood Ward, opened last year by Sir Frederick himself, there's a large bronze plaque in the foyer commemorating the occasion, and of course, the Annigoni portrait of the late Lady Hapgood, which we account one of the Happy Haven's most treasured possessions. And now, perhaps, if you'll come *this* way – ah, I see coffee – a cup of coffee awaits us – made and served specially by one or two of our patients – from the Special Research Ward, they are of course to be the subjects in the special experiment I have been explaining to you – I wanted you specially to meet them, before – ah, before we begin – (*Aside to* MRS LETOUZEL.) Where's Mrs Phineus?

LETOUZEL. She's having a little rest, Doctor. She seemed rather tired –

DOCTOR. Would you mind fetching her, Mrs Letouzel? (*In a furious whisper.*) When I said all of you, I meant *all*. She ought to be here. Why can't people listen when I give a few instructions? Hurry up and get her.

Exit MRS LETOUZEL.

Let me introduce – Mr Golightly, Mr Hardrader –

The coffee, etc., is handed to the Visitors. When the OLD PEOPLE *make conversation with them, the* VISITORS *reply in wordless goggling noises which sound both patronizing and genial.*

HARDRADER. Some five or six years now. And I wouldn't exchange it for home, goodness gracious, no . . .

GOLIGHTLY. A charming place, a very charming place, dear lady, indeed to retire to . . .

HARDRADER. The countryside, the open air, contemplation, peaceful surroundings, nature . . .

DOCTOR (*who has not taken coffee*). And of course, the beautiful scenery and fresh air in themselves as we say a continual therapy . . .

GOLIGHTLY. Oh dear me no, Sir Frederick, it is often only too stimulating here, when you reach *my* age, a peaceful and secluded existence is really the only one that charms – (*Aside to* HARDRADER.) Is it in?

HARDRADER (*aside*). Not yet. How much?

GOLIGHTLY (*aside*). About half. We don't want to overdo it.

HARDRADER (*aside*). All right. Half. (*With his back turned to the company; he carefully empties half the contents of the tube*

into a cup of coffee, and then offers it to the DOCTOR.)
Doctor, would you like a cup of coffee?

DOCTOR. No, thank you, Mr Hardrader. I don't normally
take coffee. Have some yourself. (*To the Visitors.*) And
another point, of course, the freedom from continual
contact and only too often conflict with relatives, in itself
acts as a –

HARDRADER. Doctor, if you don't care for coffee, perhaps
we could get you a cup of tea?

DOCTOR. What? No. No thank you.

HARDRADER. Oh. Very well . . .

Enter CRAPE. HARDRADER *takes him anxiously apart.*

He won't take the coffee.

CRAPE. Give him some tea.

HARDRADER. He won't take that either.

CRAPE. You've already put it in?

HARDRADER. Half of it.

GOLIGHTLY. And I often say, we were gay then, yes and
very happy. Though I wouldn't really have those days
again – but there *is* a nostalgia, ah Vienna, Vienna, and the
Emperor's mounted band riding round the Ringstrasse,
and that wonderful, wonderful Strauss music . . .

CRAPE (*aside to* HARDRADER). Give me the other half.

HARDRADER (*aside*). Why?

CRAPE (*aside*). I'll tell you later. Quick.

HARDRADER *gives him the test-tube.* MRS LETOUZEL
wheels in MRS PHINEUS.

DOCTOR. Aha, Mrs Phineus! Sir Frederick, Mr Mayor,
ladies, let me present you to our oldest, and perhaps I'd
better not say it, but she is, nevertheless, our best-loved
and best-privileged inhabitant – ah – Mrs Phineus –

CRAPE (*aside to Mrs Letouzel*). He won't take any coffee.

LETOUZEL. Then offer him some tea.

HARDRADER (*aside*). It's no good. He won't.

LETOUZEL. Leave it to me.

She goes and whispers to MRS PHINEUS.

CRAPE (*aside*). Let him just drink the coffee and we are in the clear. I've locked the communicating doors. Orderlies and nurses can't get in unless they break through the windows. We've got all the time in the world –

PHINEUS. May I have a cup of coffee?

CRAPE (*to* HARDRADER). Give it her. Quick.

HARDRADER *does so.*

PHINEUS. Thank you, Mr Hardrader . . . It seems to be rather hot. Perhaps Doctor Copperthwaite, you wouldn't mind taking a sip to test it for me, would you? I'm so afraid of burning my mouth, you see.

DOCTOR. Of course, it's a pleasure, Mrs Phineus – (*He sips.*) Oh I think you'll find it quite cool enough. In fact, it's rather cold. Been poured out a long time, I expect, it –

PHINEUS. Oh dear, it is cold? I don't think, if it's cold, I ought to take it all. No. You yourself have warned me, Doctor, of the possible danger to the kidneys, have you not? Perhaps you would drink it for me?

DOCTOR. Eh? Oh, well, I suppose I might as well, as I've got it in my hand . . . It's not very sweet. Has anyone any sugar?

MRS LETOUZEL *hands him the sugar.*

Ah, thank you, Mrs Letouzel . . . Well, I put a lot of sugar in, but it's still pretty bitter – (*To Visitors.*) Is *your* coffee all right? Sure? Do say if it's not, because –

He finishes the cupful, dubiously. Then, aside to MRS LETOUZEL.

Here, who made this stuff? I feel quite – (*He hurries off the stage.*)

The next three speeches are delivered simultaneously, in great excitement.

GOLIGHTLY. And always for ever the beautiful climate, the snow on the Dolomites, the sparkle of the wine, the roses and the music, dear lady, the sun in our blood, crying love, love, love, ah the enchantment of the South –

HARDRADER. The one thing I regret here is the absence of the river, a good strong scull up against the tide on a Sunday morning as far as Hobson's Lock, refreshing pint in the Barge and Anchor, then home again with the current and the wind with you, and every artery tingling like quicksilver – wonderful, wonderful –

LETOUZEL. Mrs Phineus is rather deaf, and perhaps a little overexcited, but she wishes to say that she is very happy indeed to meet you, Sir Frederick, and how much, how very much she has always admired you and of course dear Lady Hapgood and the wonderful things you have done for us all!

Meanwhile, CRAPE, *with his back to the others has taken the empty coffee-cup, poured out some more coffee, and is preparing to pour the rest of the Elixir into it.* MRS LETOUZEL *suddenly sees what he is up to. She comes sharply across to him and seizes his wrist.*

PHINEUS. Yes, yes, Sir Frederick, ah Lady Hapgood, dear good Lady Hapgood, I was so sorry when I heard – was it not so very sudden? But we have the portrait here. That, we shall always treasure.

MRS LETOUZEL *has been having a silent but strong struggle with* CRAPE.

LETOUZEL (*aside to him*). What do you think you're doing?
CRAPE (*aside*). Please let me do it, let me, let me – just

because I had a cold, *he* was trying to stop me but I thought that *you*, you wouldn't be so cruel as to –

LETOUZEL (*aside*). *NO!* You don't want it! It's all of us or none of us! There's no more time for tricks – besides, you and me, we need one another: if we're alone, we're lost!

She succeeds in getting the test-tube from him. In the final effort, the coffee-cup is thrown on the floor. The DOCTOR *re-enters.*

DOCTOR. All well, all well, enjoying your coffee, Sir Frederick? Mr Mayor, Mrs Mayor, er Miss, er – the biscuits all right, are they? You're quite sure, Sir Frederick? Good . . . (*He comes down to* MRS LETOUZEL. *Aside to her.*) I'd have you know, Mrs Letouzel, I've just been extremely sick. What's the matter with the coffee? Who made it? . . .

He turns back to the Visitors.

Ah, Sir Frederick, if you've finished your refreshment, perhaps we can get on to the next item in our little programme – Er, h'm, patient! Boys and girls, if you wouldn't mind clearing away the coffee things and, er, back to your rooms, and Mrs Letouzel, perhaps you could leave Mrs Phineus here with us, I believe Sir Frederick wishes to –

He breaks off uncertainly as he sees that the OLD PEOPLE *all have their backs turned and are whispering together.*

CRAPE. It hasn't worked.
HARDRADER. What do we do?
GOLIGHTLY. We'll have to do something.
CRAPE. The coffee, the coffee must have killed it!
LETOUZEL. We've still got the other half – no thanks to *you* –
PHINEUS (*suddenly*). Here: all to me!

They all crouch round her wheel-chair in a tight huddle like a football scrum. The DOCTOR *and* VISITORS *watch in bewilderment.*

DOCTOR. Well, now, I'm not sure what – we must appreciate, of course that these old people have their periodic eccentricities, it's maybe that they feel their little half-hour of recreation with us has been cut short too abruptly – we always find it best to humour them, you know, Sir Frederick –

LETOUZEL. Right. Now. Begin. Mr Crape. Mr Golightly. The bench. Quickly.

CRAPE *and* GOLIGHTLY *pick up a bench by its end and run against the Visitors with it, pinning them across their bellies against the edge of the stage.*

DOCTOR. Hey, wait a minute –
LETOUZEL. Mr Hardrader. Neck. Arms. Quickly.

HARDRADER *grabs the* DOCTOR'S *arm and twists it behind his back, at the same time bearing down with his other hand on the back of his neck. The* DOCTOR *is forced to bow right over.*

Right. Now then. Needle.

MRS PHINEUS *takes from her reticule an enormous hypodermic needle which she opens.* MRS LETOUZEL *swiftly pours in the contents of the test-tube.*

DOCTOR. Oh, oh, stoppit, leggo, ow, ouch, yarroo –

The VISITORS *gobble.*

PHINEUS. For a long time I have kept this locked up in my big box. It was lucky I thought to bring it along today. Yes. I said to myself: 'One day, it will be needed.'
LETOUZEL. Needle filled. Screwed up. Ready? (*She hauls up the* DOCTOR'S *coat and hauls down his trousers.*) NOW!

MRS PHINEUS *sticks the needle into the* DOCTOR, *who gives an appalling yell. The needle is withdrawn.*

LETOUZEL. Come on. Take him in.

She and HARDRADER *rush the* DOCTOR, *still stooping, off the stage.*

PHINEUS. You can let them go now.

CRAPE *and* GOLIGHTLY *release the* VISITORS *who still stand where they have been forced, in stunned amazement.*

This must be a most astonishing moment for you, Sir Frederick, must it not . . .

They open their mouths and gasp.

Please don't call out.

CRAPE. There's nobody to hear you. I've locked 'em all away. We're all in this together.

GOLIGHTLY. United we stand. Divided we – you know. I am not a worm. My name is Henry Golightly and I walk upon legs.

PHINEUS. But it should also be a beautiful moment because you will see how much, how very very much, we owe to you and to poor Lady Hapgood and to the kind ladies and gentlemen in the Government and in this beautiful countryside round us who take so much delight and interest in our welfare, and who always look after us like fathers and like mothers, to watch our every step and stumble, at a time in our lives when we are, as you know, no more than little children to wander and to cry and to need nothing more in life than to be continually looked after by kind fathers and mothers, who will watch our every step and stumble at a time in our lives when how few of us know what we want to do or where we want to go, or what possible good we are at all, being, as you see, like

little children wandering and crying and in search once
again of our fathers and our mothers –

MRS LETOUZEL *and* HARDRADER *re-enter, leading the*
DOCTOR *between them. He is now wearing a little boy's suit,*
with short pants, and wears a mask that entirely covers his
face. It resembles the actor's own features closely, but is round,
chubby, and childish. MRS LETOUZEL *puts a lollipop into his*
hand and he sucks at it in a formal fashion.

Ah, here he is. My baby. Come little baby, come to your
mama, sit him on my knee, dear Mrs Letouzel, I'd like to
sing him a song –

They sit him on her knee.

Yes, baby, yes, baby, yes . . .
PHINEUS (*sings*).
     Now mother holds her little boy
     And holds him to her heart,
     Fall asleep, all you children, fall asleep.
     The rising up of sun or moon
     Shall never make us part.
     Fall asleep and dream the world is all safe and sound.
ALL OLD PEOPLE (*formally*). Everybody, listen! Take warning from us. Be cheerful in your old age. Find some useful
hobby. Fretwork. Rugmaking. Basketry. Make yourselves *needed*. Remember: a busy pair of hands are worth
ten thousand times the Crown of a Queen. Go home, and
remember: your lives too, will have their termination.
VISITORS. Help. Help. Help. Let us out. Let us out.
PHINEUS. Let them out.

CRAPE *opens the door and they all run out.*

VISITORS (*cries disappearing offstage*). Help! Help!
Help! . . .

OLD PEOPLE (*bowing to the audience*). Good night. Good night. Good night.

They all leave the stage. They carry with them the remains of the coffee and refreshments. MRS PHINEUS *and* MRS LETOUZEL *carefully put the* DOCTOR *in the wheel chair, and* MRS PHINEUS *wheels him out.*

CURTAIN

Methuen World Classics

Aeschylus (two volumes)
Jean Anouilh
John Arden (two volumes)
Arden & D'Arcy
Aristophanes (two volumes)
Aristophanes & Menander
Peter Barnes (two volumes)
Brendan Behan
Aphra Behn
Edward Bond (four volumes)
Bertolt Brecht
   (three volumes)
Howard Brenton
   (two volumes)
Büchner
Bulgakov
Calderón
Anton Chekhov
Caryl Churchill
   (two volumes)
Noël Coward (five volumes)
Sarah Daniels
Eduardo De Filippo
David Edgar (three volumes)
Euripides (three volumes)
Dario Fo (two volumes)
Michael Frayn (two volumes)
Max Frisch
Gorky
Harley Granville Barker
   (two volumes)

Henrik Ibsen (six volumes)
Lorca (three volumes)
David Mamet
Marivaux
Mustapha Matura
David Mercer
   (two volumes)
Arthur Miller
   (four volumes)
Anthony Minghella
Molière
Tom Murphy (three volumes)
Peter Nichols
   (two volumes)
Clifford Odets
Joe Orton
Louise Page
A. W. Pinero
Luigi Pirandello
Stephen Poliakoff
Terence Rattigan
Ntozake Shange
Sophocles (two volumes)
Wole Soyinka
David Storey
August Strindberg
   (three volumes)
J. M. Synge
Ramón del Valle-Inclán
Frank Wedekind
Oscar Wilde

Methuen Modern Plays

include work by

Methuen Student Editions

John Arden	*Serjeant Musgrave's Dance*
Alan Ayckbourn	*Confusions*
Aphra Behn	*The Rover*
Edward Bond	*Lear*
Bertolt Brecht	*The Caucasian Chalk Circle*
	Life of Galileo
	Mother Courage and her Children
Caryl Churchill	*Top Girls*
Shelagh Delaney	*A Taste of Honey*
John Galsworthy	*Strife*
Robert Holman	*Across Oka*
Henrik Ibsen	*A Doll's House*
Charlotte Keatley	*My Mother Said I Never Should*
John Marston	*The Malcontent*
August Strindberg	*The Father*
J. M. Synge	*The Playboy of the Western World*
Oscar Wilde	*The Importance of Being Earnest*
Tennessee Williams	*A Streetcar Named Desire*